Journey into Wilderness

Life in Camp and Field; —

Comprising
Scenes, Incidents and Adventures
among
The Creek and Seminole Indians;
during their recent hostilities.
With
Descriptions of Florida Scenery;

By An Officer

late of the
Medical Staff
U. S. Army.

"The camp's harsh tumult and the conflict's glow,
The thrill of triumph and the gasp of woe,
The tender parting and the glad return,
The festal banquet and the funeral urn."

"Embellished with engravings.

Title page from J. Rhett Motte's Journal

Journey into Wilderness

An
Army Surgeon's Account
of
Life in Camp and Field
during the
Creek and Seminole Wars
1836-1838

BY

Jacob Rhett Motte

EDITED BY

JAMES F. SUNDERMAN

". . . you have men, and so have we, you have powder and lead, and so have we, your men will fight, and so will ours, till the last drop of . . . blood has moistened the dust. . . ."

(Osceola, Seminole Indian Chief, to Brigadier General Duncan L. Clinch, February 2, 1836.)

UNIVERSITY OF FLORIDA PRESS
Gainesville
1963

A University of Florida Press Book

COPYRIGHT, 1953, BY THE
UNIVERSITY OF FLORIDA
ALL RIGHTS RESERVED

LIBRARY OF CONGRESS
CATALOGUE CARD NUMBER: 53-6655

FIRST EDITION, 1953
LITHOPRINTED EDITION, 1963

LITHOPRINTED BY DOUGLAS PRINTING COMPANY, INC.
JACKSONVILLE, FLORIDA

Acknowledgments

APPRECIATION IS EXPRESSED to those who have generously assisted in the editing of the Motte Journal by providing access to manuscripts, published works, records, and other reference material, or by aiding in the research and preparation of the manuscript. Especially I should like to thank Dr. Rembert W. Patrick, head, Department of History, University of Florida, for arranging with the Florida Historical Society to make the original Motte manuscript available for publication, and for his helpful supervision and guidance during the course of my editing.

Special recognition and appreciation are due also to: Dr. W. E. Baringer and Dr. D. E. Worcester, Department of History, University of Florida, for their professional advice and assistance; Dr. John M. Goggin, Department of Sociology and Anthropology, University of Florida, for the numerous sources and facts he made available on the Creek and Seminole Indians and on the geography and archeology of the Southeast, and in particular of Florida; and Mr. Julien C. Yonge, director of the Library of Florida History, for his untiring and meticulous aid in searching for sources and in reviewing materials for authenticity and accuracy.

Gratitude is also extended to the Florida Historical Society and Mrs. Alberta Johnson, its former librarian, for making the original manuscript available; to the St. Augustine Historical Society and Mrs. Marion R. Moulds, acting librarian, for permitting the publication of excerpts from the revised manuscript; to Dr. Kenneth W. Porter, Houston, Texas, for his reference suggestions; to Dr. Mark F. Boyd, Tallahassee, Florida, for granting permission to reproduce the four pencil sketches found in this volume; to Mr. Allen S. Deas, collector of manuscripts, Mt. Pleasant, South Carolina, for his information on the life of Dr. Motte; to Dr. Kenneth F. Gantz and Dr. Frank W. Anderson, Jr., Air University, Montgomery, Ala-

Journey into Wilderness

bama, for their helpful editorial suggestions; to Ruth and Bill Takes, Montgomery, Alabama, for their assistance in collating the final narrative with Motte's original; and to Mr. William Q. Denson, Jr., Montgomery, Alabama, for drafting the maps.

To my wife, Thelma Ailene, I owe, perhaps, the greatest debt of thanks for her faithful devotion to typing, proofing, and the many other uninteresting and tedious tasks which are required in preparing a manuscript for publication.

February 25, 1953   JAMES F. SUNDERMAN

vi

Table of Contents

List of Illustrations

SKETCHES

MAPS

Introduction

I

OUR SOUTHERN FRONTIER, boisterous and lawless, was the scene of more bloody strife between the red man and the white man than any other section east of the Mississippi River. From the days of the American Revolution the Creek Indians, a strong, feared, and highly civilized confederation in Georgia and Alabama, and the Seminoles, a Creek offshoot in Florida, had seen their lands constantly encroached upon by the steady advance of white men who coveted the rich undeveloped soil of the deep South. Little by little, as the red man was forced to sign treaties and land cessions, he saw his tribal domains and hunting grounds disappear. The bloody Creek War of 1813-1814 and the Seminole uprising in 1817 were only more violent eruptions in the constant strife and bush fighting that went on for decades.

Early in the 1830's came the decree from Washington that all Indians east of the Mississippi would be removed to lands in the West. In spite of formal treaties signed with the Creeks and Seminoles guaranteeing this removal, large segments of both tribes were adamant in their refusal to leave their ancestral homes. They refused to listen to talk of leaving and vowed to resist any attempt at removal by force.

By the middle of the 1830's ill feeling between the keyed-up Creeks and Seminoles and the frontier settlers had reached the pitch of open hostilities. The United States government, determined to carry out its policy of Indian removal, ordered large numbers of regular and volunteer troops to move against the Creek and Seminole Nations. The elusive, musket-armed Indians, skilled in the art of guerilla warfare, proved no easy target for unwieldly columns of marching troops. Though the red man fought for survival, whatever moral and tactical advantages he possessed were eventually overcome by the sheer weight of numbers and the superior equipment of his foe. The wars for him were wars of attrition. Regardless, however, of the odds he faced and the quick submission he made in Georgia and Alabama, he fought for seven long years in Florida.

This clash of arms on one of America's wildest and least known frontiers provides the setting for the tales of primitive frontier life— "how fields were fought and won,"* "hair-breadth scapes by flood and field," and the "deadly breach and the cannons mouth"— which the author of this Journal vividly narrates.

II

Jacob Rhett Motte, a versatile army surgeon with a literary flair, was a proud, Chesterfieldian, Harvard-educated, self-styled Southern gentleman who one day suddenly found himself transported from the gay, aristocratic social circles of Charleston into a wild frontier. This unknown world proved a rare experience for a man of distinguished bearing who was descended from two colorful South Carolinian families of Huguenot origin.†

Motte was proud of his lineage. On his father's side, as far as available sources reveal, it went back to the Comte de la Motte of seventeenth-century France. His great-grandfather, the second generation of his family in this country, served thirty years as public treasurer of the colony of South Carolina. His grandfather, Isaac Motte, rose to the rank of colonel in the Continental Army and became known as a Revolutionary War hero through his seizure of Fort Johnson and his gallant defense of Fort Moultrie. An equally enviable lineage is found on his mother's side. Abraham Motte,

---

* Quotations used in this introduction and not otherwise annotated are taken from the original Motte manuscript.

† Sources used in sketching the author's life and background include *The Christian Register,* July 24, 1869; *South Carolina Historical and Genealogical Magazine,* IV, 1903; materials in the War Records Division, National Archives; and Arthur H. Cole (ed.), *Charleston Goes to Harvard, Diary of a Harvard Student of 1831* (Cambridge, 1940). The information embodied in the first three mentioned was furnished through correspondence with Clifford K. Shipton, custodian of the Harvard University Archives; E. G. Campbell, director, War Records Division, National Archives, Washington, D. C.; and Margaret D. Mosimann, reference librarian, Charleston Free Library, Charleston, South Carolina.

Introduction

J. Rhett's father, married Sarah Washington Quince, the daughter of Colonel William Rhett, an outstanding figure in the early history of South Carolina. The pride young Motte felt in his family heritage often prompted him to drop his first name and use the initial only. He registered at Harvard as Rhett J. Motte.

Motte was born in Charleston, September 22, 1811, and lived there during his formative years. After attending Charleston College the seventeen-year-old lad entered Harvard College in 1828, following a precedent set by his older and only brother, Mellish Irving, who had been graduated from Harvard in 1821.

Perhaps the philosophic style and the frequent intellectual approach in his writings are traceable to his Harvard background. The courses he studied there covered a wide range. In the program of his junior year alone, the humanities were represented by Latin, Greek, German, and "universal grammar," while his courses in architecture and the sciences included natural philosophy, chemistry, and electricity. Several of his required themes were on abstract topics. One he entitled "Whether genius be an innate and irresistible propensity to some particular pursuit, or merely general superiority owing to accidental circumstances?" Another bore an even more unusual title: "Crime, conscience, self-deception, worldliness, God's judgement of us and the world's judgement, etc., as exhibited in the King's soliloquy in *Hamlet*—'O my offence is rank,' etc."

His Harvard years held enjoyments as well as hard work. He was an average student—neither exceptionally enthusiastic about his courses nor prone to complain.* His friends were few, a circumstance which he himself deplored. He led a plain, moral existence, marked by abstention from dances, parties with fellow students, and other festivities. The only sports he enjoyed were riding his velocipede, swimming, and walking, the last being his favorite.

* During the latter part of his junior year at Harvard, Motte kept a diary in which he recorded his student activities, thoughts, and emotions. This diary, edited by Arthur H. Cole, librarian, Harvard Graduate School of Business Administration, affords many valuable glimpses into the early life of the author.

Journey into Wilderness

In reading his Journal one cannot doubt that his Harvard background shaped a mind which flourished on wide reading, for he exhibits a familiarity with the classics, and with the music, art, and literature of his day. In passages of reflective musing, which appear frequently throughout his writings, he quotes from writers whom we today consider among the greatest in our literary heritage. One of his recurring laments is the total absence of reading material on the frontier, the lack of which he believes produces a group of people whom he characterizes as the "dumbest . . . in the world." Never in history, he laconically observes, has there existed a class of individuals who stood in more earnest need of schoolmasters.

In August of 1832 Motte was graduated from Harvard with the degree of Bachelor of Arts. He may have remained in New England from his matriculation until graduation, for his brother was then serving as Unitarian minister of the South Congregational Church in Boston. His only sister, Anna Maria, was living at the time in New London, Connecticut, where her husband, Colonel William Lindsay of the United States Army, was stationed.

The ties between Jacob and Anna Maria were very close. He speaks of her affectionately in his Journal, in which he does not even mention his brother. In 1836 Anna Maria was living at the United States Arsenal in Augusta, Georgia, conveniently located for Motte to visit on his journey to the theater of war in Alabama. His parents were undoubtedly dead, for he often laments the fact that he has no permanent home. In his writing can be detected the maturity which only permanent bereavement can produce in a young mind. Reflecting upon the joyful anticipation exhibited by his homeward-bound army friends, he writes: "Home no longer exists for me; it is only to be found in the memory of past times and joyous youth, when hopes were bright, and the very air I breathed seemed impregnated with delight. There is no hearth-stone to which I may turn . . . meeting those loved faces which render home so dear."

Upon his graduation from Harvard, Motte failed to receive a desired appointment to the United States Military Academy and returned to Charleston. There he studied at the medical college

Introduction

and served his apprenticeship under Dr. J. E. Holbrook. Apart from mentioning service as a citizen medical doctor at the Augusta, Georgia, Arsenal in 1835, he tells little of his life and activities before his entry into the United States Army.

Leanings toward a military career had been evident during his college days. The failure of his attempt to win an appointment to West Point only postponed his desire for a "try" at the army. Hence, in March of 1836 he journeyed to Baltimore, where he was examined by the Army Medical Board. His application for admission to the medical staff was approved on March 21, and about the first of June he received orders placing him on active duty with the rank of assistant surgeon.*

His enlistment doubtless was prompted by a youthful admiration for the service. Army life in that day was not attractive, least of all in salary. One disgruntled army surgeon characterized the financial remuneration as follows: "Although I had, at my own expense, obtained through a course of eight years study and attendance on medical lectures, the degrees of A.M. and M.D., and added five or six years' experience in private practice, I found, that after expending some $300 in prerequisites, and joining the army, I would receive only $30 per month pay, and $24 for subsistence. . . . Respectable board, lodging and washing cannot be obtained at any southern station, which are the only ones with which I am acquainted, for less than $28 or $30 per month: leaving $24 for clothing, incidental expenses, and the laying up for a wet day."†

The Journal picks up the record of Motte's life, travels, and observations early on the morning of June 3, 1836, as he rode down the deserted streets of Charleston on his way to the railroad depot. He was inspired by the fact that he "was now enrolled among the elite few, the brave and honorable spirits of our small but unsurpassed Army." A year later the blunt reality of army life on a wild

* *Army and Navy Chronicle,* May 5, 1836. An assistant surgeon in the Army Medical Corps at this time had the rank of either first lieutenant or captain; a surgeon, that of major. By an act of Congress, April 23, 1908, titles of assistant surgeon and surgeon were abolished, and medical officers were ranked by purely military titles, such as lieutenant, captain, major, and colonel.

† *Ibid.,* January 21, 1836.

frontier had dampened the thrill and enchantment which his army career had originally promised. It was then he issued a warning to those of his profession who were "strongly tempted by the allurements of a military life," stating, "if you possess an impatient temper, or a character honorably proud and finely sensitive, as you value your peace of mind, do not think of taking such a step."

The quaint little Charleston-Hamburg express carried the proud new army surgeon to Augusta in a little over twelve hours. From Augusta he proceeded by stagecoach across the state to Columbus, where he reported for duty with the army opposed to the Creek Nation.

The first eleven of the thirty-six chapters of the Journal deal with the Creek Indian hostilities in Georgia and Alabama. In the winter of 1836-1837 Motte was ordered to Florida and accompanied a detachment of troops from Lowndes County, Georgia, to the Mineral Springs on the Suwannee River in Florida. The remaining twenty-five chapters relate his experiences, observations, and itinerary in Florida during the first years of the Seminole Indian hostilities. His travels with the troops in Florida took him throughout the peninsula from the Georgia border to the Everglades and as far south as Key Largo, and enabled him to tuck into the pages of his Journal a wide range of material on territorial Florida. In April of 1838, while stationed at Fort Lauderdale, Florida, he received orders transferring him back to Charleston, where the narrative of his Journal ends.

From Charleston he was ordered to Major General Winfield Scott's headquarters at Athens, Tennessee, and took part in the campaign which forcibly removed the Cherokee Indians to their new homes west of the Mississippi. After a period of service in the Cherokee country, Motte was transferred to the Michigan territory and, later, in 1840 to Huntsville, Alabama. In 1843 he was stationed at Jefferson Barracks, St. Louis, Missouri, where he drew up several interesting reports for the Surgeon General on conditions in the Missouri Valley.*

* Allen S. Deas, collector of manuscripts, to James F. Sunderman, August 26, 1950, MS in P. K. Yonge Library of Florida History, University of Florida.

Introduction

He resigned his commission in 1845, returned to Charleston, and began private practice. In December of the same year he married Mary Mahan Haig, the daughter of a Charleston doctor, and purchased a plantation at Exeter, South Carolina, apparently living there throughout the Civil War.

Civilian life again brought him the comforts of civilization. He established a home of his own, ministered to by "the soft, tender touch" of a woman's hand—a dream often expressed and long desired. And in spite of his campaign observations of mild disgust at the numerous progeny of the frontier family and the frontiersman who excelled in no "duties" except those involved in begetting "ugly little white-headed responsibilities," the Mottes had nine children—six boys and three girls. Five children survived their father's death at Exeter in 1868.

Little is known of the character and appearance of Dr. Motte except as they are revealed in his writings. A lanky, pipe-smoking army officer, he undoubtedly followed the fashion among the gentry of that day and sported a mustache. He does not conceal his love for good port wine nor his admiration for the "lovely ladies of St. Augustine." Although his heart fluttered when dancing in the arms of some exotic Minorcan lass, his determination while campaigning in the field carried him until he dropped from physical exhaustion. He complains about the drinking water, which at times was "the color and consistency of ink"; the nausea produced by walking for days in torrential downpours of a midwinter rain; the discomfort of sleeping in a saddle or in the alternative—four inches of water; the labor of wading in slimy muck, waist-deep, his clothes cut to pieces by sharp saw-grass and his shoes chewed up by the coral rocks. But his complaints, quite frequently, are couched in the humor which undoubtedly was the spirit in which they were originally voiced.

His graphic and ironic observations frequently recall the prose of the literary masters of his day. After a hot and dusty day's march, the crystal waters of Itchetucknee Springs appear to him as "an oasis in this desert which broke upon our vision like the fairyland sometimes seen in dreams." The smooth-flowing St. Johns

River appears to wind through "an avenue of o'er hanging trees
. . . their pendant branches casting mysterious shadows . . . as
they hang over its placid bosom in every variety of form and
beauty." Yet he describes other parts of Florida as "neither land,
water, nor air . . . the poorest country that ever two people quarrelled for . . . a perfect paradise for Indians, alligators, serpents,
frogs, and every other kind of loathsome reptile" . . . where "the
demon of desolation stalked with unchecked sway."

III

The Motte Journal was not written in the field. It was compiled from a volume of field notes which he kept during the campaign and which, unfortunately, has never been found. It is not
known what prevented Motte from publishing his Journal after
revising it for that purpose in 1845. This revised copy, partly in
his own handwriting and partly in the handwriting of another person, is in the possession of the St. Augustine Historical Society.
With the exception of the first four chapters, which show a small
amount of revision, it bears remarkable identity with the original
manuscript. In contrast to the original it is less irritating to the
reader because errors in sentence structure and punctuation, as well
as interpolations, additions, and deletions—the inevitable consequences of a rapidly written original draft—have been corrected.

The original version, written by Motte from his field notes not
for publication but for the benefit of his own family and friends,
is the one transcribed following this introduction. It is presumed
to be the more accurate. However, in order to give the reader the
benefit of both the original and the revised manuscripts, all informative and pertinent material not included in the original but found in
the revised version is placed in brackets in its proper place and
documented.

Both manuscripts were purchased in 1930 by William Todd, a
New England rare-book collector, from a Charleston source—un-
doubtedly the Motte heirs. The revised copy was sold to the St.
Augustine Historical Society and the original to Dr. James A.

Introduction

Robertson of Stetson University.* After the death of Dr. Robertson the original manuscript was presented to the Florida Historical Society by Mrs. Robertson. Through the aid of Dr. Rembert W. Patrick, the manuscript was lent to the P. K. Yonge Library of Florida History to be edited.

The original manuscript has been preserved in fair state. The majority of its pages measure 8 x 13 inches in folio. It is legible, although in places it is difficult to follow because of fading and water stains and the numerous corrections and interpolations made upon it. The mechanical style of Motte's script is indicative of the period. Capital letters are grandiose, and the second letter of a double "s" extends below the line. Many verbs ending in "e" retain the "e" in their participial form.

The Journal is highly informative and well written. The author's metaphorical language is superb, although sentence structure, spelling, and punctuation occasionally indicate careless composition. Indeed, many of Motte's vivid descriptions would do credit to the authors of the classics he studied at Harvard. His characterization of Captain Giles Porter, whose mustache "always exhibited by an ingenious spiral a strong partiality for the corner of each eye," and his account of sprightly social life in St. Augustine graced by raven-haired Spanish and lustrous-eyed Minorcan girls, whose figures were "of the most lovely proportions" . . . and who glided "through the labyrinthian mazes of the graceful Spanish dance," are typical examples of his literary ability.

Equally conspicuous throughout the Journal is the subtle humor woven into the descriptive narrative, which contributes one of the most entertaining aspects of the work. Motte's account of a "log-rolling, quilting, and dancing frolic" in frontier Georgia is as humorously exciting to the reader as the original performance appeared to the author. The striking comparison of a group of sage-like pelicans to the sober-faced gentry in a court of justice; the incident of an excited farmer who mistook a company of troops for a

---

* William Todd to James A. Robertson, December 3, 1931; James A. Robertson to William Todd, December 8, 1931. This correspondence is with the original copy of the manuscript.

Journey into Wilderness

band of hostile Indian warriors; and the story of Andrew Jackson's quarrel with the ladies of old Newnansville—all indicate the humoristic lens through which Motte viewed the world.

The Journal is valuable not only to the student of history but also to those who enjoy entertaining and informative reading. It is a story and a travelogue. A multitude of anecdotes, incidents, and tales of life on the little known Georgia-Alabama-Florida frontier are intricately dovetailed into the central theme—the Creek and Seminole Indian Wars. But its primary value lies in its contribution to the knowledge of the military and social history of this period. The excellent descriptions of military activities, which make the Journal a source book that has been too long ignored, include an eye-witness account of the capture of Osceola, King Philip, Coacoochee (Wild Cat), and Uchee Billy; the Battle of Jupiter Inlet; expeditions down the east coast of Florida and into the Everglades; operations in northern Florida, southern Georgia, and eastern Alabama, as well as military actions in other sections of the hostile territories. Besides sketching excellent literary portraits of various personalities, white and Indian, who played a conspicuous role in the war (the best perhaps being that of Osceola), Motte reports his impressions of pioneer settlements, military fortifications, towns, roads, frontier life and society, the geographical aspects of the country, and many other fascinating sidelights. He also projects into his Journal brief glimpses of the economic, political, and religious trends of the time.

The primary purpose of the Journal is to record what the author refers to as "occular observations." In discussing the Creek and Seminole Indian wars, he deals mainly with those events in which he took a part. He mentions, however, and at times descriptively outlines, other phases of military action, both contemporary and past, in which he did not participate. For information concerning these events he relies upon either contemporary newspaper stories or firsthand accounts of actual participants.

The transcription which follows is based upon three comparative readings, and duplicates the original manuscript insofar as possible. In the interest of clarity and readability, disconcerting errors in

xx

spelling, punctuation, and sentence structure have been corrected. In a number of instances punctuation has been added. No attempt has been made to impose strict consistency or modernization on Motte's text. The old-fashioned spellings and quaint literary style have been generally retained, and grammatical peculiarities and irregularities have been left in the narrative when they do not obscure the author's meaning. Throughout his manuscript Motte quotes a number of verses, the sources for most of which are unknown; some may be of his own composition.

I have annotated the transcription to explain various events, supplement the narrative, fill in chronological gaps, and identify the persons, places, and things mentioned by the author. This procedure, like the editing of the text itself, was motivated by a desire for an articulated presentation which would be pleasant and easy to read and to recall. If that aim has now been achieved, Motte's literary labors, despite the lapse of one hundred fifteen years, will not have been in vain.

The Journal

Preface

*D*uring a period of nearly nine years, passed amid the fatigues of almost incessant locomotion and the restlessness of continual excitement—for such I may characterize my military career, kept constantly on duty with troops in the field and on the remotest frontiers of the Union while in the Army—debarred from access to books in a great measure, in consequence of my erratic life and inaccessible positions, I resorted to keeping a journal; first begun merely to wile away moments not occupied by professional duties, it was afterwards continued under the impression that in after years it would afford some satisfaction to be able to remember old scenes and to recall them as they actually occurred.

While witnessing the dreadful scenes of Indian warfare, I was also impressed with the conviction that descriptions of horrible massacres, imminent and hair-breadth escapes, bloody battles, and dreadful murders have always been subjects of interest to the human mind, and would be more particularly so to my friends knowing my participation in them. And I might expect nothing less than to be called upon by them as soon as I should have once again assumed the appearance of a gentleman by a joyous return to the luxury of a refined suit of clothes, and look as if I had never been scratched by thorns and brambles in my life, for a full detail of "how fields were fought and won," "hair-breadth scapes by flood and field," the "deadly breach and the cannons mouth," and all that sort of thing. I therefore thought it best to write down my impressions of "scenes and incidents" while fresh in my mind and with the first glass untarnished by lapse of time; for well I knew that should I wait until I had resumed my acquaintance with a soft feather-bed,—it was a most affectionate meeting by the bye,—I should never be able to do justice in my

Journey into Wilderness

descriptions to the merits of primitive couches in soft hummocks and morasses; not after having again produced a taste of civilized food, would I feel much disposed to recount how I had revelled upon the delightsome and wholesome excellencies of gopher soup, alligator steaks, and other like delicacies.

My journal being in due time submitted to those friends who called upon me for an account of myself during my protracted absence from the pale of civilization, they have generally been pleased to compliment me by repeatedly advising its publication. I had determined several years ago, in consequence of this advice, to give to the public that portion of my journal which comprised my first two years of Army experience, obtained while campaigning against the *Creek* and *Seminole Indians;* but have heretofore been frustrated in carrying out this determination by being always kept on duty in the remotest parts of our frontier, far removed from all the appliances of civilizations.

Having recently escaped the influence which subjected me to this long continued banishment from the world by resigning my commission in the Medical Staff; and thus become enabled to resume my former and long desired position by returning to a refined and polished community, instead of being barbarized by constant contact with savages—among whom I feel I have already been too long kept for I am occasionally seized with an irresistible inclination to dress myself fantastically with leggins and wampum and utter a war-whoop—I have been again advised by some friends who perused my journal to publish it.

More in deference to their judgement than from any good opinion I entertain of my own humble abilities I now comply by making public this first two years of my "Life in Camp and Field."

I will only add that should any exception be felt to a tone of egotism that may occasionally appear in the course of these writings, the reader must bear in mind that such is inseparable from a private journal of impressions, thoughts, and feelings; but such, I repeat, it was intended to be when written; and only for my own reference in after years, or the perusal of those friends who should express any interest in my movements. These impressions of

The Journal

scenes, incidents, and adventures being noted down on the spot, and at the times of occurrence, I leave unaltered as the truest and readyest mode of imparting what would probably have been the impressions made on others in like circumstances.

Charleston, S. C.   Jacob Rhett Motte
1845

Index of Chapters

Journey into Wilderness

The Journal

Alligator—prospects of peace—reverse of feelings—Indian massacre of Mr. Clement's wife and children.

Journey into Wilderness

The Journal

Journey into Wilderness

The Journal

expedition to the interior—Indian trails discovered—description of the country—a pandemonium—Sam Jones' camp attacked—a fight and a capture—our captive—return to our boats—a break-down— another boat expedition—return to our camp.

CHAPTER XXXVI.

The 1st Artillery ordered to the Cherokee Nation in North Carolina, via Charleston—Col. Harney's perseverance—hope and despondency— 1st Artillery embark for St. Augustine—Col. Harney returns to Fort Lauderdale—reaction of feeling at the anticipation of soon seeing Charleston again—the Steamer Isis at sea—arrival at St. Augustine— hospitalities of the people there—we embark at Picolata for Charleston—the inland passage—Savannah—a man overboard—reflections on returning to Charleston—arrival at Charleston.

CHAPTER I

*I*t was on the morning of the 3rd June 1836, at the early hour of half past five o'clock, that a solitary chaise was driven rapidly through the streets of Charleston, in the direction of the Rail-Road depository.[1] That chaise contained my honored self, and my honored self's trunk, with the addition of a negro boy, who acted in the capacity of driver; the latter a very necessary appendage, for my trunk and myself were soon to be transferred to our respective cars in the long train about to start for the incipient great city of Hamburg.[2] I was on my way to join the Army in the Creek-nation,[3] having just received an appointment in the Medical Staff. I had taken leave of all my friends the day previous with one exception; and that one, dearer than the rest, postponed bidding adieu until the last moment. It was a sad parting; for about to enter as I was into scenes of strife with a savage and unsparing foe, the chances were unequally balanced whether I should ever again look upon his countenance or hear the friendly tones of his voice. It was not a moment for regret, however;—my long cherished hopes were at last fulfilled;—the dearest wish of my heart was attained; and I was now enrolled among the elite few, the brave and honorable spirits of our small but unsurpassed Army. As a Military Surgeon I was soon to experience the arduous duties of active service, the best school for a tyro in the medical profession.

We reached Hamburg that evening[4]—that is my trunk, self, and Co.—without any accident; and through the medium of an omnibus, soon found ourselves at the Planter's Hotel in Augusta. Here were collected Gen. Fenwick[5] and many other Army officers, destined for the scene of war in Alabama.[6] I remained the next day, for the purpose of visiting my sister at the Arsenal, about four miles from Augusta; and on the following morning at 9 o'clock

1

Journey into Wilderness

took my seat in the stage, with the intention of overtaking Major Lomax's detachment of troops,[7] with whom I was order'd to proceed to Columbus, Georgia, after relieving Dr. [Assistant Surgeon Joel] Martin, (who pleaded a *discomboberation* of his circulation, to escape being sent to the field). We came up with the command about ten miles east of Sparta, and passing their encampment at 11 o'clock at night, proceeded on to Sparta,[8] there to await their approach. On reporting myself the next morning to Major Lomax, I ascertained that Dr. [Assistant Surgeon Eugene Hilarian] Abadie who was despatched from Columbus by Gen. Scott[9] for the purpose, had joined the day previous, and that it would be unnecessary for me to remain with them, when my services may be more needed with other troops. This was fortunate for me; for had I joined this command, I should have had to trudge two hundred miles on foot through sun and sand; sleeping at night on the bare ground without a tent;—not having yet procured a horse or any other outfit for the campaign. I therefore proceeded in the stage in company with Lt. Waite;[10] other passengers having dropt off as we approached the Indian country.[11] The only inconveniences we experienced were breaking our heads against the sides and top of the vehicle at every jolt over the bad roads;—getting out to walk down steep and rugged hills in the middle of the night;—sinking in several mudholes, stalled, and standing ancle deep in mire, while making desperate exertions to extricate the lumbering coach;—and finally, having to stop at a house at 2 o'clock in the morning, where the inhabitants were too well secured by Morpheus to attend to our thumps, bumps, and knocks that only had the effect of waking anything but sweet music in the throats of all the curs of the establishment. [Persevering in our gymnastic exercises, we at last were rewarded with a sight of the inmates; and after an uncomfortable short nap, and an equally uncomfortable breakfast, our journey was continued.][12]

At 10 o'clock in the morning of the 7th June we reached the thriving town of Columbus, situated on the Eastern bank of the Chatahooche [Chattahoochee River]. The McIntosh Hotel kept by Mangham was selected as the place of depository for myself

2

etc., it being the principal rendezvous for the military. I here found Major [John] Erving, my rail-road travelling companion, who in the course of the morning introduced me to Major Kirby,[13] Chief of Gen. Scott's Staff; and to whom I reported myself for duty, the General being sick in bed.

The streets of Columbus presented a bustling appearance; not with business, but the constant arrivals of the mighty, valiant, and invincible citizen soldiers, in whose bosoms the flame of patriotism had furiously blazed forth. They presented a glorious array of dirks, pistols, and bowie-knives, with no scarcity of dirt. It seemed as if every ragamuffin of Georgia, deeming himself an invincible warrior, had enlisted under the standard of Mars, which many from their conduct must have mistaken for the standard of Bacchus, as they observed the articles of the latter god with much greater reverence.[14]

I seized an opportunity to visit the camp of some friendly Indians on the Alabama side of the Chatahooche.[15] After crossing the bridge which connects the two states, and walking a mile, I soon discovered their wigwams. They are built of the bark of the pine-tree stretched over four poles driven perpendicularly into the ground. The sides were open, and afforded an entire view of the internal domestic arrangement. This was simple enough; merely a blanket or two spread upon the ground, upon which were sitting the squaws engaged in making moccasins, or chilli-pika as they are called in the Creek language; and around them were playing the little naked papooses. Upon a log outside sat the dignified heads of families, engaged either in smoking their pipes, or in the enjoyment of luxurious indolence. In the chief I found a venerable looking old gentleman, who glorified in the title of Col. Blue;[16] he had served under Jackson in the last war with the rank of Col. which title he had retained in preference to his Indian cognomen of Blue-Warrior. He sat in silent grandeur at the entrance of his wigwam, a white flag waving over his head in indication of his amity. When informed that I was a *hillis-haia* or physician, he was anxious that I should give him something to cure his rheumatism, which he said prevented his hunting. He

3

appeared to be about eighty years of age. It was easy to defy the fascinations of the young squaws, their divine forms of redundant proportions not answering to my standard of beauty; corsets and all the other miseries of a refined figure not finding favour in their estimation. There were some half-breeds, however, whose brilliant black eyes and beautifully chiselled features would rival many of our celebrated city belles.

This visit afforded a melancholy theme for contemplation during my walk back. Here was a people, once mighty and magnanimous, who owned no equal; a race intrepid and unslaved, who roved happy and contented o'er the boundless wild, about to be swept from their ancient inheritance by the withering proximity of the white man; from that fair soil on which their forefathers lived and died. The spirit of time and the spirit of whiskey are indeed working dreadful changes among these once noble savages,—nature's chiefs.[17]

On the 13th June an order was put into my hands to report myself to Capt. Munroe[18] of the 4th Artillery, who would arrive with his command next morning and immediately proceed to Woolfolk's plantation,[19] situated ten miles below Columbus, on the Chattahooche river and directly opposite to Fort Mitchell.[20] Some Indians had lately attacked an adjoining plantation and shot several negroes; to prevent a similar outrage, Woolfolk had requested of Gen. Scott some troops to be stationed there. At sunrise the next morning Capt. Munroe's company marched through the town. I joined them, and proceeded on foot to the designated place. With proper precautions against an attack, we selected a place of encampment in an old Indian field, near the ferry which crosses the Chatahooche towards Fort Mitchell. We were excessively annoyed by the mosquitoes, but more so by a jackass, whose solitude had been so seldom interrupted, that on the appearance of so much goodly company, he gave tone to the exuberance of his joy in the most discordant notes. No sleep could be got for his incessant braying during the nights. As peculiarly appropriate we designated this place Camp Balaam. One of the sentinels became quite excited in the night, swearing that he heard

4

SECTION OF ALABAMA
LOCALE OF THE
SECOND CREEK WAR
1836

MOTTE'S ITINERARY····

the Indians whooping to one another quite close to him. We heard the same sounds, but our more experienced ears immediately recognised the peculiar cry of the owl, which bears a strong resemblance to the whoop of the human voice. The only officers beside Capt. Munroe & myself, were Lt. Bainbridge[21] and Lt. [William Helmsley] Emery [Emory]. Our amusements were rather limited, consisting in walking to the spring and drinking water, then walking back to our tents. We were sometimes amused, however, by witnessing the squaws of the friendly Indians swimming in the river; they would strip and dive in with perfect nonchalance, and when in [the water], defying any one to catch them. [Which would indeed have been a difficult matter for the rivers appeared to be their natural element, with such ease & familiarity they frolicked upon and beneath its surface, disappearing in one spot to rise at a remote and unexpected distance.][22] Their general demeanour was always very modest, never permitting any one to take liberties with them. The day after our march, the Capt. and myself crossed over the Chattahooche to Fort Mitchell. The fort was a square formed by pickets [12 feet high] with a block house at two diagonal corners. I here found my old acquaintance Lt. Peyton,[23] from whom I got an article I stood very much in need of, a blanket; having left Columbus in a hurry without one. We dined at the public mess, being waited upon by Indians. We returned before dark, as there were many hostile Indians hovering about the vicinity and the fort was a mile from the river. A few days after, we received an acquisition to our numbers by the arrival of Lt. [Robert Harris] Archer and company.[24] On the 19th June we were ordered to Fort Mitchell, and encamped in a grove of trees without the pickets. We were not permitted long to remain quiet, for on the evening of the 20th June, we again crossed the Chatahooche on our march down to Roanoke,[25] a village on the Georgia side of the Chattahooche in possession of the enemy. I had fortunately received intimation of this in the morning, and immediately despatched a messenger to Columbus, to purchase me a horse, and all the necessary paraphernalia. They arrived as we were marching out of camp about dark. [Intending

The Journal

to cross the river that night, and camp on the east side, for an early start next morning.][26] The next morning Major Pierce[27] and his battalion joined us; and soon after we were joined by Major Lomax with his battalion; our whole force now amounted to 500 men [under the command of Major Pierce].[28] We marched that day fifteen miles, and encamped near a log house, in which we found a fire burning and some pans of very fine clabber, upon which we luxuriated, the occupants having apparently but just left it. This excited our suspicions that Indians were about us; and soon our hopes were verified, for while spreading our camp blankets for the night, the alarm was given that Indians were seen near us; immediately the long-roll was heard calling every man to his post, and after standing under arms one or two hours while a scouting party examined the neighboring bushes without success, we retired to our tents. An amusing incident occurred during the alarm, but which might have proved serious. The Sergeant of the Guard, who was a Polander, while visiting the different sentinels, came to one who knew as little about the Polish language as the Sergeant did of English. The Sentinel hailed,—the Sergeant answered in his unintelligible tongue, which sounding very much like Creek to the Sentinel, he concluded the safest and surest way would be to make the approaching person a target at which he might try his skill in shooting; he did so, and fortunately for the Sergeant discovered he was no great shot. That Indians were about us was evident, for they were distinctly heard yelling in the woods all night. I was startled from a sound nap just before daylight, by the report of a musket close to my ear, quickly followed by another, and another, until a dozen reports were heard, among which I could distinguish the sharp ring of the rifle. Now we certainly will have some sport, thought I, as I felt for my pistols in the dark. In less than one minute from the first report, every man was wide awake, and anxiously awaiting the foe. But none had the temerity to show themselves. Five or six had crept up close to our line of sentinels, and were indulging their curiosity by investigating our strength, when their desire of increasing their information was suddenly checked by the whistling of balls about

7

their ears. Not relishing such music, they had retired in disgust; but not before they were heard to say that we were too strong for them. The next morning it was ascertained by the trail they made that 100 Indians had crossed the road near us, going in the direction of Florida.[29]

By sunrise we were again on the march, and continued it uninterrupted until noon, when a negro was seen running after us with the speed of the wind, terror depicted in every feature. "The Indians! the Indians!" cried he; well, what of them? "Dem coming up de road arter you fass." What do they look like? "Like de berry debble; dem heap, and all naked." Naked Indians; that could not be Paddy Carr's band, whom we expected to follow us; and the hostile Indians are known to fight naked. "Semper paratus" is the safest principle of action; so our men were drawn up in battle array across the road. We had not remained in this state of suspense many minutes, when this formidable band of savages made their appearance. They proved to be Paddy Carr[30] and his band of 100 friendly warriors.

Paddy Carr is a half-breed Indian of dark complexion, about forty years of age, five feet eight or nine inches, handsomely proportioned, and muscular in his person, very intelligent in conversation, and has no doubt received a good education. He speaks our language with fluency, is correct in his deportment, and rather polished in his manners. Our men received them with a loud cheer, as they defiled past in Indian file. Instead of being naked, as the terror of the negro caused them to appear in his eyes, they were each decked out in a scarlet turban with a strip of white cloth around the centre,[31] in indication of their friendly disposition and a scarlet scarf was thrown over one shoulder, beside their usual dress of calico hunting shirt, and buckskin leggings. Some of them also wore a small looking-glass suspended round the neck, for the purposes of the toilet and in the hand unoccupied by the rifle was held a fan [made of the feathers from the tail of a wild turkey],[32] which as they marched was kept in constant motion. Indeed, this latter article was by no means a superfluous appendage, under a sun darting his rays with torrid fervour. Paddy gave an amuseing account of the negro's terror on first discovering them; how he tumbled from the cart he was driving, and made tracks in an opposite direction to his original course, leaving horse, cart, and everything else to their mercy. Also of a white man, who was on horse-back with a bag of meal under him, and who on discovering them made desperate exertions to slip the bag from under him, that his horse may travel the lighter and enable him to escape. Soon after being joined by these warriors, we stopt for the night, having come 15 miles since morning. [Our heavily laden baggage-wagons frequently detaining us by getting stalled in the numerous mud-holes and other bad places.][33]

CHAPTER II

$\mathscr{S}$oon after reveille next morning, while we were scalding our mouths and throats in hurried attempts to drink hot coffee from tin cups, the only ware used in camp, the reports of distant firearms in rapid succession fell upon our ears; the sound appeared to emanate from Fort Henderson[1] eight miles off, and it was the opinion of Major Paddy Carr,—for we had dubbed him with this title,—that the Indians had attacked that place, and they were now "fighting like the very devil," as he expressed himself. A council of war was immediately held, and the resolution adopted of proceeding to their assistance with part of our force, leaving a sufficient guard for the baggage. Dr. [Assistant Surgeon Alfred W.] Elwes and myself, the only surgeons present, were instructed to furnish our pockets with tourniquets and whatever instruments might be necessary for the wounded, and to proceed with the rescueing party. Our eagerness for a brush with the yellow dogs made us use quick despatch; and in five minutes all was ready for a start, when the idea occurred that the fireing arose from the garrison dischargeing their loaded arms, which had become wet from a heavy rain in the night. Disappointment was painted upon every countenance, and particularly among the band of Indian warriors, who at the first prospect of a fight, exhibited their savage joy by a shrill yell [or war-whoop].[2]

We continued our march towards Roanoke, and at noon arrived at Fort McCreary [McCrary],[3] garrisoned by militia. We stopt a couple of hours near the margin of a bubbling fount, whose very sparkle seemed to infuse new vigour into the men after their fatigueing march under the heat of a summer's sun in a southern latitude. After resting, and refreshing ourselves with the contents of our haversacks, we resumed the line of march, the Indians in the van.[4] It was a beautiful sight as we proceeded through the

10

forest path, catching occasional glimpses of sky, and stream, and glade. My elevated position on horseback as I sometimes followed in the rear, enabled me to overlook the extended line of troops as they wound their course through the serpentine path of the open pine-woods. Their white cross-belts upon a ground of sky-blue,— the colour of their fatigue uniform,—and black leathern caps glittering in the sun, as they proceeded in double-file, gave them, in their route-step, fluctuating motion, the appearance of a huge snake "winding its slow length along," the body of leading Indians on horse-back in their picturesque dresses representing the head. This resemblance was heightened when overlooking them from the summit of an elevated hill, which I frequently had an opportunity of doing, on account of the undulating surface over which we marched. Far ahead of all rode Major Paddy, on a cream coloured horse, his saddle covered with a scarlet blanket; and at his side hung an Indian bullet pouch or *sukchahoo-ché,* highly ornamented with party-coloured beads; his turban distinguished from the rest by the graceful floating of an eagle's feather.

Passing Fort McCreary, we immediately entered upon the scene of Indian devastations. For eight miles before we reached Roanoke, the road presented nothing but a continued series of black heaps of ashes, all that remained to mark the once happy homes of many now houseless families. Few escaped without some of their members falling victims to the devilish craft and subtilty of this insidious foe. Showing themselves in moments of unsuspicious security, invests their system of indiscriminate hostility with tenfold horrors and calamities. Sad indeed is the day which calls forth an Indian's vengeance; and still more sad, when rising in his might he swears to be avenged for all his wrongs.

The sun had just set, and a few bright streaks still brightened the west, the evening star appearing in serene beauty, when we entered what a few weeks back was the beautiful village of Roanoke.[5] Dark was the scene that spread before us. Nothing marked the place where once it stood but heaps of ashes and a few charred logs. Of many proud mansions which lately reared their fronts to the admiration of the beholder, not one was left.

The firebrand of the savage had but too well done its work. My tent was pitched upon the very spot where stood the house of Col. Gibson, from the smouldering remnants of which were picked up the bones of two unfortunate persons, who unable to escape, had been burnt to death. The Col. was in his house when the attack was made, and the first intimation he received of it was the whistling of rifle bullets through every window. It was just before daylight, the favorite time for an Indian attack, yet he could distinctly see that every egress was well guarded by the tawney devils. His determination was soon formed; so seizing a loaded double barrel gun, he threw open a back door, and discharging both barrels into a crowd of Indians who stood there thirsting for his blood, he immediately made a rush, and succeeded in escapeing their vigilance by concealing himself in a neighbouring stream with only his nose out. In another house which these devils had set on fire, was a woman concealed under a box with her infant; on their retireing she extinguished the fire. The Indians thinking they had not done their work effectually, returned and again set fire to it, and while in the house sat upon the very box which concealed the woman and the child. This was repeated several times, until the woman succeeded in escaping unobserved to a stream, where she hid as the Col. did. Many similar incidents of hair-breadth escapes are told by those who saved their scalps, but which I shall omit in these desultory notes of a campaign, intended merely for my own reference in after years, or the perusal of those friends who take an interest in my movements.

On the evening of the 24th June we heard the distant sound of drums and fifes, heralding the approach of Gen. Sandford [Sanford][6] with his army of 2000 Georgia Militia. [They appeared in all the panoply of glorious war, with the thrilling notes of martial music sounding in their ears, and banners of gaudy hues waving before their eyes, rallying points on the destined fields of victory for these brave defenders of their country's rights.][7] They encamped near us. Gen. Scott and Staff also made their appearance soon after. The scene now presented upon the site of the late desolated Roanoke,—the animation, stir, and bustle of so large a camp,—was in striking contrast to the dark and smothering ruins around. It produced sensations of a novel kind in my breast. Although I had entered the Army with all the military ardor and feelings as it were of an old campaigner, yet the sudden transition from the ease and indulgences which a city life afforded, to the privations and exposures incidental to a camp in the vicinity of an enemy, rendered the task of identifying myself in this situation at times difficult.

At first the camp fare of bacon and hard bread washed down morning and evening with coffee without milk, and from a tin cup, was not disagreeable on account of its novelty; but a continued repetition of the same routine of diet awakened feelings of an unpleasant kind whenever the stated hours of replenishing exhausted nature approached. To vary our fare, we set the Indians at catching some stray pigs that were seen about the place, which they did much to our amusement as well as satisfaction. The cunning and swiftness of foot displayed by them in entrapping the swiney tribe were subjects of general admiration throughout the camp. The result proved that I was not alone in desireing a variety upon the mess table. . . .[8]

The night of the 25th exposed the equanimity of my temper to its severest trial. The thunder rolled, the lightening flashed, and the rain came down in torrents. I had been able to procure only one of the common tents, which covered a space six feet square, and whose sides rose obliquely from the ground to a sharp ridge, not permitting the privilege of standing erect. In this diminutive affair did Dr. [Assistant Surgeon Madison] Mills,[9] who had just joined us, and to whom I had offered the shelter of my tent until his own deficiency could be removed, and myself attempt to be comfortable; we spread our blankets upon the ground, and sought in sleep to drown the noise of the rageing elements. But little repose were we to get that night. The tent was pitched upon a gentle decline, and it seemed as if all the water that fell from heaven had selected a channel through the spot we occupied. My tent was not water-proof in such a storm and we were soon favored with a sprinkling from above in addition to the foot of water under us. [To avoid lying in the water I perched myself upon a small box I had in the tent, between one and two feet square, and there sat all night meditating, and vowing I would quit that sort of life as soon as a return of daylight would enable me to write my resignation; for never had I thought amid the luxurious and refined life of a city, that I should ever be reduced to this.][10] The morning at last appeared, but with it a continuation of the storm. [. . . notwithstanding the storm as violent as ever, I had determined to postpone my resignation; for it occurred to me, the vicinity of an enemy was not the proper place for carrying out such a resolution.][11]

Preparations had been made for crossing the Chatahooche, and orders being issued for a move, on the 26th by eight o'clock A.M. the "general"[12] was sounded throughout the camps, and at the third roll every tent fell simultaneously, leaving no protection against the drenching rain which still came down in torrents. The whole day was consumed in transporting the baggage wagons and men, the only means of transportation being upon a flat[13] built for the occasion. A rope was carried across and tied to a tree on the opposite bank, under the protection of a six-pounder, as we expected to meet with resistance; but none was made, and the only obstacles we met with were the swift current and the high, precipitate bank up which the wagons unloaded were obliged to be pulled by the men.

Fresh trails of Indians were observed on the Alabama side of the Chatahooche, in the vicinity of our crossing place, apparently as of persons who watched us. *Major Paddy* with some of his mounted warriors were immediately put across and set upon the signs, and soon succeeded in capturing an Indian negro[14] and pony [sent by the Indians to spy on us].[15] We encamped upon an old Indian field near the river, and designated the place as Camp Sandford. The rain had poured the whole day, and right glad were we to gain once more the feeble protection of our canvass houses.

The next day increased the number of medical officers in our

14

camp by the arrival of Dr. Lawson,[16] Medical Director of the Army in the field, accompanied by Dr. [Assistant Surgeon Burton] Randall.

As there seemed but little prospect of the Indians coming to us, Gen. Scott determined upon going to seek them, and on the 25th June issued his orders to that effect.[17] The country we were in being Indian territory, was almost "terra incognita" to any but an Indian; and it was very well known that these children of the forests never have larger roads than foot-paths or trails. It was therefore necessary to leave all the wagons behind, and carry only what might be required for four-days rations[18] on pack-mules. There were many sick also, who would be unable to endure the fatigue of scouring the Cawaggee swamps,[19] and these were left behind with the baggage and wagons; also one company of militia as guard. The duty was assigned to me of remaining behind to attend the sick; no sinecure, as the sick list reported between 60 and 70, and most of them cases of dysentery and diarrhea, from drinking the rotten lime-stone water of the country [. . . and exposure to the vicissitudes of camp life].[20]

We felt rather insecure with our small and inefficient guard of militia, while the capture of so much baggage,—there being upwards of eighty wagons,—held out so strong an inducement for an attack from the Indians.[21] To strengthen our position as much as possible, we had all the wagons drawn up in close array around us in the manner of a stockade, leaving an open space on one side, through which a six-pounder threatened destruction to all who should attempt the approach.

Those of the invalids who were least indisposed were made to mount guard; [knowing the laxity of discipline among our militia soldiers, we were not altogether disposed to trust our safety entirely to militia vigilance],[22] and on Dr. Elwes' recovery, we took our turns in being officer of the day. Never were the duties more strictly performed by any one than by us on these occasions; for not feeling much confidence in our militia sentinels, we scrupulously kept awake, and went the grand rounds several times in the night, by which we incurred more risk of a shot from them than from the savages. Our precaution was not thrown away; for notwithstanding the imminent danger threatening them, the eyelids of these votaries of Morpheus had so great a desire of associating together, as to exclude all remembrance of their being on post, and frequently were these valiant defenders found indulging in dreams of their comfortable homes, while the duties of the tented field demanded their utmost vigilance. [One of these militia sentinels whom I found asleep on post, pleaded for excuse, that he had so violent a tooth-ache he could not possibly keep awake. Happy fellow! To have such a remedy!]²³

On the second night an incident occurred which enabled us to ascertain the energies of our men. About midnight the alarm was given by one of the sentinels: immediately—

"Fixed at his post was each bold patriot formed,
In well-rang'd squadron strongly circled round;
So close their order, or disposed their fight.
As Pallas's self might view with fix'd delight;
Or had the God of War inclined his eyes,
The God of War had own'd a just surprise.
A chosen Phalanx, firm, resolv'd as Fate,
Descending Indians and their battle wait."

But no descending Indians made their appearance; only an Indian dog; and the alarmed sentinel had fired, under the supposition, that an Indian and his dog were inseparable.

After four days absence Gen. Sandford and his army returned to our camp; Gen. Scott having proceeded on to Fort Mitchell with all the regulars except Major Lomax's battalion, which returned with the militia. Gen. Sandford now in command, took advantage of that circumstance to order me to Fort McCreary, where Gen. Lowe and his regiment of [Georgia] militia were stationed, and who being dissatisfied with their own Surgeon, had made a request that a surgeon of the regular army might be sent to them. It was with great reluctance that I obeyed this order; but there was no alternative, so on the 1st July I obtained a passage in the Steam-boat American, as far as the landing within a mile of Fort McCreary. This boat had been fitted up with barricades, and was occupied by seamen and officers of the Navy, for the purpose of plying up and down the Chatahooche to intercept any Indians who might attempt to cross;[24] and was on her way up to Columbus when I thus became an [honorary] passenger in her. [Lt. Johnston of the Navy was in command.] These fellows lived like fighting cocks aboard, having an abundance of every luxury; and it really did my heart good to see their dinner-table arrayed in all the appliances of civilization; and my mouth watered in anticipation of the dinner hour with its attendant comforts, for latterly I had been smitten with a scarcity of provisions. But alas! that hour was never to arrive for me on that day, either aboard the steam-boat or any where else. We reached the place of my destination just before the dinner-hour, which had been delayed for the purpose of preparing something extra in honor of their guests,—for there were other officers aboard as passengers besides myself. At the landing I found a portion of the garrison who were discharging the duties of guard to some stores that had been left there. Leaving my baggage under their charge until I could walk to the fort and send for it, my horse which I had sent round by land with my attendant not having yet arrived, I started off at a rapid pace in hopes of getting there before their dinner-hour past. The walk proved longer than I desired, and here I was too late. Among my baggage left at the landing was a champaign basket, which I used as a mess chest, and which I recollected to be well stored with ready-cooked edibles. My only chance of a dinner was to send for that, and in the interim act the part of "patience on a monument," smiling at an empty stomach. I was destined to more noble suffering, for on the arrival of the aforesaid champaign basket, my prospect for a dinner was very much darkened; I found myself now reduced to great extremity and small means, for with a superfluity of appetite I found a plentiful deficiency of the wherewithal to satisfy the same; the basket was empty, its contents having been appropriated by the hungry sentinels at the landing.

CHAPTER III

I remained at Fort McCreary until the morning of the 4th July, when Gen. Lowe having received an order to proceed to Columbus, I departed with him; but hearing that a party of hostile Indians who had been captured were to be sent immediately west of the Mississippi to their new home, I took the road to Fort Mitchell, hoping that my services as Surgeon to Emigrating Indians,—on which special duty I had been detailed,—might be called into requisition.

I passed on the road several companies of Gen. Sandford's army, on their way to Columbus, to be paid off; their time of volunteering had expired, and fighting Indians not being what it was cracked up to be in their opinion, all their valorous and patriotic feeling had evaporated and the desire of glory having yielded to the desire for domestic rest, they were hurrying home.[1]

The sky was sketched in broad yellow radiance in the west, and the lengthened shadows had disappeared when I reached the foot of the eminence upon whose summit the stockade called Fort Mitchell is situated. I had passed this day of feasting and celebration throughout the Union in travelling through dreary woods, beguileing my tedious and fatiguing progress by conjuring up in every whispering leaf a patriotic orator, and dwelling in fancy upon the fine odours emanating from innumerable viands that were then undergoing the fiery ordeal, preparatory to the task of blunting the keen edge of patriotic appetites. Such cogitations had the inevitable effect of exciting a congenial feeling of patriotism in my own stomach; and it was with a due degree of anxiety about the normal dinner-hour I looked out for a chance of obtaining the necessary accompaniments of mortality. I did not long despair; for soon—

The Journal

"I knew by the smoke that so gracefully curl'd
Through the dark pine-trees, that a log-hut was near,
And I said, 'if there's corn-bread to be found in the world
A stomach that was hungry might hope for it here.' "

On arriving at Fort Mitchell I put up at Johnson's; a log-house which assumed the dignified appellation of Hotel. I found that after lodging in the open air I could not sleep with comfort in a house, and the two or three first nights after my arrival were sleepless ones.

I was too late for the emigrating party of hostile Indians, Dr. Abadie, who was on the spot, having been assigned to accompany them before my arrival.

It was a melancholy spectacle as these proud monarchs of the soil were marched off from their native land to a distant country, which to their anticipations presented all the horrors of the infernal regions. There were several who committed suicide rather than endure the sorrow of leaving the spot where rested the bones of their ancestors. One old fellow was found hanging by the neck the night before he was to leave Fort Mitchell for the far West; preferring the glorious uncertainty of another world, to the inglorious misery of being forced to a country of which he knew nothing, but dreaded every thing bad.[2] This indifference to life was displayed by the Indians on many occasions; for though apparently great in open battle, yet death by their own hands presented no terrors to them.

On one occasion when a party of them were overtaken and attacked in Georgia while trying to get to Florida, one of them being wounded in the leg could not escape, and seeing a white man approach him as he lay upon the ground, rather than be taken prisoner, drew out his knife and deliberately cut his own throat.

There is a more noble instance of self-sacrifice told of an Indian Princess, who being seized with the small-pox, immediately killed herself to prevent the infection from spreading among her tribe.

Journey into Wilderness

One of this very party of emigrating Indians on his arrival at Montgomery [Alabama] attempted his escape; but when caught and secured in a waggon, by some accident got possession of a very dull knife; with this he made several ineffectual efforts to cut his throat, but it not proving sharp enough, he with both hands forced it into his chest over the breast-bone, and by successive violent thrusts succeeded in dividing the main artery, when he bled to death. Similar instances of suicide were very common, and served forcibly to exhibit how strong the "amor patriae" burned in their breasts. With them their country was life, and without the former the latter was valueless. To them how applicable the words of Horace—"dulce et decorum est pro patria mori."[3]

A party of five hundred who had been taken captive, and brought to Fort Mitchell, were necessarily sent off in chains. The men were handcuffed two together, and a long chain passing between the double file connected them all together. The stoical disposition of these forest philosophers was strongly displayed, for neither their physical nor mental sufferings could elicit from them the least indication of distress, except occasionally the utterance of an emphatic "ta" whenever two of them pulling in opposite directions would jerk one another by the wrists. The women followed drowned in tears, and giving utterance to most distressing cries; the children joined in from sympathy, for they were yet too young to participate in the unenviable feelings of their parents. The smaller ones were comfortably disposed off [of] in the waggons, which followed in the rear.[4]

I here had an opportunity of seeing the celebrated hostile chief, *Neah-Mathla* [*Eneah Mathla*], who has on every occasion during his life manifested the most inimical feelings towards the whites. It was he who headed the Seminoles in the last war against Genl. Jackson, and who even now, tho' he is a prisoner in irons, glories in being the avenger of his people's wrongs. He does not attempt to disguise his hostile feelings, but justifies himself on account of the extensive frauds committed by the white men upon his tribe. He is now eighty four years of age; has a remarkably fine fore-

The Journal

head, and still possesses an eagle eye, and his countenance gives the impression of his being a brave and remarkable man. He has a son in captivity with him for whom he displays great affection; he is quite "unconcerned as regards his own fate," he says, "but spare his son." At the time they were captured, a manifestation was made to kill his son, when the old man broke loose from his guards and posting himself in front of his son, bared his breast and entreated his captors not to touch his boy, but to kill him instead.[5]

I remained at Fort Mitchell until the 8th July, when an order was sent me to proceed without delay to Tuskegee, Ala: and there report myself to Gen. Jessup [Jesup][6] for services with Major [Sylvester] Churchill's battalion of Artillery.

As the country was still infested with hundreds of hostile Indians, and Tuskegee was fifty miles off, it would be running the risk of almost certain death to attempt the journey alone; so I delayed a few days until Major Slaughter of the Alabama volunteers, who expected to leave in a day or two, should be ready to go with his escort.

On the 11th July we left Fort Mitchell and proceeded in a westwardly direction on the old Federal road,[7] directly through the heart of the hostile nation. All along the road was presented a repetition of the devastated scenes which met the eye at Roanoke. Bridges destroyed; houses burnt; and new made graves, where the murdered travellers had been hastily buried beside the road; half-burnt remains of stages and waggons that had been pillaged by the Indians blocked up the way; and in one spot the road was filled with empty coffins, scattered in all directions by the Indians, who had taken them from a waggon, sent out for the purpose of bringing in the dead for burial.

We reached before dark the only house left by the Indians on the road; there we found Col. Brooks[8] of the artillery with his command encamped; and there we concluded to stop for the night. This house was occupied by a man named Stone, and by a sign-board which swung from a tree in front, I inferred that it had been a tavern in times of peace under the title of "Creek Stand."

21

Journey into Wilderness

The next morning we resumed our journey at an early hour, and being now in that part of the Creek nation which remained friendly, passed through several Indian towns that were still inhabited. At one of them we were introduced by the Lieutenant of our escort to his father, a venerable old Indian.

Until that moment I was not aware that Lt. Monroe [Moniac][9] was other than a white man; but on enquiry I ascertained he was a half-breed; had been educated at West Point Academy, and on the completion of his studies received a commission in the Army. He soon after resigned; a visit to his family having revived in his breast in all its former force the roving disposition of his people. Since then he has ranged with native freedom over the woods and plains, until the recent outbreak of the Indians afforded him an opportunity of showing his gratitude to the government which had fostered him in his youth.

After exchanging courtesies with these sons of the forest, we continued our course, and entered Tuskegee about midday. I reported myself to Capt. Lane,[10] Gen. Jesup's adjutant, he being absent, and immediately retired to bed at Wm. Dent's hotel, being seized with a most confounded head-ache and fever. By proper care I was up and moving the next day, and began to look around at the place I had got into.

Tuskegee is a specimen of American cities in their infancy, when only a few hours old. A selected spot in the primeval forest had been laid out in town lots, and a few buildings had arisen from among stumps and burnt trees. Although but a year has elapsed since the birth of this place, it now boasted a jail, several stores, and rival hotels. It also as a matter of course had its law-offices, but what was remarkable no physician. I should have marked this latter circumstance as an unaccountable phenomenon, but was informed that the physician had been killed by his horse running away and throwing him against a tree a few days back. Poor fellow! I knew him well; he was a townsman of mine, and had but recently graduated. We attended the same course of lectures together for two years in Charleston, I preceeding him by one year only in becoming an M.D.

22

The Journal

Tuskegee is situated midway from Columbus, Ga: and Montgomery, Ala: on the principal mail-route between New Orleans and Charleston, and was before this war, the medium of much travelling. I found it filled with Alabama mounted volunteers. A thousand or more were mustered out of service the day after my arrival, and—happy fellows!—took up the line of march for *home*. Major Churchill, who had gone with his command to Montgomery as a guard for the emigrating party of Indians until they should be safely deposited on board steamboats, returned on the 14th July, when I reported myself to him for duty, having received an order to that effect. In consequence of there being no physician at Tuskegee, but myself, while I remained there my services were in constant requisition among all classes, ages, and sexes.

CHAPTER IV

I continued dispensing medicine and health in Tuskegee until the 1st August, when I received an order to repair immediately to Camp McClenden, fifteen miles from Tuskegee on the road to Columbus, and to remain there as long as Dr. Elwes the Surgeon at the station should continue sick. In the afternoon I started in company with Col. Brooks and Lt. Emery, and when we had got half-way, a soldier was seen riding towards us full speed. On meeting us he put a letter into Col. Brooks' hand. After the perusal of it, the latter turned to me with an order to put spurs to my horse and proceed on as rapidly as possible, for my services were needed immediately in camp. Military orders must be obeyed without questions, so away I went, wondering what under the sun could be the matter. The Indians certainly could not have attacked the camp; and Dr. Elwes surely cannot be dying. It was near dark when I reached the encampment, and soon ascertained that a different job awaited me than what I had anticipated when I started. One of the men in a fit of derangement had attempted to shoot his orderly sergeant, when Sergeant [William] Rea, who was Sergeant of the guard, interfered and received the contents of the maniac's musket in his right arm. On examining the arm I found that a ball and two buck-shot had passed obliquely through the right elbow joint, fracturing the extremities of the bones forming the joint in so dreadful a manner that I deemed immediate amputation necessary. Lights were procured, and with the assistance of one of the soldiers who acted as hospital steward I performed the operation. No doubt to the great admiration of all the officers and men who were witnesses of my skill. The Sergeant displayed great firmness under the knife; while I was taking up the arteries, he observing one of the candles which were of tallow burning rather dimly, with the

24

fingers of his remaining hand very coolly pinched off the long wick, at the same time chiding the holder for his negligence. I felt much interested for the success of this case, it being my first operation of any magnitude, and performed under such disadvantages.

Dr. Elwes in a few days recovered sufficiently to leave his bed, when he obtained a furlough, and departed for the "Merryweather Mineral Springs" in Georgia.[1] The first week of my stay at this station, there were two companies of Artillery present, one commanded by Major Erving, the other by Capt. Harvey Brown;[2] the latter at the end of that time was ordered with his company to the "Big Warrior Stand."[3]

Most of my time while at this station was occupied with the sick, of which there were many, and some severe cases of dysentery and congestine or typhoid fever, for these diseases prevailed extensively among the men; there were several Tennessean Volunteers also who had been left under my care affected with the latter disease. I, however, had cause to congratulate both myself and my patients on the success of my treatment. In three weeks after the operation I had the gratification of discharging Sergt. Rea from the Hospital perfectly well [. . . after giving him a certificate for pension, as being disabled in the discharge of his duties while Sergeant of the guard].[4] Such unremitting attention was too much for me; I soon had to take my own medicine, and for a week was confined to a sick bed.

While in this neighbourhood I met with a remarkable case of recovery from a wound which would in general be considered fatal. A negro woman belonging to Col. Watson, whose plantation is situated near the Chattahooche river, was shot through the body by some Indians during an attack upon the plantation. She was in an advanced state of pregnancy at the time, and soon after the accident was brought to bed, when it was ascertained that the ball had passed through the head of the child while in the womb. The woman soon recovered without any difficulty.

Occasionally I found time to ride to Echo Hadjo's camp[5] of friendly Indians, five miles off. On one of my visits I found their head men in full assembly and going through the ceremony of taking the black-drink.[6] This is only done on very important occasions, such as the declaration of war, etc., of which this was one, for they were met in council to deliberate upon the expediency of going to Florida to fight against the Seminoles. The place of assembly was a large square area, bounded on the four sides by long open sheds, under which, upon a platform of canes raised three feet from the ground were reclining the dignitaries in various attitudes; some sitting cross-legged like a taylor [tailor], others resting upon their elbows, while not a few were stretched off at full length upon their backs, and all decked out in their savage finery. In the center of the square was a fire, over which was suspended from a cross-stick a large earthen pot, containing the ingredients of the black-drink. Two men who superintended the process of preparation, were engaged with long ladles in skimming off the froth which rose to the surface of the liquid in considerable quantity. After a due time had elapsed in this way, the ladles were supplanted in the hands of the two masters of ceremony by gourds with long handles and an aperture on one side an inch in diamitre [diameter]. Having filled these with the precious liquid, they proceeded to opposite sides of the area and commenced handing it round. As soon as the hole in the gourd and the mouth of the drinker came in contact, an apparent rivalship commenced between the two waiters, in a singular song of but one note, consisting of the sound ah-ah-a-a prolonged with a shrill key without drawing breath until the drinker finished his task. This they seemed in a great hurry to do, for the drink is said to be remarkably bitter and nauseous. I was told that the reputation of the drinker for eloquence was always measured by the number of mouthfuls he took; he who stood at the top of the ladder of oratory always drank the longest, while the occupant of the lower round could not take more than one swallow. The drink had the reputation of clearing their minds and making bright ideas flow, preparatory to making a speech. From its effect upon the stomach I do not doubt its capability of purifying the brain; for after swallowing a dose, the poor orators seemed much distressed as if

The Journal

laboring under the operation of an emetic, with this difference only, that instead of discharging the nauseous stuff at once, they would sit for an hour after swallowing it, belching up the contents of their bread-baskets every five minutes into their mouths, and from there, discharge it with a squirt towards the centre of the square.[7] The sight was extremely ludicrous after the drink had made the entire circuit, to see so many grave and dignified figures sitting around in perfect silence, engaged in squirting from all directions towards one spot. [Can this, however, be considered as presenting any more disgusting sight than the practice in all our own legislative assemblies of squirting filthy tobacco juice over the floor? The savages indeed have the better claim to wisdom, for theirs is a purifying process; and by clearing the stomach, bring their minds to a proper condition for business; whereas tobacco chewing can produce no other effect than endangering the health, and weakening the intellectual faculties. Of the two practices let us rather adopt that of the Indians as far more civilized, and refined, and characteristic of wise people.][8] Observing a singular appearance of stripes upon the legs of all the men, I was induced to inquire the cause, was told that it was a universal custom with them to scratch their legs with needles fixed into a piece of wood, until the blood flowed. They asserted that when fatigued this operation afforded them immediate relief and considerable pleasure.[9] They are also remarkably fond of being bled, particularly the women; the sight of a lancet in the hand of any one is sure always to elicit from them a request to have it used upon them, whether sick or well. They frequently bleed themselves with a piece of glass, preferring that to a lancet which they cannot use themselves. I became quite proficient in the Creek language, by mingling with our Indian neighbours, and will give a specimen of the Creek tongue in some of their words and phrases. I shall first give the words used by them in counting, which according to their arrangement may designate any amount.

1—*Hum*p*kin.*
2—Ho*c*olin.

3—Tut*che*nin.
4—*O*stin.

27

5—Cho-*ci*pin.
6—Ep*a*kin.
7—Colo*pa*kin.
8—Chinapakin.
9—Osta*pa*kin.
10—*Pa*lin.
11—*Pa*lin-hump*k*iligen.
12—*Pa*lin-hocolo*ca*gen.
13—*Pa*lin-tutcheno*ca*gen.
14—*Pa*lin-osta*ca*gen.
15—*Pa*lin-choce*po*ca*gen.
16—*Pa*lin-spaco*ca*gen.
17—*Pa*lin-colipo*ca*gen.
18—*Pa*lin-chinipa*ca*gen.

19—*Pa*lin-ostopa*ca*gen.
20—*Pa*lin-hoco*lin.
21—*Pa*lin-ho-*co*lin-humkiligen.
22—*Pa*lin-ho-colin-hocolo*ca*gen.
30—*Pa*lin-tut*che*nin.
40—*Pa*lio*s*ten.
50—*Pa*licho*ke*pin.
60—*Pa*lio*pa*kin.
70—*Pa*licolo*pa*kin.
80—*Pa*lichina*pa*kin.
90—*Pa*liostapakin.
100—*Ch*opki-hum*pkin.

1000—*Ch*opkithl*u*cko.

I have spelt the words so that in pronunciation the vowels should be sounded according to the French rule of pronunciation. I shall now give a few of their words. [The entire language being very limited as regards words, the same is frequently used to express different things; the meaning communicated by the emphasis and tone of voice, which in the Indian is capable of the sweetest modulation. Tis music itself to hear the Indians conversing in hours of social intercourse.][10]

Arm—Chehsak *pah*.
Apple—Satatla*koo*.
All gone—Suks-*cheh*.
Are you sick?—Chech no *kah?*
Bed—To*pah*.
Blanket—A-*chit*-tah.
Breech-cloth—E-*goph*-ka.
Bad—Holy-waugus *cheh*.
[Boot—E-*fa* teh-ka.][11]
Belt—*Shee*-wan-a-le-ta.
Book—Nako *cheh*.
Bread—Tutle*keh*. or Ta-ka-*li*-ka.
Boy—Whaunan *cheh*.
Big—Lak-*kits*.
Beads—Ho-*nai*-wah.
Black man—Ista *lust*ch.
Cup—Alo*wah*.
Cat—C*a*t*eh*.
Cow—*Wa*ukah.
Child—Ista *cheh*.
Camp—Cheh ah *pah*.

Creek—Hatcheh.
Corn—*Ah*cheh.
Day—*Ni*ttah.
Dog—Ehf*ah*.
Day before yesterday—Pox-ung-keh-
ah-si-ung-keh.
[Dollar Gone—Dollar-humpkin.][12]
Eye—Sattatlo*hah*.
Father—*Chilth*-keh.
Fire—*T*oot*kah*.
Fence—Tohope*kee*.
Fingers—Chankeh wasah *kah*.
Foot—Chatteh.
Green—Lan-*nits*.
Give me—Ah mis *cheh*.
Good—*Hin*clus.
Very good—Hinclus ta *ma* hich.
Very good indeed—Hincla *mas* cheh.
Horse—Cholocko.
Hunting shirt—Yo kofe kitt*ah*.
House—Sookoo.

The Journal

Head—Sakkah.
Hair—Sakkah sischeh.
Half—A-pul-*hump*-kin.
Indian—Ista *chatt*eh.
Leggins—Ah fah *teh* kah.
Little—Chope-kut-zin.
Little girl—Hocteh *cheh*.
Log—Cheh hatch kah *wah*.
Lie down—Waugus cheh.
Moccasin—Chilleh *pika*.
Mine—Cha-*na*-kits-chey.
Much—Mas.
More—*Hat*-tum.
Milk—Waukah *pis*seh.
Money—Chatta kanah *wah*.
Man—*Wha*nan. [or Ista.]¹³
My hands—*Chon*keh.
Your hands—*Chin*keh.
Mouth—Sattat ko *hah*.
Moon—Nekleh hossee.
Make haste—La*kow*.
Me, or I—Ena.
[Merchant—Is-nees-ca.]¹⁴
No—Cush.
Night—*Neth*-lee.
Nothing the matter—*Stone*kus.
Pouch—Sugcha *hoo* cheh.
Pouch strap—Sugcha hoo cheh fugkah.
Physician—Illis *haiah*.
Physic—Illis-*wah*.
Peach—Pacaneah.
Rice—*Alo*so.
River—Withla*koo*.
Little River—Withlakoo*cheh*.
Run—Li kus *cheh*.
Stop—Hattits cheh.
Listen—Cheh wun weh.
Say again—Nakin.
Son—Chat-pots-zen.
[Sister—Cheh-mun-wah.]¹⁵
Spurs—E*schief* kittah.
Sit down—*Lag*us cheh.
Saddle—Opat*ak*ah.
Sun—Netah Hossee.
Sugar—Asoko*lah*.
Segar—Hit-chy-ah-*pal*-kah.

Stone—Sa*tow*.
Stars—Koto chumpah.
Strong, or bitter—Homis-cheh.
Very sick—E-ah-kal-e-*mas*-cheh.
I don't know—Kith-lucks.
Very handsome—Helittah ma *hich*.
Tobacco—*Hit*-chey.
[Tobacco pipe—Hit-cheh-pak-ah-wah.]¹⁶
Tomorrow—*Pox*eh.
Today—Mo-*cha*-mit-tah.
What's the matter?—Estomah?
Too much—Ti-tai-*mas*-chey.
What's your name—Nakin *chief* ka *teh*?
Woman, or girl—*Hoc*teh.
White man—Ista *had*keh.
My wife—Cheh ah *wah*.
Water—Owe*wah*.
Yesterday—Pox-*ung*-keh.
Yes—Kah [or Inca.]
You—Chee-me.
Yours—Hat-ta-mais-chey.
I am your friend—An hisseh elittah *mas* cheh.
I love you—Cheh mokah *is* cheh.
I love that woman a great deal—Hocteh ahcheh attanokah *tamas* cheh.
That is a pretty girl—*Hoc*teh elittah mas cheh.
You are a pretty girl—*Hoc*teh cheh elittah fon.
Where do you live?—Istah ma ehootah cheh?
That's my house—Sacheh sookoo.
How old are you?—Cheh ma solehta estoma cheh?
Do you want it?—Cheh-ah-che-teh.
[I drink your health—Is-ea-la-mus-cheh.]¹⁷
I want it—Chi-ah-chis-cheh.
Buy it—Nis-us-*cheh*.
How much?—Nah-*cho*-mah?
Come let us go—A-la-kus-*cheh*.
Very well, it is so—Mo-mus-*cheh*.

29

Journey into Wilderness

I speak to you—Cheh-no-kahis-*cheh*.
I give you—*Che*-mai-*lanits*-cheh.
I am going—I-ee-pus-*cheh*.
My daughter—*Chits*-hotes-teh.

Eight of a dollar—Ka-lai-*zu*-cheh.
Quarter of a dollar—Kan-*zat*-kah.
Sixteen of a dollar—Pick-eh-*u*-chee.

Verbs.

Ligiton—Infinitive mode [mood]—To lay down, or ride.

Indicative Mode

Present tense—Ligico—I ride.
 Ligitska—you ride.
 Ligue—he rides.

Okagen—we ride.

Okaga—they ride.

 Imperfect tense—Ligungis—rode.
  Ligungst.
  Ligungi.
  Okagunga.

 Future tense—Ligathlonis—will ride.
 Singular—Ligatlomitska.
 Plural—Okagatlonis.
  Ligofen—when I ride.
 Imperative—Ligue-cheh—ride thou.

Aieton—to go.
Aiepus—I go.
Aiungis—I went.
Aiepotlonis—I will go.
Aiefen—When I go.
Aiepus cheh—go.
Hateton—to stop.
Hattits cheh—stop.
Haieton—to make.
Nisseton—to sell.
Ateton—to come.

Watiis—I come.
Atloniis—I will come.
Atits cheh—come.
Ista na' atitska?—Where do you come from?
Tuskegee n'atiis cheh—I come from Tuskegee.
Ista n'aiatlonitska?—Where are you going?
Hatchee tabaia—Across the creek.

[The Creek and Seminole Indians speak the same language, having been originally the same people; there is some slight difference in unimportant idioms but [they are] easily understood by both tribes.][18]

CHAPTER V

*O*n the 7th Sept Major Erving received an order to repair with his command to Fort Mitchell, as soon as relieved by a company of marines.[1] I, of course, expected to go with him, and was in high spirits at the idea of escaping from the dull woods and once more mingling with the inhabitants of the civilized world. But my evil genius still haunted me. Dr. Elwes, who had long before recovered, and remained at Columbus, loathe to return to this his proper post, when he heard of this anticipated movement, he immediately posted down to report himself, and proceeding instantly to head-quarters at Tuskegee, requested that my situation might be given to him, and I left behind with the marines. He succeeded in obtaining his request; and on the arrival of Capt. Harris[2] and marines, with a sad heart, I saw those depart for Fort Mitchell whom by right I ought to have accompanied.

I remained with the marines at McClenden until the 14th Sept when Major [William L.] McClintock of the Artillery with the last of the Regulars who had been in the interior, passed by our encampment on their way to Fort Mitchell, at which point all the Army were collecting, preparatory to entering Florida, the Creek war being considered at an end, as only a few hundred Indians remained in the swamps without surrendering. My heart leaped with joy, and a host of splenetic imps was put to the route when the Major handed me an order from Gen. Jesup to join these troops.

We marched into Fort Mitchell about 1 o'clock the next day. In this vicinity was the camp of seven hundred Indian Volunteers, who had entered the service of the United States for the purposes of proceeding to Florida, and fighting against the Seminoles. They were only induced to this step by their reluctance to emigrate to the West, their families being allowed to remain in Alabama until

31

they should return from the Florida expedition. They presented a formidable array against Osceola and his band of hostiles.[3]

I was witness to their amazement at the sight of the India-rubber or Ponton [pontoon] bridge invented by Capt. [John F.] Lane of the Army; and which was then undergoing an examination on the Chatahooche before the Committee appointed for that purpose. It consisted of large bags of pontons, something like cotton bags in shape made of India-rubber cloth, which being filled with air and attached sideways together formed a bridge of fourteen feet width, and any length, according to the number of bags used; upon these were laid light timber to support boards placed laterally, which forming a smooth, level, surface, admitted the passage of wagons, horses, etc. A detachment of six hundred men with all their arms and accoutrements, including the officers mounted upon horses, marched on it at once, and after remaining a quarter of an hour going through the evolutions to test its strength, they countermarched with as much facility as if on *terra firma*. Field pieces with their complement of matrosses,[4] and their caissons filled with ammunition, and loaded wagons were also driven over it with the same ease. It was said that a troop of horses arriving at night at a river where this bridge was stretching across the river, and seeing it, crossed upon it, under the impression that it was a common bridge. The great advantage of this bridge is its portableness, all the pontons and cordge [cordage] for a bridge of three hundred and fifty feet being capable of transportation in a single wagon; whereas the former ponton equipages consisted of cumbrous and bulky pontons of wood, sheet iron, and copper.

A few days after my arrival I witnessed the departure of this tawney regiment in steamboats for Florida, under the command of Capt. Lane, of the Regular Army, who held the ex-officio rank of Colonel. They went off apparently delighted at the prospect of having some body to fight, no consequence to them with whom.

In the last Seminole war, when one of their chiefs was asked why he made war upon the whites, who had always been their friends, and were ever willing to be at peace with them; he replied,

ENN. N. CAROLINA

THE STATE OF
GEORGIA

MOTTE'S ITINERARY...

SAVANNAH

OCONEE

OCMULGEE

TO CHARLESTON

Augusta

SOUTH CAROLINA RR

Sparta

Hamburg

FEDERAL   ROAD

RIVER

Milledgeville

OGEECHEE

OLD

Ft. Hawkins

RIVER

RIVER

Savannah

Columbus

Creek
Agency

RIVER

shell

Ft. McCreary

KICHAFOONE

RIVER

ALTAMAHA   RIVER

Roanoke

on

Pinderton

CHATTAHOOCHEE

Ft. Gaines

FLINT   RIVER

OKEFINOKEE

WITHLACOOCHEE RIVER

UPPER

ALAPAHA RIVER

SWAMP

RIVER

Franklinville

SUWANEE

ST. MARYS

RIVER

RIVER

APALACHICOLA RIVER

Tallahassee

Jacksonville

FLORIDA

St. Marks

ST. JOHNS RIVER

St. Augustine

SUWANEE   RIVER

SANTA FE RIVER

GULF

OF

MEXICO

that he knew the whites had never injured them, but that making war was such a manly exercise he liked to practice his young men at it.

Col. Lane went off in high spirits; and well he may, for the command of such a regiment would be an honor to any man and particularly under existing circumstances with the prospect, as every one supposed, of their immediately terminating the Seminole war. Just before his departure the Col. rode up to a group of us, who were standing conversing together, and shook hands with all, evidently very happy. As he went off, some one observed, "there goes Lane on the road to glory."[5] [Alas! none anticipated what was soon to be his fate.][6]

On reaching Fort Mitchell this time I had hoped for a little respite from the severe privations and trials I had been so long subjected to but my expectations were not to be realized;—they were only to be enjoyed in perspective. In consequence of the great alarm excited in the southern counties of Georgia by murders and depredations committed by the Creek Indians who were endeavouring to escape into Florida from Alabama, Governor Schley[7] had petitioned Gen. Jesup to station some troops in Ware or Lowndes County, that being the least populous and most defenceless portion of the country through which the Indians were passing. It was also liable to invasions from the Seminoles, as it bordered upon Florida. In compliance with this request, Major [Greenleaf] Dearborn with two companies of Infantry was ordered to proceed immediately to the above counties in Georgia, and there establish himself. These counties being so far south and in a low swampy part of the country had the worst possible reputation for health, and going there at this season of the year was almost considered certain death to a white man and stranger unacclimated. It was necessary then to send some surgeon with the troops, that it may not be said they died without proper medical attendance; and also that they might have a chance of a surgeon in the other world to physic them. Dr. Lawson, the Medical Director, was therefore instructed by Gen. Jesup to select some one of the surgeons for this duty; and the Doctor with his usual friendly discrimination, whenever there was any particularly disagreeable duty to be done, picked upon me. So away I was ordered, to die of fever as I thought amidst the swamps of Lowndes County. Major Dearborn to whom I was ordered to report myself was at Irwinton, sixty miles below Fort Mitchell, on the Alabama side of the Chatahooche. It was therefore necessary for me to proceed there forthwith alone.

The country I had to traverse in going to Irwinton was still infested by the straggling parties of hostile Indians who had not yet submitted. I should also have to spend a night in the woods, as not one of the few houses in the intermediate country had escaped the wrath of these devils. A travelling companion would therefore have been very desirable; but none such could be found, except my good steed, who had already on several occasions been sole companion of my wanderings. Although not capable of affording much counsel and conversation, yet his presence was by no means superfluous under a sun which darted its torrid rays like lightning upon my devoted head.

On the 25th Sept I mounted my horse, and with a good pair of well loaded pistols in my holsters commenced my solitary journey. My path at first lay through frowning woods, whose gigantic columns upheld tops of dark green hue, which seemed to ascend into the clouds. All was wild, dismal, and unknown, and the melancholy sighing of the breeze which seemed to mourn the desolation of the scene, was the only sound which broke upon the ear, except the occasional plaintive whistle of the partridge, who suffered themselves to be approached without any apprehension [of danger].[8] As I proceeded through these wild glens, seldom trod by any but the Indian or wolf, a few long hillocks enclosed by logs would sometimes direct my eye to the final resting place of a savage. After proceeding fifteen miles, the fresh print of a moccasin upon the ground made me cast a more scrutinizing look into every bush and behind every tree which lay in my path before I made its proximity. But no Indian would afford me an opportunity of exercising upon him my skill as a marksman.

The sun was throwing its rays through the trees in golden

lustre, and the shadows had begun to lengthen when I came in sight of the Chatahooche river, at a spot where a river [flat][9] boat was tied. A fortunate circumstance for me, as I thus escaped the disagreeable alternative of lodging that night in the woods upon the bare ground, with a chance of waking up next morning and finding myself minus a scalp. I immediately introduced myself to the Captain, who informed me in return that he claimed the indefinite cognomen of Capt. Smith; that his boat was engaged in the service of the United States, and that my company for the night would by no means be disagreeable to him. I soon made myself at home, and in a few minutes was hale-fellow-well-met with all the crew, who, though most of them were black, seemed upon a perfect equality with the captain. After my hot ride a swim in the river was a luxury not to be neglected; so, according to the Canadian boatman's song—

> *"Je trouvais l'eau si belle,*
> *Que je m'y suis baigné."*[10]

I was afterwards indulged in a supper of Chowder made of fish and bacon served up in a tub, and coffee in a tin [that] was [a] hand basin. Although a day's fasting and a bath are good promoters of an appetite, yet I cannot say that I did much credit to the beatific excellence of Capt. Smith's fare. He and his black crew, however, soon made a clear deck. They were a hardy looking set of fellows, and though the life they lead is very laborious, [they] seemed the most cheerful and light-hearted people in the world. They were constantly stretching their mouths beyond every rule of Chesterfield, and "rending heaven's conclave with their merriment." The boat was nothing but a square flat, adapted to the navigation of these rivers when the water is too low to admit the passage of steam-boats. Going down stream they are allowed to drift with the current, only needing a particular attention and watchfulness where the rivers contracting their waters are precipitated with increased current over a shallow and rocky bed. The toil and trials are encountered in poleing up stream against a rapid current.

36

The Journal

I sat up until a late hour admiring the beautiful and sparkling splendor of the stars, which beamed in rich clusters from a moon-less sky, and were seen through the avenue of primeval forest which lined both shores of the river.

It is in such an hour of stillness and loveliness, when no sound is heard but the rustling of foliage stirred by zephyrs freighted with native fragrance, and the soft purling of gliding waters, that we love to revel in recollections of early scenes and attachments— that we hear the sweet tones of far distant friends from whom the fluctuating contingencies of the world have severed us—that we recall the scenes of happiness which those friends were wont to share with us. The soothing effects of this universal silence sued so sweetly to my senses, that they were fast settling into a congenial tranquillity, when several exceedingly loud and discordant ex-plosions of laughter, reiterated by the echo of the circumjacent forests, burst upon my auricular organs, and putting to flight fancy with all her visionary train, recalled me to a consciousness of my true situation. A soul possessing the least claim to sensibility could not resist suffering at this interruption. I found that the unpleasant strains issued from some of the crew, who having just awoke from their early slumbers, had commenced exercising their waking faculties, of which laughing in the unChesterfieldian man-ner was the principal. I smothered the expression of my wrath with the consolatary and phylosophic reflection that, "it is the destiny of man to be forever subjected to his little pittance of en-joyment, and poison those moments of sunshine, which might otherwise be consecrated to happiness." After this, I retired for the night under the Captain's mosquito bar, which he had gener-ously surrendered to my use, and slept until sun-rise next morning.

I bid farewell to my kind entertainers, who, while expressing their regret at my departure, were grinning from ear to ear, and in a few moments was again enveloped in solitude, and pursueing my way to Irwinton, where I arrived about 3 o'clock in the after-noon, without the occurrence of any further moving incidents by either flood or field.

CHAPTER VI

$\mathcal{T}$he village of Irwinton is beautifully located upon a bluff more than a hundred feet high at a bend of the Chatahooche, and afforded one of the finest views on the river, which from here extended in a straight course for several miles above. It contained many handsome frame houses that were finished, and several others were seen rapidly rising from amidst stumps and fallen trees. Among the latter I observed one with something like a steeple, which induced me to believe the salvation of the soul was duly attended to; but on inquiry I was undeceived, its destination being a public eating house, the wants of the body being held paramount to those of the soul as is usual in most new settlements.

I heard an amusing anecdote of some Alabama Volunteers who were stationed here for the protection of the place. Under the impression that Uncle Sam would pay for all their wants, they luxuriated extensively on sugar-plums, champaign, Spanish segars, and other such delightsome delicacies, and the shop-keepers were told to present their bills to the United States for payment. After the departure of the valiant soldiers for their respective homes, all the sugar-plums being consumed and therefore deeming their services no longer needed, the bills were in due form presented to Gen. Jesup; his usual gravity was quite overcome by such an anomalous circumstance, and after giving vent to his unrestrainable laughter, dismissed the poor shop-keepers with a flea in their ear and nothing in their pockets, their accounts not acknowledged by Uncle Sam.

I found Major Dearborn encamped two miles from Irwinton, and after reporting myself to him rode over to visit Major Lomax, who was also stationed in the neighbourhood with his battalion of Artillery.

On the 29th Sept we took up the line of march for Lowndes

The Journal

County, Georgia, and after crossing the Chattahooche advanced fifteen miles the first day over the most wretched roads that ever disfigured the face of the earth. We proceeded by easy marches, generally resting in the middle of the day when we took our food, which was prepared before we started in the early morn and again when we encamped for the night. The second night I slept in a church by the roadside.

A laughable occurrence took place while the men were resting in the middle of the day. We were in the midst of an open pine-woods, and the men were sitting together upon the ground under the trees in some very high grass, which left only the upper part of their bodies visible; about this time two travellers on foot happened to come along, and observing from a distance such a large body of men together in so remote and dreary a place, and having received no previous intimation of regular troops passing through, immediately took to their heels, and had retrograded a mile at double quick when they met our baggage wagons; they communicated to the teamsters the alarming information that a large army of Indians were just behind them in full chase, and advised them to leave their wagons and flee for their lives. On describing the said Indians, they were told whom they had honored with their suspicions. Indeed, our appearance might have deceived the veritable simon-pures themselves; we had become bronzed by an exposure to the sun in Alabama the whole summer; our black leather caps may easily be metamorphosed by an excited imagination into the glossy hair of the Indian at a distance, and colour of the men's jackets were the same as most of the Indian hunting shirts, their white cross-belts representing the Indian pouch strap, and their knapsacks the latter's pack; moreover, we were on the very track of the Indians who were endeavouring to escape to Florida. The two fellows looked very sheepish when they passed us.

The third night we slept in the midst of a pine-barren. The fourth, near the banks of the Kichafoona river, upon the site of an old Indian town, which was the scene of one of Jackson's slaughters in the last Seminole war.[1] The fifth night I tried to sleep, but could not, for I was tossing upon a sick bed. The next morning I made out to mount my horse, and endeavoured to keep along with the troops.

We crossed Flint river, and had got beyond Pinderton[2] in Baker county, when the exertion proved too great for me, for fever with its dreadful hold had seized on my very life-springs; and finding myself unable to keep my saddle, I was forced to dismount and lie down upon the road until one of the baggage wagons came up, when I was helped into it. The torture I endured for four days during which I was conveyed in this vehicle of torment cannot be expressed in language. My anxiety, however, to continue with the troops, enabled me to support the greatest agony for some time. The thin covering to the wagon afforded my burning brain no protection against the heat of a vertical sun in this latitude, and the constant jolting over the rugged roads and roots of trees was fast driving me into a dreadful tempest of delirium. Human nature could endure such suffering no longer, and with reluctance I was compelled to be left in a log-house which stood beside the road in Thomas county ten miles from Florida. The occupant, whose name was Adams, seemed a kind-hearted man, and he promised to bestow [upon me] all the care in his power. Fortunately I retained my reasoning faculties, and I was enabled to prescribe for myself the proper medicines. Yet it was with a morbid dread I found myself affected with typhus fever, a phasis of disease which is always associated in my mind with an accumulation of terrors,—its slow and silent progress, and the entire prostration of strength with which it is accompanied. I had full leisure to meditate upon my unenviable situation, for seldom was the solitude of my sick chamber ever disturbed. Afar removed from kindred and those I loved, with body weakened and mind bereft of its energy—no watchful cares and hallowed tendernesses to alleviate the pangs of sickness—no tender woman to linger like an angel with hush'd step and serene smile of love around my pillow of suffering and gently hold my aching head; for in sickness man always turns to the bosom of woman, for that soothing sympathy and everduring kindness which alone can bear with the querulous repinings so natural to his situation—

The Journal

"No eye to mingle sorrow's tear,
No tongue to call me kind and dear.—
'Twas gloomy and I wish'd for death!"

At night, when all else was hushed in silence and in sleep, I'd lay wakeful upon my pallet, and listen to the rushing wind as it swept around the humble edifice; and through the wide apertures between the logs would gaze upon the stars and pale moon which shone brightly pure in heaven except when some vapoury clouds tinged by her light would cross her path like messengers of heaven; with what sincerity did I exclaim with Schiller—

"Eilende Wolken! Segler der Lüfte!
Wer mit euch wanderte, mit euch schiffte!
Grüsset mir freundlich mein Jugendland!"[3]

By aid of a good constitution I was at last enabled to master the disease, and after ten days confinement to bed, again stood upon my legs. From this moment I convalesced rapidly, and was much indebted to my kind host for a speedy recovery of strength. He would spend a whole day in the neighboring streams catching the delicious trout to indulge my appetite; and a hint was not needed to induce him to hunt the wild turkey for me. I would frequently visit his fields of sugar-cane, and seated upon a log would spend hours in sucking the delicious juice.

On the 21st Oct I had regained sufficient strength to ride my horse; so on that day I bid farewell to my kind and hospitable host,—whom I shall always bear in my heart with grateful remembrance,—and following upon the trail of the troops, proceeded to rejoin them.

Autumn with its refreshing sunshine had now superceded the heat of summer, and its hollow winds, with mournful sound announcing the approach of dreary winter, were driving the leaves about in eddying course; their rustling alone broke the stillness of the scene as I journeyed slowly on through the wide forests, which were now throwing off their garb of sturdy vigour and assuming the ostentatious and gaudy livery of the season. The beauty of woodland scenery is always heightened just before the chilly winter throws its icy influence over their bloom, and envelopes them in a robe of dusky brown. Then it is that the gorgeous and fantastic blending of green, yellow, crimson, purple, and scarlet, which tinge the distant prospect, defies the art of the painter, who endeavours in vain to imitate successfully the varied hues of nature.

On the evening of the 22nd Oct I arrived at Franklinville,[4] which is the only town in the whole of Lowndes county, and contains only three log-houses; one of which is a court-house, and another the Post-office; the third is a store. This great place is situated on the upper Withlacoochè, and here I found the troops encamped. They were preparing to move farther south, and nearer to Florida; and the day after I joined, the tents were struck, the Withlacoochè crossed, and after marching ten miles in a southerly direction, a new place of encampment was selected near the plantation of a Mr. Townsend.[5]

CHAPTER VII

*T*he situation at Camp Townsend[1] was not celebrated for many beauties and excellencies to make it an object of peculiar attraction. It was in one of the most extensive and most barren of all the pine-barrens in Georgia, where nothing is to [be] seen but pine-trees and saw-palmetto. To the North it was sheltered by lofty pine-trees; to the East it looked upon an extensive forest of over-grown pine-trees, most charmingly variegated by pine-trees of a smaller growth. A fine grove of majestic and venerable pine-trees protected the camp from the sun (whose heat was now acceptable) towards the South; and to the West, the eye was carried along over a glittering and smiling quagmire, abounding in toads, and tadpoles, and the view [was] terminated by the towering and thickly growing trunks of pine-trees, whose numbers were doubly increased by reflection in the puddles which beautifully diversified the aforesaid quagmire. A tender air of repose pervaded the whole scene. The croaking of the thousand varieties of toads and tadpoles with which the quagmire abounded formed a concert of simple melody; the lowing of the cattle, which rove in native freedom through these woods; the grunting of the hogs who enjoy the same rural felicity; and the strokes of our men's axes, partook of the softness of the scene, and fell tunefully upon the ear. Amidst such elysian happiness my mind could not fail being disposed to gentle pleasures and tranquil enjoyments. The other senses also had their full share of delight; for I revelled in the good things of the land, which abounded with all manner of fish and flesh, and such like delightsome and wholesome excellencies. I slept on Buffaloe skin—sat on Bear skin—and fed on venison and wild-turkies, with an occasional sprinkling of squirrel. I here acquired the qualifications for presiding over any Epicurean association in the world, by being able to discuss most learnedly

43

on the merits of not only a haunch of venison, but all the other delicacies enumerated above. I used often to add to my stock of happiness by riding out into the pine-woods, where I could enjoy in perfection the varied and romantic scenery of burned and decaying trees, pig-pens, pine-flats, and log-huts; could watch and admire the little tadpoles and polywogs as they frisked and frolicked in the muddy pools, and listen to the inspiring melody of the more sedate frogs that croaked upon the margins with dignified solemnity.

Our enjoyments were not confined to daylight only, for soon as the last rays of the sun had beamed their farewell radiance on the high pine-tops, our attentive neighbours the screech-owls and whooping cranes would commence entertaining us in the most delicate manner, at the expense of their melodious voices. These flattering attentions, however, were not properly appreciated by us; owing no doubt to our not possessing a correct taste for music. Nor must I omit to mention—for it would be the height of ingratitude if I did—the nightly visits of our equally attentive neighbours —the hogs. In their comings they displayed the wisdom of Solomon. Not a snout was visible before tatoo [tattoo];[2] but soon as that signal for an exit into retiracy was completed, on they came, grunting, snorting, and squeaking,—old boars, little pigs, and all; forming a concert of sweet sounds that would have astounded and put to the blush any Pierian sodality. Their serenades were met on our part with base ingratitude; by the shade of Mozart! instead of listening to their dulcet tones with marked applause, and inviting them to partake of refreshments after such exertions, as is usual among a refined and serenaded people, we impolitely and ungratefully gave the sentinels peremptory orders to expel them at the point of the bayonet, whenever seen near our canvassed domiciles. To do credit to their wisdom, I must state that they always made it a rule to return to whatever spot from which the sentinel may have so unceremoniously expelled them, and submit it to a close examination so soon as his back was turned upon them. Such conduct gave rise in camp to a suspicion that their serenades were mere cloaks under which they might conceal their foraging designs; and these wise animals doubtless reasoned logically, that, as no one ever takes any trouble without a cause, ergo, there must exist some cause for the trouble of driving them from any particular spot; being of a phylosophic turn of mind and desirous of gathering information on every subject, these sages therefore persisted in returning to investigate the matter thoroughly. What staggered my belief in their wisdom a little was, that instead of approaching silently in the dark, as all sensible thieves do, they always announced their proximity to forbidden ground with loud and continuous grunting. To remove this inconsistency in their character, I have arrived at the conclusion that this grunting had the same effect upon them that martial music has upon the soldier in the battle-field,—it spirited them up to deeds of daring. It had become necessary for them after a while to have some such stimulus to keep their courage up; for on finding that this family of snouts and boars, like many other bores in the world, were unacquainted with the polished science of taking a hint administered in a gentle way, we resorted to a more effectual mode of bringing their music to a finale. We flattered ourselves that we hit upon the only method of insulting them; attended with another advantage,—that of perfecting ourselves in the art of pistol-shooting. I would not myself have adopted this fashionable mode to settling our quarrels with the pigs, if the brutes had not annoyed my family—consisting of an old black hen and a red chicken rooster—disturbing their dreams at night, and causing them to look very drooping, doubtless from loss of sleep at night, which they could not indulge [in] by day in consequence of their being constantly engaged in desperate exertions to get loose from one of my tent pins, to which my great attachment for them had caused me to have them tied by one leg.

I had frequent opportunities of increasing my family by the offers of ducks, etc., but fearing the cares of a large family would be too burdensome upon me, I was compelled to decline any extension of my affections.

The two members mentioned above, were presents from some of my country patients in the neighbourhood of our camp. I had

not been on the grounds many minutes, when swarms of applicants
for medical advice, hearing of the arrival of a physician in the
country [which was too poor to entice one of the faculty to select
as his stamping ground],[3] came thick upon me. Indeed, the arrival
of the President of the United States could not have created a
greater sensation. My presence was solicited in forty different
directions at once by man, woman, and child. I was waited upon
by messengers express from thirty miles distance. These applica-
tions were redoubled as soon as it was known that I would take
no fee. Some, who were sorry to lose so capital an opportunity
of taking medicine, which may never occur to them again as long
as they might live, began to rake their memories for some old
complaint, the ghost of which had disappeared forty years before.
There was one man who took me six miles to see one of his
children, whom I found having ate a larger dinner than usual,
the repository thereof—like that of a little puppy after a full meal
—had increased proportionally, and this frightened the good man.
His generous heart prompted him to bring me a pair of chickens.
Another man who had salinated himself severely by imprudent use
of calomel, a common thing in this part of the world [where it
cannot be said that ignorance is bliss],[4] sent for me in the night
three miles off; he magnanimously rewarded my exertions in his
behalf with a hen;—the identical black hen which I adopted into
my family circle. Another opened his heart, and out came a
peck of groundnuts [peanuts].[5] Some gave venison; others deer
skins, dressed and in the raw state. One poor fellow, who had
nothing to give which he thought would be acceptable, offered to
lend me his rifle for as long a time as I remained in the vicinity.

I have made two valuable discoveries in the course of my
country practice; the one is, that the approbation of my own heart,
the consciousness of well-doing more amply rewarded me for my
kindness and attention to the sick than any money could have ever
done. All the money in the world could not cause the exquisite
happiness which is felt by the benevolent physician, who in his
visits to the afflicted knows that his coming is hailed as the glad
tidings of consolation, that his presence will spread a calm over

hearts torn by agitation, and will soothe the disquietude of grieving friends;—that he brings comfort to the mind afflicted as well as to the body—is the comforter of sensibility—the controler of the "feeling's agony,"—the highest attribute of mortals. It is this reward which inspires in the finely sensitive physician's breast that indifference to danger, to which he is so necessarily exposed while pleading with patient and persevering humanity for the lives of his patients—that prompts him to inhale the poisonous atmosphere of malignant disease—which makes him become familiar with scenes of the most loathsome and disgustful, while endeavouring to alleviate suffering humanity. "Those who think that the discharge of the pecuniary debt cancels all obligation to their physician are vastly mistaken; money given, even without a grudging hand, but with a thankless heart, can never requite such services as the physician renders."

The other discovery which resulted from my experience among these people is also of a happy tendency; it will serve to reconcile me to whatever situation the fortuitous circumstances of life may condemn me. By it I am convinced that in the general distribution of misery, no one is exempt; that privations, to be endured, are found in every situation of life; that "rural fields and banks of crystal streams, that murmur and meander through verdant vales and whispering forests," are not always the abodes of a race of beings exempt from the common calamities and, miseries of human nature. But by pursueing our course usefully, whether in town or country, in crowded streets, or in solitary roads, is the surest method of attaining happiness; and by alleviating the miseries and sufferings of others is the surest way to forget our own. We should, indeed, as some author has expressed it, constantly bear in mind that "in proportion as we minister to the happiness of others we take the most effectual means to augment our own." Or as the poet White[6] says—

> "To be happy here is man's chief end,
> And to be happy, he must needs be good."

I have somehow slipt into a digression, which are always

47

troublesome things; just like the Indian paths in the Pine-woods; if a man gets into one there is no telling when he will come to a stopping place; and the farther on he goes, the more distant seems the termination.

There is a universal feature in most country families, which was particularly conspicuous here, the innumerable children; Oh! Goddess Lucina, why do you inflict such a calamity upon these poor people, for such I considered the numerous and hopeful off-spring, who eat them out of doors.[7] Some persons would call this the "smiling of heaven upon their union"; if so, heaven must smile by doublets; or as Salmagundi[8] says, the women must certainly "throw doublets" every time.

CHAPTER VIII

*S*oon as frowning winter had gained the supremacy with his withering grasp, our camp assumed the form and arrangements best adapted to that inclement season. The constant felling of pine-trees for fuel was a source of much annoyance to me. From morning to night the strokes of the axe were constantly heard at my ears; and the soldiers who performed the duty of woodsmen seemed to be very ambitious of showing how near to my tent their skill could fell a pine-tree without knocking out my brains. Frequently while sitting in my tent engaged in a fit of abstraction or something equally important, I would be aroused by hearing a great whizzing overhead, as if all the comets of the universe were taking a race, when starting from my tent and looking up, I would see rushing towards me with the velocity of a rail-road locomotive a pine-tree ninety or a hundred feet high; I had but to dodge back into my tent again, until a repetition of the whizzing could be heard. I was not the only dodger, for when a tree is about to fall, the axeman usually cried *"look out,"* and in all directions over camp men may be seen bobbing their noodles to escape the shower of branches and pine-burrs that are scattered far and wide. We were, however, well repaid for our bobbing by the fires these trees made. It took six pine-trees of the largest size to make one campfire every night. It was made in this way; the largest trees in the neighborhood were selected, generally from two to three feet in diamitor [diameter]; these were cut into lengths of twelve feet, and then rolled up to the front of the tent, distant from it about ten or twelve feet; two smaller pieces are laid upon the ground perpendicular to these, and parallel to one another to serve as andirons, lying towards the tents; upon these other large logs are piled to a height of five or six feet. We each of us had a brobdignag comforter of this description in front of our tents, and as soon as the sun set they commenced blazing with the fierceness of so many volcanies [volcanoes]. As our camp consisted of twenty tents, each of which had a fire in front, the scene presented at night was awfully grand and magnificently comfortable. We burn'd such a large quantity of wood, that we cleared and used as fuel an acre per week of pine woods; and had it only been good soil, no squatter could have seen our clearings without immediately settling, building a log-hut, and fencing in his fields, after which nothing would have been necessary but to put seed into the ground.

One night we witnessed the dazzling effect of our fires upon a flock of wild geese who were emigrating to the South, as usual on the approach of winter. In passing over us, they were so bewildered by the uncommon glare presented to their eyes amidst the surrounding darkness, that for two hours they kept up a wild-goose chase in a circle over our heads, not being able to leave the magic spot. I was told the country people frequently employed this method of decoying them from their nocturnal flight to within shooting distance. The above incident was commemorated by some of the occupants of camp, in the following beautiful effusion and specimen of the sublime; doubtless an effort at consolement for not being able to get a goose for supper. The caption is particularly fine; but it was the usual style of language among the country people of that remote portion of our country.

A flock of wild geese flusterated, and discomboberated, but not dumbfungled.—

Our fires burn'd bright;—
Some geese in their flight,
Were dazzled by the noonday lustre;
They stopt on their course—
They mustered their force,—
For they were in a terrible flustre.

We threw on more wood—
As much as we could,—
To make our fires burn brighter;

The Journal

We then could count seven,
Between us and Heaven,—
For it now had become much lighter.

We got our guns out—
The geese—they flew round about,
All the while making much clatter;
They moved somewhat slower,—
They came somewhat lower,—
For they wished to know what was the matter.

We wanted them nigher,
Before we would fire,—
For in shooting we like to be sure;
But we waited in vain,
Full two hours in the rain,—
When they cleared out, and came back no more.

While we were encamped near Townsend's, I enjoyed the uncommon felicity of a fire-hunt, a sport of which I had often heard, but never participated in; and hope never again. Major [Thomas] Staniford and myself had been long contemplating a ride to Franklinville, for the purpose of a deer-hunt by day and a fire-hunt by night with the nimrods of that place; and we one day put our design in execution. We started in the afternoon,—he on Neahmathla,—a villainous Indian pony, of which more anon, and I on my blooded steed Columbus; each armed with a musket and all the customary paraphernalia of a hunter. To a stranger accidentally meeting us, we might possibly have raised a suspicion that Quixotism was not quite defunct. Not that either of us had a visage approximating in the slightest degree to ruefulness; or that my companion's pony was a jackass, but in other respects— I could not refrain from laughing myself at the conceit. In the first place, I was mounted on a horse whose graceful proportions only made more apparent by strong contrast with the entire want of symmetry in the other animal; and am myself rather inclined to be of the lean kind. On the other hand, the Major with figure of fair rotundity was jogging along with his saddle-bags on a little, round, scrubby devil, not knee high to a mosquito. In short, the *tout ensemble* was remarkably unique and sufficiently striking to knock one down—with laughing.

But Neahmathla must subject his character as well as physical appearance, like all immortalized individuals, from Gen. Jackson down to Tom-Thumb,—to examination. He was born and educated among the Indians, and must have been a docile youth to his instructors, for never was there a better exemplification of the proverb, as "the twig is bent, the tree is inclined." I know not whether to call his chief endowment phlegmatic patience, or the stubborn insensibility of a stoic phylosophy. Doubtless a touch of both. He was never known to express astonishment at anything, but on two occasions,—once, the Major being in a hurry intimated in the customary manner to the Indian the necessity of trotting; I was present at the time, and immediately observed the muscles of his physiognomy relax from their usual expression of Indian indifference, whilst a look of perfect astonishment usurped its place;—he was astonished that any one should attempt to get him out of a walk. It was a failure on the Major's part. The only other occasion was when the Major first led him up to a stump for the purpose of mounting him, the circumstance of his [the Major's] having just ate breakfast and more than usual rendering such a procedure necessary; Neahmathla's stoicism was quite overcome!—the idea of a stump being necessary to assist any one to the back of such a diminutive devil as he knew himself to be, was too much for his phylosophy; never did I see astonishment more expressively depicted on any phiz. The Major wanted to insinuate that it was only an expression of fear at the sight of the stump. But that could not have been the case; an Indian pony has been in contact with too many stumps not to know one when he sees it. Since that moment he always carried his head a half an inch higher.

Revenons à nos moutons [Let's come back to our business], or rather to our venison, we reached Franklinville in due season,— that is, in time for supper. Next morning we started on the projected deer-hunt, intending to try for deer by daylight first. Such

The Journal

sports being very common in all parts of the world, I shall not notice it farther than to state that we got but one deer. This did not satisfy us; so it was unanimously determined to try that night what could be done in the way of hunting by fire,—a mode of procuring venison very common in thinly settled frontier regions but made illegal in thick settlements. Should I be asked for a description of this sport, and were to attempt to give it from that night's experience, my definition of fire-hunting would be, that it consisted in two individuals stumping at night through brushes and briers, swamps, and quagmires, treating themselves to an occasional stumble over the prostrate trunks of trees, and diving headforemost into a concealed gopher hole on the other side; one of them bearing over his shoulder a blazing pine-tree, while the other followed in his wake, Indian fashion, carrying upon one shoulder a gun and upon the other an axe; the latter for cutting down more pine-trees, as fast as one burnt out, in order that they might not be left in the dark, and commit the egregious blunder of going round a quagmire instead of through it, and lose thereby considerable felicity, particularly on a cold night as that was. The gun was apparently carried, as far as my observation extended, by way of giving an ostensible motive for thus perambulating the forests at a time when all *compos mentis* individuals were asleep in their beds.

I returned from this my first essay at fire-hunting fully convinced that it must be an invaluable amusement to those who are fond of wet feet on a cold night and a prodigious deal of unnecessary fatigue instead of reposing comfortably in their beds. But not being particularly partial to either of these exquisite delights myself, I determined to avoid fire-hunting for the future.

I frequently was nightly entertained in my visits to our unsophisticated neighbours, by their endeavours to edify me with precepts of political wisdom, and sublime disputations on the science of legislation. No where have I ever met a more ignorant people, and who stood in more earnest need of schoolmasters. They actually knew nothing beyond the necessity of eating to support life, and of being clothed to defend themselves from the

53

weather;—mere vegetables. Their huts, with but few exceptions, you could hardly have induced a sensible dog to occupy, without his shedding tears of dissatisfaction, and making strong opposition. And yet, so true it is, that "ignorance is bliss," these people seemed contented; and knew not but what they possessed their amount of earth's luxuries.

How wisely has Providence ordained that all mankind should not be endowed with similar tastes and dispositions; otherwise a large portion of Georgia would never have been settled,—at least many parts that I have seen. Put a rifle into the hands of a *Piney-wood* Settler, however, and as long as squirrels and deer are not extinct he is owner of the world in his own estimation. I have frequently gone out with these expert marksmen that I might be astonished at their skill,—or at least seem so,—for these indirect compliments often brought to my larder a wild turkey or a quarter of venison.

I had just got out of my buffaloe-skin, one morning, and had not quite finished dressing, when the front of my tent was raised, and in walked a man "a good deal how come you so." He immediately commenced embracing me in the most affectionate and Frenchman-like manner; burst into tears, and swore he loved all soldiers better than his life, etc. He soon soothed down and stated that he had brought his wife a distance of seven miles to hear the drum and see the men stand in a straight line; phenomena she was as unacquainted with as a sucking dove. He concluded by stating that he had left her in a log-house close by, which had been built for a church, but was brought into requisition for that purpose only once or twice a year, and that he would go and bring her immediately to my tent. This honor I tried to evade, at least until I had put on my clothes, and congratulated myself on the fact of its raining very severely at the time. I hinted to him very politely, the gratification a visit from his better half would afford me, but that the fair lady had better stay where she was for the present, as it would be highly improper to endanger her health by exposing her delicate person to a ducking. "Oh no," he replied, "she was remarkably fond of society, and would not mind the rain, but would prefer to come and sit with me in my tent." She came; the shower continued; so the visit was long, they having discovered the impropriety of her getting wet. My breakfast hour having arrived, and the repast being ready, I could not avoid inviting them to partake. A second invitation was unnecessary. The meal despatched, I took a segar as customary, and offered another to "the gentleman." The fair lady intimated how grieved she was at not being able to join us, as she only smoked pipes, and unfortunately had left hers at home. I felt distressed for her situation; so cutting up a segar, I filled a small dutch pipe I had with me, and thus enabled her to luxuriate with us in her own way. "She was *mightily* pleased with the pipe; *reckoned* it was a *nationest* costly thing"; and intimated that "the possession of it would make her *powerfully proud.*" I could not consistently with politeness avoid asking her acceptance of it, and she very condescendingly complied with my request. It was a happy thing for me; the present producing such an exhilirating effect, that she could no longer keep quiet, but took herself off, and her husband with her; but not before a *squeezing* invitation to be sure to come see them. A day or two after, they repeated their visit. As soon as seated to their liking in my tent, my fair visitor most graciously unfolded her pocket handkerchief and took therefrom a dozen tallow candles, which she as graciously tendered for my acceptance, enhancing their value by asserting that she had made them with her own delicate hands for my especial accommodation. Such a mark of attention from one of the fair sex was quite overpowering. But her inferior half was not to be outdone in liberality; so with unequalled magnanimity and generosity he invited me to a conjuration he was shortly to edify the natives with; and also stated, if we let our men come, who would each be charged twenty-five cents for admittance, the officers should be admitted for nothing. Such kindness and marked distinction was unlooked for, and though we were all impressed with a deep sense of gratitude, we did not honor ourselves by attending the wonderful exhibition.

Journey into Wilderness

On making some inquiries about this singular personage, I learnt that he had such a high opinion of his talents, that the year preceeding he actually offered himself a candidate for the State Legislature, and got one vote; but that was put in by himself.

CHAPTER IX

*W*e had been encamped near Townsend's clearing about three weeks, when our neighbours began to be too troublesome for a longer proximity. They displayed too great an affection towards our men by supplying them with—a soldier's greatest luxury—whiskey,—thereby injuring their morals and keeping them constantly in the guard-tent. The Major commanding[1] saw the evil, and concluded to get out of its way. He therefore issued his orders on Monday night the 13th November, that we should all be ready to march the following morning by sun-rise.

The hour arrived; our tents were struck; and pursuing a South East course, we proceeded fifteen miles from our old encampment; and selected a spot in a Pine-barren near the clearing of a Mr. Clyatt,[2] and within five miles of Florida. Had we fallen asleep at Camp Townsend and awoke at Camp Clyatt, we never would have discovered the change of locality. We were here surrounded by the same Corinthian pines; the same Sabbath stillness pervaded the whole scene, where nature reposed in silence; the same barrenness of even a blade of grass to throw a solitary bloom over its sterility. In short, the same dull, silent, and insipid pine-barren, where the listlessness of blank vacuity hung upon the flagging spirits, causing the lingering moments to "drag their slow length along" in indifference and heavy-hearted despondency;—where even the mirror of memory only added to our misery and sadness by reflecting the contrasted beauty of other scenes with increased charms;—and where our brightest hopes and affections were lost on a wide waste of cheerless existence.

[Lord] Byron has somewhere expressed the wish "that the desert were his dwelling place"; now he certainly could not have been serious, or his notions of a desert must have been very erroneous; for a desert and a Georgia pine-barren being synonymous terms, from my experience and knowledge of the latter, I am decidedly of [the] opinion that neither are very well calculated to "soothe the sad bosom of joyless despair," but to produce a diametrically opposite result, as was the case in myself. To be sure, there's no telling what influence "the one fair spirit for a minister" might exercise in such a locality; and I would advise any one who feels disposed to test the efficacy of Byron's prescription for "joyless despair," by resorting to a wilderness, not to forget "the one fair spirit." Byron has also seriously expressed the opinion that "there is a pleasure in the pathless woods, there is society" etc; all humburg; and very well for those to assert who never felt the stagnation of life in "the pathless woods"; my homestead has been the pathless woods for many weary years [months] and never could I derive any other feeling than ennui from looking at nothing put pine-trees; nor could I make up my mind to consider "the wood-peckers tapping the hollow pine-trees" for worms, as agreeable society, they not evincing sufficient sociability, and, they constituted the only society to be met with in these said "pathless woods." I can, however, vouch for the truth of there being many spots where, "no flowers gaily springing, nor birds sweetly singing," existed; for such were the characteristics of the Georgia pine-barrens, where we vegetated for many months.

During our progress from one place of encampment to the other, I was much diverted at witnessing the graceful and surprising evolutions of my feathered family—the aforesaid black-hen and red-chicken-rooster. Two boards which had been nailed together as substitute for a table, and which formed a surface about two feet square, were placed upon the top of the baggage in one of the wagons; to the centre of this the two objects of my affection had been tied, for the better security of their valuable lives, by strings attached to their legs, which allowed them merely the liberty of this surface; either the jolting of the wagon over the rugged road not permitting them to enjoy much satisfactory repose on such a smooth surface; or being ambitious to exhibit their agility from so favorable an elevation, they amused themselves by dancing quadrilles during the whole journey. At every jolt of the

The Journal

wagon, away they would start in a graceful sidelong *chasette a chasette,* then balancez [Chassez et du Chassez then balancez],[3] and after crossing over and turning partners round, would back to their places and finish the figure with a pigeon-wing or a pirouette that would have excited envy in the bosom of any Frenchman. I was apprehensive such violent exertions might prove fatal to the old lady; for I noticed she kept her mouth constantly open during all her exercises, as well as her younger partner. A day's rest, however, restored them both to their usual equanimity.

The conjurer and candidate for the legislature having given out that on a particular day he intended to have a log-rolling, quilting, and dancing frolic, and having sent an especial message to Major Staniford and myself to attend; our curiosity was excited to witness the originality of such an affair of which we had heard, but never witnessed; so we determined to go. We had to ride six miles and arrived there about sun-set not caring much to participate in the log-rolling part of the entertainment; the conjurer was busily engaged erecting a long table out of rough boards in the open air; while his wife was as busily engaged in cooking pork and cabbage in the kitchen, into which we were invited, being informed that it was the reception room. We there found the company assembled, and on entering would have removed our hats, to show our breeding in the presence of the fairer sex; on looking round, however, we noticed that such a procedure would not have been in conformity with the rules or customs of the company, and being decidedly outré[4] would only have exposed us to their ridicule; so quaker-fashion we remained; and the fair angels whose gaze were fixed upon us, seemed by their approving smiles not to take our conduct amiss,—probably liked us the better for appearing to disregard their presence. The pork and cabbage were in due time despatched, and a few of the gentlemen put to bed, in consideration of not being able to use their legs from a too free use of our host's whiskey.

Then began preparations for the double-shuffle. There were three fiddlers; but unfortunately for the exercise of their united talents, only one fiddle; and that deficient in some of its strings.

Journey into Wilderness

The three votaries of Apollo therefore exercised their functions successively upon the cracked instrument, and did not fail to produce such sounds as would have attracted the admiration of even the mighty goddess of Discord herself. Their chief merit seemed to consist in all producing a similar concatenation of sounds, which they persisted in dignifying with the appellation of tune; the name of which, however, was more than the brightest faculties could call. The Major could not be induced to venture his carcase in the violent exercise of double-shuffle and cross-fling; so I had to support the credit of our camp by my own exertions; and so successfully, that the conjurer was in raptures, and made an attempt to exhibit his admiration by embracing me before the whole company; but I could not stand such a flattering display, so bolted.

The intervals of the dance were filled up by the gentlemen handing round in a tumbler, what I thought was whiskey and water, but which the Major asserted, from closer inspection, was unadulterated whiskey; the younger ladies were generally satisfied with one or two mouthfulls from each tumbler, but as the same ceremony was to be gone through with each gentleman in rapid succession, the fairest of creation did not lose their proper allowance. The old ladies, who were veterans in the business, never loosened their grasp of the tumblers until their lips had drained the last drop of the precious liquid. As a necessary consequence it was impossible for them to sit up long, and soon all the beds were occupied by these ancient dames; the gentlemen who afterwards got into a similar predicament were compelled to lie wherever they fell.

At one o'clock fighting commenced, when the Major and myself, not being ambitious of distinguishing ourselves in the pugilistic art, made a retreat; and at two in the morning we were in our tents, after a bitter cold ride.

We soon after received an addition to our society by the arrival of [First] Lt. [Silas] Casey from Florida, who had received an order to join Major Dearborn's company. We now had some amusement by occasionally breaking the monotony of our life, in a game of whist without a resort to [a] dumby [dummy].[5]

The Journal

In the intervals of replenishing nature, Major Dearborn and myself had been industriously employed in manufacturing chess-men out of pine-chips; as much for immediate pastime as future amusement. Having little to divert our attention from such useful occupation, there being no books attainable in camp, our labours were soon rewarded with a beautiful and original set of chess-men. We then occasionally escaped the heavy pressure of idle hours by indulging in this civilized and scientific game.

In accordance with the already expressed opinion,—the result of both experience and reflection—that to make ourselves contented in any spot where necessity should place us, the best way is to make ourselves useful, by endeavouring to alleviate the miseries of those around us; I visited all the country people who sent for me, or whom I heard stood in need of my professional services.

I visited one day a very worthy man who lived forty miles from our camp. He had been shot through the body in an engagement with the Indians in the month of July previous, and from the want of surgical advice had been lingering on the brink of the grave ever since, and enduring the greatest suffering. I found that the ball had entered at a point a little to the right of the lower extremity of the sternum, or breast bone, and had come out at a point of his back diametrically opposite. From the symptoms and an examination I made, I found that the ball had struck a rib which it splintered. He was sinking rapidly from hectic and injudicious treatment; and it produced feelings of the happiest kind that I might thus be enabled to save the life of this poor fellow by timely interference. In pursuance of my adopted plan I refused all fee, but his expressions of gratitude more than compensated me. He however insisted on my accepting a very fine bear-skin, having incidentally heard that I was anxious to procure one.

On my return to camp I passed by the abode of two singular individuals with whom I left my present to be dressed. These were two aged brothers of the name of Moodie, who had been living in the blessed state of celibacy all their long lives, for no other purpose evidently than that of being blest with one another's society through life. It was said that one of them did marry a woman once, in what was called the Spanish mode; that is, took her on trial for six months before the nuptual knot should be tied; but at the end of the third month, he discovered they were not destined for each other, or calculated to augment one another's happiness; so he returned to the bosom of his brother, and had never made a second attempt to sever the ties of brotherly love.

They were living representatives of the "Scout" and "Indian John," as described by Cooper in the "Pioneers," both in character and mode of living. Their edifice was a miserably small pile of logs, eclypt a house in that country. It was situated in a solitary spot of the pine woods, remote from any other habitation. They attended to all their household duties themselves; made all their own clothes, and cooked their own food; not another living being was to be found about them, except an old gaunt stag-hound,— probably a descendant of the Scouts' "Hector." Not even that 'sine qua non" pet of an old bachelor—a cat—was to be seen. Their ostensible occupations were making shoes and dressing skins; and whenever speaking of one another, the one spoken of was always designated by the other as "the shoe-maker," or "the tanner," according to which one it was, for each flourished in his respective branch exclusively. The pen of a Cooper or an Irving would have made much of their eccentricities.

In consequence of a requisition of Major Dearborn on the county for one company of mounted militia, for the defence of their own frontier and homes against the Indians, who began to threaten the neighborhood, a draft was to be held at Franklinville, the county-town, on a certain day. In accordance with a request from the Major that I should attend on that day and take a letter to the Colonel of the Country, I mounted my good steed Columbus, and after several hours hard riding, found myself at the scene of action at the appointed time. About two hundred men were assembled; and most of them in a dangerous state of effervescence, because the Colonel had ordered them to muster without first consulting their wishes. One of the privates was particularly exasperated, and told his Colonel, if he would only strip off his coat and step out into open ground he would soon thrash him for his impudence; but as the commanding officer declined any such display of courage, declaring he was not a fighting man, the other proceeded to draw the sword which hung at the Colonel's side, and showed a disposition of returning it in a way which the Colonel did not relish, for there were serious demonstrations of running him through the body. It was a lucky thing that our Major did not attend; for he would certainly have been made acquainted with the process of *slicking,*[6] in return for attempting to have these valiant citizens drafted for the defense of their homes and firesides. At one moment I was under serious apprehensions that they intended to make me the Major's representative in being *slicked,* but they had sufficient reason left them to see the impropriety of the attempt, and I was permitted to make my retreat without molestation, and in a dignified manner.

Several times, and at several distant points of its track, have I crossed in my rides one of those "storm's dark paths,"—those terrific evidences of the wind's might, when suddenly roused to its wrath in these Southern latitudes. For miles in extent, beyond the knowledge of those inhabitants whom I have questioned about it, did this hurricane[7] pursue its undeviating course, prostrating every thing before it, even the largest tree of the forest; leaving in its wake a broad belt of open space a quarter of a mile wide, over which but a moment before the lofty woodland monarchs had reared their heads in vigorous pride; but now, their giant stems and rugged shafts strewed the ground in wild disorder, admitting the sun's rays for the first time to places which had been shrouded in gloom from their creation.

Such a scene was well calculated to recall vividly to memory those lines of Barber,—[8]

"When winter's tempests are abroad, oh! what sublimer sight,
"Than when the broad-armed forest oaks, in unapparelled might,
"Stand, like embattled skeletons upon the storm's dark path,
"And toss and writhe their groaning limbs beneath its howling
    wrath!"

CHAPTER X

*A*gain was the general sounded; again our tents were struck; and again did we take up the line of march for a new camping ground. On the 3rd December we left the neighborhood of Clyatt and proceeded about five miles into the vicinity of Squire Swilley.[1] We again encamped amidst the towering pine-trees, still the same in every change of scene. The prospect was slightly improved by an oak tree presenting itself here and there; but as their summer's leaves had become sere, these also, who not long back wore mantles of a thousand hues, now presented one expanse of dusky brown. Our tents were pitched upon the brow of a fine hill; a gentle slope extending from the left of our encampment to the margin of a limpid mill-pond, on the edge of which was located the Squire's Mill, which sawed boards, ground corn, and gin'ed cotton, all by the powerful propulsion of the above pond. Casting our vision beyond the surface of this pellucid sheet of water, the eye rested upon an extensive corn-field, once presenting a glorious array of waving foliage, with a prospect of comfortable realities, but which at this time exhibited the *"yellow melancholy"* of winter. In the centre stood a few negro log-huts. On the verge of the forest, beyond this field, and just peeping into view, stood the Squire's abode; a log-house; for though the Squire possessed the proximate advantage of a saw-mill, and an abundant supply of the requisite materials for a more comfortable dwelling, and one more consistent with his elevated position in the world,— for the Squire was a member of the State Legislature—yet the force of habit, and natural indifference to the comforts of life made him contented with this humble edifice.

The Squire was a very clever fellow, and did not lose any opportunity of being attentive to his new neighbours. A few days after our arrival, we were invited by the Squire to assist him in

64

routing from his quarters a large bear, whose tracks he had recently discovered in a swamp not far off. Major Staniford and myself were always ready for agreeable excitement, and among them the sports of the chase; so one morning immediately after an early breakfast we started for a visit to bruin. Unfortunately he was not at home; neither could one ascertain in what direction he had gone; but to make amends for not finding the bear, we commenced an attack upon the wild-turkies, which were innumerable around us. I shot with my rifle—the largest gobbler I had ever seen; he weighed over twenty pounds, and falling from the top of a very lofty pine-tree, his contact with the ground sounded like a young earthquake. We returned in the evening to camp with scratched hands and faces, and torn clothes, the result of our day's sport, in addition to a stag and a cart-load of turkies.

With a good rifle and a good hound—for I had also added one to my family—and in a country abounding in game, and with few settlers to kill them, as that was, and a little to occupy the mind it proved impossible not to become a keen sportsman, and I soon considered myself a perfect Nimrod. With very little sickness among the men to engage my attention, I find [found] abundant leisure to indulge in this exciting amusement.

There was within half a mile of our camp a dense and boundless swamp; the resort of bears, wolves, deer, turkies, etc; and of myself, whenever I felt disposed to indulge in shooting or in meditation, notwithstanding the suspicion that it concealed Indians. Its solitude and silence, however, I never found interrupted except by the barking of the squirrels, which as I sat in the enjoyment of luxurious listlessness upon the fallen trunk of some woodland veteran come gambolling around me; or by the scarlet tufted woodpeckers as they industriously plied their busy hammers; or by the graceful stag who would occasionally be seen stalking at a distance through the natural arcades, which extended in all directions to the forests verge, followed by the timid doe, who, startled by the rushing and swelling wind as it sighed through the branches of the grove, came bounding along the forest walks, apparently seeking protection from her equally frightened mate. Oft has evening's shades come on, and eve's pale star in her lonely watch found me sitting there in thoughtfulness alone, my rifle idly resting against my shoulder. For it was at such times that my soul was wafted upon the wings of memory from the presence of cold reality, to scenes where its dearest "fantasies were temporarily embodied into action." It was at such times that I'd hear the voices of my youthful home—

> "*The blessed household voices, wont to fill*
> *My heart's clear depths with unalloyed delight!*
> *I'd hear them still unchanged:—though some from earth*
> *Were music parted, and the tones of mirth—*
> *Wild, silvery tones, that rang through days more bright!*
> *Had died in others,—yet to me they come,*
> *Singing of boyhood back—the voices of my home!*"

It was then, too, that the memory of their virtues would press on my heart, and a thousand endearing recollections arise to my remembrance, saddening the feeling already under the gloomy influence of the place, by the distressing reflection that home no longer existed for me.[2]

The aforesaid swamp was the scene of a very disagreeable adventure to me on one occasion. It was the afternoon of a bleak, comfortless wintry day, after being confined by rain to my tent the whole morning, that with my rifle I sought this place in quest of turkies. Finding interesting companionship in my own thoughts, which were busily engaged in traversing the scenes of by-gone days, I had unconsciously wandered farther than usual into the blind mazes of the forest. I was at length aroused to the sudden consciousness that the night shades were gathering around, by the deepening twilight gloom in these dense woods. Cold and tired I turned to retrace my steps, but had not proceeded far, when the last glimmer of day faded from the sky; which was doubly darkened by intervening foliage, and heavy masses of clouds. I wandered on, picking my steps with difficulty in the darkness of the gloomy recesses, unable to pursue any definite direction; one moment extricating myself from some bramble; then again dashing through

The Journal

a bog; occasionally running against the twisted branches of some hoary tree whose rotten trunk lay mouldering away in the moss. The laborious task of gaining a way through the many obstructions which surrounded me in great numbers, was much aggravated by the reflection that every step might be carrying me farther from instead of towards our camp; and my chagrin was greatly enhanced, too, by the agreeable prospect of spending the night in this rare place, with bears and wolves for bed fellows and hostile Indians for neighbours. These thoughts which rolled tumultuously through my mind, and the cold wintry wind that whistled over me, nerved every energy of my frame into double vigour. I soon, however, became exhausted by my exertions, and despair like a leaden cloud began to settle upon me; for even patience was wearied. Hungry, exhausted, and desperate, I felt that it was useless to strive any longer, but that it was necessary to make some preparations for passing a supperless night in this place, where bleakness and desolation reigned supreme. While engaged in attempts to strike a fire, a sound most exhilarating and spirit stirring suddenly fell upon my ear; the sound of a bugle. A rush of joy poured in upon my soul, and hope again filled my heart. I sprang up, and collecting all my energies, made the best of my way in the direction from whence issued the notes of our camp bugle sounding tatoo. With unmingled satisfaction I, that night, lay upon my buffaloe-skin, under the shelter of my tent, and listened to the pattering of the rain upon its canvass roof, after the enjoyment of a fine supper of venison and hot coffee.

The settlers in the south east corner of Lowndes County became terribly alarmed by the Indians shooting one of their number, whilst he was out hunting; and another while sitting at supper in the midst of his family. They consequently entreated Major Dearborn to march his troops into that quarter. In conformity with this request, the Major issued his orders for a move, and on the 18th Decr we commenced our march.

The distance was not great; yet there were many impediments to our rapid progress. About one o'clock we found ourselves on

67

the bank of the Lapahoochee, our further progress impeded by the usual place of fording being of a swimming depth. Fortunately we found a small canoe tied to a tree, and in this we succeeded in transporting our baggage and men over. We were obliged to swim the horses, and drag the wagons through the water as well as we could. This delay brought night upon us before we could trim ourselves for prosecuting the march. There was no alternative but to remain where we were until next morning; so in a few moments our tents were pitched;—our fires made; and every one except the sentinels stretched out upon his camp blanket, in the enjoyment of luxuriant repose.

Reveille next morning started us anew; and until two o'clock P.M. we were busily engaged in cutting our way through the "pathless woods." A tedious job, when roads wide enough for passage of wagons are to be cut as we proceed through the primeval forest; and every step to be delayed by the felling of trees.

We reached the Allapahaw [Alapaha] river about 2 o'clock P.M., and found our troubles were not yet finished. At a place called Troublesome ford,—certainly a very appropriate if not euphoneous title,—we were to attempt the dangerous passage. It was necessary that some means of conveying the baggage over dry land should be procured, and as no accommodating canoe made its appearance, the men were set to building a raft. This was by no means an expeditious job; so our tents were pitched for the night, and every preparation was made for an early start in the morning; and that we may not be detained too long next day, we had one wagon dragged over that night.

How futile are all the expectations of man! That night we witnessed as severe a rain as ever visited the earth; this immense fall of water had produced a contrary effect upon the river, for in the morning we found its waters had risen several feet higher than they were the night previous, and the ford of a swimming depth. We launched the raft, and it immediately sunk, the logs being too green. Fortunately a straggler came along, and informed us where a canoe was to be found three miles below us. We sent for it as a last resource. After a long delay it arrived,

The Journal

and we succeeded in getting the baggage and men across. Now arose the chief difficulty, and we had to twist our brains *"pretty considerably"* as the people there say, before we hit upon a good idea, for transferring the other wagon from one to the other side of so wide, and deep, and rapid a river. We at last thought the best chance would be to twist the hide of an ox, which we had shot for supper the night previous, into a rope, and by attaching one end to the wagon, the other end might be carried to the opposite bank, and by launching the wagon into the water it might easily be floated over. The attempt was made; the wagon reached the middle of the stream, when the strong current upset it; the body went down stream with the current while the wheels disappeared from sight,—finding greater attraction in the rocks at the bottom. We were now in a quandary; but soon out of it; for all the men were immediately set to work and after spending the whole morning fishing the several parts of the wagon from the water, we found ourselves, wagons, etc., all on the same side together, and that the right one. Three miles farther brought us to the place of our intended encampment. This was in a still more dreary part of a pine-barren than any we had yet visited, and in the immediate vicinity of a block-house, which the settlers had erected as a place of resort from the savages, who were passing through constantly from the Creek Nation to Florida.[3]

About a mile from this spot, a party of Creek Indians were attacked on the 31st July 1836 by a small body of Georgia scouts, and every one shot, except two, who escaped by diving into the river and swimming down with the current under water. The bones of the killed were still bleaching on the bank of the river, where they fell, and which had been beautifully cleaned by the wolves, and polished by the sun. I got possession of the chief's skull who was shot by Squire Swilley, as he stood apart from the rest in the act of loading his rifle, and whose name was *Tustenuggee John*.[4] Their wives and children were taken prisoners, and sent back to Alabama under a guard of Georgia Militia; but on their way, they one night eluded the vigilance of their guards; and the women after poisoning all the children made their escape. However unnatural this act may appear, twas a common feature of Indian character during this war; and on several occasions when pressed in pursuit, have the Indians deserted their children after suffocating them by filling their mouths and nostrils with swamp-mud.[5]

CHAPTER XI

*W*e were now in the extreme South East corner of Lowndes County near the great Okefinokee swamp, and in the very tracks of the hostile Indians, passing from Alabama to Florida; so we expected before long we should find something to amuse us in our monotonous way of living. The only alteration to the routine of camp-life in which we had been engaged since entering these eternal pine-barrens, where we only found that "one day telleth another," was the adoption of a little more precaution, lest the "yellow nagurs," as the Irishmen called our enemy might attack us; and which we from our hearts were most sincerely wishing they would do; for a life of inaction in such an unexciteable position as we occupied was far from agreeable.

To vary the dullness of doing nothing, occasionally I offered to ride to Franklinville for the mail on the usual mail day, which occurred once a week; my professional visits had brought me acquainted with many bye-paths and trails through the woods, and by following these, ten miles of the forty-five on the route might be cut off; my offer was therefore generally accepted and off I'd start, only accompanied by the usual companion of my solitary wanderings, than whom I wish I may never need a better; I mean my steed, of noble blood and high breeding. The dreary route was varied by having to swim my horse over four rivers and creeks going and returning; there being no bridges nor ferries then established in that wild and frontier country, where scarcely any roads deserving the name were yet to be found. And even if they were, the little travelling that was done there would not have supported the expense of their proper superintendence. In general the only roads were old Indian Trails; and the only directions, a piece of bark cut from a tree, commonly called a blaze. I have sometimes travelled along these blazed roads for thirty miles before any vestige of humanity would meet the eye; and when it did appear, it would be in the uncivilized shape of a pile of logs eclypt a house; this consisted of a covered pen eight or ten feet square, which served for parlour, kitchen, chamber, fowl-house, and pig-pen.

On Christmas morning I found myself on one of the above mentioned errands, jogging along one of these tracks of the wild-woods, through whose waving roof occasional glimpses of the sunny sky might be caught, breaking sweetly in upon the twilight gloom, cheering the lonely wearied traveller, who wandered there, and infusing into his mind visions of peace and brightening hope. Thus has it ever been; amidst all my manifold grievances, there would always appear some small but vivid rays of sunshine to brighten my path, cheer my steps, and invite me to persevere. The day—the place—were peculiarly adapted to contemplation, and the soft, low murmuring of the full-foliaged pines fell gently upon the ear of memory, speaking of other and dearer spots. It whispered tales of my former pleasant home.[1] Its gentle breathing also produced the sweet tones of far distant friends and jocund companions; with whom were associated the memory of many enjoyments,—who had mingled in all my felicities. The annual return of such days as this always served as a looking-glass to reflect past times, and recall a train of half worn-out impressions, only softened by the lapse of time. With what a sweet-souled melancholy did I recall the days of my boyhood, when only the bright side of life was visible, and before the rude jostles of the world had severed the dearest ties. Twas then I looked eagerly forward through the opening vista and thought—

"How pleasant, as the man, world taught, with high determined heart,
To tread life's busy, crowded stage, and act th' allotted part."

Experience is a sad instructor, and inflicts many disappointments in the course of her lessons; already has she made me alter my tune, and my world's song is now on a different chord for—

The Journal

"I'm fretted with its noisy scenes, and wish I had a home,
And wish there was a spirit there, to gladden when I come."

Fondly did I anticipate the time when I might turn from the "pomp and circumstance of war," to seek the fireside of social life; there to confide my dearest affections.[2]

On the 28th December we left our camp for a scouting expedition into Florida, taking nothing with us but our arms, and three days' rations in a haversack slung to our side. After plodding all day through mud and water and saw-palmettoe, at sunset we found ourselves twenty miles within Florida, and near the plantation of a Captain ———. On entering the domicile of this said personage, we were met at the threshold by his mulattoe housekeeper, who informed us that her master was very sick in bed, and could not be seen. We were about retiring, when a voice was heard issuing from the adjoining room swearing that it was a lie; that he was not sick, but only d———d drunk; and insisted on our immediately entering. On complying, we found an elderly man in bed, with a beard of a week's growth; and very soon ascertained that he had not belied his situation. It appeared that he had been on a frolic two days before Christmas and getting into an elevated state of exhilaration had been put to bed, where he remained, keeping up Christmas by keeping up "the old drunk," or rather lengthening it out by continous potations of brandy, night and day; for which service he kept a little negro boy constantly in the room, to supply him with the delicious beverage. I observed that the little fellow made the mixture of brandy and water always in favour of the former, so as to remove the necessity of frequent repetitions, by speedily inducing undrinkable felicity, thereby gaining some little respite.

We bivouacked in the woods that night; not having any tents with us. On the next day Major Staniford and myself crossed the Suwannee river in a flat, and rode to the Mineral Springs of East Florida.[3] We there found the public-house picketed in, and surrounded by miserable little temporary shelters erected by the settlers of the neighbourhood; who were congregated here thick upon one another for mutual protection; their own houses either burnt, or rendered insecure by the savages.

The Suwannee Mineral Springs is a remarkable sight; it issues from the Eastern bank of the Suwannee; the spring and the river mingling their waters together and imparting to that of the river its yellow colour half way across and a considerable distance down stream, and depositing upon all the surrounding rocks sulphur in sufficient quantity to make their yellow colour apparent at a great distance. By standing upon a projecting rock I could immerse one hand in warm water characteristic of the spring while the other was dipt in the cold water of the river not more than a few inches distant. In summer the temperature of the spring appears to ones altered feelings as remarkable for coldness as in winter for warmth. We were told that many invalids resorted here for the benefit of the water before the Indians rendered it a dangerous place of residence as well as difficult of access.

On our return at 1 o'clock to where we left the troops, the place was deserted; Major Dearborn had marched off leaving us to find them as well as we could. We trailed them; and came up as they were about halting for the night; and were cutting down trees for their bivouac fire. The fire was made in this way; several pine-trees were piled upon one another in a straight line extending seventy or eighty feet; half of the men arranged themselves in a line on each side of its length, in the manner one would place oysters at a fire to be roasted in the shell; with this difference; that oysters are generally placed with their mouths to the fire, whereas we were arranged with our feet in that direction, our heads resting upon a pine-tree rolled up parallel to the line of fire, and about ten feet from it. The night was bitter cold, and although very close to the fire, I found it too cold to continue in the incumbent posture without any covering, for the ground was whitened by the frost. The next morning we returned to our tents after three days' absence.

New Year's day found us [veg]etating amidst the dull pine trees and saw-palmettoe flats, with most exemplary patience and perfect tranquility. Seven months had elapsed since I left the

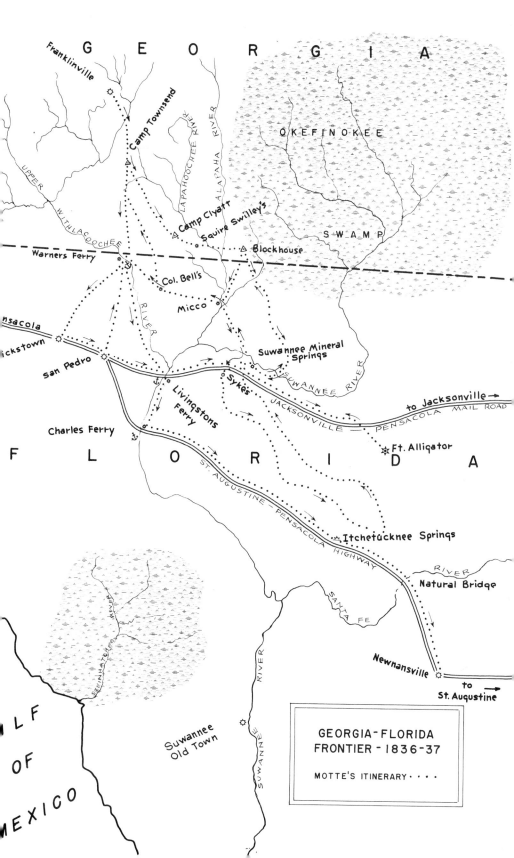

Journey into Wilderness

scene of my past happiness for those of privation and danger; (seven months since my longing eyes were blessed with a sight of the spot I hold dearest on earth). Seven months had my cherished hopes and affections been confined to the cheerless existence of a camp life;—seven months had I been abideing among the forest denizens, a canvass roof my only shelter from the rains and storms and withering wintry blasts; and occasionally without even that slender protection. Still was I "condemn'd to hopes delusive mine"; no brightening prospect appeared of a termination to that waste of existence. The desolation of the scene only increased with every move we made, no doubt caused by the mind casting its own dark hues o'er nature's bloom. It is indeed true, that "beauty is only an ideal outline, changing beneath the capricious hand of association—meeting the eye, but to take its coloring from the heart." Or to express the same idea poetically, "it is our feelings give their tone to whatsoe'er we gaze upon." Thus accomodating all the scenes of nature to my own state of feeling, it was not wonderful that—

> "Nothing gave pleasure—that nothing seem'd fair,
> For the lingering moments were numbered with care."

The sun of a New Year had indeed risen to the world, diffusing gladness around, and cheering the hearts of happy men; but to me the smiling morning shone in vain; it brought no new-born pleasure to cheer the dreary sameness of a life which made the bright world desolate, and caused earth to appear a desert.

There was I withering away my youth's glorious pride and brightest period of existence, gaining nothing, acquiring no new knowledge to enable a retrospect of the past day without disgust; the social feelings going to decay for want of [an] intelligent, accomplished, woman "to raise the manners and improve the heart," in hours of social intercourse. [It made my heart feel heavy, cold, and dejected, that life's verdure when all things bright were beaming for me, should thus pass away.][4] The sadness which accompanied these reflections, brought the remembrance of departed joys with a sensation of exquisite pleasure; for the consciousness of having

76

been blessed is, after all, worth more than the unreal anticipation of joys, which are always uncertain in this precarious life. It is to memory that we are indebted for much of our happiness. When the mind is darkened by sorrows, memory comes with its redeeming light, by which we retrace the "dim foot-path" of bygone years, to the hearth-stone of our earlier days, and youth's happy hours, when sorrows and cares were not in our vocabulary. It is òn this day particularly that memory awakes thoughts of early and shadowy recollections,—thoughts which laid mouldering and unheeded at other times in the dim chambers of the mind. It is indeed true, that the further we are removed from the time and place of our earliest and sweetest associations, the more they become endeared to us; my own experience asserts this fact for

> *"To the past my heart would cling,*
> *And still alloy the future hour!"*

In that land of unsophisticated habits, where steamboats, railroads, and newspapers never invaded the sight;—where books were yet unknown articles;—nothing was left to the unfortunate sojourner for means "pour passer le tems [temps],"[5] but a resort to memory or fancy,—and by their aid I managed to wile away the heavy hours transporting myself into the narrow and distant circle which contained all the objects of my affection.

We one day received a countermand to an order which Gen. Jesup had sent us, to join the Army in Florida. Much to our disappointment and mortification the express bearing the countermand arrived before the receipt of the order countermanded; and we thus missed an opportunity of having something to do. We were however allowed the privilege of moving into Florida, and there encamping.

No time was lost in making use of this permission to escape from Georgia pine-barrens. Accordingly, on the 10th January 1837 we marched with all our paraphernalia into Florida, and proceeded to Micco,[6] the site of an old Indian town on the west bank of the Allapahaw river, and ten miles from the Georgia line.[7] We encamped the first night on the east side of the river;

and on the following day crossed the Allapahaw in an old flat, ferried over by an old negro named Abram—the original, I suspect, of Jim Crow;—he had been the property of Daniel Bell, the person who owned the adjoining plantation, who, in consideration of the important services rendered by this Jim Crow and his old wife to him, in getting and raising a family of twelve children, had emancipated them, and given them a piece of ground to plant corn and potatoes in, and this ferry to gain something to eat with their corn and potatoes.

In honor of his dignified position and useful capacities he was dubbed Capt. Abram. The river had swelled to a great height by a succession of severe rains; so much so, that at the point we crossed Capt. Abram had to lay aside his pole, not being able to touch bottom with it, and take to oars; yet at this very spot in dry weather might be seen one of those freaks of nature with which this country abounds. This river after flowing hundreds of miles with a broad, rapid, and deep current, will here suddenly make a precipitate descent through a large chasm into the earth, and flowing under ground several miles will again rise to the surface and continue the "even tenor of its way."[8] After excessive rains, the subterranean passage is not large enough to admit the increased body of water which then overflows; and where it is now forty feet deep is sometimes so dry that travellers cannot find sufficient water for their horses. Nearly every river and creek in this territory presents similar phenomena. There is a water course within two miles of our encampment called *Rocky Creek,* which sinks in this manner and never appears again to the knowledge of any one.[9]

CHAPTER XII

*O*n the 25th January Major Dearborn received a letter from the inhabitants at the Suwannee Mineral Springs fifteen miles below us, entreating our assistance in pursueing a large party of Indians, who had the night previous attacked the house of a Mr. Sykes [Sikes], three miles from them, and murdered some of the family. Orders were immediately issued for a forced march.

Leaving our tents, baggage, etc., we started about 3 o'clock in the afternoon, and stopt that night on the West side of the Suwannee river. Soon after reveille next morning we crossed over into East Florida,[1] and delayed at the springs only enough to procure some provisions and a guide, and immediately proceeded towards the scene of attack.

We found that the old man Sykes by wonderful coolness and presence of mind had been able to defend his house single handed against about thirty Indians from 4 o'clock in the afternoon, the time they made the attack, until after midnight, when the sudden appearance of a mounted party, who had been apprised of his situation, and started to his rescue, frightened the Indians off. The house was situated on the Mail-road between Jacksonville and Tallahassee,[2] near a hammock. On the afternoon of the 24th Janry, Sykes was in his corn crib with his little grand-child shucking corn, when he heard a volley of rifles at a spot where his son-in-law Smiley was cutting wood, one hundred and fifty yards from the house. Immediately after, the war-whoop was yelled out by the savages, which was sufficient hint for Sykes, who, taking his grand-child in his arms, made for his house, gathering up in his passage through the yard several little negro children whom he also took into the house with him. He succeeded in gaining the shelter of his log-house without injury from the bullets which were sent after him by the savage devils, who came rushing up in

79

pursuit from all directions, yelling most horribly. Fortunately he had in his house at the time seven loaded guns of all descriptions, rifles, muskets, and double-barrelled shot guns. He at first seized his double-barrel gun with the intention of giving them a broad-side as they approached, concluding his own death inevitable, but determined to die game; observing, however, one of the savages running up from where Smiley had been killed, priming and re-loading his rifle after the murderous deed, Sykes felt a strong inclination "to split this fellow's heart," as he expressed himself, by way of appeasing the departed spirit of his son-in-law; so laying down the double-barrel gun, he seized a rifle to make sure work; and taking deliberate aim at the Indian shot him through the breast, one inch from his heart, and stopt his yelling in this world forever. His body was afterwards found where the Indians had dragged and endeavoured to conceal it with bushes; and a fine looking fellow he was; the very *beau ideal* of an Apollo. This successful shot put the Indians all "aback," as the sailors say, and "brought them up all standing"; for they instantly checked their advance, and got behind trees in the yard. This gave old Sykes time to let them know he had other guns for their benefit, and with his shot-gun put another scamp *"hors de combat,"* by break-ing his back; of all the horrid yells and bellowings which ever issued from a human mouth, Sykes said this fellow gave the best sample, when he found himself wounded. He managed to drag himself to a fence, but was unable to get over it; so by way of something to do, commenced vomiting in a very praise-worthy manner. I examined this spot, and found quantities of eggshells and blood which he had thrown up. He was finally dragged off by a couple of his swarthy brethren, and that was the last seen of him, altho' his cries were heard long after.

This unexpected resistance intimidated the Indians so much, as to keep them at a respectful distance;[3] where they continued firing and yelling from behind trees. The window shutter from which Sykes fired upon them was completely riddled by their bul-lets, yet he escaped unhurt; and to this fortunate circumstance the lives of all with him were indebted; for by keeping up a constant firing until rescued, he kept the Indians at a distance, by inducing them to believe that there was a strong force in the house; whereas there were only his wife and daughter, and two negro women with several little children. After dark, the light from his burning corn-house, which the Indians had fired, was very serviceable to him by enabling him to see the position of the Indians. At 10 o'clock he ripped up a plank from the floor of his house, and making one of the negro women strip herself, told her to get under the house, and crawling on all fours along the fence, would in the darkness, deceive the Indians into the belief that she was a hog, of which there were many about; and in this way might escape to the springs and inform the people of his awkward predicament. She succeeded in the attempt, and about midnight a few of his friends from the neighbouring springs arrived to his relief; when the Indians gave a farewell yell and took to their heels.

Sykes asserted that there was a white man with the Indians; but that he was so careful of himself, as to avoid all opportunities of being shot; which compliment Sykes was very desirous of paying him. This devil with a white skin seemed very anxious to retreat when he found what unexpected resistance was made, and was distinctly heard by all in the house to cry out in English to the Indians, "Let us go, they fire too hot from that house."[4]

We took possession of the premises for the night, quartering the men in the dwelling house, as being the largest, while we made headquarters of the kitchen; and upon my bear-skin spread upon the floor before the kitchen fire I enjoy'd a comfortable sleep until daybreak. We then proceeded towards a spot designated as the most probable hideing place of the Indians. A company of mounted volunteers from the Springs were expected to meet us there, that while we started the game they might take stands and shoot them as they broke cover; or while we were scouring the hammock[5] they might watch the borders that none escaped. We waited several hours at the rendezvous for the expected company without any signs of them. At last their Captain accompanied by two men only rode up; and after making many apologies for his delay, said it was caused by his men refusing to obey his orders and turn out; and failing in his endeavours to make them, had at last determined to come without them, so as not to keep us waiting longer. It could not be expected that so few footmen, as our command consisted of, could do much without some horsemen; however, we determined to advance and do our best.

We proceeded first to the deserted house of a Mr. Wells, that had been attacked by the Indians a short time previous, when they killed one man and wounded another. We quartered there the second night, and found an abundance of potatoes and sugar-cane syrup which had escaped the hands of the Indians. These and a beef we killed, constituted all our provisions while out on this scout. The next morning we were joined by a company of mounted militia, and advanced into Florida about forty miles; but could find no other traces of the enemy, except a few moccasin tracks. It rained so incessantly that all our exertions were so much lost labour; it being impossible to trail the savages over ground that was inundated by the quantity of rain that fell during the night, and continued falling. After being drenched to the skin and enduring a great deal of fatigue, we got back to the shelter of our tents on the 31st Jany after seven days' absence.

On the following day, we removed our encampment ten miles in a westwardly direction, to the neighbourhood of Col. James Bell.[6] I soon had my hands full of business, for in consequence of the men being exposed to so much wet while the Influenza was raging epidemically around us, they very soon were able to out-bark all the dogs in the neighbouring plantations. Major Dearborn was among the first to adopt this new order of things. Besides the sick of our camp, I was called upon to visit many of the settlers, whole families of whom were down at once with the measles in a severe form. (Among the rest was a very interesting and handsome daughter of a Mr. Morbla, whom I found scarcely able to breathe, but by judicious treatment was restored to health before we left the vicinity. She was interesting to me because she very much resembled an absent friend, independent of her sufferings.)

We remained at Col. Bell's until the 22nd Febr., when we

struck our tents and proceeded to Warner's ferry on the Upper Withlacoochee, close to the boundary line between Georgia and Florida. While there, we built a stockade, for the protection of the neighboring inhabitants, when [after] we should have left, as a place of refuge for them.

In consequence of an alarm at Hicks-town,[7] caused by a body of Indians attacking a plantation in the neighbourhood, on the 1st March we crossed the Withlacoo-chee and marched to the relief of its inhabitants. The swarthy devils, however, had made themselves scarce by the time we got there; so all we had to do was, as the Scotchman says, "to coome back agen."

We visited San Pedro,[8] which is seven miles from Hicks-town. In truth the latter was nothing but an extensive field, which had once been the site of an important Indian town; but at the time we saw it [it] presented not the least vestige of its former life and bustle or indeed of any life at all. San Pedro was a County-town [county seat, Madison County]; and we found it the resort of many fugitives who had left their desolated homes to escape the rifles and scalping-knife; and were dwelling in miserable shantees that could scarcely protect them from the slightest shower. The few settlers on the road we travelled on our return, who had not deserted their clearings, were suffering very much from alarm of Indians, who were known to be concealed somewhere in the vicinity; for they would frequently, when prompted by their necessities, leave their lurking place, in the swamps, and commit depredations, and then retire with impunity loaded with their plunder.

On the 7th March our camp was alarmed by night by a sentinel discharging his musket. We were all immediately under arms and at our respective posts; when the Sergeant of the guard reported that the Sentinel had fired at some one who was attempting to steal my horse. This was certainly a bold attempt, but done in a way charactertistic of an Indian. My horse was always kept tied to a tree in the rear of my tent, and not six yards from where a sentinel was posted. There were a number of hogs constantly prowling about the horse, to pick up the corn he dropt in eating. Taking a hint from this circumstance, the thief had crept up on all fours and imposed himself upon the Sentinel as one of these animals, until he had untied the halter from the tree, but, turning round to lead the horse off, he disclosed his true character. The Sentinel observing he had a turban on his head after the Indian costume immediately fired at him; but fearing to hit the horse unfortunately missed the man, for he scampered off in one direction and the horse in another. The latter was found next morning quietly grazing close by the camp.

On the 18th March we left our camp and proceeded in a South-East direction, with the intention of meeting a body of recruits who were at Newnansville,[9] awaiting an opportunity of joining us.

We crossed the Suwannee river at Livingston's ferry[10] that evening, and bivouacked for the night on its Eastern bank, having accomplished a march of nearly thirty miles in one day; a severe task for men loaded with their muskets and accoutrements and heavy knapsacks. The second day we marched eighteen miles, and took possession of a house which had been deserted by its owner named Clements, and where we found an abundance of corn and fodder for our horses. We finally reached Alligator Fort,[11] and determined there to await the arrival of the recruits, as Newnansville was distant but a day's march.

The place called Alligator Fort from its vicinity to Alligator [village of] the Indian chief's [Alligator's] tribe, was an asylum of many families who had been routed from their homes and obliged to receive sustenance from the United States, being deprived of the means of supporting themselves by this cruel Indian warfare, which respected neither age nor sex.

We got back to our camp on the evening of the 25th March, after marching one hundred and forty miles; but with light hearts and buoyant hopes, for the agreeable tidings of anticipated peace had reached our ears. The Indians were, according to report, at last subdued; and were surrendering themselves for emigration; and by the 10th April we heard were to be on their way Westward; when we would probably receive orders to proceed Northwards to our posts.[12]

The Journal

In accordance with the principle of the mind's colouring imparting its hue to surrounding objects, everything assumed a new and brighter aspect, with the first rekindling of hope in my desponding heart. The sun again seemed to glance with joyous smile gaily and brightly on earth, arraying every object under its influence with beauty and promise of happiness. Under the soft breath of spring the woodlands had long been decked with gay verdure; and wild flowers had long been springing in splendour and beauty unobserved around me; but not until this revival of decaying hope infused into my heart its sunshine, and lit my eye with joy, did nature put on her loveliest vestments for me. Flowers the most ambrosial had exerted their pleasing sway in vain; the "warblings of wood notes wild" fell unheeded upon my ear; but now seen, inhaled, and heard through a relieved weariness, which gave the most ordinary objects an interest. Creation seemed filled with a beauty which nature alone could scarce have imparted. There was now a brilliancy in the atmosphere which threw a softness around the verdure of the trees, and doubled the melody of their feathery occupants; perfumed flowers and blossoming trees, enriching the balmy air with their united scents, had their fragrance now justly appreciated.

Already in bright eyed fancy I looked upon those well remembered, fondly cherished scenes, so dearly loved in childhood's happy hour, and which the recent cessation from carnage and wars alarms held out a promise of my soon revisiting; when all my hopes of happiness were suddenly blasted in the bud by the commission of an atrocity by the treacherous, murderous, rascally Indians, which exceeded in savage barbarity and ferocity all their previous works of death and desolation. It seemed strange how sympathy could ever have been excited in one's breast for these bloodthirsty, cowardly demons; whose only glory was butchering defenceless individuals; raising the ruthless rifle and keen-edged scalping-knife against unoffending and helpless infancy, decrepid old age, and weak women; never risking an encounter with men like themselves but under the most advantageous circumstances; and flying at the least symptom of danger.

Journey into Wilderness

On the announcement that hostilities had ceased, many families had returned to their deserted homes, from the rude stockade defences erected in many parts of the country for the protection of the panic struck inhabitants. These fortified houses were crowded with women and children; mothers pressing their infants to their bosoms had here fled for safety; often fancying they heard the stealthy tread of the savages; and listening in agony for their horrible yells, while their husbands and brothers were out in obedience to the call for volunteers to assist in driving from their fastnesses the ruthless Seminoles, and rid the territory of such vermin. Among the first who availed themselves of declared peace to return to their domestic avocations was Clements and his family. Their home was the house we had occupied one night on our march to Alligator Fort, but only a week previous to the bloody tragedy. Clements had left his home for the purpose of drawing rations at Livingston's ferry eighteen miles off; and returned to find it desolate. His whole family had fallen victims to Indian barbarity; mercy was extended to none; the rifle-bullets pierced mother and child at the same stroke. Who can depict the consternation and horror of the husband and father on finding his wife and five children, whom he had left alive and well but a few hours before, all stretched lifeless on the ground, weltering in their own blood; their scalps torn from their heads and borne off as testimony of triumph by their savage murderers; their bodies partly devoured by the hogs! It was a scene to make humanity mourn and tremble.[13]

CHAPTER XIII

*O*n the 1st April Major Dearborn left us under command of Major Staniford, having received a leave of absence to visit his family in Maine. A few days after, we returned to our old ground of encampment near Townsend's; and there vegetated until the end of the month; when an order was received from Gen. Jesup[1] for our detachment to proceed immediately to Newnansville, E. Florida. We took up the line of march on the 30th April; crossed Warner's ferry over the Upper Withlacoochee on the 1st May; and encamped that night on the south bank. From that point until we reached Livingston's ferry on the Suwannee, we had a continued series of stoppages, stallings, etc., from the roads having been under water when the river overflowed its banks and inundated the country for miles in extent a short time previous. Great indeed was the toil and fatigue endured on this march; and when the state of the roads is considered, nobly did our soldiers accomplish it, although we occupied three days in passing over the same ground that we had traversed in one but a short time back. At every mile the teams had to be unhitched, and the men take the traces in hand and drag the wagons through swampy bogs and spongy flats, where no horse could move; they were often in water up to their waists, much of the way being through ponds left by the falling river.

Time will run through the roughest day; and it finally brought us to Livingston's ferry; which we crossed in a flat, and pitched our tents on its eastern bank. Here we remained one day to rest and procure wagons for transportation, for we found the state of the roads rendered it necessary that we should lighten our present loads. This accomplished, we once more got under way, and proceeded down the east bank of the Suwannee towards Charles ferry,[2] where we designed striking the main road to Newnansville.

Journey into Wilderness

We encamped for one night near Charles ferry, and renewed at an early hour next morning our weary march. We were apparently the first to travel over this route with wheels since the war commenced; and a slow and tedious time we had; stopping every five minutes to clear away the fallen trees which blocked up the road; sinking through the soft spongy ground if we deserted the beaten track to circumvent the obstructions. We found great scarcity of water also upon the route; and suffered much from thirst while marching through sun and sand, both very abundant amidst these eternal pine-barrens. Never were mortals more grateful than our men, when one afternoon after a hot day's march through burning sands without a drop of water to moisten our parched lips, a shower dropt like mercy from heaven, which drenching us to the skin, was more refreshing and invigorating than a day's rest could have been. I overheard some of the men say that if this shower had not come when it did, they would certainly have dropt dead.

About noon of the second day's march from Charles' ferry we reached an oasis in this desert, which broke upon our vision like the fairy-land sometimes seen in dreams. Itchetuckney was the name of this terrestrial paradise,[3] for such it seemed to our weary faculties, where man once dwelt in peace; until disturbed by the savage foe; who exercising the wily caution of a beast of prey stole with noiseless step upon his victim. In a hollow dell where the very air seemed concentrated in coolness, a grassy slope of the most rich and velvet green extended to the margin of a translucent and placid spring, whereon was faithfully reflected the green foliage that thickened over it; and in its transparent water might be clearly discerned the tiniest object at the bottom, clothed in the blent hues of the o'er arching sky; the babbling of the stream, and faint rustlings of the foliage as the breeze passed gently over the impending shrubbery, were the only sounds heard in this sweetest of sylvan solitudes. Various kinds of fruit trees glowing with blossoms were bright in loveliness around us.

As the sun was at his meridien strength when we reached this spot, we determined here to await his nearer approach to the hori-

The Journal

zon before we should continue our route. So, reposing on banks covered with flowers, we took our midday meal amid this beautiful scenery. Our refreshment was simple, but attended with wholesome appetites; after which, we slept extended on the grass until the hour arrived when the fiercely burning sun was somewhat shorn of his power. We soon after passed upon the road the carcass of a horse, who with his rider bearing an express had been shot by the Indians a little while before.

About eight miles from Newnansville we crossed the *Santa-Fee* [Santa Fe] river, over the natural bridge.[4] Had we not been told by our guide at the moment, we should never have suspected that there was anything like a river in our vicinity. This spot exhibited another specimen of Nature's freaks, which I have already noticed; but here it was on a much larger scale. The river, which a week previous had overflowed this spot to a swimming depth, and a width of half a mile, now passed quietly under ground a distance of three miles, forming a natural bridge of that width; when it again emerges into daylight, and shows itself flowing in a broad and deep channel.

As we approached Newnansville, the County Town of Alachua [County] where are to be found the most valuable lands in Florida,[5] our road lay through a beautiful country, watered by sparkling streams, and enlivened by richest verdure. We here found fields of tassell'd corn growing as it were *"upon their own hook;"* for the houses to which the fields pertained were all abandoned by their owners through fear of the Savage.

On the 14th May we approached our destination; and being sent forward by Major Staniford to select a suitable camping ground, I selected with the assistance of Col. Mills,[6] of the Florida Volunteers who was here in command, an eligible spot on a wooded hill, a few hundred yards to the South East of Newnansville.

Three miles from this place was the scene of a severe contest between the Indians and Capt. Tomkins [Tompkins],[7] of the 1st Artillery, the previous summer. He was stationed here in command with his company and a few Florida Militia; when hearing of the approach and an intended attack by the savages upon New-

89

nansville, he determined to go out and meet them in the open woods. He had proceeded but three miles when the enemy were seen advancing up the road in great force towards their white foes; upon seeing whom [the Florida Militia], they immediately commenced the most frantic yelling; and leaping about, exhibited many extravagant demonstrations of their delight at the approaching contest; finally extending to the right and left, they took to trees and awaited the advance of our troops. Capt. Tomkins had brought out with him a small howitzer, and loading it with grape shot he first gave them a serenade "a la distance"; they not relishing such unexpectedly deep tones with the accompaniment of bullets, endeavoured to drown the music with their yells and treble rifle notes; but this was "no go" and only served as an "encore"; for it caused a repetition of the tune ten or more times, when they concluded to retire in disgust. This was done at double quick time by the whole band, with the exception of a few of their number who were left upon the ground to verify the poet's assertion of "music having charms to soothe the savage breast." In the absence of rocks, which are very scarce about that spot, the pine-trees served as admirable substitutes for verifying the rest of the poet's assertion; for they were so split by the Captain's barrel organ, that many generations yet unborn will see in them tangible proofs of splitting by "music's charms."[8]

Newnansville, before this war, could boast of only one block house, eclypt a court house, and one tavern, built in the same primitive style of architecture. Now it consists of two rival hotels, a fort, shops in abundance, and dwellings, alias shantees, so numerous that for several days after my arrival I could scarcely find my way through the labrynth of streets and lanes, laid out with a pleasing disregard to all rules of uniformity.

This sudden increase of population and consequent prosperity to the incipient city was caused entirely by an innate dread and very natural dislike of its inhabitants to being scalped.[9] They were mostly small farmers who had emigrated from different States and settled in Alachua County to plant corn, hoe potatoes, and beget ugly little white-headed responsibilities. Which occu-

The Journal

pations they pursued with praise-worthy industry and perseverance in the pipeing times of peace; but imagining it much easier to be fed by Uncle Sam, they provoked the Indians by various aggressions to a retaliation, and then complained to their venerable Uncle of the mischievous disposition of his red nephews. He immediately issued his mandate to the said curiously coloured relations, that as they could not live in brotherly affection with his white nephews and nieces, their health must be in a bad state, and a change of air would be very beneficial; whereupon he prescribed that west of the Mississippi as being very pure and wholesome. Uncle Sam's red relatives not coincideing with him on the subject of their health, and discovering the authors of their Uncle's displeasure, undertook to revenge themselves upon their white cousins who immediately congregated in spots, built pickets or stockades—which they called forts—drew rations—as they designated themselves "suffering inhabitants"—and devoted their attention entirely to the last of their former occupations.

Finding this a very agreeable way of living, they occasionally united together, and riding through the country in strong parties managed to kill a stray Indian or two. This so exasperated the rest of the tribe that they would break out anew and swear they wouldn't cease hostilities so long as a white-skin of them was left. [I state this as a general opinion, not mine.][10]

The mansions of Newnansville were certainly unique in appearance. Each abode consisted of a shed built of slab-boards enclosing an area about twelve feet square; and were evidently calculated for exercising the rights of hospitality; for the occupants excluded nothing; even the rain always finding ready admittance. In some sheds there were several families living huddled together under the same roof, each occupying a corner of the room, and occasionally a fifth family in the center. They must have found this mode the most agreeable,—upon the principle of "the more the merrier," for they even allowed some one or other of the families to take in boarders; as I could testify from my own experience on several occasions.

We were frequently invited to attend the balls that were nightly given by this fashionable community; and I always made it my duty to attend; not only to show my respect for the society of this enlightened metropolis; but also because these exhibitions always afforded a fund of amusement after the monotonous routine of a day in camp, on account of the original style of dancing the *"double trouble,"*[11] and the high tone of refinement which pervaded the conversation of the polished gentlemen and accomplished ladies.

On the occasion of a dinner given by the inhabitants to Col. Mills, we were invited to attend. At the hour stated in the notes of invitation we presented ourselves at one of the rival hotels, the scene of operations upon this festive occasion. We found a long arbour erected in the yard, back of the house, and an equally long table extending under it, with all the appliances of the feast. All the inhabitants of the country, men, women, & children, were present. The ladies dined first; the children next; and after them upon the remnants of the feast the gentlemen and invited guests. This order being observed apparently, for want of a better reason, that the gentlemen might not be interrupted in the patriotic duty of drinking toasts. Unfortunately, in the midst of Col. Mills' speech in reply to a sentiment which was thought to confer everlasting immortality upon him, a heavy shower poured its malice upon our poor devoted heads, which were all uncovered out of respect to the orator. This proved but a slight damper to our enjoyments, or the martial speaker's eloquence, who with exemplary fortitude continued his speech without flinching; and only sat down and put his hat on at the end of the peroration, when the welkin rang with three times three from the admireing and flattered audience.[12]

The ladies sent in a toast which would have withered Old Hickory into a nonentity had he been present. It was an outpouring of the overflowing bile, which some severe remarks of the General upon the courage of the Florida gentry had caused to be super-abundantly secreted in the livers of these fair Alachua dames.[13]

The General had observed in one of his letters, to some one, which was published in the newspapers, that the Florida men were

The Journal

all cowards; and recommended to their wives that they should be discarded and new husbands from other States substituted who would get [beget] brave children with the courage sufficiently to protect them. The sentiment of the ladies was highly condemnatory of this sensible advice; [they] expressed their perfect satisfaction with their present helpmates; and stated that they were not in the habit of swapping husbands nor disposed to adopt such a mode of procedure, notwithstanding the amiable example offered them in the General's own conduct in former times.[14]

Capt. Gilliland of the Alachua Militia presided at the table; and not until the scraping of a fiddle in the adjoining house informed us that the ladies had opened the ball, which was to finish the day's entertainment, did we quit the social board.[15]

The arrival at Newnansville of Capt. B. Beall[16] with his company [D] of U. S. 2nd Dragoons, which occurred a week after our own, produced quite a sensation in our camp. These were the first Regular troops we had seen since leaving Alabama eight months previous. They had been scouting in the vicinity of Suwannee river, and had come here for a few days' rest.

We soon after had our society further increased by the arrival of Major Ashby,[17] U. S. 2nd Dragoons, just from Charleston where he had been spending the winter to recruit his health injured by a severe wound received in a skirmish with some Indians the previous summer in Florida.[18] Major [Thomas T.] Flauntleroy [Fauntleroy] also arrived soon after with three companies of U. S. 2nd Dragoons from Suwannee Old Town[19] and took position here for the summer. With him were Lts. Spalding,[20] Thornton,[21] Hunter,[22] and [First Lieutenant George A.] Forsyth of the same corps; and Dr. G. R. Clarke[23] of the Army; all very clever, agreeable companions, and a valuable acquisition to our society. Fun and frolic now prevailed to a great extent; balls and double shuffle without end; the ladies very amiable and duty in camp not very irksome. We anticipated making ample amends during the summer for our privations and fatigue the past winter.

CHAPTER XIV

I had began to feel very happy and contented in my situation at Newnansville among so many delightful companions; and was looking forward to spending an agreeable summer, when an order arrived from Gen. Jesup, directing me to proceed without delay to Fort Mellon on Lake Monroe;[1] in consequence of the reported indisposition of Dr. Laub[2] the Surgeon on that post; and the extreme sickness among the troops there, rendering the constant attendance of a physician necessary. This was another link in my chain of disappointed hopes; another instance of the fallacy of human expectations.

Military orders must be obeyed; and with promptness; so on the 6th June I left Newnansville in the company with Lt. Thornton of the 2nd Dragoons, who had obtained leave to go home on account of ill health. Thornton was too sick to ride horseback; so we borrowed a small wagon from Lt. Spalding; and making a soldier ride my horse, I drove the wagon.

We started off at 2 o'clock in the afternoon, and reached Fort Harlee[3] on the Santa Fee river about dusk. There we were hospitably entertained and lodged for the night, by my friend and old fellow campaigner Major [William L.] McClintock, who was commandant of the post. As Black Creek was only twenty seven miles distant, we waited for the decline of the sun next day before we recommenced our journey; and at 1 o'clock bid our hospitable entertainers adieu. The roads were so bad from the deep sand, we made but slow progress; and sunset found us seven miles from Garey's ferry.[4] At the very moment I was whipping up to accomplish our journey before dark, the hind axle-tree of our vehicle broke in twain; and down we came upon the ground with an awful crash. Here was a dilemma; in a hostile country; surrounded by hammocks, which were the lurking places of blood-

94

thirsty savages, as merciless as the prowling lion or crouching tiger; night coming on, no means of repaireing the shattered axle-tree; one of us too sick to walk, or even to ride horse-back without danger of falling off. There was but one alternative, which we put into execution. I mounted my horse, and having unhitched the other animal from his harness, Thornton managed to get on his back, and remain there, while the soldier walked; leaving wagon, baggage, etc, to take care of themselves, until we should send for them the next day, if not otherwise appropriated in the interim.

We reached Fort Heileman[5] at Black Creek just as tatoo was beating, about 9 o'clock; and crossing Garey's ferry, were soon comforting ourselves over a cup of old Garey's tea; and though without cream, yet having been so long accustomed to the absence of that luxury, we did not the less enjoy our tea after our fatigue and mishap.

There was no boat going to Fort Mellon on the next day; which fortuitous circumstance allowed me time to explore the mysteries of this much talked of place. I found it remarkable for nothing, except flies, fleas, and heat. As the principal depot for the Army in Florida, however, it presented a more civilized aspect than scenes I had been accustomed to for the last twelve months. There were frame houses with glass in window sashes; steam-boats were moored to the banks of the stream; and a stirring business-like air prevailed everywhere; which impressed me strongly with a consciousness of my proximity to the haunts of civilized man. This consciousness produced a soothing effect upon my spirits, after my long sojourn in the wilderness.

On the 9th June I left Garey's ferry, and embarked in the U. S. Steamer Essayons[6] for Fort Mellon at 10 o'clock in the morning; and proceeding three miles, stopped to take in wood from the bank where it had been collected for this purpose. This done, we continued our way through the dark and deep rolling current of Black Creek, which flowed between mossy embankments, beautifully bordered by varied flowers and blossoming trees, whose tops bending o'er the water, cast shadows which may indeed be said to resemble "fairy islands in a sunny sea." We passed many little creeks and nooks, which expanding themselves into broader basins, slept in profound repose amid the foliage, scarce a ripple disturbing their liquid surface, except where some lazy alligator raised its head to wonder at the passing boat.

In what bright contrast did the broad bosom of the St. John's river first burst upon my sight! Never shall I forget my sensations at that rare and beauteous sight. It shot a gleam of joy to my heart which only those can appreciate who like myself have been raised in sight of the boundless ocean with which was associated all of past happiness; and then shut up for a twelve month [period] in the forest, unblest with even a view of the horizon. I had been suffocating as it were in a dungeon; I now felt as if once more admitted to the free air of heaven. Thick, dark forests formed the boundary on every side; when on a sudden turn in the creek, I beheld before me, through an avenue of o'er hanging trees, the magnificent expanse of the St. John's; whose bright waters seen dancing in the sun beams afforded an inexpressible relief to my wearied eyes, which had so long dwelt on gloomy pines. I swallowed with open mouth the exhilarating air, whose freshness infused new energy into my whole being. As we emerged from Black Creek into the great expanse of the river glittering in the sunlight;—which was like putting out to sea;—a schooner with her swelling canvass wooing the breeze rose full upon my sight; the silver crested waves gently curling under her bows as she skimmed like a sea-bird o'er the watery plain. She was just from Charleston; the home of my memory and hopes. Imagination immediately took wing and soared; conjuring me back to the hallowed circles of my childhood's brightest hour.

Wrapt in the fantasies of "fond memory's spell," the hours flew unconsciously by; and the departing glory of the sun was announcing that another day had passed when we deviated from the centre of the river towards the east bank where Picolata[7] stood. We there stopped only long enough to deliver despatches to Capt. [Charles Spencer] Merchant the Commandant of the post; and continued our progress uninterrupted, until the narrow and crooked windings of the river rendered a passage through

ATLANTIC

OCEAN

TO JACKSONVILLE

NORTH FORK

⚓ Gareys Ferry
Ft. Heilman ⚓

BLACK CREEK

SOUTH FORK

RIVER

SANTA FE RIVER

Ft. Harlee ⚡

SANTA FE POND

ST. AUGUSTINE PENSACOLA HIGHWAY

ewnansville

Ft. Fraser ⚡

Ft. Marion ⚡
St. Augustine

Picolata

Ft. Peyton ⚡

NEWNANS LAKE

ALACHUA PRAIRIE

t. Walker ⚡
cahoote ⚡

ORANGE LAKE

RIVER

⚓ Paynes Landing

Ft. Gates ⚡

ST. JOHNS

Bulow's Plantation

Ft. Drane ⚡

arlie Emathla's Town

OKLAWAHA

LAKE GEORGE

Dunham's

⚓ Ft. King

Dunlawton

⚡ Ft. Volusia

Camp Izzard ⚡

GAINES BATTLE

OCHEE

RIVER

⚡ Ft. Kingsbury

LAKE MONROE

BATTLE OF WAHOO SWAMP

WITHLACOOCHEE

Pilaklikaha

Ft. Mellon ⚡

⚡ Ft. Armstrong

DADE'S MASSACRE

NORTHEAST FLORIDA
NEWNANSVILLE - ST. AUGUSTINE -
FORT MELLON AREA

REPRODUCED FROM THE
BRUFF MAP 1846

MOTTE'S ITINERARY · · · ·

them by night a dangerous experiment. We therefore dropt anchor; and after the luxury of a segar;—best enjoyed always amid the glories of the night; and its enjoyment enhanced on this occasion, by the freshness of the night breeze upon deck, which was cool and strong enough to keep off moschetoes [mosquitoes]; —after luxuriating in a real havannah, I sought my berth, with heart overflowing with delicious sensations; and slept sweeter for being lulled by the rippling waters.

We were again under way at the first dawn, and long before Morpheus had removed his heavy finger from my eyelids. A succession of glorious scenery was constantly presented to the sight, as we rapidly stemmed the St. Johns; whose banks, now receding, now approximating so as merely to admit our boat between them, were bright in loveliness on either hand with every species of tree and shrub. From orange groves, whose golden fruit and snowy blossom stood in beautiful contrast with their dark foliage, we'd pass on to long rows of tall and slim palmettoes; their graceful trunks shooting up along the river banks for miles. Then a change would come over the beauty of the scenery; and in place of orange and palm trees, would appear the spreading oak, the bay, the beautiful cedar, and stately magnolia; their pendant branches casting mysterious shadows on the St. Johns, as they hang over its placid bosom in every variety of form and beauty. In the early part of the day we entered upon the broad spreading Lake George; which is a mere expansion of the St. Johns; forming a lake about seventeen miles long, and half that distance in breadth. At its southern extremity,—where there is a bar which it was necessary to cross before further progress could be made into the St. Johns, —we found the Steamer Camden at anchor; having on board a detachment of troops commanded by [Second] Lt. [Christopher Quarles] Tompkins of the 3rd Art. destined for Fort Mellon. The Camden being of too great draught to cross the bar, we dropt anchor to lighten her, by taking from her these troops. As this was a job not to be quickly accomplished with all their baggage in one small yawl boat, the Captain of our boat concluded to remain here until morning.

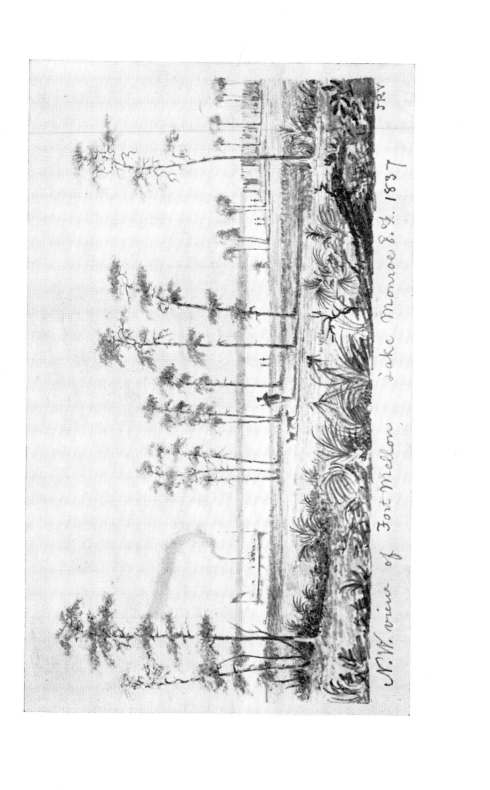

N.W. view of Fort Mellon. Lake Monroe E.F. 1837

The Journal

On the 11th June, we were once more steaming up this wonderfully beautiful river; its sylvan shores presenting the same varied aspect of beauty as already described. We stopt for a few moments at Volusia,[8] to take off a couple of Dragoons who had got thus far on their way to Fort Mellon riding express. They left their horses in quiet possession of the pasturage near the abandoned post; which seemed deserted by every living creature but these two poor quadrupeds. This post had been broken up a week before, in consequence of its extremely unhealthy location. Not an individual of the whole garrison, officer or private, had escaped the influence of this miasmatic region. Several deaths had occurred there, and the living were not sufficiently well, and scarcely strong enough to bury the dead. The same destiny was said to await those at Fort Mellon, if not speedily abandoned; which prophecy seemed about being fulfilled at the time, for I heard its sick list was daily increasing; and that several deaths had already occurred among both officers and men.

Volusia's appearance, associated with the cause of its recent desertion, to my eyes looked hideously desolate. The pickets were located near the river, at the base of a far reaching hill; a clearing of many acres, begirt with hammocks, extended around. This was the scene of Major Gates' alledged improper conduct in not sending for the body of one of his men, killed by the Indians within sight of the pickets; for which he was summarily and unjustly struck from the Army roll by President Jackson without a trial; but was afterwards restored upon the acquittal of a court of inquiry, which he rightfully demanded upon his conduct.[9]

It was a high-handed and unauthorized act of President Jackson, thus to strip a meritorious officer of his commission and blast his reputation without the shadow of an examination into the alledged offence, but merely on his own individual and biased opinion. Such acts of vindictive injustice have characterized others in high places at Washington, who, contemptible as individuals, think by copying a man, who however excellent he may have been yet had failings, that it will make them appear great to the world, and remove from them the insignificancy of character which will ever be their attribute whatever adventitious position they may have attained through the misguided kindness of another rather than from any merits of their own.

The Court Martial which was ordered for the trial of Major Gates totally exonerated him from any slightest cause for criminations; but on the contrary, the testimony, offered before it, proved that the Major deserved great credit for his prudence in not suffering himself to be drawn out from his defenses and caught in an ambuscade, as was the evident design of the Indians. Volusia was the depot of stores for the left wing of the Army, and on it alone could they rely for supplies. Major Gates when left in charge of it with invalids principally for a garrison, was instructed to defend and preserve it at all hazards. If the Major had made a sortie, he would have been obliged to take all his available force, which must have been very small, leaving the stockade unprotected, and open to the Indians, who were no doubt awaiting such an opportunity to rush in from an opposite direction. After enduring a year of anxious suspense, this worthy and accomplished officer finally had justice done him, by an honorable acquittal, and restoration to his proper rank in the Army.

We reached Fort Mellon about 4 o'clock in the afternoon of the 11th June; after having crossed another expansion of the St. Johns, called Lake Monroe, upon whose south-western edge Fort Mellon was situated. Immediately upon landing I reported myself to Col. Harney[10] of the 2nd Dragoons, who was there in command. I found several old acquaintances at the post; and among them Paddy Carr with his band of Creek warriors; who had volunteered to leave Alabama and come to Florida to fight the Seminoles. I here also found my old friend Lt. Peyton of the 2nd Arty.

This place of which I have given a sketch,[11] drawn by my friend Capt J. R. Vinton[12] of the Army, is memorable in the annals of the Florida war for the battle which was fought here on the 8th Febry last; a week after the first landing of the troops.

Two hours before daylight on that day the Sentinel's attention was attracted to a rustling noise in the bushes around, and had barely time to give the alarm, when the rifles and throats of six hundred[13] blood-thirsty Micasukies, led on by *King Philip*[14] and his son *Coa-coo-ché*,[15] or *Wild-Cat,* opened in full chorus upon the ears of the sleeping garrison. Too well aware from experience that night assaults and surprises constituted the peculiar warfare of these devils, every man had orders to lay down at night with his belts on, and his arms in his hands; luckily being thus prepared, every man in an instant was at his proper post, behind a low breast work of logs at the time only two or three in height, that had been hurriedly erected the day previous; and of whose existence the Indians were ignorant; for while rushing forwards in the darkness, supposing no obstacles in the way, their headlong career was suddenly checked on beholding this breast-work; and their yells changed into a cry of *Tohopeka,* the Indian word for fort or strong-place. They retired a hundred yards, and from behind trees kept up an increasing fireing and yelling until eight o'clock; when a sudden stillness usurped the place of all this noise and uproar, and nothing more was either seen or heard of them. At the first discharge, Capt. Mellon was shot dead at his post; the only individual killed of our party;[16] and but fifteen men slightly wounded. Lt. McLaughlin[17] of the Navy, who was acting as aide to Col. [Alexander C. W.] Fanning the commanding officer, was struck to the ground by a rifle ball in the breast; but subsequently recovered. Capt. Mellon, after whom the post was named, was buried in an angle of the breast-work as it then stood, close upon the margin of the lake. The position of works being altered since, his grave is now enclosed in palisades, over which waved the mossy branches of a wide spreading oak. A rough stone—the production of the spot—rests upon the grave within the small enclosure; and upon it some devoted friend has scratched the name of the hero who occupies a soldier's grave in this lonely spot.

The officers engaged in this action were highly spoken off [of] by Lt. Col. Fanning, commanding at the time, in his official despatch. In making honorable mention of them he says, "Lt. Col. Harney commanding the four companies, displayed, during the contest, the greatest boldness and vigor, and inspired his newly enlisted men with great confidence. I have at all times received from him the most energetic support. With the officers of his battalion I have every reason to be well satisfied. My eye was upon every one, and I discovered nothing but firmness and confidence in all. In justice to them their names must be mentioned: Captain [William] Gordon, Captain [Jonathan L.] Bean, 1st Lt. John Graham, 1st Lt. [Marshall Sax] Howe, 1st Lt. [James W.] Hamilton, 1st Lt. [George A. H.] Blake, 2nd Lt. [John Winfield Scott] McNeil, 2nd Lt. Thornton, 2nd Lt. [Charles E.] Kingsbury, and 2nd Lt. [Charles A.] May.

"On the fall of Captain Mellon, Captain J. R. Vinton, of the 3rd Artillery, assumed the command of the two companies of Artillery. I have long known his great military attainments. On this occasion I witnessed his conduct and courage. 1st Lt. [William B.] Davidson took command of Mellon's company during the engagement. It could not have fallen into better hands. I have already spoken of the service rendered by 2nd Lt. [George C.] Thomas of the 4th Artillery. He has always volunteered his services on every dangerous scouting party. Lt. Piercey,[18] of the Navy, Captain of the friendly Indians, with his Indian force, fought among the regular troops; and he is always foremost in danger.

"Assistant Surgeon Laub dressed the wounded under the fire of the enemy. Paddy Carr, the Creek chief, fought well. He has generally headed the scouting parties, and has performed those laborious and dangerous duties with great promptitude and cheerfulness. If I have mentioned all, it is because all deserve mention. Never was officer, charged with a delicate and hazardous enterprize, served with more zeal and promptitude."

And well did they deserve this praise of Col. Fanning, for becoming intimately acquainted with them myself I can add my mite of commendation and vouch for the fact of their being true and steadfast in the service of their country, and unflinching in the hour of danger. Of the officers mentioned as engaged in this affair, six in a short time of one another fell victims to either the rifle bullets of the savage; or the diseases of the climate, rendered malignant by the unparalleled exposures and hardships of camp and field in such a country, and in such a warfare.[19]

102

The Journal

Two nights before this attack was made, a couple of officers had a very narrow escape from the Indians. Lt. McLaughlin of the Navy and Lt. Thomas of the Army, had mounted their horses in the afternoon for a ride. Having rode as far as seemed proper, they were about turning their horses' heads towards the fort, when they discovered the disagreeable fact of their having lost their way, not being able to recollect in what direction the fort was; there being of course, no roads in this neighborhood. In riding about to discover the way, they suddenly found themselves in the centre of an Indian encampment; and at the same moment the Indians raised a yell, and gave chase after them in their rapid retreat. Knowing that certain death awaited them if taken, they did not spare their horses; but putting spurs to them fled like deer chased by the hunters. Despairing of finding their way back to the fort in the dark, and not knowing but that every step taken might increase their distance from it, they finally dismounted; and concealing their horses in a dense hammock, the poor hunted fellows proceeded some little distance, and crouching under the flimsy covering of some saw-palmetto that grew about them, hoped to escape the vigilant eyes of these human hounds, who were following in their track. Their yells were heard nearer and nearer; in a moment torches glared through the trees, and the forest seemed girdled round with light, and echoing to the infernal yells of hundreds of savages thirsting for blood. No doubt their terrors magnified the numbers; but to them there seemed a legion, who with blazing torches that now flared close around them, threatened for hours to lay open their insecure place of refuge. Towards morning, silence and darkness again spread over the forest; and long after daylight, one of them raised his head to reconnoitre, previous to exposing his person. And well for his scalp that he used this precaution; for not many yards from where he lay, his eyes fell upon a group of warriors sitting around a fire; their rifles in their hands ready for immediate use. After the lapse of what seemed hours to them, they again ventured to look; and finding the coast clear, crawled from their uncomfortable position; and soon succeeded by aid of daylight in finding their way back

103

to the fort, and giving the first intimation of Indians being in the vicinity of any force.[20]

I found a long sick list awaiting me at the hospital next morning; which spoke strongly in favour of an immediate abandonment of this post. Lt. Kingsbury of the 2nd Dragoons had been buried only the day before my arrival; and there were now sick, besides several officers, about seventy men. Col. Harney had received orders to break up the post immediately; but with his usual daring enterprise still delayed the execution of them that he might put in practice some theoretic plan of his for catching the Indians; which however, proved as feasible as, and somewhat similar to, the old and well established recipe for catching birds by putting salt upon their tails, wherein the only difficulty is found in making them stand quietly till you can approach the said tails.

As this was a time of truce, the Seminoles were constantly coming into our camp, and mingling in friendly intercourse with Paddy Carr's band of Creeks.[21] *Coa-coo-ché* alias *Wild-Cat* was a constant visitor of my tent; and ever since he got drunk there one afternoon on superfine port-wine I found it difficult to keep him away. Whiskey is the "summum bonum"[22] of Indian felicity;[23] but Coacooche having once tasted my port, declared it very fine medicine; and discarded all attempts to get his drunk on the meaner beverage; no doubt supposing it more consistent with his dignity as a King's son to be aristocratic in his tastes.

There were frequent ball-plays between the Creeks and Seminoles; and among the former alone. Back of our camp there was a wide level plain, the scene of these exercises; where several hundred Indians might every day have been seen, quite naked, enjoying their favourite amusement.

CHAPTER XV

*O*n the 17th inst three steamboats arrived, at Fort Mellon, with positive orders that the post should be broken up without delay. Col. Harney could no longer hesitate; so by dark of the same day we had all our baggage on board, and all the men soon after; and early dawn of the 18th found us on our way down Lake Monroe, bound for St. Augustine; leaving Coacooche in possession of Fort Mellon; of which, it is presumed, he immediately assumed command.

We stopt at Volusia to destroy a large quantity of corn, which had been left there when the post was abandoned in such haste, on account of the unhealthyness, and the mortality among the garrison.[1]

We arrived at Picolata on the evening of the 19th after dark; and remained there until the next afternoon, while Col. Harney rode over to St. Augustine and back.

We reached Jacksonville by 1 o'clock at night; where we stopt until morning, for the purpose of taking in wood. I had time enough to walk through this miserable little place with a brother officer, while the operation of wooding was going on; but saw nothing worthy of commemoration in its dozen scattered houses and sandy streets.

We were again under way by 7 o'clock; and crossed the St. John's bar a few hours after.

Now arrived the acme of my delight; once more was I bounding o'er the billowy plain, where sea and sky presented a boundless source of joy. With the first gleam of the mighty ocean, and with the first roar of its wild unmastered waves, all control over my excited feelings vanished; and with sensations of the most exquisite happiness, I could not refrain from leaping about the deck. The sea-birds seemed to partake of my feelings; for great numbers

105

of gulls and pelicans were around us, either delightedly reposing upon the sunny water, or skimming o'er the silvery crested waves, which were gently curling under the influence of the breeze; while our boat boldly dashing onward sent showers of glittering spray o'er her bows.

We reached St. Augustine at 4 o'clock in the afternoon of the 21st June. As we were making fast to the only wharf of which this place can boast, a letter was handed aboard to me, whose contents threw a blighting influence o'er all my hopes. It was an order from Gen. Armstead [Armistead][2] for me to proceed without delay to Fort Harlee, and report myself for duty there, in consequence of the sickness of Dr. [Assistant Surgeon Edward] Worrell, the Surgeon at that post. Heigho! So, instead of being allowed a reprieve during the summer months with the other officers, after my long and tedious inhumation in the sombre woods and depths of the wilderness; which I had borne with a patient resignation that was truly edifying; and after which I very much needed the recreation of a fresh, cool sea-air, so as to be reinstated in vigor and efficiency for the next campaign; instead of being permitted to recruit my constitution with a new infusion of health and spirits, after the debilitating service and severe hardships of the field; by breathing a pure atmosphere, and by entering into the enjoyments of society, with those who had not been half as long deprived of them, and therefore did not need their refreshing influence so much; I alone was permitted only to touch the threshold, and immediately was packed off to some sickly post in the interior; there to abide the heats and perils of a Florida summer.

The duties of an Army Surgeon in Florida allowed of no relaxation, either winter or summer, night or day. His post was always that of danger too; during winter, in the field sharing alike with all his brother officers their fatigues, privations, and perils. In summer, while his fellow campaigners were resting from their past toils and dangers, in anticipation of new ones the coming winter,[3]—following in beauty's train, and indulging in the softer luxuries of the heart; he was pressing the pulse of languid sickness,

The Journal

and breathing the pestiferous exhalations of crowded hospitals, in some unhealthy "Ultima Thule" of the wilderness. He had but one consolation; the consciousness of doing good. This alone supported him through such continued hardships; and he was always eager to encounter any danger which the glory of his profession required of him. The Army Surgeon has been truly called the soldier's peculiar friend,

> *"Who cheers him in camp, in marches lead,*
> *And with him in the battles bleed."*

As such, ought he not be an object of particular solicitude to all military men? Though a non-combatant ought he to be regarded with a less favorable eye than those whose enviable lot it is to hold commissions in the line?[4]

The ocean sunrise of the 22nd June found me outside of St. Augustine bar, on my way to Black Creek, in the same steamer, the Camden, that brought me to St. Augustine the day previous. The glorious diffusion of golden beams which streamed o'er the bright dancing sea, and the balmy breath of early morn, failed of their usually exhilarating influence o'er me; I was sick; not only at heart, but in body; for serious indisposition soon drove me to my berth, where I lay until we arrived at Black Creek the next day, and which I left only to occupy a sick bed at old Garey's.

On the 29th June I felt sufficiently recovered to proceed to my post in the sombre woods; and on the afternoon of that day reported myself to Captain [Samuel] Ringgold of Fort Harllee. This post was situated between Garey's ferry and Newnansville; twenty seven miles from the former, and eighteen from the latter. It was situated on a branch of the Santa Fee river, where a bridge had been thrown across the stream, and designated as the Santa Fee bridge. Major Harllee [Harlee][5] of the South Carolina Volunteers, who was here the preceeding winter, erected pickets with two block-houses at diagonal corners, after the fashion of Florida forts;[6] and hence it was dubbed Fort Harllee. A low pine-flat extended around in all directions, and nothing interrupted the monotonous view of russet pine trunks but a few miserable shantees, hurriedly erected,—some of pine-bark only,—and occupied by cracker families, who had left their homes and resorted hither to be under the wing of our protection.

In compliance with an invitation to spend the Fourth of July at Newnansville, where the day was to be celebrated with all due observance, particularly with a public dinner; I mounted my horse on the morning of that day, and rode over the eighteen miles. My solitary ride through the forests afforded a fine opportunity for indulging in the retrospection of events which were intimately associated in my heart with this day; the annual return of which for many years had never found me twice in the same part of the world.

The chief characteristic of military life may very properly be said to consist of *locomotion,* or constant change of scene. Such has been my experience of it, for nearly nine years never abiding in one spot more than a few months at a time, and previous to the day about which I am now writing, I had never remained quiet longer than a week or two in one place. Though in a different latitude and longitude from that spot which claimed my presence on the same day twelve months previous, I was forcibly reminded during my solitary ride, of the similarity of my occupation on the two days by a recurrence of the same train of thought relative to this our Nation's natal day, which I have recorded in the early part of this work. Here was I riding *"solitaire"* through a pine forest, under the scorching sun of Florida; not knowing at what moment my solitude might be unpleasantly broken in upon, by the unwelcome apparition of some tawney devil of an Indian "upon hostile thoughts intent." In Chapter 3rd is described how this day a year back, found me riding through a pine-forest among the Creek Indians. My privations seemed much greater during the first of the above mentioned rides, for I was then but a novice in the art of self-denial, and had not received the profitable experience of twelve months passed in the severe discipline of life in the field and camp, which somewhat modified my reflections during this my second 4th of July ride.[7]

At 1 o'clock I reached Newnansville, and dismounting at the

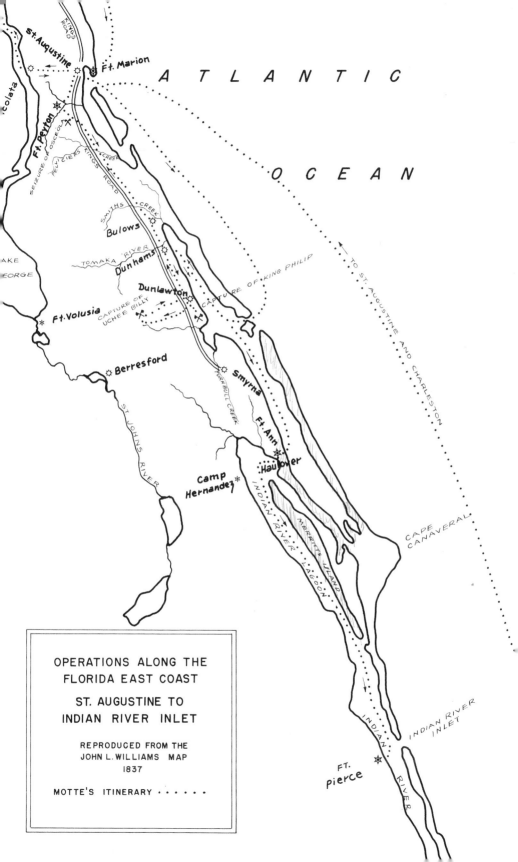

ATLANTIC

OCEAN

St. Augustine

KINGS ROAD

Ft. Marion

Colata

Ft. Peyton

SEIZURE OF OSCEOLA

PELLICIERS CREEK

KINGS ROAD

SMITHS CREEK

Bulows

TO ST. AUGUSTINE AND CHARLESTON

TOMAKA RIVER

Dunhams

Dunlawton

CAPTURE OF KING PHILIP

Ft. Volusia

CAPTURE OF UCHEE BILLY

LAKE GEORGE

Berresford

ST. JOHNS RIVER

TURNBULL CREEK

Smyrna

Ft. Ann

Haulover

Camp Hernandez

INDIAN RIVER LAGOON

MERRITTS ISLAND

CAPE CANAVERAL

INDIAN RIVER INLET

Ft. Pierce

INDIAN RIVER

OPERATIONS ALONG THE
FLORIDA EAST COAST

ST. AUGUSTINE TO
INDIAN RIVER INLET

REPRODUCED FROM THE
JOHN L. WILLIAMS MAP
1837

MOTTE'S ITINERARY • • • • • •

tavern where the dinner was to be served up, I entered the *"salle a manger."*[8] A very different scene presented itself to my eyes from that I expected to behold; instead of a long table extending from end to end of the hall, covered with all the appliances of a feast, "Linden saw another sight." Twas certainly a table in the center of the room, and that table covered,—but with what?—a winding sheet covering the corpse of Stanley the late master of the house. He had died but a few minutes before of congestive fever; and the house of feasting was thus turned into the house of mourning. The celebration of the day was consequently postponed; and the 4th of July occurred somewhat later in the month that year at Newnansville. I returned to Fort Harllee next day, to resume the process of vegetating.

While sitting one day in my tent at this post, engaged in the interesting occupation of removing the exuberant superficies of my face; vulgarly called shaving; suddenly I felt a shock as if the earth was shaken to its axis, succeeded by a noise similar to the rattling musketry of contending armies. As soon as my astonished faculties would permit, I started up, and lo! a huge pine tree of gigantic proportions, not more than a hundred yards from where I was, stood shattered and withered like a scorched blade of grass. A thunder cloud had discharged its potent electricity immediately over the camp, while all nature elsewhere was in repose, and striking this giant of the woods, ceased to be.

In consequence of a summons to attend as witness before a court martial sitting at St. Augustine, on the 23rd of July Lt. Davidson and myself set out for that place. We remained at Black Creek on the 24th, and the morning of the 25th found me once again on board a steamer, ploughing the St. Johns on my way to Picolata; where we arrived at 1 o'clock; and immediately mounted our horses which we had brought with us, and gallop'd over the eighteen miles to St. Augustine. I took up my quarters at Livingston's Hotel;[9] and getting into a civilized suit of clothes felt once more like a gentleman.

At my previous visit to St. Augustine, my stay was so short and inauspicious, having arrived at night and left the next morning soon after daylight, that I had no time for seeing the place. I did not neglect the present opportunity; so at an early hour on the morning after my arrival, I strolled through this ancient city. It is said to be the oldest town in North America except those of Mexico. And faith! I should think so from its appearance. It was built in 1565. Fort Marion on the northern outskirts of the town was built many years ago by the Spaniards. It now presents the appearance of an antiquated castle of the 14th Century, with its regular battlements, moat, and drawbridge; its rampart is twenty feet high, bastioned and casemated. The first thing that strikes a stranger in St. Augustine is the remarkable appearance of the houses. They are built in a peculiar style of a kind of stone, or tabbia [tabby],[10] containing, or rather formed of, a vast accumulation of marine shells. This material is dug up along the sea-shore, on the opposite Island of Anastasia. At a distance, the houses present the appearance of fancy work on a large scale. Like all Spanish towns, the streets are very narrow; and not being paved, the clouds of dust, which every equestrian seemed to think it his peculiar priviledge to keep up in your face, are exceedingly annoying in dry weather.

St. Francis' barracks occupy a position at the southern extremity of the city, facing the water to the east. Built for a nunnery, and used as such in former times, when Florida was a Spanish territory, and therefore interesting from its association; I have annexed a correct sketch of the building by my friend Capt. J. R. Vinton of the Army. The flag staff which might be mistaken as proceeding from the roof of the building is placed in the centre of the barrack yard. From the observatory a very commanding view of St. Augustine and its suburbs could be obtained. The building as here represented has been since demolished, and the present barracks tho' different in all respects from the old edifice built upon its walls. [The whereabouts of this sketch is unknown.—Ed.]

The night after our arrival we were favoured with an invitation from the lady of Judge Smith[11] to attend a party at her house. This opportunity of sharing the blandishments of converse with the fairest specimens of creation, and of enjoying the looks of beauteous maidens with lustrous eyes and wreathed smiles, was not to be neglected. The appointed festal hour found me properly attired for the presence of beauty; and with palpitating heart—for I had become rustified by my long exclusion from the influence of ladies' society—I made my bow, amidst "gladdening strains and chaste bewitching smiles." As soon as I had sufficiently recovered from the effects of this operation, I ventured to look around upon the assembled company. The dance went joyously on; and figures of the most lovely proportions, fit models for sculptors and painters, and arrayed in dazzling beauty, were gliding through the labyrinthian mazes of the graceful Spanish dance. Myriad dark and fawn-like eyes shed a pure radiance of glad light with their kindling beams; while the rich black tresses and olive complexion sufficiently attested the claims to Spanish descent, in strong contrast to the lighter locks and whiter skins of America's daughters. The moments flew, for I was in Elysium.

With sad thoughts at the necessity of my leaving such scenes and sources of happiness, to go and vegetate at Fort Harllee, I returned to my lodgings at a late hour; went to bed, and dreamed I was in Charleston, gazing on brighter eyes than those I just left.

I found the society of St. Augustine, composed of American, Spanish, and Minorcan families, to be characterized by refined intelligence, and polished manners; and their elegant hospitalities I shall always bear in mind with grateful feelings.

We attended several parties during our short stay, and a grand ball given by Col. Harney of the Dragoons at his quarters, the night before we left St. Augustine. The Spanish dance seemed deservedly to prevail over all others except the waltz; but it was a very different thing from that which is called the Spanish dance in our northern cities; here all was grace and ease, like the floating of down upon the breath of morning.

The St. Augustine ladies certainly danced more gracefully, and kept better time, than any of my fair country women I ever saw in our more northern cities. It was really delightful to see the beautiful Minorcan girls moving through their intricate waltz to the music of the violin and tambourine, which discoursed most

The Journal

sweet harmony under the scientific touch of Marcellini the black fiddler in one of his Spanish tunes, which are very beautiful, and peculiar to this place alone.

There was also a strange fascination about the Minorcan beauties, which operated as a kind of fairy-spell. It always seemed as if I was in a dreamy trance at their balls. The scene always vividly recalled to my mind the black-eyed houri we read of with which the faithful are to be solaced in the world to come, for their trials and hard suffering in this vale of tears. I never felt ennui at these balls,—although they were kept up to 3 or 4 o'clock, and sometimes till daylight.

I left St. Augustine with regret on the 5th Augst to return to my post. Judge Read [Reid][12] the Attorney General, and several lawyers accompanied us. They were going to Newnansville to try two negroes for the murder of Capt. Gilliland; the same who presided at the dinner given to Col. Mills at Newnansville in May last. He had started alone from Charles ferry for Newnansville, but not making his appearance in due time, his friends became alarmed, and established a search, when his body was found with two bullet holes through it at Ichetuckny, that sylvan paradise, where we rested at noon on our march from Lowndes County. These two negroes were apprehended under suspicious circumstances; and finally confessed their guilt; but could not be hung without the formality of a trial.

We stopt at Black Creek during the 6th Augst that Gen. Hernandez[13] might have the benefit of our escort the next day as far as Fort Harllee, he being engaged on a tour of inspection through his brigade.

I remained at Fort Harllee in a state of quiescence until the 23rd Augst, when an order arrived for me to proceed to Fort Peyton and report for duty there, as soon as I should be relieved by Dr. [Assistant Surgeon William James] Sloan. Fort Peyton being only seven miles from St. Augustine, I was on tenter hooks of anxiety for the appearance of Dr. Sloan; which did not occur until the evening of 29th Augst; and at daylight next morning I was *ai-e-pus-cheh* [on my way], as the Seminoles say. I felt no

Journey into Wilderness

inclination to delay at Black Creek, but pushed on with all speed. While [I was] crossing the St. Johns, the weather suddenly changed. The deep and beautiful serenity of a clear blue sky soon disappeared behind black-clouds, which gathered in dense masses over the heavens and covered the whole horizon; the wind first increasing to a low moan, suddenly rose to a whirlwind's roar, and swept onward with the force of a tornado. The river moved in a sullen swell at first, reflecting the dark and heavy clouds that rolled above; but its aspect soon changed under the wrathful influence of the tempest, which lashed it into a thousand furies. The rain began to fall, first in drops, then poured in large streams from the surcharged clouds. The cabin of the "Forester"[14] afforded a snug shelter from the "pelting of the storm"; while I could listen with comfortable indifference to the clamours of the tempest roaring over the sounding waters, and contrast in my mind the present comfortable mode of locomotion with that I had been practising for more than a year. We arrived at Picolata in the height of the storm at 1 o'clock; but my impatience wouldn't allow me to delay on that account; so mounting "in hot haste" I dashed off for St. Augustine, splashing through mud and water, defying both wind and rain, which whistled and poured in torrents around my head, while the blasts wailing through the ancient forest of pine sent forth awful sounds. Before I reached St. Augustine, parting day had thrown its dark shadows across my path, and a solitary supper was the consequence.

The next day I rode out to Fort Peyton, and reported myself to Capt. [Gustavus S.] Drane, who was in command. This post was situated on an elevated piece of ground in the midst of a pine-barren near Moultrie Creek, seven miles south from St. Augustine. It consisted of four log houses built in a hollow square; two occupied by the troops; one by the officers, the fourth used as a hospital and commissary store.

It was not very far from this place that an act of great gallantry was performed by an officer of the Army; and which, through his modesty—always the attendant of valour,—remained long unknown; and was only accidentally discovered by another officer

114

overhearing some soldiers speak with admiration of Capt. Dimick's particularly cool and courageous behaviour in a certain skirmish with the Indians. The officer's curiosity being excited, he was induced to question the Captain; but could draw from him only a brief and reluctant account. Not satisfied, he questioned the Sergeant who was with the party, there being no commissioned officer with Capt. Dimick at the time; and from him he learnt the following details.

In the affair alluded to, which took place between a small party of U. S. Troops, and a superior force of Indians, the latter were routed with considerable loss. In the midst of the action, whilst Captain Dimick of the 1st Artillery, on horseback, was directing, and by his coolness and courage animating his little party, he was suddenly, and as if by concert, set upon from different directions by two Indians of huge stature. They fired simultaneously, and wounded Captain Dimick in the leg, at the same time bringing down his horse; disengaging himself from his horse, with great activity, he gained his feet in time to bring down one of his antagonists, as, with fearful yells, they rushed to take his scalp, thinking their fire had killed him. On seeing his companion fall, the other Indian took to flight, but not in time to save himself. Captain Dimick wheeled about, and, with great coolness, shot him dead with the other barrel of his fowling piece. In the mean time, the wounded Indian, though unable to rise, had seized a gun, but before he could use it, the gallant Captain despatched him with his sword.[15]

CHAPTER XVI

*O*n the 4th Sept four negroes belonging to Major Heriot,[1] who were captured by the Indians at the commencement of the war, delivered themselves up at Fort Peyton, having succeeded in escaping the vigilance of their captors. They presented a very pitiable spectacle, looking haggard and emaciated, and with no other covering than a cloth about the loins. They complained of having encountered intolerable hardships and very scant fare among the Indians, who gave them nothing to eat but *coonte*[2] and alligators; and that they were subjected to severe beatings on every occurrence of ill temper in their tawny and savage masters. They exhibited the greatest delight at rejoining the whites; and communicated important information relative to the plans and situations of the enemy, whom they represented as reduced to very "short commons." They also stated that they left in the vicinity of Mosquito [Lagoon], engaged in preparing *coonte,* a number of Indians, who had already burnt the buildings at Fort Mellon and Volusia since we left them, notwithstanding their promises to the contrary.

This did not look much like peace; notwithstanding all their promises and peaceful talks; in fact, the more they talk about peace, and the greater their overtures, the more cause is there for suspecting that treachery lurks within their breasts; and until we have them safe on shipboard, no faith can or ought to be placed in them.

In consequence of the report of these negroes that Indians were near Mosquito which was prohibited ground to them,[3] Lt. Peyton—the commandant of our post [Captain Drane being absent at the time][4]—issued an order for Lt. [Charles Augustus] May to proceed immediately south with his company of Dragoons, and endeavor to capture as many of the enemy as possible. A

116

The Journal

guide being necessary, measures were taken to procure one from St. Augustine. This caused some delay; when Gen. Hernandez hearing of the expedition, immediately issued orders for a larger detachment to proceed for this scout, not knowing what force of Indians might be encountered. He also gave notice that the detachment would be accompanied by himself, at the same time issuing orders for me to go also, the most agreeable order ever issued to me, for we felt perfectly assured that something would be done. The detachment consisted of one hundred and seventy men in all; two companies of 2nd U. S. Dragoons under [Second] Lts. McNeil and May; one company of 3rd Art. under Lt. [William] Fraser, and two companies of Florida Volunteers from St. Augustine under Lts. [Francis] Pellicier and [Daniel W.] Whitehurst; the whole battalion commanded by Lt. Peyton of the 2nd Arty. under the supervision of Gen. Hernandez, whose staff consisted of Lt. Graham[5] of 2nd Dragoons and myself.

On the 7th Sept, at dawn, we were all in our saddles, eager and ready to find the savages in their fastnesses; and taking up the line of march, with what provisions and baggage we could carry on our horses, and in two wagons we proceeded south; intending to bivouac at Bulow's abandoned plantation the first night.

Our road for twenty miles lay through wet pine-barrens.[6] About noon we reached a small oak grove, whose umbrageous and wide spreading foliage, impervious to the sun's rays, afforded a desirable shade for resting our horses, and refreshing ourselves with the contents of our haversacks. This important duty accomplished, we resumed our march through heavy sands and occasional swamps; succeeded by thick scrubs, until near dark, when the ruins of Bulow's fine Mill and mansion[7] pointed out our resting place for the night, having marched over thirty miles since morning. We turned down the broad avenue, once flanked by noble oaks, but whose scathed and blackened trunks and leafless limbs alone remained to test their former magnificence. On either side were extensive fields, most luxuriant once with richest [sugar] crops, but now presenting a scene o'er which the demon of desolation stalked with unchecked sway. On our left arose through the calm twi-

Journey into Wilderness

light of a summer's evening the ruined arches and columns of the once stately [sugar] Mill; while before us lay a smouldering ashy heap, the only vestige to show where once had stood the hospitable mansion, before the dark demon of ruin commenced his riots. Amid these ruins we built our bivouac fires; the river Halifax smoothly gliding nearbye through green meadows of pastoral beauty. After swallowing our frugal supper, we wrapt ourselves up each in his camp blanket, and stretching our limbs upon the dewy ground, slept on our primitive couches, pavilioned by the broad vault of heaven studded with myriads of brilliant worlds, as sweetly and soundly as we ever did on a softer bed.

With morning's dawn we were all astir; and our bivouac soon presented a bustling scene; here and there were seen men rubbing down their horses; others saddling; while around the various fires were seated or standing groups of swarthy Minorcans and mustachoed Dragoons engaged in cooking or eating their simple breakfasts.

While preparing to mount our horses for a move, five negroes suddenly made their appearance from the bushes nearby. Upon being questioned they stated that they had escaped from the Seminoles, and were anxious for the protection of the whites. Four of them belonged to Major Heriot, the owner of the four negroes who had escaped to Fort Peyton [on 4 September] and given us [the original] information of the [hostile] Indians [encampment]; the fifth was John [Philip],[8] an Indian negro, the slave of King Philip; but who fled from his master on account of his [Heriot's] attachment to his wife, one of the other negroes owned by Heriot. They reported the Indians had no intention of coming in or emigrating, and at that very time there were parties of them south of the Tomoka river[9] and east of the St. John's preparing *coonte*. This rencounter was a fortunate circumstance for us; for with such a guide as this John we could proceed to the very spot where he had left these tawny devils; and without the guidance of one possessing Indian sagacity, it is impossible to detect the lurking place of Indians, or to trace them in their devious path.

Leaving all the negroes except John under the charge of Lt.

118

The Journal

Fraser with his company of Artillery, who was ordered to remain at Tomoka ferry until our return, we pushed forward with all speed. So long a time had elapsed since this part of the Territory had been visited by a white man, that the paths were obliterated by overgrowth, and the brambles embracing us too endearingly in their tenacious gripe [grip] we had literally to carve a path for ourselves with our swords as we progressed. We soon struck into a pathless tract of spongy pine-barren, for road there was none, except of our own making; and after passing over several morasses, we crossed the head of Tomoka river through an almost impassable swamp, our horses bogging down to their saddle girths. In this way we continued until sunset, when the sight of an Indian smoke gently curling above the tree tops indicated the proximity of the savages. We now entered a dense hammock, and emerging from the opposite side, after a fatigueing and difficult passage, saw before us at the distance of half a mile the blackened ruins of the Dunlawton Mill,[10] and moving about among the rubbish we observed several dark objects, which our guide recognised to be Indians. Fearful of giving alarm too soon, we kept under cover of the hammock until their departure; when, advancing with the utmost caution, we ventured to approach the ruins. All was still; the Indians had retired to their wigwams, which we discovered by their fires to be a mile from us. We took up our position amidst the ruins, under the light of a young moon, in perfect silence, while a party was sent out to make a reconnaisance. They soon returned and reported the feasibility of the contemplated mode of attack, in which every precaution was taken to prevent the escape of the savages. About midnight the volunteers under Lt. Whitehurst dismounted, and leaving their horses, quietly obtained a position in ambuscade on two sides of the Indian camp in its immediate vicinity; all the rest of us continued mounted and were drawn up in line on the opposite side but far enough to elude the keen sight or hearing of the enemy. Just as day began to dawn, the signal for a charge was given; on we rushed; every man trying to be the first in at the death. We soon found our-selves unexpectedly in the presence of royalty, for there stood King

Journey into Wilderness

Philip the principal chief on the St. John's river naked as he was born, except the breech-cloth; and covered with most unkingly dirt; for Lt. May like a second Hernando de Soto, "striking in his spurs had dashed up to the savage prince," who not standing "as serene and unmoved" as the haughty Inca of old, was compelled to cut divers involuntary somersets on the ground, under the powerful impetus communicated by May's charger.

Though a captive, there was still a sternness in this chief's dark eye,—which black as a thundercloud and emitting flashes like its lightning,—plainly told his spirit was unquelled.[11]

We captured the whole party except Philip's youngest son, a lad of eighteen years who escaped into the neighboring hammock by his uncommon agility. Among the prisoners taken was an Indian called *Tomoka John,* who ultimately as will appear became very useful to us. There were also a number of women and children captured; the former, miserable, blackened, haggard, shrivelled [smoke-dried and half-clad][12] devils; the latter, ugly little nudities. Although a few guns were fired, this capture was effected without loss or blood-shed on either side. A large quantity of *coonte,* both red and white,[13] was found in the camp; of which we brought off what we could, and destroyed the remainder. We also found several ponies.

On questioning the prisoners, we learnt that there was a camp of Uchee Indians among whom was *Uchee Billy,* their celebrated and formidable chief, who was once thought to have been killed, about ten miles off.[14] *Tomoka John* offering to guide us to their place of concealment if we would untie him, he was taken at his word. This Indian led the way in silence for several miles; then gave us to understand that we must perform the rest of the distance on foot, having to pass through a very intricate and extensive cabbage hammock impassable for horses.

Taking one hundred men with us on foot, and leaving the rest to guard the horses, we started afresh about 4 o'clock in the afternoon. Silently and cautiously we wended our way through the old woods, where possibly a civilized being had never before voluntarily ventured. A deep and beautiful serenity pervaded nature;

for all was silence, save when at long intervals, the cry of some solitary bird broke on our ears with startling shrillness; or when a rustling among the dry branches made us pause in breathless silence, till a deer, bounding across our path, would plunge into the opposite thicket; while we dare not send a bullet after him, lest the report of our guns should alarm the wily enemy, who might even then be lurking close beside us. We entered the deep hammock at sunset, and guided by the Indian warrior, pressed forward, at first with all the speed the nature of the place allowed. *Tomoka John* however soon checked our rapid pace, intimating that there might be some outlying Indian, not yet returned from hunting, and that we must use the utmost caution in approaching, to avoid discovery. The darkness of night soon enveloped us. We advanced with caution, crawling through the hammock like so many Nebuchadnezzars, until midnight; when the Indian suddenly paused, and whispered to the General who was leading that we were near the spot. He then sank on his hands and knees, and crept softly forwards like a cat circumventing his prey [so that he] soon became invisible in the gloom. Returning after a short lapse of time in the same manner, he informed us that the fires of the Uchees were not very far from us, and that we had better at once make the intended disposition of our men for attack, and again represented what desperate warriors those Uchees were in this Indian camp with whom we were about to engage; and that they would certainly give us hot work. Dividing our force into two columns [50 men each],[15] Lts. McNeil and May in command of one, and Lt. Peyton taking command of the other; we were directed to surround the camp by creeping cautiously to the right and left of it; the men in single file and at ten paces apart so as to include all the fires and form a perfect circle around the whole of the enemy. As soon as in position we were to crawl within a hundred yards of the fires, and there lie prostrate upon the ground, concealed by the low saw-palmetto bushes, until the signal should be given at dawn to rise and charge.

We succeeded in attaining our assigned positions; from which I could distinctly see the forms of savages lying listlessly around their fires; and occasionally felt a thrilling sensation at our proximity, lest we should be too soon discovered for the success of our enterprise, whenever any of them got up to add more fuel to their fires. But after scratching themselves, throwing a few sticks upon their fires, and giving a shake or two, they would again lie down, unsuspicious of what dangerous bed-fellows were lying upon the same couch with themselves. A short time before day their dogs commenced barking and their fires being immediately extinguished, the Indians must have suspected or were fearful that all was not right and we therefore expected to find them on the alert.

The air was calm as an "infants breathing," with occasional light gales faintly quivering through the dark and shadowy trees. Nothing else interrupted the silence of creation. The gloom of night first began to deepen; then came the dawning hour of day so anxiously looked for by us. Twilight with all its shadows and solemn gloom gradually disappeared before the cheerful advent of light; the sky was clear and grayly tinged with the returning light.

> *"What various scenes, and oh! what scenes of woe*
> *Were witnessed by the red and struggling beam!"*

A moment of breathless suspense, and the signal is given; up jump a hundred impatient men simultaneously from their crouching posture in the grass; and with a shout which "rent heaven's conclave," charged forward at full speed. The Indians as we expected were ready to receive us, for instantaneously all the heavens around us were ringing with their horrid war-whoop and the clear sharp reports of their rifles, blended with the shouts of our men and the louder reports of our carbines [for tho' instructed not to kill if capture could be effected without, twas impossible to restrain our men under a falling fire from the enemy, and remain passive to be shot down ourselves].[16] The wildness and interest of the scene was considerably augmented by the glaring eyes, streaming black hair and red painted faces of the savages, as they danced and skipped about in their fruitless efforts to escape. They evidently had not had time to make their toilet becomingly, for the reception of their early visitors; for we found them either perfectly naked, or only half clad with hunting shirts, their faces however covered with war-paint. We succeeded in capturing the whole party, which consisted of several warriors, with *Uchee Billy,* and his brother *[Uchee] Jack,* and a number of women and children. One Indian warrior was killed by Lt. Peyton who captured with his own hand another. Several were wounded; while but one of our party was injured.[17] Unfortunately, that one was Lt. McNeil. He fell mortally wounded within a few feet of the spot where *Uchee Billy* had crouched with deadly aim behind some bags of *coonte* hastily piled up into a breast work, from whence came the fatal bullet.[18] I was near at the time, and immediately stopped to render him my professional assistance; but soon ascertained that his wound was beyond all human aid.

We found large quantities of *coonte* and other Indian spoils, which we were compelled to destroy. [The most active in gathering plunder, and who carried off the largest pack, was our Indian guide *Tomoka John,* so lately a visitor and friendly occupant of this very camp. I strongly suspect it was the desire to plunder his own friends, that induced him to offer his guidance to us in finding their place of concealment. One of the features of Indian character.][19] A number of Indian ponies also were captured. As soon as litters could be constructed for McNeil and the wounded Indians, out of pine saplings and blankets, we retraced our way back to where we had left the horses, leaving the dead Indian where he fell, his flesh to be gnawed by the wolves and buzzards, and his bones to bleach in the wilderness.

This position selected by *Uchee Billy* was one well calculated to baffle the penetration and vigilance of any one not endowed with the peculiar sagacity of an Indian; and without our captive guide, this lurking place of the enemy could never have been detected. It was a small pine-barren placed like an island in the midst of an almost interminable and impenetrable palmetto swamp nine months of the year under water and inaccessible to any one unacquainted with its many tracks.[20]

CHAPTER XVII

*W*hen it is considered what difficulties had to be encountered, and were surmounted, to elude the untiring vigilance and activity of a bold, active, and wily foe, thoroughly acquainted with all the passes of the swamps, and whose peculiar warfare makes them perfectly familiar to all kinds of stratagems, night assaults, and surprises, the zeal and persevering courage of our little Army were worthy of all praise. Were the days of chivalry not passed, their courage and constancy would have been fit themes for poets and the songs of minstrels. Indeed, when the nature of the Florida expeditions is considered, both as regards the climate, country, and foe; the "torrid realms of more than burning day,"—sad haunts of death and putrid air; the wily and uncertain Indians for enemies; who constantly practising stratagems, ambuscades, and surprises, and thoroughly acquainted with the passes [fords] of the rivers and morasses which intersect the country in all directions, hovered about our marches, and concentrated their numbers with unexampled rapidity at every difficult pass; where, lurking in ambushed security, they delivered a deadly fire at an unexpected moment; destroying unseen, until, dispelled by the brave hearts and firm hands of our troops, they fled from the ground with a swiftness that baffled the pursuit of the white man through the devious paths of swamps impenetrable to the eye, only to renew their harassing and destructive work at the next inaccessible hammock; eternally thinning the ranks of our gallant army, who in discharge of a patriotic duty, were encountering the dangers and privations of an arduous service in the sickly swamps of a territory where the foe lurked in comparative security. Considering all this, the world must justly acknowledge that these expeditions were undoubtedly fraught with more real perils than the adventures of many proud knights, whose deeds are recorded

The Journal

in historic legends, and emblazoned in the scutcheons of their descendants.

Not knowing but that the whole nation, apprised by Philip's son of this capture, would be upon our little band to the rescue of such master spirits as *King Philip* and *Uchee Billy;* we delayed not an instant longer than necessary for a little rest; and started on our return to St. Augustine, that we might make sure of our slippery and important prisoners, by securing them in the stronghold of Fort Marion.

The rude litters, constructed of green poles with the axe and knife alone, and covered with blankets, and dry hides,—the latter being found in great abundance at the hostile camp,—were conveyed, suspended from the backs of the captured ponies, with as much ease and comfort to the sufferers as they could have been in ambulances of the most approved and modern construction. *King Philip,* out of respect to his age and high station, was allowed to ride one of his own ponies; the other Indians were made to walk, the males tied in couplets.

We prosecuted our toilsome march in solemn silence, only interrupted by the clangour of our steel sabres against the stirrup, and the tramping of our horses upon the parched sod, as they fretted under the intense heat of a burning sun. Lt. May and myself had alternately to go ahead in some places and cleave a way with our swords through the densely overgrown path, that the litters may pass.

The stars began to twinkle, and twilight to thicken into night, but there was no interruption to our onward progress. A gentle breeze ruffling the branches of the trees on the approach of evening, soon however commenced, cooling the air, and affording an agreeable relief after the mellow heat of a sultry day.

At ten o'clock at night, faint with fasting and toilworn with long travel, we reached the southern bank of Tomoka river. Here we found it necessary to stop until morning; and having stationed a strong guard over our captives,—one of whom died in the course of the night from wounds received,—we satisfied the cravings of appetite; and stretching ourselves upon a couch of leaves, canopied

125

by heaven, and lulled by the occasional howl of a wolf in the distance, the drowsy god soon shed his influence o'er us.

At daylight next morning we were all astir; and after swallowing some hot coffee, from which we had been so long debarred not having been permitted to light a fire for fear of discovery, immediately commenced swimming our horses across the stream, which was a quarter of a mile wide at this spot. Fortunately we discovered an old canoe, in which we transported the wounded across. On the northern bank we found Lt. Fraser with his company of Artillery, where they had been left to guard the baggage train. After transferring the wounded into the wagons, as well as the women and children, we again proceeded *en route* towards St. Augustine.

Nothing interrupted our march during the day; and the obscurity of night found us in our saddles, wending our way with drooping heads to a proper place for bivouacking. Lt. McNeil, whose side I never deserted one moment after the reception of his wound, and who received my constant attentions, lingered until 10 o'clock at night, when the spirit that animated his manly form took its flight for that place where the brave have their final repose; his campaign over—his fighting was closed; and his country was deprived of a brave and efficient officer.

> *"No more would the reveille wake him at morn,*
> *Nor the tatoo proclaim another day gone.—*
> *No more upon his ear would come,*
> *The war beat of the gathering drum,*
> *Or the trumpet's rousing blast."*—

Such is the common fatality of war—and such is the death "when come it must," that the brave man covets. Such also the incidents in life which now and then forcibly call upon us to pause in the wild career of our thoughtless existence; which remind us that life is attended with uncertainty; above all the life of a soldier. The gradual approach of death through the slow operations of disease undermining the strength and weakening the functions by degrees, is not calculated to make such warning impressions on our minds, as when we see one suddenly struck down in the vigor of youth and manhood; receiving the fatal blow while the eye is bright, and the pulse beats strong; falling unwarned and unprepared. To a reflective mind death is terrible at any time, and in any shape; but it is in the sudden death of the young and vigorous, of one who holds the prospect of a long life of health and usefulness, that the grim monster assumes his most terrific aspect. Then it is that we exclaim—

> ". . . 'tis a dreadful thing to die
> *When the youthful heart with hope beats high,*
> *When visions of the future crowd*
> *Around the mind in vesture proud,*
> *And fancy gayly pictures forth*
> *The high and mighty things of earth—*
> *The hero's high renown; the fame*
> *That clings around a mighty name;*
> *As objects of pursuit in life,*
> *Of dauntless and increasing strife—*
> *To leave them all, and pass away,*
> *And with forgotten men to lay,*
> *Unknown, unhonoured and unblest,*
> *'Tis terrible, indeed!"*

But such thoughts are as ephemeral as the fleeting moment to the soldier. He enters the field with his mind made up to meet dangers of no ordinary nature. At the sacrifice of every comfort, he is ever ready for battle; and holds his life cheap in the service of his country; and if it be his fortune to meet death in the perilous fight, he falls in the flush of excitement, congratulating himself that he will not be reported as one who died unhonored.

McNeil's death was an additional inducement for hastening our return to St. Augustine, that his remains might be interred in holy ground, and with those military honors which a gallant and honorable soldier should always receive from his bereaved comrades.

As the night was clear and serene, and the cloudless sky was studied [studded] with millions of brilliant luminaries, that sparkled like diamonds, and shine with more than ordinary lustre in this latitude, we decided to prosecute our march by night.

Up to this time strong excitement had kept my energies awake, and free from the sensation of fatigue; but there is a limit beyond which exhausted nature cannot pass, and soon my wearied frame began to sink, and my eye-lids to close. With my hands braced upon my rifle resting transversely across the pommel of my saddle, I was enabled to retain my seat on horseback, notwithstanding Morpheus had complete possession of my faculties, and rendered utterly fruitless all my endeavours to retain command of them.

With my eyes closed in sleep, which I cannot say was very refreshing, being frequently broken by the stumbling of my horse, who had taken advantage of his riders oblivion to follow his example, nearly throwing me over his head, in the middle of a dream wherein soft beds held a conspicuous place, I continued till past midnight; when the order to halt was given. It was not necessary to be repeated; for though every man in the command slept profoundly in his saddle at the time, his ears were open; especially to such glad sounds. In the twinkling of a wink were our respective bodies transferred from the uncomfortable perpendicular on horseback to the comfortable horizontal on the ground, and with the recumbent forms of our captive Indians stretched close to us upon the turf, we sank to slumber.

With the morning's dawn we were on the alert; for our place of bivouac was the last hammock on our route where a successful attempt could have been made by the enemy to rescue their king and his fellow captives; and we were suspicious that this spot might have been selected for an attack upon us. From the expression of Philip's countenance and the eager glances he cast around we detected a similar suspicion in his mind; but as daylight advanced, and the sun arose upon our quiet bivouac, we felt reassured, and Philip's hopes took flight. Until now he had entertained hopes of a rescue; but from this moment he was the personification of submissive despair.

We reached Fort Peyton about mid-day, where we stopped to rest ourselves and horses, Lt. Graham 2nd Dragoons having

The Journal

been sent forward to have preparations made for Lt. McNeil's funeral on our arrival, the intense heat rendering his immediate interment necessary.

As the success of our expedition was supposed to be attended with more beneficial advantages to the country than any preceding it; and as the capture and bringing into certain security, such master spirits as *King Philip, Uchee Billy* and other desperate warriors gave promise of a more speedy peace than all the military achievements of the previous two years; our entree into St. Augustine, which took place in the afternoon, was attended with all the "pomp and circumstance of a glorious war." The air resounded with acclamations from the male portion of inhabitants, who rushed in crowds to the public square, as we passed along with our prisoners to the fort, and every window and balcony was thronged with dark bright eyes smiling on us, and fair hands wafting us a welcome with their white kerchiefs streaming through the air.[1]

The only cloud which rested upon the successful result of our enterprise, arose from the reflection that one who had so lately gone forth with us in all the flush of youth and joy; whose manly form buoyant with hope and expectation we so lately gazed upon with admiration, returned not with us; tis true his pale form was with us, but the spirit that gave it light and animation had fled. But a few days back he went forth in the full vigor of early manhood, redundant with life and health; he was now brought back a cold and lifeless corpse, only to be deposited beneath the soil of Florida. His career had been brief, but his end was glorious; and the best and only consolation we could offer his bereaved relatives and friends was that he died for his country; and as those who fall upon their country's battle field are esteemed most happy, they should not mourn over his honourable end. They had also the satisfaction of knowing that though his form rested in a far distant land, he received a soldier's glorious grave, and soldier's tears; and—

"When a soldier weeps o'er a brother's bier,
We may know that the brave is dead;

129

Journey into Wilderness

For never yet was a soldier's tear
Shed over a craven's head."

Though his lifeless relics may rest in the land of flowers, his name shall live in the bright pages of his country, for whose honor he gave his life; and every passer-by will pause at his grave, and say, "here rests a brave and patriotic soldier,—a gallant officer."

Lt. McNeil was not more than 19 years of age;[2] was the son of [Brigadier] Gen. John McNeil, late of the U. S. Army, and grandson of Gen. Benj. Pierce, of New Hampshire, a hero of the revolution. Urged on by the brave blood of heroes which filled his veins, his honorable end was only consistent with his upright course in life. His many excellent virtues and social qualities, caused his loss to be severely felt in his own intimate circle of companionship; to which he was endeared by ties of friendly fellowship, and of cordial regard.

After having secured our prisoners in the fort, we turned our attention to performing the last sad duties to our deceased comrade. His body was escorted to the grave from Gen. Hernandez's house by the battalion in whose presence he received his death-wound; and followed by all the officers at the post and the most respectable of the citizens.

We remained at St. Augustine a few days to recruit our energies after the recent fatigues, and then returned to our post at Fort Peyton.

CHAPTER XVIII

*I*n consequence of King Philip expressing a desire to have his family sent for, Gen. Hernandez permitted Tomoka John, one of the Indians recently captured, to be the bearer of a message from his royal majesty to his family and relations, desiring them to come in; and appointed the 24th Septr to meet them at Bulowville, whence he would conduct them in person to St. Augustine. Accordingly, orders were issued that on the 21st Septr the battalion should be in readiness to depart at daylight for Bulowville; there to await the appearance of King Philip's envoy and family.

The dawn of the 21st arrived, ushered in by torrents of rain; while the bleak wind roared, and thick storm clouds scoured the sky. But it found the heroic band in their saddles; swords girded and carbines slung; ready to take the field against the savage foe; to arrest the deadly rifle and scalping-knife. Gen. Hernandez and staff were there also, including myself, always ready to bind the wounded and raise the drooping head.

Nothing daunted by the wild and dreary aspect of the weather, we took up the line of march; each one carrying on his horse his prog[1] in a haversack, and a bag of forage for his horse, with a single blanket thrown over the saddle for protection against the storm at night. No tents nor other baggage embarrassed our progress, as we steadily wended our course through mud and water, perfectly indifferent to the cold gusts that swept across our path, and the drenching torrents that incessantly poured upon our heads. Thus it continued all day;—

> *"Nor till the lingering day is done,*
> *Our toilsome march we stay."*

On reaching our destination late in the evening it still rained.

131

We immediately took possession of the small picket work that had been erected the previous year at Bulowville; and after stationing our sentinels, we set about providing shelter against the storm, each man the best way he could, thereby verifying the adage that "he is the best soldier who takes the best care of himself." The General and Staff established headquarters within the pickets, where we fortunately found a few boards; these leaned up against the sides of the pickets, formed tolerably snug, if not very elegant quarters. The soldiery erected for themselves, with palmetto leaves, and boughs of different trees still retaining their leaves, picturesque little huts, sufficiently large to admit an individual on hands and knees. In the midst of our bivouac stood the remains of Mr. Bulow's mansion, which had been burnt by the Indians; and the scene presented at night was wild and savage in the extreme. Around the fires built amid the ruins, shedding a bright glare in cheerful contrast upon the smoked walls, might be seen many recumbent and wrapped up figures; some slumbering, while others listlessly sat watching the glowing embers, resembling brigands in their secret haunts; here and there were displayed haversacks and canteens suspended, and carbines resting against the walls, or the trunk of a tree; while in the back ground, indistinctly visible through the gloom and shadow, were horses picketed, and near them a cloaked sentinel. The moan of the melancholy wind, among the forest trees, with the alternate roar and whistling of the midnight storm, added to the wild and desolate aspect of the scene.

Though we could not boast a roof impervious to water, and my couch of leaves, over which was thrown a solitary blanket, was not the dryest nor softest my limbs had ever compressed, yet never did I sleep sounder in the habitations of my kindred beings.

Nothing occurred to interrupt the monotony of our little encampment until the evening of the 24th Septr, when eight negroes, who had been stolen by the Indians at the commencement of the war from Messrs. Cruger and Depeyster,[2] discovering our situation, succeeded in escaping from the Indians and flying to us for protection. They were immediately sent to St. Augustine under an

escort. The General being disappointed in not seeing Tomoka
John return at the appointed time, determined to wait a few days
longer; and accordingly despatched an order for a wagon load of
provisions for ourselves and horses, to be sent from St. Augustine
with the return of the escort.

We continued to vegetate in our interesting little huts—for the
rain which had never ceased falling since we left Fort Peyton,
prevented our stirring about much; when on the afternoon of the
26th Sept our ears were gladdened by a cry from one of the
sentinels, that he saw a white flag approaching through the avenue
leading to our position. Instantly the whole command was roused
from apathy and on the *qui vive;*[3] and very soon we descried
several Indian warriors, one of whom was mounted and bearing
a white flag, approaching with slow and dignified gait. Our interpreter was sent out to meet and conduct them to the General's
quarters; when I recognised with *Tomoka John* my old Fort Mellon acquaintance *Coa-coo-chee,* or Wild-Cat, Philip's son. He
was accompanied by *Blue-Snake,*[4] and two other warriors of considerable note, who had come in to confer with Philip as to future
proceedings. Notwithstanding the rain which poured a deluge
at the time, and the late hour of the day, orders were issued for
an immediate return to St. Augustine; and at 5 o'clock P.M. we
were all mounted and on our way back, leaving Bulowville as
desolate as we found it.

We continued to press on, though it soon became so dark that
our horses heads could not be distinguished amid the surrounding
obscurity; and the fall of huge trees, torn up by their roots, crash-
ing and echoing through the forests, under the influence of the
powerful equinoctial storm, contributed to the dreariness and
gloom of our situation. Slighting all difficulties, we allowed nothing
to impede our progress until midnight, when arriving at a stream
swollen by the rain to a dangerous depth, it seemed most prudent
to wait for daylight before we should attempt to cross it.

Wearied and sleepy I threw myself from horseback, and crawling under our only baggage wagon where it had stopped in the
road, stretched myself upon the wet ground; and in spite of the

roaring of the storm, the mournful whistling of the chilling wind as it went rushing by, and the pouring of watery torrents around my head, I slept soundly, with the thick clouds for curtains to my place of rest. My slumbers were destined to be of short duration; for scarcely had an hour elapsed when I awoke with sensations of suffocation, and found my couch of rest the bed of a rapid stream, which flowing with accumulating force and depth, threatened soon to merge the unconscious slumberer in a "sleep which knows no waking." Extricating myself from this dangerous situation I was fain to seek one of the bright pine-trees which by this time were blazing in all directions, shedding their cheerful light upon the dripping, shivering, and woe-begone figures which stood around them in groups. Thus slowly waned the night; no one daring to assume the recumbent posture lest he should be drowned by the rushing waters. To while away the time and assist in keeping our eyes open, we at last resorted to singing; and daylight dawned upon as merry a set seemingly as ever trod shoe leather.

With the first gray streak in the east we were off, as fast as our stiffened horses could move; and that was but a snail's pace. About 10 o'clock the rain ceased; the clouds disappeared; and with the reappearance of the sun all nature both animate and inanimate assumed a smiling and cheerful aspect. Two hours afterwards we came in sight of Fort Peyton; but prior to entering, *Coa-coo-chee* wishing to present himself with the utmost effect, thus evincing the pride of appearance, which pervades the savage equally with civilized life, retired back in the woods to robe himself. He soon reappeared in all the pomp of scarlet and burnished silver; his head decorated with a plume of white crane feathers, and a silver band around his gaudy turban. His leather leggings were also superceded by a pair of bright scarlet cloth. He insisted upon being mounted on a spirited horse; and attired in his picturesque native costume, he rode with a great deal of savage grace and majesty.[5]

We stopped at Fort Peyton merely to breath our horses; and continued on to St. Augustine, where after parading our Indian delegates through the streets for the gratification of the inhabitants, as well as of Coa-coo-chee, they were transferred to the fort.

In *Coa-coo-chee* we had a valuable acquisition. He was a young enterprising chief;—the Napoleon of the Seminoles; and his safe keeping was a matter of much consequence, for his influence among his people was even greater than that of his father, and there is no doubt that he will rise to be the principal chief of the Seminoles. He, however, stated that in coming in of his own accord he expected to be permitted to return; and being very anxious to do so, promised that if allowed to go out he would come back and bring with him all the negroes and cattle, which have been stolen by his tribe, and as many of his people as he could get. Philip, his father, objected to his going; but wished some other Indian sent, and Philip's wishes in this matter were worthy of being consulted, he knowing best his son's probable intentions.[6]

In consequence of the benefits expected to result from our recent expeditions, Gen. Jesup issued the following order, to be read at all the military posts in Florida.

Head Quarters, Army of the South
St. Augustine, Septr 27th 1837

Order No. 187

Par. 1. The Major General Commanding returns his thanks to Brigadier General Hernandez and the officers and troops of his command, both regulars and volunteers, for their excellent conduct in the late expedition south.

A force of less than one hundred and eighty men have killed or secured fifty three Indians and negroes; among the former five principal and important chiefs, whose loss to the enemy will be irreparable; and several Indians and negroes who will be most valuable as guides to the Army.

The Major General assures Brigadier General Hernandez of his approbation of the measures he so promptly adopted, and so gallantly carried out; and he congratulates him, and his command, on the success of the enterprise; a success which cannot but have an auspicious influence on the future operations of the Army.

By order of Major General Jesup.

(signed)   J. A. Chambers
A. D. C. & A. A. G.

CHAPTER XIX

I returned to my post at Fort Peyton, and on the morning of 2d Octr *Coa-coo-chee* visited us, having stopped on his way to his tribe, where he was going with messages to the chiefs and warriors from Philip, by Gen. Hernandez's permission, to induce them to come in. He was to be back in fourteen days.

True to his promise the 16th Octr saw his return, bringing with him Philip's brother [Ta-co-sa-Tustennukkee][1] and Philip's youngest son [Captain Sam].[2] He stated that *Oceola* [*Osceola*],[3] and some other chiefs, with about a hundred Indians, would be in, in a few days, to hold a talk; and that he had left them one day's journey behind, and had come forward himself to give notice of their approach. He also gave information, that a large number of negroes were at Volusia; but advised that they should not be sent for until the result of the talk is known. He advised, however, that as they were in a starving condition, provisions should be sent to them; otherwise they would die, not knowing where to get any thing to eat.

The same night I rode to St. Augustine, where I attended a ball at Col. Cleland's,[4] for occasionally,

> *"Our stern alarms change to merry meetings,*
> *Our dreadful marches to delightful measures."*

There we danced till 4 o'clock in the morning; and in less than an hour after I was in my saddle, ready to accompany Gen. Hernandez to the Indian camp twenty miles distant.

We arrived at the camp,[5] after passing seventy nine negroes on their way to St. Augustine, sent in by the Indians. We had an interview with some of the inferior chiefs, *Oceola* not being present; and immediately started on our return anxious to get back in time to attend another grand ball to be given at Gen.

The Journal

Hernandez's that night, in honor of his daughter's marriage; for the ladies of St. Augustine are such lovely creatures, and waltz with such perfection, an opportunity of basking in the light of their eyes was not to be missed.

We reached the city at midnight, and immediately changing my apparel, which was better suited to the hard service of war, for more festal attire, I soon transferred myself to where bright eyes beamed and beauty sighed, and light feet tripped to music's swell, witching the heart, and captivating the senses.[6] Daylight dawned upon our festivities;[7] and a few minutes after, I mounted my horse and returned to the monotony of Fort Peyton.

In the course of the day, two runners came in; and desired an interview with Gen. Hernandez. One, who was the spokesman, said: "He came as the representative of *Micanopy*,[8] *Ho-la-too-chee*[9] and *Jumper*;[10] that the road was white, and he had a short but straight talk from *Oceola* and *Coa-hadjo*;[11] that the snake had two tongues; he had but one;—that his heart was white;—that *Oceola* had sent him to say that he would be in to hold a talk in person,— that a man, no matter how bad he was, would some day or other be convinced of his errors;—that he was sorry for what had past; —that he had thrown away his rifle a long time since, and that he had now brought nothing but his ball sticks.—That he would hold a talk and then have one or two days ball play,[12] when he hoped they would be at peace once more. That they meant to trifle no longer with the white flag; would rub their faces with it, and play with it no longer. This he said was Oceola's talk, and as he received so he gave it."

That the Indians were sincere in desiring peace, there could be no doubt; but as they said nothing about emigration, their peace was attended with the proviso of being permitted to remain in the country. Their treachery was proverbial; and notwithstanding all their *straight talks,* they were not to be trusted. *Oceola* and his band come [came] with the avowed intention of having a talk; but there was not the least doubt with the real one as was afterwards ascertained, endeavouring to rescue Philip, who was held in high estimation by them, and to massacre the inhabitants of

137

St. Augustine, if they should find them weak and unprepared, hoping probably that the negroes whom they sent in advance would assist them.

On the 20th Octr *Oceola,*—or more properly *Assyn-ya-hola,* as it is pronounced by the Indians,—and his band of Indian warriors encamped about a mile from Fort Peyton; and sent in an ambassador (*John Cavalho*),[13] to Gen. Hernandez, desiring to see and converse with him at their camp, but without an escort; saying, he would be perfectly safe among them without troops. Gen. Jesup, knowing that wherever *John Cavalho* was present, foul play might be expected, forbid his going without a strong escort. At the same time, Gen. Jesup sent a confidential order to Lt. Peyton commanding at Fort Peyton, to seize *Assyn-ya-hola* and his party should they come within the fort; but not to attempt it unless the whole force should place themselves within his power.

On the morning of the 21st Octr. Gen. Hernandez, arrived at Fort Peyton from St. Augustine, accompanied by a number of officers and citizens, and soon after proceeded to *Assyn-ya-hola's* camp[14] with an escort of two hundred Dragoons, regulars and volunteers. *Assyn-ya-hola* met Gen. Hernandez, and immediately a ring was formed and the talk began. It was a very short one; for Gen. Jesup had instructed Hernandez to seize all the party if the answers to his questions were not satisfactory.[15] The Indians stated that they had been invited by Philip to come and hear what propositions were to be made to them; that they did not come to deliver themselves up as prisoners; and said nothing that seemed to indicate that they were yet conquered. As soon as this fact was ascertained, and their answers to questions put proving evasive, Gen. Hernandez told them that we had been deceived by them long enough, and that we did not intend to be deceived again. He immediately gave a preconcerted signal, and instantly they were surrounded by our troops under the command of Major Ashby, and the whole of them taken prisoners. So promptly and suddenly was this done, that the Indians had not time to raise a single rifle, though each had one by his side, leaded and primed, ready for action. During the talk, *Oceola* evidently did not like

Oseola at Lake Monroe
during the Armistice. May 1837

The Journal

the aspect of affairs, for he evinced a good deal of uneasiness, kept his eyes constantly and quickly wandering about; but the moment he found himself a prisoner, he became perfectly quiet and calm, and not the slightest symptom of emotion could be seen in his countenance, or indeed in that of any of his warriors.[16]

We thus by "one fell swoop" secured *Oceola, Coa-hadjo,* with other war-chiefs,[17] and eighty of their picked warriors,[18] thus breaking in a great degree the force of the nation; and though the war was continued, we had "drawn the fangs from the reptile." Gen. Jesup who arrived at Fort Peyton during the talk, gave orders to have them immediately marched to town, and safely secured under lock and key in the fort.[19]

While these warriors were marching between a double file of soldiers to St. Augustine, I was standing on a stump some little distance off observing the procession, when I noticed one tall warrior over six feet high named John Hicks, or *Inchebatche-a-hajo,* son of Hicks late head of the Micasukies, casting his eye quickly about as if anxiously endeavouring to discover some body. As soon as his eye fell upon me, his countenance lit up, and he beckoned to me with eager gesture. I approached to learn what he wanted. All he knew of English was a word or two, but seeing no interpreter near, and not aware that I understood Seminole, he endeavoured to express himself in my language; but all he could say was "money-house"; this he frequently repeated, not much to my enlightenment however, for I was at a loss to know what he was driving at; by gestures he finally made me understand that money-house meant pocket-book, and that he wanted some money which he had asked me, to whom he had unaccountably taken a fancy, to keep for him in my pocketbook, he having none of his own, and the money being in bills ran the risk of being destroyed in his rifle-pouch,—an Indian's only pocket. This money he had earned during his short sojourn near Fort Peyton by driving a brisk trade in deer-skins, and by making them into leggings and moccasins; some of which I still have, made by him. As he was about to visit the metropolis of Florida, he thought he would require all his money to indulge in the fashionable extravagances of a great city.

These warriors were said to be nearly all *Micasukies;*[20] and if so, there was no shadow of a doubt that *Oceola* had some hostile intentions, which made this capture doubly important.

We had now in our possession the bone and sinew of the Indian nation; we had all the war-chiefs and instigators of the war except three, viz, *Sam Jones,*[21] alias *Apiaka, Alligator,*[22] and *Cloud;*[23] we had *Emathla* (Philip), *Coa-hadjo, Miccopotokee,* and *Euchee-Billy,* all principal chiefs; *Coa-coo-chee, Oceola, Chitta-Yahola,*[24] *Tustenuckee* [*Tustenugee Hadjo*], and several other important sub-chiefs.

The capture of these chiefs we knew would by no means increase the friendly feelings of the Indians toward us, but would tend rather to render them more vindictive and desperate than ever; and it was therefore expected by many that there would still be some hard fighting.

Though we expected to have a few months more of hard service, the existing state of affairs at this time, we thought, most evidently tended to bring about an early termination to this disastrous war.

Oceola was always represented as an upstart in the nation; *a novus homo;* but having an unbounded ambition, he had obtained his high elevation, by energy and great talents. Although not an hereditary chief, he was a ruling spirit among those wretches, and exercised with autocratic power the sway he had acquired by his superior shrewdness and sagacity over their stern minds, and exacted from them the homage of vassals and dependents. Exercising more influence over these disorganized bands than their hereditary chiefs possessed, these latter through jealousy had always denounced his power in the nation. If only half that has been said of this indomitable warrior be true, he was a most remarkable man. Though this war was believed to have originated, and been carried on, mainly by his influence with his savage compeers, yet in consequence of being averse to murdering women and children and prisoners in cold blood, according to an Indian custom, his popularity was in some measure considerably weakened. He was at the time of his capture about thirty five years old; and his person, rather below than above the common height, was elegantly formed, with hands and feet effeminately small. He had a countenance expressive of much thought and cunning, and though when captured evidently sad and care-worn, the fire of his flashing eyes was unsubdued. His forehead was tolerably high, and cast in an intellectual mold—the upper portion which was generally concealed by his hair being worn low and hanging out in front expressed dignity and firmness, while the full arched brow indicated a man who thought much and intensely. His eyes were black and piercing; and when animated were full of dark fire, but when in repose they were softer than the soft eye of woman. His mouth, when relieved by a smile, wore an expression of great sweetness;—and his lips were chiselled with the accuracy of sculpture. His address was easy, and his bearing affable and courtly; in his salutations full of smiles, and like most of the Indians, hearty in the shake of his hand. I have been furnished by Capt. J. R. Vinton with a full length portrait of this remarkable Indian chief, which I can testify to being the most correct likeness ever taken of him. The face is a remarkably striking likeness, as he appeared previous to his capture.[25]

There were some individuals who pretended to condemn the capture of Oceola and his warriors as dishonorable on the part of Gen. Jesup;—as a base violation of a flag of truce.[26] Tis true they had a white flag flying; but they were never told that it would afford them indemnity from capture on this occasion. On the contrary, they had been repeatedly told that the only terms with which they could be received were those of actual surrender and that no flag would be received on any other terms. Indeed, there was too much sympathy extended upon these treacherous, murderous savages. Even had they been enticed in under the immunity of the white flag, Gen. Jesup would have been perfectly justified in making prisoners of them, for he was dealing with the very individuals who had repeatedly and treacherously trifled with the flag of truce; had forfeited their plighted faith, and flagrantly deceived him, in forcibly carrying off hostages left by them in his hands; and when we recollect that this interview was sought by them with the worst of motives, public opinion ought not only to justify, but commend him for the transaction.[27]

The day following *Oceola's* capture, twenty nine more Indians were secured near Fort Peyton,[28] and two days later a family of five were taken. These were probably part of the retinue of those chiefs, who came with Oceola to hold a "talk."

There were now confined in the fort at St. Augustine one hundred and forty seven Indian prisoners.[29]

A few days after, Gen. Hernandez again proceeded south, to make a reconnaissance about Spring Garden,[30] and to take any stragglers that may fall in his way. In consequence of being unfortunately confined to my bed by sickness at the time, I could not accompany him, Asst. Surgeon Forry[31] taking my place. He returned after a few days absence, having succeeded in securing fifty three Indians and sixteen negroes, without any trouble however.[32]

CHAPTER XX

*T*he winter campaign was now about to be opened. It was to be a vigorous one, and active preparations were accordingly being made in all quarters. Gen. Jesup was determined to end the war if possible; and if matured plans, fresh troops, ample supplies, energy, and perseverance could have accomplished so desirable an end, it would have been done.[1]

Sam Jones (*Apiaka*) was now the whole head and front of the Seminole war. He was represented by those who knew him as a great rascal; and assuming the attributes of a prophet, assisted by the fortuitous and frequent occurrence of our horses dying on the road, which he ascribed to his own spells and incantations,[2] great confidence was reposed in his power of saving them by the hostile Indians, who at one time were said to have even deposed the pacific and imbecile *Micanopy,* their hereditary chief, and elected him in his stead.

It was reported that the Micasukies were determined to remain in the country at all hazards, and that there were then concentrated at the head of the St. John's river, and near Indian river, about 1500 warriors with *Sam Jones* at their head, waiting for a fight. The ardent prayer of all was that they would remain concentrated until we could meet them; for should they only make a fair and stand up fight, our troops we knew *"would stand up to their fodder,"* and soon bring matters to an end. But should the Indians adopt the Fabian system and scatter into small bands, they were expected to give a great deal of trouble; and by pertinaciously retreating to their hiding places when pursued, which they could easily do, in country rendered almost impenetrable by the wide spread morasses and everglades, the dense hammocks and fastnesses that cover its surface, in which no troops in the world could operate, but which afforded a safe shelter to

143

the Indians, who had secret beaten trails with which they were familiarly acquainted, the war could have been prolonged "ad infinitum," or until they deemed it proper to surrender. This is the true secret that so long retarded the victorious termination of Indian hostilities in Florida.[3] It was the character of the country, not the want of valor or persevering energy in our army; notwithstanding the abusive comments of some civilians,[4] who reclining on cushioned chairs in their comfortable and secure homes vomited forth reproaches, sneers, and condemnation, wantonly assailing the characters of those who alienated from home and kindred and all the comforts of life, were compelled to remain in this inglorious war, checking the depredations of the savage, and pressing forward in the defense of their country; traversing unexplored tracks; marching over burning sands; wading in morasses and swamps waist deep, exposed to noxious vapours, and subject to the whims of drenching rains or the scorching sun of an almost torrid climate, whose mid-day beams burned the skin and fermented the blood; surrounded by the dangers of savage warfare, and encountering toils, hardships, and privations without a murmur, and of which no one can have the least conception who was not a participant; and finally, when worn out by arduous service, sent home with ruined constitutions, to drag out a miserable existence, to be ended most probably in poverty, if not previously laid under the sod of Florida by an Indian bullet, or midnight dews, whose imperceptible damps imbibed by the thinly-clad-body, soon infected it with the disease that layed many in the silent tomb.

The true causes of the delay in terminating this war I repeat, can never be fully known but by those who participated in the war; for they were of such a nature that only a participant could become familiar with their difficulties. It was easy to make comments upon, but not so easy to be actually engaged in such a climate as Florida['s] in constantly making roads, building bridges, erecting defenses, transporting supplies, guarding the sick, fighting the enemy, driving him to his fastnesses, and then beating up his hammocks; and all this to be done under a sultry sun or in drenching rains. Campaigning in Florida, at least when I was there in the early part of the war, was only characterized by every species of privation and disease. And yet the world may have observed with admiration officers of finished education, and minds as well drilled as their companies, of polished manners, and talents qualifying them to adorn any civil station, enduring with patient long suffering the toils and discomforts of an inglorious war, with no sphere for the display of strategy, and no prospect of gathering laurels; but all endured from a high and unselfish *esprit de corps,* and a cherished enthusiasm in the service of their country.

It was an easy matter for those at a distance to look at a map of Florida, and ask "why did not they surround the hammocks, and destroy the enemy in detail (as we would cows in a pen), or starve them out?" An ocular observation of the territory would soon have convinced these sapient critics that [surrounding] a hammock twenty miles long and ten broad, if easily surrounded in their bright imaginations, was not a very feasible act. And as for starving them;—in a country filled with beef, deer, and turkies, whose streams and ponds abound with the finest fish, and where *coonte,* the Indian bread-stuff, grew spontaneous on every foot of ground, I may truly say that the Seminoles subsisted from sources that were inexhaustible.

Though all expected from the Army by the public was not achieved at the first out-break of this war, enough was done to prove that the American Army cannot be exceeded in energy, courage, and patriotism; that from the very commencement of operations in this ill-fated war, our gallant little band displayed the greatest zeal and devotion to the service amid the most trying scenes; while the loss of life in battle incontestibly proved how nobly its character and reputation has been sustained. The public was disappointed and dissatisfied because no brilliant and decisive victories were achieved; they were not aware that such victories were out of the question; that the enemy had an espionage over the whole country, and knowing all our movements, was met or not, at his own convenience; that they always fought from their own positions, and never took any from which they could not secure a safe retreat; that this position was always on the edge of some hammock, whence every Indian, posted behind some covert, made his deliberate shot;—the fact of his being near not known until the crack of his rifle and savage yells were heard, and our men were seen falling; and when charged upon, they precipitately retreated. Thus it was in every engagement with these Indians; nothing but a succession of running fights from hammock to hammock, and swamp to swamp. Very different from an encounter between civilized troops, who will stand up and take hard knocks upon hard knocks, until one party is fairly knocked under, and yields to the other a decisive victory.

I challenge the world to cite nobler deeds of daring than have been evinced by our little army in this inglorious war. They may speak of Thermopylae, and cite the chivalrous acts of olden times but in deeds equally worthy of admiration, and with no other incentive but moral courage to support the spirits amid the dangers which every where beset their path, no other army has ever before surpassed this.

Gen. Jesup's plan of operations for the winter's campaign, as well as could be previously surmised, seemed to have been the following. The whole army in Florida was to be divided into four detachments, each of sufficient strength to encounter the united force of the enemy. Leaving a sufficient garrison at each post for its defence, these four columns were to enter the country now occupied by the Indians by four different routes, sweeping down the peninsula southwardly, in sporting phrase *driving it.* One division under Gen. Hernandez was to proceed from St. Augustine, scouring the whole country between the St. John's river and the coast. While Gen. Hernandez was pursueing his devious march along the eastern side of the St. John's, Gen. Eustis[5] was to move with another column towards the south on the Western side. A third column under Col. Taylor[6] was to operate from Tampa Bay; and the fourth under Col. Smith[7] from Charlotte harbour.

The posts at Mosquito,[8] Volusia, and Fort Mellon, which were vacated during the summer on account of their unhealthy positions, were to be immediately re-established by parties sent in advance; and vessels laden with provisions were to proceed south, and await

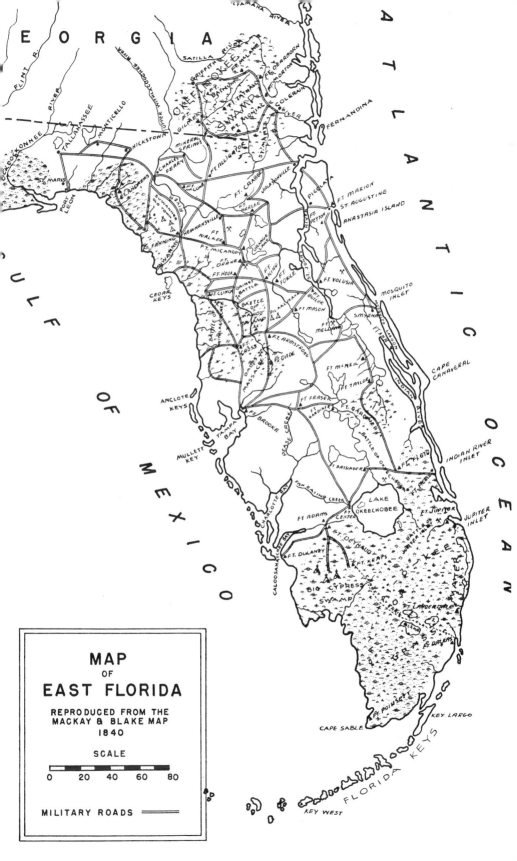

MAP
OF
EAST FLORIDA

REPRODUCED FROM THE
MACKAY & BLAKE MAP
1840

SCALE

0   20   40   60   80

MILITARY ROADS

at designated spots the approach of the troops. It appeared impossible from this judicious arrangement that the Indian could avoid coming in contact with some portion of our forces, or being driven into the sea.[9]

CHAPTER XXI

*O*n the 3d Nov an order was received at Fort Peyton directing Capt. Drane and Lt. Peyton to proceed with their companies to St. Augustine, and there embark for New Smyrna[1] at Mosquito. There being no intimation about my accompanying them in the order, I experienced rather gloomy forebodings at the prospect of being left at Fort Peyton to enjoy inglorious ease. In the afternoon of the same day Major Ashby arrived with three companies of the 2d Dragoons, to relieve the Artillery companies; and the latter proceeded immediately to the place of embarkation, at St. Augustine.

My fears in regard to spending a tame and uninteresting winter immured within the pickets of Fort Peyton, were removed by the arrival on the evening of the 4th Novr of an order for me to join and accompany the detachment that was going to Mosquito. From the lowest abyss of despair my spirits were instantly elevated to the highest pinnacle of exuberance, as with hasty preparations I obeyed the welcome order.

We were detained at St. Augustine longer than was anticipated, in consequence of all the preparatory arrangements for our departure not being completed. This delay afforded me an opportunity of witnessing the arrival of the Cherokee delegation, deputed—under the sanction of our Government,—by John Ross[2] principal chief of the Cherokees, to bear a talk to the Seminoles; advising them to be good boys, and not give their great Father at Washington so much trouble. It was hoped they might succeed in their philanthropic mediation; but feared it would turn out rather a humbug.[3] The names of the plenipotentiaries were 1. [Tekahskeh, alias Hair] *Conrad,* 2. [Taskeketchee, alias Jesse] *Bushyhead,* 3. [Oosahetah, alias Richard] *Field,* 4. [Ahnahstaquah, alias Thomas] *Redwood* [Woodward], and 5. [their interpreter

Telahkahquahlah, alias the] *Pole-cat;* who were accompanied by Col. Sherburne [Sherbourne], agent of the U. States.[4]

On the night of the 6th Novr 1837 I embarked with the 1st Regt of Artillery, who were distributed after great difficulty on board the Schooners Medium and Oscar, and the Steamer Florida, the largest portion of the men being prematurely more than half seas-over; their parting libations having been too copiously imbibed. The scene presented on the wharf during the greater part of the night beggared description. The Paymaster had been among them during the day; and about to go probably where there was neither buying nor selling, most of the men had got rid of their cash in a way most luxurious to common soldiers; that is, after filling their canteens with liquor, which their officers as adroitly emptied upon the ground, they had undertaken to fill their interior man; but in so doing neglected a proper attention to the outer man, whose movements being somewhat vibratory, resulted in an unpleasant application outwardly of the weaker beverage salt water, by a tumble into [off] the dock. The narrow wharf being crowded with baggage,—provisions,—guns, both little and great,—men taking leave of their wives, and men who had no wives to leave, there was but small space left to turn about in during the process of loading the different vessels; and morning was close upon us when the last man was marched aboard, and the vessels hauled off into the stream.

In consequence of an adverse wind, the steamer Florida,—in which were Gen. Hernandez and Staff, including myself;—had to tow the schooners over the Bar. She succeeded in giving a good offing to the Medium; but a heavy sea rising, and the tide falling, we had to defer repeating that operation with the Oscar until the day after. At daylight on the morning of the 8th Novr we were again under way, with the Oscar in tow; and soon found ourselves beyond the obstacle which rendered assistance necessary to our sailing companions; when casting off the tow line, we left them with their white sails spread to a favourable breeze, and finding ourselves again basking in the splendour of an ocean sunrise.

The Journal

Eight miles south of St. Augustine, and two and a half miles from land, we passed the singular phenomenon of a subterranean or more properly submarine Mineral fountain at Sea. I am told they are not uncommon along the coast of Florida; and are supposed to be connected, or have a similar origin with the subterranean streams which abound in every part of that territory. The one we passed had the appearance of a shoal two hundred feet in diameter, from the yellowish colour, and ebullition of its waters. This yellowish colour shows it to be homogeneous with the numerous limestone fountains of Florida; they being encrusted with a white deposit which refracted through the transparent water, makes an illumination, and this to the eye at some distance seems a yellowish loom. Refractions of this sort are said to be familiar to those who have sailed among the calcareous shoals of the West Indies. This mineral fountain is said to be unfathomable in the center to a line of 25 fathoms, although just beyond its margin bottom is found at 9 fathoms seaward, and 14 fathoms land-side; and its water is described as cool, brackish, and sulphurous, sometimes fresh, and emitting a sulphurous odour that may be discerned half a mile off when to leeward of it. The volume of water discharged by this fountain is conjectured to be as large as a column of 100 feet [in] diameter.[5]

Leaving this remarkable marine spring to the speculations of those who love to investigate the causes of nature's secret works, we continued the undulating tenor of our watery course, and reached the haven of our destination at 5 o'clock in the afternoon.

We found the Medium at anchor within the bar of Mosquito; and taking up our berth along side of her, remained until the following morning, and the arrival of the Oscar, to effect a landing.

The bright rays of the setting sun, which in this Southern clime always imparts a richness to nature's scenery before it becomes enveloped in evening's obscurity, added to the beauty and romance of the neighbouring shores, gorgeous in Autumnal tints of the mellowest softness; and in addition to the most exquisite beauty, the scene presented all the attractions of novelty. Long after the sun had cast his farewell glance upon earth and sea,

and the shades of night had veiled the smiling face of the surrounding landscape, I retained my position on deck; gazing at the
silent beauty of the heavens, whose gem like orbs glowed through
this transparent atmosphere beautifully in the overarching firma-
ment; and listening to the dashing of the impetuous waves,
sparkling like fretted gold upon the neighbouring beach. It was
the place and hour for the imagination to work, and illusive fancy
soon conjured up with all the distinctness of reality things and
persons long past away. Voices hushed forever in the still tomb
again cheered my heart with melodious accents;—eyes closed forever in the darkness of death, once more cast their smiling glances
upon me. A thousand remembrances rose like a dim land-like
cloud to gladden the heart with the semblance of happiness,
destined the next moment to sink and melt away into aerial
nothing.

At daylight next morning we hauled up the river to a spot
more favorable for landing, and immediately in front of the ruins
of Judge Dunham's[6] place known as New Smyrna. Though almost reduced to a state of primitive wildness from its long desertion, the scene presented many beauties, which conspired to render
it one of the most romantic spots I had yet visited. In the midst
of orange, lemon, fig, and other blossoming trees, with a sprinkling
of the slender and stately palmetto rising lightly and gracefully
above the dense mass of foliage, there appeared the ruined columns,
towering upwards, like gigantic sentries of the place, of Judge
Dunham's once princely mansion; all that remained visible; the
walls having been blown down as twas said by the explosion of
a keg of powder, which unknown to the Indians who fired the
building was concealed in the cellar. This was the spot where
Turnbull first established his Minorcan colony, and the ruins of
the original occupant's dwellings are still visible in the distance,
adding a melancholy feature to the landscape, from a retrospective
association of the sufferings there endured. An untamed forest
filled up the back ground; its dark shades impressing the mind
with the mysteries of its extensive and gloomy labyrinths, only
traversed by the wild beast, and the wily savage, more blood-

thirsty than the beast of prey;—the prowling lion or the crouching tiger. The abundance of Pelicans and other wild-fowl added much to the interest of the scenery, as floating in groups upon the river, they rose and sunk with the undulations of the water; or circling the air either in serrated files or alone, they changed their location for the greater facility of securing their food.

We were all soon on shore through the medium of the numerous large flat-bottomed boats, called Mackinaw boats,[7] brought with us, having been constructed expressly for the navigation of these shallow lagoons.

We pitched our tents amid the ruins, under the protecting shade of wide spreading live oaks, and other umbrageous trees. I selected a spot for my tent near the base of a gigantic column; and towering over it grew an orange tree, in solitary and stately grandeur. Capt. Drane, who was in command immediately commenced the necessary improvements for rendering the ruins useful as places for storage of provisions.

At leisure moments we amused ourselves in fishing, and revelled most extensively upon the wholesome and excellent produce of these waters, abounding with fine oysters and sheep-head; the latter too plentiful to be long regarded as a luxury.[8]

A few days after our arrival, twenty one negroes were discovered in our vicinity, endeavouring to escape from the Indians. They were brought into camp slightly removed from a state of nudity, and fed; after which necessary operation we were informed by them that they had been stolen by the savages from the estate of Messrs. Cruger and Depeyster; some from those of Major Heriot and of Major Woodruff.[9] They stated that a large number of Indians were assembled near Indian river ready to fight. They were sent to St. Augustine on the departure of the steamer Florida the day after. Gen. Hernandez also left us by the same opportunity, having returned to St. Augustine to accompany the mounted part of his command by land to *New Smyrna*.

We remained *in statu quo* until the 20th Novr, when our camp was enlivened by the arrival of Gen. Hernandez and mounted force, consisting of part of 2d U. S. Dragoons under Major Ashby;

a regiment of Florida volunteers most of them descendants of the Minorcans already alluded to,—under Col. Hanson;[10] and the Tennessee Volunteers. They established their bivouac near us; and immediately commenced the laudable exercise of recruiting themselves on the fine supply of oyster and fish; that an order to march might find them in good strength, health, and condition for active service.

About the same time Lt. Col. Pierce arrived in [the] Steamer Richmond from St. Augustine with the remaining companies of [the] 1st Art., accompanied by Major Kirby and other officers of the 1st Art. Many of them very fine young fellows just from the Military Academy at West Point; Dr. [Assistant Surgeon Philip] Maxwell arrived at the same time. Lt. McLaughlin of the Navy, previously distinguished by his gallantry in Florida, having volunteered again for duty in Florida, also arrived, bring with him about twenty sailors who were to be employed in navigating the lagoons and Indian river.

CHAPTER XXII

*T*he busy hum of preparation resounded from all sides of our large and miscellaneous camp. In one part nearest the water, distinguished by an odd assemblage of tarpaulins and oars formed into something like tents, may be observed our amphibious cooperators, busily engaged in recaulking the barges preparatory to transporting provisions to Indian river; where it was intended that the forces east of the St. Johns should concentrate for supplies, previous to proceeding farther south.

By the active cooperation of all hands, everything upon which our farther progress depended was speedily accomplished; and on the 29th Novr at daylight, Lt. McLaughlin,—commodore of the fleet,—hoisted his broad pennant, and made signal for weighing anchor. His fleet consisted of about ten or a dozen Mackinaw boats, and one fast-sailing sloop-rigged boat used as the flag ship and whipper-in of the others. The boats had been laden the day previous, that no delay might occur on the morning of starting; and immediately after reveille, three companies of 1st Artillery commanded by Lts. Magruder,[1] Mackall,[2] and French[3] embarked; the men being distributed among the boats, about twenty soldiers and two sailors in each. Lt. Magruder as commander of the forces, and myself as Fleet Surgeon accompanied the commodore in the Flagship. Our course was south, towards Mosquito Lagoon; and destination a place called the *Haulover* at the S. Western extremity of the Lagoon; and so called from its being a strip of land nearly a mile wide, which separated the Lagoon from Indian river, over which the Indians were accustomed to drag their canoes from one water into the other. At this place we were to await the arrival of Gen. Hernandez with the rest of his forces, who intended following us to the designated place by land; leaving one company of 1st Artillery at New Smyrna with Capt. Drane in command.

Journey into Wilderness

We got under way, and were soon prosecuting our voyage with hearts as light and spirits as buoyant, as zeal in our country's cause, and a bright sky above our heads could produce. The first half of our way, we had to thread our course through a labyrinth of low mangrove islands, partly inundated, and inaccessible, and packed in closely upon each other, being separated by innumerable narrow and shallow channels, their width barely sufficient in some places for the passage of our boats. The scenery was anything but prepossessing; nothing visible but the dried and tangled limbs of the dead mangrove trees, which had been all killed by a frost during the severe winter of 1835;[4] nothing green, not even a blade of grass met the eye to enliven the view. Though everything like vegetation was absent, life of another kind abounded; vast numbers of aquatic birds covered the waters, those unfrequented lagoons being the resort of millions of all the varieties of water-fowl that were generally found in that latitude. Innumerable species of wild-ducks, pelicans, gulls, etc. floated around us, whilst in all directions as far as the eye could see, the dark and leafless limbs of the closely growing mangrove were dotted with thousands of white cranes, as with flakes of feathery snow, giving to the scene the peculiar appearance of extensive cotton fields after a frost. Ever and anon would a flock of *Pink-Curlews* [*roseate spoonbills*], —commonly so called from their beautiful colour,—a rare and highly valued bird, hover over our heads, looking like the leaves of a rose that had been broken and given to the streaming air.

At midday we stopped at the only accessible spot on our route, to give our men some respite from their laborious duties at the oars, and to procure some fresh water from a spring which we expected to find there, from the fact of the spot having once been inhabited, the remains of an old Indian lodge being still visible upon the top of the mound. This accessible spot was nothing but a firm mound of small extent, rearing its head high above the surrounding level of inundated mud and mangrove. The mound seemed to be composed almost entirely of shells, and presented very much the appearance of artificial formation. Upon the summit I discovered several human bones, apparently very old, some of which I brought away. This excited in my mind a suspicion that the spot upon which we stood was one of those Indian burial mounds many of which are to be found in Florida. But if so it must have been a strange freak to select a place of such difficult access, and so remote from "terra firma." I have procured a sketch of one of these mounds situated near Fort Taylor on the upper St. Johns, upon the summit of which our men built a block-house.[5] The height of it may be judged by the appearance of the horses grazing at the base. These mounds have [been] and always will be a mysterious subject for speculation; relics of greater power than now exists among the Indian tribes; and proofs of the superstitious veneration with which once the red man regarded the resting place of his ancestor's bones, a veneration which now exists but in history. I pocketed the parts of a skull,—perhaps one owned by some warrior "great in battle as in council wise,"— perchance the remnant of a royal head. Of whosoever knowledge box it once formed a part, it must have done him service under hard knocks, for a thicker skull I never saw, being half an inch thick. I returned to my boat, and replenished exhausted nature by swallowing "cold victuals."

After an hour's rest we resumed our voyage; and soon put out into *mosquito lagoon,* an open lake-like sheet of water, where the wind being favorable, those boats that had them [sails] were put under sail; while the crews of those not so supplied, exhibited their ingenuity by the substitute of tents, blankets, old counter-panes, etc, presenting a grotesque and motley assemblage, worthy the pencil of Cruikshank.[6] Here the commodore's ship became particularly useful, for with such difference in rigging, there could not but be a difference in sailing; and very soon our fleet was scattered far and wide. This inequality was remedied by the superior speed of our flag-ship, which enabled us to bring up the sternmost by towing; and by sailing along the line, to encourage the crews of the dullest boats to exert themselves at the oars. In this way we got along swimmingly; and the sun, which on approaching the West, had shed his light gloriously over the waters of the lagoon in a flood of gold, soon cast his farewell glance upon us, leaving the western sky a bright and burnished sheet; its clouds richly rolled and tinged with gold, exceeding the gorgeous descriptions of oriental story.

As a hen gathering her brood under her protecting wings on the approach of night; so did our prudent Commodore make the signal for concentrating the fleet before darkness enveloped us. We dropt anchor beyond gun shot from the shore, and prepared to pass the night as well as circumstances would allow, being rather confined in our quarters with so many aboard such small craft. The small open sailing boat of the Commodore contained during the night besides the crew of four men, all the officers of the detachment, five in number; and by placing boards, brought along for the purpose, over the seats, we formed a temporary deck; upon this the whole party arranged themselves by means of dove-tailing, and bringing heels and points together. There we lay all night closely wedged and immovable, canopied partly by the heavens, partly by the mainsail of the boat saturated with dew.

Nothing could be seen but the "fair stars clustering high," with their reflection bespangling the smooth water of the lagoon; and the dark line of thickly wooded shore obscured in heavy gloom, extended in profound repose.—Nothing could be heard but the gentle murmuring of the water as it rippled within a few inches of our ears against the boat. Long familiar only with the gloomy grandeur of the forest and its melancholy moaning, the novelty of my situation charmed me; long desirous of beholding these strange waters, I felt my longing realized. The perfect stillness of the scene,—the absence of every sound but such as harmonized with the character of the place, far removed from towns and civilization,—twas fascinating; it seemed as the illusions of magic,—the sorceries of the imagination.

Before the bright arising star of morning had become eclipsed by the kindling beams of the brighter luminary, we were all awake; and ready to pursue our course. Ignorant of the exact locality of the spot we were in quest of,—for all this part of the country was wild and unknown to the whites,—we continued our way at random, trusting to our instinct, and the slight knowledge

The Journal

which our Minorcan guide may have retained of the land-marks. Slight indeed; for it was barely possible that through the lapse of many years since he had visited this place on a hunting excursion, nature should have retained the same appearance. The shores lay in all the wildness of nature; in some spots towering forests rose; the perennial palmetto—the russet-trunked pine—the silver shafted water oak, and a variety of other trees proudly tossed their high heads in the wind; as if defying the usurpation by us of their dominion, which for ages they had held in undisturbed possession. In other spots,

> *"Vast plains, spread out on every side,*
> *Stretch to the sloping skies."*

These were covered with a tall rank grass, or prairie reed; presenting a sea of grass in one unbroken expanse, gently waving their tops about in obedience to the breeze which coquettishly toyed with them, as it wandered over the dreary waste. Nothing obstructed the eye, save here and there a melancholy looking palmetto tree relieved in solitary grandeur against the blue sky on the horizon.

We had proceeded up to the head of the lagoon under the influence of a favorable breeze, without discovering the *Haulover;* and in order to renew the search, were working our way back with oars against a head wind, which began to behave roughly with the waters of the lagoon, here expanded to a breadth of many miles, and which seemed to glow beneath the fervid rays of a glaring sun; when suddenly there appeared along the distant margin of the shore a long extended line of moving objects. The distance was too great to enable us to distinguish clearly, but the immediate impression was that they were a large body of Indians watching our movements. This impression was strengthened when we noticed the sun's rays brilliantly reflected, as if from the bright silver ornaments generally worn around the head and upon the breast by the savages. We gradually approached to make a reconnaissance, and soon discovered that they were all mounted, amounting to upwards of five or six hundred horsemen; and that they

159

were moving slowly along the waters edge in single file. We were deliberating upon the proper manner of landing to attack them,— the idea of backing out never entering our noddles, notwithstanding our inferior force,—when suddenly the truth flashed up before us;—they could be no other than Gen. Hernandez and his mounted force, who had left Smyrna after we did; and being as ignorant of the localities as we were, notwithstanding their Indian guide *Blue-Snake,* whose silver ornaments we had observed glittering in the sun, had passed the *Haulover,* and were following the boats, supposing our organs of locality to be better developed.

We landed our Minorcan guide, who after holding a consultation with *Blue-Snake,* proceeded with that worthy in search of— not the promised—but the unpromising land; which they soon discovered.

Our Commodore wishing to make an imposing landing in true Naval style, ordered the boats into line, with their bows shorewards, and gave the signal to advance;—in military phrase "forward by the front." We proceeded admirably for a little way; but were yet several hundred yards from the shore when our boats grounded, notwithstanding their slight draught. In fact, the lagoon was nothing but an immense extent of flat land overflowed by the sea, giving it the appearance of a large lake, the water no where I believe exceeding six feet in depth. It had the peculiarity of being excessively salt, which may be accounted for by the continual influx of the sea, and the great evaporation constantly going on. From this circumstance, the lagoon and Indian river, which has the same peculiarity, were the constant resort of the Indians, for the purpose of procuring salt, which they manufactured by a simple process of boiling.

We landed at last, after a long wade through the water, amidst a thick growth of prairie reed and saw-grass higher than our heads, through which we had to force our way to the spot selected for the encampment. This was nearly a mile distant, on the Indian river shore, at the other side of the *Haulover;* across which we afterwards found a rude path, if the scarcely visible track, left by the savage, may be thus denominated.

160

The Journal

The site of our camp was an open prairie, upon a strip of land, which may easily be found by looking at any map of Florida, presenting one unbroken expanse of scrub-saw-palmetto from two to four feet high, and entirely bare of trees, except where here and there a palmetto tree waving high, tossed its umbrella-shaped head in sulky loneliness. On one side, Indian river, which is six miles in breadth at this spot, rolled along its majestic and expansive stream towards the ocean, a distance of ninety miles; its opposite and distant shore presenting a wilderness of cypress and pine forests, sacred from the invading plough share, or the axe of the woodman; their impervious wilds,—where the deer browsed and the wolves cried to each other in undisturbed and savage communion,—as yet untrodden by human foot, except by that of the roaming Indian. On the other side of us, the placid waters of Mosquito lagoon displayed its silvery surface, in which the blue sky, pure, deep, unspotted, lay mirrored; the clearness of its waters disclosing to view its finny inhabitants, who

> "Shooting with quick glance,
> Showed to the sun their waved coats, dropp'd with gold."

The charm of the whole scene was greatly heightened by the innumerable flocks of ducks, who disturbed by our unwonted intrusion upon their retiracy, where a complete eternal silence had previously reigned, were constantly hovering backwards and forwards in frightened thousands over our camp, filling the air with the noise of their quickly moving wings; the velocity of their flight considerably increased by our efforts to bring about a better acquaintance, by means of our guns. The air also, which at that period of the year was elsewhere under the withering supremacy of frowning winter, was there as soft as the breathings of June.

CHAPTER XXIII

*T*he morning after our arrival, the boats were sent back to New Smyrna for more provisions, and not being relieved from duty with the boating party, as a matter of course I returned with them. The distance being only thirty miles, and the way being now known to us, we reached there the same night, after a fatiguing row, the men being nearly exhausted.

The boats were quickly laden; and at half past nine the next morning we commenced our return. Nothing occurred to interrupt the monotony of the voyage; watching the various birds affording the chief amusement. Among these the Pelicans contributed the most to our merriment, although next to the owl they are the most solemn looking of all birds. They sometimes congregated in an immense flock on an isolated shoal in the lagoon, and presented the appearance at a distance of a regiment under arms. By a slight stretch of the imagination one might have conceived them —as they gravely eyed you askant—an assemblage met to consult on the affairs of their community; you might have perceived several grave and solemn looking dignitaries detach themselves from the rest, and strut up and down with an air exceedingly impressive. Then one might have imagined them met to try some offender, who sat on a shoal detached from the rest, with wings and bill drooping; the rest were eyeing him with a gloomy and indignant frown, and each individual seemed to be deeply occupied in revolving in his cranium the most condign punishment. Then as we approached we'd see the assemblage gradually merge the public interest into individual safety; until at last they would rise with one accord, and sail away to some less frequented spot.

We reached the *Haulover* long after dark, after a severe day's labour, and proceeding to the camp, found most of the officers assembled,—as usual in the evening after the duties of the day,—

around one of the camp fires; speculating on persons and things in general, and this campaign's movements in particular. There were several oracles among us, who lifted up their voices in the wilderness and uttered most sapient and profound maxims, while the rest listened with awe and wonder depicted upon their faces, which presented by the light of the camp fires a most ghastly appearance, augmented by the uncouth garb in which some were arrayed. Bob McL———— [First Lieutenant Robert Milligan Mc-Lane] for example, had encased himself in a huge monkey jacket, which approached the nature of a frock-coat very much in one respect, viz, its lower edge terminating at a close proximity to his knees. There were some, however, who were dressed as neat and trig as if prepared to enter a lady's parlour; these were the new comers of course. The old campaigner could always be distinguished by his off hand, free, easy, and dont-care-for-nothing sort of manner, whose prevailing expression of countenance, it was remarked by some one, was a gloomy frown.

There was also with us Capt.—[Giles Porter] who, a medley of quirks and quiddities, as I heard him once called, was no bad companion on a dull campaign; his quaint and quizzical remarks, generally made with a withering sneer, and always full of sarcasm, afforded a fund of amusement.[1] He stood six feet three. His sword—a most formidable weapon of the dark ages—a family relic no doubt—was generally seen trailing three feet behind him, to the imminent risk of every person in his vicinity. His greatest pride however, was his mustachoes, which of a dun colour, always exhibit[ed] by an ingenious spiral a strong partiality for the corner of each eye. This gave him an appalling expression, which tickled his fancy not a little; and whenever anything annoyed him, it was immediately discovered by his curling his mustachoes most sedulously. A good joke was told of him, as having occurred in Florida. The company he commanded was mounted; and the Orderly Sergeant, who bestrode a mettlesome sorrel mare, more than once called forth the Captain's ire by the ungainly manner he sat his saddle. "Zounds Sergeant," cried the Captain one day, as the company was practising the evolutions, "you bestride your horse as if he was a beer barrel; dismount sir, and let me show you how to manage her." Thereupon the gallant commander vaulting valiantly into the saddle, buried spurs deep into the horse's sides, as he theatrically exclaimed "Thus!" The next moment the Captain was seen describing a parabolic curve similar to the trajectory of a ten inch shell; his neck and head resembling the fuse, and alighting on his seat of honour at the feet of the unskillful Sergeant, who commenced condoling with his splenetic commander, continued seated, making spasmodic efforts to smile. "Ah! your honor, that was an ugly fall." "Sure the earth thrembled [trembled] under you, Captain, your honor, faix!" "I felt the shock like an earthquake here," exclaimed one of the men. "You may say that, and niver lie," quoth another. "Silence Sirs," cried the enraged commander; "dismiss the company Sergeant, and the next time I attempt to break a young jade of a filley, may I never be promoted."

We remained quiet in camp, without any change, until the 7th Decr; when Gen. Hernandez with the Cavalry left us for the opposite side of Indian river, going round its head to get there. Upon reaching the spot, his fires were to be signals for us to join him with the boats, which had been hauled over land from the lagoon into Indian river.

During the General's stay in our camp, his Indian guide *Blue Snake* and myself became sworn friends; indeed, his friendship became at times troublesome, for he insisted on spreading his blanket in my tent *cheek by jole* [jowl] by the side of mine, as long as we were together, and thus remaining inseparable even during the dark hours of night. He knowing nothing of English, and I understanding the Seminole language very imperfectly, our conversation became of course very limited in the dark where signs could not be substituted. At such times he would lie upon his back drumming his fingers upon his breast, all the while chanting a melancholy ditty in a monotonous whine; probably some love song; which, however, was far from being disagreeable; for the low tones of an Indian voice are music itself.

After the departure of the Dragoons, our camp life became

The Journal

still more monotonous; nothing doing, nothing done. Our amusements consisted in shooting at the ducks, and hunting *gophers*. This latter is a species of land turtle, that grow to a large size. They are a solitary animal preferring the society of the black and rattle-snakes to that of their own species. Their habitations are holes dug by them into the ground to a depth of ten or twelve feet, where the black and rattle-snakes very amicably take up their abode with them, to all appearances living quite sociably and happily together. We dug into one of these holes in the centre of our camp once, and one of the men had extended his hand to grasp the gopher, when an enormous black snake protruded his head from the hole and reconnoitred us very suspiciously. The man was terribly alarmed, and with difficulty could any one be persuaded to approach the hole. We at last succeeded in drawing his snake-ship from his hiding place; when we found by measurement, his dimensions to be nine feet in length, and twelve inches in circumference. As he lay extended on the ground, he presented a pretty formidable appearance. These *gopher* holes, by the bye, are not the only favorite resort of those snakes; for on one occasion, while stretched on my blanket in my tent, I lay thinking of exactly nothing at all, a slight rustling in one corner of it attracted my attention; when there I beheld, apparently quite at home, one of those black gentlemen. Upon my moving, he calmly glided by, and disappeared beneath the folds of the canvass. Visits from the reptiles I was quite accustomed to; for never did I enter my tent, after however short an absence, without finding several lizards and toads in quiet possession of my blanket.

An express from St. Augustine arrived at our camp on the 12th Decr bringing news both cheering and dispiriting. With regard to the first kind; the accounts from the Cherokee delegation were so far favorable. One of their number who had been sent in advance with despatches, represented the Seminoles as disposed to come in without any further hostilities; and soon after, the whole delegation returned to Fort Mellon from their visit to the Seminoles, accompanied by *Micanopy, Cloud,* and about thirty principal warriors, who surrendered themselves at that post.

Journey into Wilderness

The Cherokee delegation had sat in council two days with the Seminoles, at a place called *Fowl-Town;* at which were *Sam Jones* and three hundred of the *Micasukies* under him. *Micanopy* was said to have received them with much joy, and gave them a talk, stating his determination to abide by the treaty, and go west. *Sam Jones* also agreed to come in; but changed his mind afterwards; deciding to send his nephew first, to enquire of Gen. Jesup, if it was true that he had threatened to put the said Sam in petticoats when he caught him, and whip him around the camp. If so, he must either retract or apologise, or the aforesaid *Sam* would have no dealings with him. I think the General ought certainly to have offered Sammy the personal and honorable satisfaction, which every gentleman is entitled to receive who feels that his insulted honour cannot be otherwise appeased.

The same express also brought intelligence of a dispiriting kind, as regarded the submission of the Seminoles. *Wild-Cat,* with one other chief, and seventeen warriors had effected their escape from the Fort at St. Augustine. The whole of these were confined in one room and by some means or other had been furnished with files; thus enabling them to saw off the iron bars that had been placed across the window. By tying their blankets together, they descended into the moat, and then twas with them *"ai-e-pus-che!"* This escape of *Wild-Cat* we expected no doubt would produce a revolution in the minds of the Seminoles, even if they had been seriously inclined to submit;[2] and the termination of the war we therefore considered as postponed *sine die.*[3]

On the 18th Decr another express arrived, bringing intelligence, various and contradictory. One version of the reports was that a council had been held at Fort Mellon which lasted three hours; at which were present *Micanopy* and all the Seminoles, the Cherokee *plenipotentiaries,* and all the officers of the Army then at that post; that it was decided that the Cherokee deputation should return with Sam Jones' nephew and bring in that worthy gentleman; that other warriors should be selected to go out and bring in the women, children, and all the *other* cattle; and, more-

166

over, the express said that Gen. Jesup, who was at Picolata, declared the war was over.

Another version,—which we thought the most probable—was that Gen. Jesup had sent a threatening message to *Sam Jones,* or *Abiaka,* that if he did not give up the Indian Chiefs *Wild-Cat* and *Tuskenuggee* [Halpatter Tustenugee or Alligator], whom he intended to hang, he would give him no quarter; and that he would give him ten days to consider about it. We thought if the latter piece of news be true, an energetic and general movement of the Army would soon follow, and we were expecting immediate orders.

While awaiting the movements of our Commanding General, Col. Pierce did not allow his regiment to lie idle but had them out every day at battalion drills. Capt. ———— [Porter], the wag of our camp, used to say in reply to expressions of impatience at our remaining inactive so long, that the 1st Artillery had gained already sufficient honour in the field and was only resting upon its laurels.

In order to clear a sufficient space for drilling, the Col. turned out the whole regiment and had the prairie set on fire on all sides. I never beheld a more magnificent spectacle. The flames appeared to rise to the clouds, and all nature seemed to succumb to the fiery tempest. Not the least sublime or beautiful were the varied hues of the dense columns of smoke that obscured the light of the sun. The most beautiful wreaths of all the varied hues of the rainbow would detach themselves from the dense mass of lurid black vapour, and float into mid-air, undergoing changes that vied with that most beautiful phenomenon. Then as a sudden gust of wind would dispel the smoke, a gorgeous ring of fire would appear to girt the horizon many miles distant, progressing northwards, withering every living thing in its path, from the gigantic pine to the smallest shrub.

CHAPTER XXIV

*L*t. [L. M.] Powell of the Navy; who had been ordered to proceed on an exploring expedition along the coast and rivers of South Florida, and to cooperate with the Army against the Indians, arrived at the haulover a few days after we did. His command consisted of about two hundred men, comprising sailors, soldiers, and volunteers.[1] The officers of that expedition were Lt. Powell, commanding; Dr. Leitner [a Naval Surgeon] of Charleston So. Ca. surgeon and naturalist; passed Midshipman Harrison; Midshipmen McArthur and Murphy; [First] Lt. [Henry W.] Fowler, commdg. company I of 1st Artillery U. S. A. attached to the expedition; Capt. [James R.] Irving and [Second] Lt. [Oliver LaThrop] Sheppard [Shepperd] of the Washington City Volunteers, also on duty with the detachment; and Mr. Jos. Johnston[2] formerly of the Army, Topographical Engineer. These were embarked in thirty three small light boats well calculated for the business they were on. Their first object was to explore Indian river; and with that intention, immediately after pitching their tents in our vicinity they commenced transporting their boats across the Haulover from the lagoon into that river. They occupied several days in completing their preparations; during which time they were frequently exercised by their commander in drilling. When drawn up in line they presented a curious blending of black and white, like the keys of a piano forte; many of the sailors being coloured men. There was also an odd alternation of tarpaulin hats and pea-jackets, with forage caps and soldiers trip roundabouts; soldiers and sailors, white men and black, being all thrown into the ranks indiscriminately, a beautiful specimen of mosaic; thus modifying sailor's ardour with soldier's discipline.

Christmas found them with us, and we determined to give them a jollification in celebration of the day. Our situation debarred the possibility of providing such an entertainment as we wished, but the enjoyment was not less from the absence of what generally constitutes a Christmas dinner. We revelled upon *gopher soup* and whiskey toddy, which were the chief luxuries that graced our board. By the bye; as regards *gopher soup,* no epicure in the world but would smack his lips could he only get a taste of this rare dish, known only in Florida; and the whiskey toddy was highly relished also, to judge by the quantity that we stowed away, though its chief recommendation was the fact of its being the only liquor that was attainable at Camp Haulover. Had Sammy Veller [Weller][3] been present he would doubtless have been sorely grieved at seeing the destinies of so many individuals thwarted in not having been born oysters, from the uncommon powers of suction displayed. But then it was Christmas, which only comes once a year; and to many of us about those times, only came once in several years. Though unable to boast of a very great variety of viands, yet we had in abundance what was even better, "a feast of reason and flow of soul." Music too lent its charms to enliven the day; for in Lt. French we had a perfect "night-ingale in the wilderness" as I once heard him called. His powerful and melodious voice with the accompaniment of his guitar, frequently having had the effect of charming away ennui, and dispelling the most inveterate "azure demons" or Indigoes, that ever capered in the brains of mortal. McGruder [Magruder] also occasionally contributed his mite on the same instrument and his voice was not disagreeable, and always in tune for "Quoi Liset est ce vous."[4] In fact we abounded in singers. [First Lieutenant James Lowny] Donaldson and [Second Lieutenant Arthur Middle-ton] Rutledge sometimes favoured us with the melody of their voices; and when piously inclined Aisquith[5] was always on hand for a hymn. And when "Cigars and Cogniac" was sung, every man in camp disclosed the development of tune in his cranium; which was made known in a most stentorian manner; much to the dismay of all the sedate owls within hearing, who on such occasions, manifested a strong disapprobation, by the most approved man-ner of hooting.

Journey into Wilderness

On the following morning Lt. Powell with his command embarked; and with three cheers, which were returned from the boats; we saw them start on their exploring expedition down Indian river. One of their objects was to select eligible sites for depots; and we were soon to follow and build forts at the places selected.

In consequence of our anticipated departure, [First] Lt. [James R.] Irwing [Irwin] of the 1st Art. was ordered to superintend the erection of some kind of fortification at the haulover, capable of being defended by one company, which were to remain as a guard when we had left.

In the evening of the 26th Decr an alarm was spread through camp, and orders issued for proceeding immediately across Indian river to Camp Hernandez, where the Cavalry were encamped, ten miles obliquely from us, in consequence of a great firing heard in that direction. The officers of our camp all volunteered, but as all could not leave, as many as were required and could be spared moved across the river with two hundred men, expecting to find the enemy in great force by the noise and number of the guns we heard. On reaching the supposed scene of action, we found the cause of the uproar in the arrival of a reinforcement of five hundred Tennessean Volunteers, who were discharging their guns after exposure to a heavy rain.

We had begun to grow restless at the postponed movement of the Army, not doubting but that hostilities would be continued, and that nothing but the most imperious necessity should delay our operations, in a country, where seasons and climate had to be regarded, when the arrival of the express confirmed our worst anticipations. The *Cherokee Mediation* had proved a failure, for Sam Jones and his people had "let the words of the talk enter one ear and pass through the other like the listless winds." The talk it seemd [seemed] proposed nothing but peace with the white man; and left the terms to be proposed by the Seminoles; which having always been the point at issue, ended as usual in dissatisfaction on both sides. In consequence of this termination to the truce, the different divisions of the Army had renewed their hostile

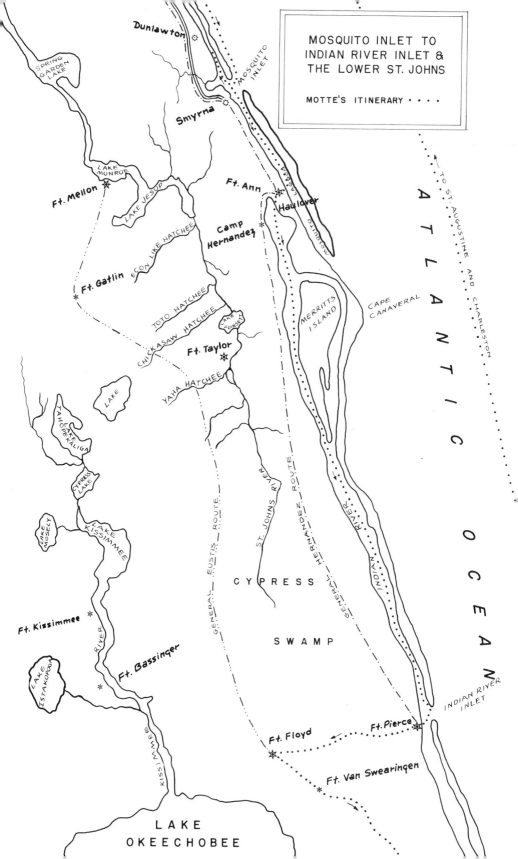

operations. That portion under the immediate command of Gen. Eustis, amounting to fifteen hundred regulars, had taken the field from Fort Mellon; which had been left with a garrison of a hundred and forty men under the command of Major Staniford. Their first destination was *Sam Jones'* town,[6] in a South Eastern direction from that post, and about two miles from the St. John's river, where all the Indians under *Sam Jones* were supposed to be collected. Col. Taylor with his command of a thousand men, composed principally of regular Infantry, with a few volunteers, and two hundred Delaware and Shawnee Indians, was on the Kissimmee, about thirty miles in the rear or S. E. of *Sam Jones.* The express also said that *Alligator* and *Jumper,* two of the most important chiefs in the nation,—the former commanding at Dade's Massacre,—the latter *Micanopy's* sense keeper,[7]—had gone in with their families to Col. Taylor.[8]

This news, and orders for the 1st Art. to move down Indian river to the bluffs opposite to the Inlet, created quite a sensation in camp; and stirring times again commenced. On the evening of the 29th Decr. orders were issued that the Regt. should be in readiness to embark at 3 o'clock next morning. Our camp in consequence presented all night a scene of "life and light," the men being busily occupied in cooking their rations, for the voyage of ninety miles in open boats. At 3 o'clock A.M. the 30th Decr after the tents were struck and stowed away in the boats, some of the men in pure wantonness set fire to the palmetto houses that had been erected over the tents as protection against the sun's rays. Immediately the flames spread in all directions, blazing, crackling, and snapping amongst the dry stuff with terrific violence. Some apprehension was felt lest the fire should extend to the Store-house and magazine, which were made of the same light material; but fortunately the flames were quelled after great exertions.

By daylight we were all aboard, and under way, bidding adieu to *Fort Ann;* the fort at the Haulover being so called by Lt. Irwin, the architect and builder, who named it, as he said, after the prettiest girl in Pennsylvania. We stopped for a few minutes at

Camp Hernandez, whence Capt. Porter was ordered back with his company by Gen. Hernandez to remain in command at the Haul-over during the winter campaign.[9]

We continued all day quietly gliding down Indian river, whose placid surface had remained unbroken for so many ages, by any other voyagers than the beautiful and timid duck, the dignified and unwieldy pelican, and occasionally an Indian in his light canoe. In whose undisturbed and transparent waters the fishes had increased and multiplied, meeting no death but nature's. The thickly wooded shores, wrapt in silence and solitude, displayed to the view all the various shades of colouring which the imagination could fancy; and many green and sunny islands, clothed in gay verdure, and diversified by the richest and most luxuriant foliage in this southern clime, exhibited much of the picturesque, as we floated past with noiseless progress before a gentle and favoring breeze. The shades of evening gathered around us; but as we had a fair wind behind, and a bright sky above us, we did not check our career, but continued all night under easy sail.

Nothing occurred to disturb the quiet of the night, except the wolves in the neighbouring forest responding howl with howl as they threatened one another. At one time the reflection on the heavens of a distant Indian fire in the woods served to beguile a few minutes of admiration, as the contrast between the part of the sky which was illumined, and that in the shade, was exceedingly beautiful.

At 4 o'clock in the afternoon of the 31st Decr we reached *Indian river Inlet;* distant 90 miles from the Haulover; and again feasted our eyes upon the broad Atlantic spread out before us in all its witching sublimity. We there found Lt. Powell and his command encamped near the sea-beach, waiting the arrival of his supplies from St. Augustine. With any other than disagreeable sensations we picked ourselves out from the chaotic mass of living and inanimate matter which crowded our open boats; amidst which we had been for so many successive hours stowed in an almost incredible small space; the boats being filled to the gunnels with baggage and provisions, and twenty men added to each, to fill up the chinks.

Journey into Wilderness

We pitched our tents upon the white sand of the sea-shore, and once more I experienced perfect happiness; a happiness arising from the pleasurable associations so intimately connected in my mind with such localities. To one born and bred upon a sea-coast, accustomed from earliest infancy to the ocean view, I can conceive no punishment so productive of misery as a banishment from its fascinating vicinity; no pleasure so perfect as a return to its familiar scenery, rendered doubly beautiful by the privation, as—

"Blessings brighten when they take their flight."

How often when dragging out a weary existence in some remote and gloomy inland forest, or even when reposing upon the "flower enamell'd margin" of some limpid brook or babbling stream, with the rich and glowing beauties of the scenery heightened by the soft and aromatic perfume which pervaded the air, have I felt in full force Mrs. Hemans'[10] "Song of a Greek Islander in Exile";

Where is the Sea, I languish here;
Where is my own blue Sea,
With all its barks of fleet career,
And flags and breezes free;
I miss the voice of waves,
The first which woke my childhood's glee;
The measured chime, the thundering burst,
Where is my own blue Sea?
Where is my own blue Sea?

Oh! rich your myrtle's breath may rise,
Soft, soft, your winds may be;
Yet my sick heart within me dies—
Where is my own blue sea?
I hear the sheperd's mountain flute,
I hear the whispering tree,
The echoes of my soul are mute—
Where is my own blue Sea?
Where is my own blue Sea?

Never did sweeter sleep ever visit my wearied eyelids than I

174

enjoyed while at this sandy encampment, hushed as I was by "sea blasts wild," and the music of the waves dashing their foam against the beach.

At reveille next morning, New Year's day, I was up, and with several of my brother officers proceeded immediately to the beach for a bath. Though it would have been esteemed inconsiderate, and rather unseasonable in a more northern latitude to undress by the sea-side on the 1st January, for the purpose of bathing as a mere matter of choice; yet with the thermometer at 80°, we did not apprehend much danger from taking cold; indeed, it was particularly luxurious, and would have been much more so if the moschetoes [mosquitoes] and sand-flies had been less sociable, during the process of dressing ourselves.[11] After breakfast the morning was devoted to a stroll along the beach.

What scenes and events, recalled from history, or conjured up in fancy's mould, brought to view by a walk along those lonely shores. What sufferings had this very beach at different periods been witness to! Strewed on every side were visible the remains of unfortunate vessels; whose crews had only escaped the dangers of the boiling deep to meet on this inhospitable land a more dreadful fate from the wily and blood-thirsty Indian, who, a stranger to every feeling of humanity and compassion, plunged the deadly steel into the bosoms of his supplicating victims, while with vain entreaties they pierced the air with agonizing cries for mercy. How often, in times long past, on these very shores, whose stillness was now only broken by the "waves wild moan," have those foes to mankind, the cold-blooded Buccaneers, held their noisy and obscene revelries. Many a bitter tear has been shed by distant relatives at the prolonged absence and unknown fate of a husband or son; a lover or brother; whose whitened bones now lie there concealed by a little sand; their only requiem the wild voices of the stormy winds.

CHAPTER XXV

*O*n the morning of the 2nd Janry 1838 we moved over to the west side of Indian river; to a spot four miles south of the Inlet, designated as "the bluff," *par excellence;* being the highest point of land on the whole river though only about ten or fifteen feet above the water. We there established ourselves; first by pitching our tents on a narrow esplanade between the river and the bluff, which rises perpendicularly behind us; next by erecting a block-house upon the top of the bluff. Being pretty much like all other block-houses in Florida, except that this one was built of palmetto logs, we deemed it worthy the title of fort, and the distinction of a name; it was therefore dubbed *Fort Pierce,* after our worthy commander.[1] My tent was located with its front but a few feet from the water edge, and but a few inches above the river's surface. Here was a luxury! To lie upon my blanket, and have the water constantly in view, and almost within reach of my hand. The spot upon which we were encamped bore traces of having not long previous been the site of an Indian camp; and at a point jutting into the river, a few hundred yards south of us, were still left standing the poles and palmetto leaves of some of their lodges. A dense forest, in which the palmetto tree held a conspicuous place, bounded the view immediately in our rear. The formation of the ground adjoining the bluff presented strong indications of its having been thrown up in a regular manner of a fortification; but when, or by whom made, will probably forever remain a secret; the antiquity only of its date made known by the enormous trees growing out of the embankments and entrenchments, which were easily to be distinguished.[2] It may possibly have been the retreat in olden times of the Buccaneers; for, to quote the words of history, "The coast of Florida was long the favorite resort, and her bays and inlets, but little known to the

176

rest of the world, long continued to be the safe retreat of that bold, desperate, and reckless race of beings, who, during the seventeenth century, so much infested the Southern Seas. It was from this coast that they drew their main supplies; and when driven from the ocean, it was here in these unknown regions that they sought safety. And according to tradition, it was to the Spanish forts and settlements along the coast, that they carried much of the blood-stained wealth, which they had gathered by piracy from the four corners of the earth." Or perchance it is the work of the adventurous Spaniards; whose traces are to be found at almost every step in Florida, where two hundred years ago they made their settlements.

Inadequate are words to express the quantity and quality of the fish that abounded in those waters. In one hour one may take as many *Bonetas, Redfish, Groupers, Sheephead, Bass, Trout,* and myriads of other kinds, unknown elsewhere, of the finest flavour, and of large dimensions, generally from two to three feet in length, as will feast a regiment. The finest kind of Sheephead we very soon discarded from our mess tables as noisome things, in comparison with the other fish caught there, and which are peculiar to these latitudes. As for the oysters; six are a comfortable meal for one person, indeed, without exaggeration, the greatest abundance may be easily obtained, which after removal from the shell, measure six or seven inches in length, and two or three inches in breadth. A whole Army might be subsisted here upon the produce of this river, if fish diet agreed with them, and not fear an exhaustion of supplies. We all of us began to grow so fat upon this good living, that we were afraid unless something turned up very soon to produce a change in our felicitous mode of life, that we should have had to borrow from our neighbours, the Indians their style of dress, for our clothes every day became tighter.

A few days after settling on our new ground, Lt. Powell followed us with his command, and encamped a few hundred yards distant on the river shore. He, however, remained but a day or two, when he again pulled up stakes, and embarked his detachment to prosecute the object of his expedition. From here, he was to proceed first to explore the St. Lucie, one of the tributary streams of Indian river twenty miles south of our position. His boats having proved insufficient for the comfortable accommodation of his whole party, the Washington Volunteers were left with us.

Soon after the departure of Powell, Gen. Hernandez and mounted force arrived; having threaded their way with difficulty through an unknown and never before visited tract of country. They, however, had the advantage of carrying but little baggage; only what could be packed upon the backs of mules.

In consequence of this accession to our numbers, and of the non-arrival of the vessel expected from St. Augustine with forage for the horses; orders were issued for part of the 1st Artillery to return to the Haulover in the Mackinaw boats, and bring back with all possible despatch a supply of horse food. Consequently, on the 8th Janry Col. Pierce and the greater part of his regiment departed on their voyage up Indian river; Major Kirby remaining in command of that part of the Regt. which was left, to take care of camp, and defend the sick.

On the 14th Janry our remote and quiet little post presented quite a scene of bustle; occasioned by the arrival of Gen. Jesup and Staff, accompanied by part of the 2d Dragoons under the command of Col. Twiggs,[3] amounting to four hundred men, and about six hundred mounted volunteers from Alabama and Tennessee. They had left a part of their detachment encamped about thirty miles from us in the interior, at a place called Camp Lloyd;[4] and had come seeking this post through the wilderness in quest of provisions for themselves and horses; and where Gen. Jesup concluded to remain and recruit his troops on the fine oysters and other fish until Gen. Eustis with his division should arrive at Camp Lloyd. The general had with him as guide an Indian recently captured personally by Lt. Searle[5] of his staff. They had passed many heavy trails, which were recent and all tending to the south. The Indians were therefore thought to be in force in that direction, and as the whole of that part of Florida was represented by our Indian guides as uninhabitable, except a very nar-

LAKE OKEECHOBEE
AND
THE EAST COAST

REPRODUCED FROM THE
MACKAY-BLAKE MAP
1840

MOTTE'S ITINERARY · · · ·

row strip of land between the Atlantic ocean, and the *Okechobee* lake, our troops were expecting soon to give a very good account of the enemy, it being impossible for them to escape unobserved; or retreat much farther south, without being stopped by the water.

By the arrival of Capt. H. [Harvey] Brown we first learnt the particulars of a disastrous victory, which the division under Col. Taylor had gained over the Indians,—disastrous, inasmuch as he lost five officers, twenty five privates killed, and over a hundred wounded.

It seemed that on the evening of the 24th Decr, Col. Taylor captured an Indian on the Kissimmee river, from whom he learnt that *Alligator* with all the war spirits of the Seminoles, and *Sam Jones* or *Abiaka,* with a hundred and seventy five Mickasukies were encamped not many miles distant on the east side of the Kissimmee, and near the Lake *O-ke-cho-bee.* The Colonel consequently under the reluctant guidance of the captured Indian, who had no taste for being hung, went in search of the enemy; and after passing several cypress swamps and dense hammocks, reached the vicinity of their encampment on Christmas morning.[6]

The Indians in expectation of an attack, had selected one of the most difficult places to approach in Florida; having a swamp nearly a mile wide in front, which was unpassable for horses, and almost for foot. They had also cleared away the palmetto from before the hammock in which they were stationed within rifle range of the skirts; and as the Army charged, received them with a deadly fire, which brought nearly one tenth to the ground.[7] Notwithstanding the warm and destructive fire which was kept up, the sixth and part of the fourth Infantry pressed forward; gained the hammock; and after fighting severely for more than an hour, completely routed the enemy;[8] who were driven in every direction; leaving the field with ten of their number dead upon it, in possession of our troops, and innumerable traces of blood where they had dragged others off.[9]

The sixth Infantry suffered most severely. It lost its Lt. Col. A. R. Thompson,[10]—Adjutant J. P. Center,[11]—Capt. Van Swearingen,[12]—and 1st Lt. F. J. Brooke,[13]—its Sergt. Major, and nineteen rank and file. It had wounded Capt. G. Andrews,[14]—Lt. W. H. T. Walker,[15] and seventy six rank and file. It must have been a hard contested struggle, in which every officer of four companies of one regiment, including the orderly sergeants, were either killed or wounded, while its commander and staff fell where they fought, in the hottest of the action.[16]

The Missouri Volunteers, who were with Col. Taylor, met with a serious loss in the death of their commander, Col. Gentry.[17] He fell mortally wounded at the head of his regiment—while gallantly encouraging his men to the charge.

Thus did our gallant little army once more prove its intrepidity and invincibility, though at so great a sacrifice; but I trust not greater than was counterbalanced by the advantageous results that no doubt accrued from this victory.[18] And it only remained for Congress to show a nation's gratitude by providing for the families of those martyrs in their common country's cause.[19]

CHAPTER XXVI

On the 15th Janry the boats returned from the Haul-over. And on the morning of the 16th our camp was thrown into a state of excitement, by the sudden return of Lt. Powell's detachment;[1] which had encountered the enemy in force the day previous, near the head of the Jupiter river, and been repulsed with severe loss, having five killed and twenty two wounded. Among the former was their Surgeon Dr. Leitner, which rendered it necessary for them to hasten back with all speed to this post, that the wounded might receive proper surgical attendance. Thus the work went bravely on.

A proof of the extremity to which they were reduced in the retreat to their boats, was the circumstance of their leaving their dead on the battle ground. Every officer of the party was wounded except Mr. Johnson, formerly of the Army, and acting adjutant to the detachment, who had seven balls through different parts of his clothes; two passing through his hat. Lt. Fowler of the Army who commanded the company of 1st Artillery, on duty with the detachment, by whose gallant conduct in covering the retreat of the sailors, the whole command was saved from total annihilation,—was wounded twice; as also were Midshipmen McArthur and Harrison.

The account of the affair was, that finding a fresh trail near the head waters of Jupiter river, they followed it up; and suddenly came upon a large herd of cattle and horses; amongst which they captured a squaw. From this woman they ascertained that several parties of Indians were encamped in the neighborhood; and taking her as guide, they determined to go in search of them. After marching five miles, they struck a large beaten trail at the head of a cypress swamp, and at the same instant heard the war-whoop raised before them. Lt. Powell having his small party extended in line, and divided into three divisions, immediately charged across the swamp. At the first fire Harrison was shot down; and his division being left without an officer, became confused. Notwithstanding, the enemy were driven seven or eight hundred yards to the margin of a larger swamp; where they made a more determined resistance. Here McArthur was badly wounded, at the head of his division, cheering his men on; and Dr. Leitner at the same time received a mortal wound. The men falling fast; and evening closing in; with no prospect of being able to carry to the boats more wounded than they already had, the order was given to retire. The sailors, most of whom were raw undisciplined hands, instead of firm veterans of the Navy, immediately broke and fled in utter confusion. The handful of regular troops having more confidence in each other, the effect of discipline, stood steady; and by closing the rear and keeping up a judicious fire, covered the retreating sailors. And thus to their courageous conduct, and that of the officers, was the whole command saved from being cut to pieces; and mainly indebted for the comparative security in which they regained the boats. After Lt. Fowler was shot down, Mr. Johnson took command of the regulars; and the coolness, courage, and judgement he displayed at the most critical and trying emergency was the theme of praise with every one who beheld him. He was the last to retreat; and the last to embark; and through his disinterested zeal to see every man safely aboard, was himself nearly left behind to the tender mercy of his savage foes; it being half past seven o'clock at night, and the darkness causing him to be unobserved upon the shore by those in the boats. The captured squaw was brought off, being closely guarded during the fight; which lasted from 4 o'clock in the afternoon until past seven.

The cause of the defeat was ascribed to their meeting a larger force than was anticipated;[2] so large as to cover their flanks; their own force amounting to only eighty men, Midshipman Murphy, with part of his division being absent at the time on detached service, and twenty three men having been left with the boats. Unfortunately, in the darkness and confusion, one of the boats was left behind with all its contents; among which unfortunately was a keg of powder.[3]

At the time Dr. Leitner was shot down, his hospital Steward hastened to his assistance; and immediately shared a similar fate. It was said that Leitner was not quite dead when last seen; but requested those who came to bear him off, to look to their own safety, and not to regard him, declaring that he was mortally wounded, and could not live long; and that it would therefore be unnecessary for his friends to encumber themselves with him. Poor Leitner! he was my friend and fellow-student, [we] having pursued our professional studies together in the same office in Charleston, under the auspices of Dr. J. E. Holbrook. A German by birth, he had made Charleston his place of residence for the previous seven years. He was a man of rare ability, and singular modesty; excelling in the characteristics of the German scholar, and enthusiastically devoted to the sciences; of which botany was his favorite branch. Zealous in acquiring knowledge pertaining to natural science, he had devoted himself for the last three or four years of his life to exploring the unknown regions in the southern portions of Florida; which he found to be fertile in objects of interest to the naturalist. Anxious to pursue his researches, and denied the privilege of doing so alone, by the hostility of the natives, he had attached himself to this expedition in the capacity of acting surgeon; as he had done to a similar one under Lt. Powell the year previous; in which he proved himself very useful as a guide through this "terra incognita." He had but a short time before issued a prospectus for publishing the results of his labours in that section of Florida; of which he alone of all scientific individuals was capable; when death thus suddenly terminated his career of usefulness; depriving science of one of her most indefatigable votaries; and mankind of the benefits of his laborious researches.

At a later period to this when we were encamped near the scene of Leitner's death, I spared no pains, and missed no opportunity of ascertaining every thing relative to his probable fate. The Indians who were engaged in the conflict which proved fatal to him having become our prisoners, I sought all occasions to learn from them what had become of my friend, for his body could never be found, nor any trace of it. They always attempted to evade the enquiry by giving some absurd answer, and generally contradictory at different times. At first they informed us that he was captured alive tho severely wounded by the Indians, who ascertaining that he was a Surgeon, determined to save his life that they might profit by his professional services. That with this intention, they endeavoured to make his situation as comfortable as possible; and had carried him many miles into the interior on a litter, when one day an Indian warrior who had lost his brother in one of the battles, rushed upon him with a yell, and plunged his knife into his heart.

Some of the Indians told a different story. They said that six days after the fight, a couple of Indians met him walking upon the bank of the river in the vicinity of the battle-field and shot him dead on the spot. Alas! what a fate, if this story be true; but what a relief must death have been to him, in his abandoned situation, suffering from wounds and starvation, and no prospect of relief in any other way but from death.

Which of these accounts deserves most credit, if either does, is very problematical. The Indians being such proverbial liars, I doubt if the real ultimate fate of poor Leitner will ever become known to the whites authentically.[4]

CHAPTER XXVII

*T*he whole of the 16th Janry was occupied by Dr. [Samuel G. I.] DeCamp and myself in attending to the wounded of Powell's command; and that night Gen. Jesup issued orders for the mounted force to proceed immediately to Jupiter river, the late scene of Powell's fight, there to seek and give battle to the enemy. Dr. DeCamp having become almost worn out by his recent long march with the 2d Dragoons from Jefferson Barracks in Missouri,[1] seemed to require some little respite from the fatigues of active service, and being myself anxious to proceed where more stirring service than that of a post afforded, I willingly exchanged places with him, he remaining at Fort Pierce, while I proceeded with the Dragoons into the field.

Thus it was that on the morning of the 17th Janry, at daylight, I again found myself in the saddle, armed and equipped once more for land service, as I then thought, but which turned out to be water service with a vengeance, and of a much severer nature than boating had been.

We pursued a westerly course; and after emerging from the dense hammock which borders upon the river, we passed through a narrow strip of pine barren, and then entered upon the famous and undefined Al-pa-ti-o-kee Swamp.[2] A watery region indeed! Behind us arose the forest of pine, like a dark wall; while before and on either side of us, the scene presented to our view was one unbroken extent of water and morass; like that of a boundless rice-field when inundated. No obstruction offered itself to the eye as it wandered o'er the interminable, dreary waste of waters, through which our course lay, except the tops of a tall rank grass, about five feet or upwards in height; and which harmonized well with the desolate aspect of the surrounding region, exhibiting a picture of universal desolation. The water which covered this immense grassy savannah was in depth from half-leg to saddle-girth, and extended far beyond the horizon all around. We floundered along our Stygian way, where never a bird sings, or even a cricket chirps, but where the complete silence which ever reigned was first broken by the splashing of our horses; no shady wood afforded its refreshing shelter from the unrepelled heat of a glaring and summer-like sun; not a breath of wind stirred the rank grass. At intervals of several miles, we would pass small clusters of trees, ornamentally disposed in clumps and groves, principally palmetto, grouped together upon slightly elevated spots, forming so many verdant islands in this submerged prairie, and which afforded a pleasing relief to the immense expanse of water. These islands were the only spots approximating to dryness in the whole surrounding country; and to which alone we could look amid this wide watery waste for a resting place at night. In the sketch of an Indian mound near Fort Taylor may be seen one of these clumps of trees, and by imagining the ground in that sketch covered with water, some idea may be formed of the appearance of the Alpatioka swamp.

Nothing occurred to vary the monotony of our day's dreary march, except the shooting of a Dragoon's horse, which was done in consequence of the poor beast having broken his leg while endeavouring to extricate himself from the mire.

On the approach of evening, we began to feel some anxiety to discover a place sufficiently free from water—from wet was impossible—upon which to spread our blankets; and where our jaded horses might procure the rest of which they stood in so much need, after such laborious and fatiguing exertions. With great difficulty we at last found an island large enough to accommodate the whole party; and there we rested our aching bones for the night.

This great accumulation of water is no doubt caused by the overflowing of all the neighbouring streams; and forms an inexhaustible reservoir for all the streams in this part of Florida. It is considered the real source of the St. Johns river.

At daylight the next morning we were again in the saddle;

and wending our amphibious way o'er this trackless wild. In the afternoon we reached *Camp Lloyd*, at the head of the St. Johns, and not many miles from the scene of Col. Taylor's late battle. Here we found Gen. Eustis; who had arrived a day or two previous, with ten companies of the 3d and the 4th Artillery, and a large train of ambulances and baggage wagons; having accomplished a march of two hundred miles through the wilderness, in which they had to be constantly cutting roads through dismal swamps, and almost impenetrable hammocks, and bridging streams for the passage of the wagons; all the while exposed to the scorching beams of a tropical sun, or drenching torrents of rain.[3]

On the 19th at 1 o'clock P.M. the whole of our united force, except a guard left to garrison the stockade built at Fort Lloyd, took up the line of march south; in the direction of Lt. Powell's battle ground, where we expected to meet the enemy.[4] Our force consisted of six hundred Dragoons; four hundred Artillery; and about five hundred Tennessee and Alabama Volunteers. We proceeded only a few miles the first day and encamped for the night.

The dawn of the 20th found us in marching array; the order of march being as follows. The Artillery, wagons, and pack-mules proceeded in column in the centre; the Dragoons in single file at a hundred yards distance on the right flank, the volunteers at the same distance on the left flank, thus forming three columns. Our course this day lay through a scattering growth of dwarf pine, and under-brush of saw-palmetto; and we encamped at night in the vicinity of a marshy bog,—partly in it. Our fatigue, however, rendered us indifferent as to where we lay our wearied limbs, and acheing heads; the foulest ditch would have proved a bed of hops. In the course of the night we were joined by thirty five Delaware Indians; volunteers to Florida; who had been sent to overtake us from Col. Taylor's division; and who came up with us while we were encamped.

Long before daylight on the following morning, we were all astir in the Dragoon part of the camp. Our baggage being conveyed on pack-mules, instead of wagons as with the Artillery, it required more time to fold the tents and fasten them to the pack-saddles; which was done while we are [were] taking by fire-light our early breakfast of hot coffee and hard biscuit. In a few minutes the bugle sounded to horse; and soon nothing remained on the spot but the embers of our numerous fires; where but a short time before the hum of hundreds filled the air.

The country through which we passed this day might be considered one continued swamp; being very low and wet, or more properly speaking, a succession of cypress swamps and saw-grass ponds, our men on foot were frequently wading nearly to their middle, it being absolutely necessary to take to the water, which offered generally a firm sandy bottom, to avoid the dense growth of scrub, and saw-palmetto on the comparatively dry flats, in penetrating which we would have had to encounter great labour. The interest of our route was occasionally varied, and the fatigue of our footmen lightened, by passing through low, wet flats of scattering dwarf-pines, interspersed with wet, grassy plains, and diversified with saw-palmetto scrubs, and cabbage-hammocks. The saw-palmetto proved very effective in tearing our horses' legs, and reducing our nether garments to tatters. The former had to groan and bear it; the latter were patched up with old corn bags, rendering our appearance very variegated and picturesque.

We did not make a full day's march; being stopped earlier than usual by a stream, which required bridging before farther progress could be made. We encamped therefore about noon, on the edge of a hammock bordering the stream.

The first care after halting on a march was to take off our arms and accoutrements, and carefully place them so that each man could find his equipments instantly. The next, if Dragoons, was to attend to unpacking the mules, unsaddling the horses, and pitching the tents, while others were gathering wood for the fires. Soon the cheerful blaze would crackle in all directions, and around each fire might be seen groups of men, cracking their jokes, and speculating on the probability of soon coming up with the enemy. On some occasions while thus sociably employed, the sharp crack of a rifle will be heard, followed by a peculiarily uncomfortable sound produced by the pinging of a ball as it strikes amongst the men. "The Indians, the Indians," is the cry; and all start to their feet and seize their arms. The long roll is beat, and everyone repairs to his post. It probably turns out to be only some wary savage, who has crawled within rifle range, and sent his deadly messenger into the very heart of camp. The sentinels are questioned; "Did you hear a noise, or see anything?" "No, your honour, I hav'nt heard a pin drop." Shortly the excitement ceases; all resume their occupation, taking care not to stand in the glare of the camp fire. Meanwhile, the officers are patiently awaiting for their suppers, which the attendants are preparing; and wile away the time by criticising the last engagement; consigning Government to *Old Nick* for its want of gratitude; and coming most complacently to the conclusion, that we are a most unfortunate, and ill-used set, to be compelled to waste the best of our days in a wilderness, and perchance fall in a nameless engagement with a worse than nameless enemy.

The *coup-d'oeil*[5] presented by an army encamped for the night is extremely picturesque. Frequently have I deserted my blanket to wander through the tented avenues and canvass streets when midnight has thrown its deep shadows o'er the sward, and the sounds of camp are all hushed; when nothing is heard but the piping of the wind through the branches of the trees. On one side was seen a long line of horses fastened to ropes stretched from tree to tree, and extending from one extremity of camp to the other. In another direction might be seen innumerable wagons drawn up in solid squares; their white and clean looking tops glancing in the light of the camp fires, which every where threw up a flickering blaze. All around are the temporary abodes of hundreds of human beings; here today; gone tomorrow.

On the next morning at dawn we crossed the stream, the corps of Pioneers under the command of Lt. R. Anderson[6] having thrown a bridge over it during the night previous. We proceeded through the same uninteresting kind of country; our march being but a repetition of yesterday's; with the exception that the ponds seemed to increase in numbers, and magnitude, and depth, and the dry land to become scarcer, as we proceeded south. We continued wading in water until evening; when coming to an extensive swamp, part of the Al-pa-ti-o-kee, forming the head waters of the St. Lucie river,—through which it would be necessary to pass,— we deferred this anticipated pleasure until next morning, and encamped for the night.

In the course of this day's march I enjoyed a fine opportunity of witnessing the agility of a deer. While marching along in the usual order, one of these animals, who was asleep in the bushes between the line of Artillery and that of the Dragoons, suddenly started up when the centre of the column was abreast of it. At first it ran from us towards the Artillery; then back to our line; and seeing no outlet, finally became desperate, and making a charge at our line of Dragoons as we slowly followed one another in single file, our horses' heads touching the tails of those preceeding, made one flying leap, and cleared a Dragoon's horse which was a short distance from mine. Many a finger tingled to pull trigger in behalf of a venison supper, but orders were peremptory that on no account should a shot be fired.

The next day we crossed the head waters of the St. Lucie river; floundering through mud and water for a mile and a half up to our saddle flaps in depth. On emerging from this swamp on the south side, we came upon the site of an extensive Indian camp, which presented signs of having been recently abandoned. As we proceeded we also observed numerous well-beaten Indian trails; all tending south. Our route all this day lay through submerged scrub flats, and saw-palmetto swells, interspersed with cypress and bay-ponds. These ponds generally exhibited in their centre picturesque clumps of cypress trees and willows, ornamentally clothed with long hanging moss, gracefully and fantastically disposed in festoons, forming fairy looking islets reposing in verdant loveliness on the bosom of the water, and so nearly level with it, as to appear floating upon its shining surface; fit abodes for the genii of these unearthly regions, which come nearest the description of that fabulous place, that we read of, which was neither land, water, nor air. Indeed, the whole country, since leaving Fort Pierce, had been one unbroken extent of water and morass; a very little land; much saw-palmetto; and more snakes, mosquitoes, and other venomous *"critters"* than one can shake a stick at. Nothing, however, can be imagined more lovely and picturesque than the thousand little isolated spots, scattered in all directions over the surface of this immense sheet of water, which seemed like a placid inland sea shining under a bright sun. Every possible variety of shape, colour, contour, and size were exhibited in the arrangement of the trees and moss upon these islets, which, reflected from the limpid and sunny depths of the transparent water over-shadowed by them, brought home to the imagination all the enchanting visions of Oriental description. As we threaded this maze of countless islets, studding the unbroken surface of water in loneliness and silence amid all the wild romance of nature;— far secluded from the haunts of civilized man and marked only by the characteristics of wildest desolation, augmented by the entire ignorance which envelopes these regions; upon which, how-ever, a landscape painter would delight to dwell; we felt the most intense admiration, and gazed with a mingled emotion of delight and awe.

CHAPTER XXVIII

*O*n the night of the 23d we encamped in the midst of high saw-palmetto, on the edge of a pond; and sent up a few signal rockets; to the great consternation of all the horses in camp. They were—I mean the rockets—unanswered by Col. Taylor, for whom they were intended; and who was proceeding south, farther west, and along the edge of the *O-kee-cho-bee* lake. This *O-kee-cho-bee* is a sheet of water of immense extent, lying directly across the promontory of Florida, from about thirty miles of Fort Pierce to within nearly the same distance of Charlotte harbour on the west side of Florida. It contains several large islands, on which the families of the Indians were supposed to be concealed. It was their strong-hold, and last resort. This is that ocean-like lake, laid down on all the maps as Lake Macaco,[1] and which for a long while had been thought entirely fabulous in existence.

On the 24th we renewed our march, as usual, at daylight; and continued to encounter the same obstacles we had to overcome for the previous week; cutting roads through dense hammocks; passing innumerable cypress swamps, and pine flats, interspersed with an almost impassable growth of saw-palmetto; and wading in water nearly up to the men's waists; many of whom were barefooted, and their clothes torn off, and flesh badly lacerated by the saw-palmetto.

About 12 o'clock word was brought from Capt. [William M.] Fulton, who was four miles in advance with Lt. R. Parker[2] and his company of Dragoons, which formed the advanced guard, that the enemy were strongly posted in a dense hammock; and had fired upon his leading files, when about to enter, and had wounded one of the horses. Gen. Jesup immediately gave orders for the Dragoons and volunteers to move forward with all speed, and attack the enemy. We were not slow in obeying; and soon

the palmetto bushes and scrub were making a tremendous cracking, as
—*"rushed our steeds to battle driven."*

We quickly arrived in sight of the hammock where the Indians
had posted themselves, and were awaiting us. In front was an
almost impassable cypress slough, nearly half a mile wide; in
passing through which we were up to our saddle girths in mud
and water, our horses constantly stumbling over the cypress knees.[3]

The disposition for battle was immediately made;[4] the Dragoons
dismounting, and leaving their horses in the care of one man to
every seven horses, charged the hammock in gallant style. Then
came the terrific Indian war-whoop; with a running accompaniment of sharp rifle shots; "rending heaven's conclave." The Artillery soon came up, and joined in the conflict; some entering the
hammock, which was so thick a man could not see two feet ahead
of him; while others stood by the field artillery [a six pounder]
and howitzer at the edge of the hammock, which not being able
to enter, did effective service by throwing grape and shells into
the thickest of the bushes. Congreve rockets[5] also contributed
their terrible whizzing toward increasing the stunning uproar
that raged on all sides. The Indians yelled and shrieked; the
rifles cracked, and their balls whistled; the musketry rattled; the
congreve rockets whizzed; the artillery bellowed; the shells burst;
and take it all in all there was created no small racket for awhile.

On gaining the centre of the hammock, we found a rapid and
deep stream flowing between us and the Indians, who were deliver-
ing a deadly fire from behind trees on the opposite bank. The
stream was about thirty yards in width;[6] nothing daunted by
this obstacle, our men hesitated not a moment, but plunged into
the swift torrent, and crossed in the face of a shower of balls which
whistled about their ears. The stream proved deeper than was
anticipated; and many could only reach the opposite side by
swimming. Such unexpected conduct in direct opposition to their
own mode of proceedure so astonished the savages, that they immediately *"absquatulated."* And well it was for our men that
they did so, their guns being useless without ammunition, which

The Journal

had been spoiled by the water, while they were swimming the stream.

When charging the hammock, some of the Tennessee Volunteers thought it very foolish to expose their valuable lives against a pack of savages, so held back at a respectable distance. This so enraged Gen. Jesup, that seizing a pistol in hand he dismounted from his horse and ordered them to follow him immediately. Saying this, he rushed forward into the hammock; and on reaching the edge of the stream, stopped and looked around to ascertain if he had been obeyed. He found himself alone; and at the same instant a ball struck him in the face, breaking his spectacles, and laying open the left cheek just below the eye. He picked up the pieces of broken spectacles and retired; his high opinion of the efficiency of volunteers, which had been previously exhalted, very much lowered.[7]

As soon as we gained the opposite side of the stream, which was called *Locha-Hatchee,* the enemy scattered up and down the hammock in the greatest alarm; and ceasing their yells soon disappeared altogether.

The number of Indians engaged were estimated from two to three hundred warriors and there were with them probably as many negroes; but situated as they were in an almost impregnable position, they ought to have held it against five times that force.

Our loss was seven killed, and thirty wounded; many of whom afterwards died from the severity of their wounds. That of the enemy could not be ascertained from the density of the bushes. We found one warrior shot through the head; but it might be presumed that they carried off and concealed their dead, according to their custom.

All the regular troops behaved as they always do, with the most consummate daring and courage. It is to be regretted that the same cannot be said of the volunteers who were engaged. They, however, behaved as volunteers have generally done, being entirely devoid of discipline, and not having confidence in one another, and therefore acted consistently. It was but another proof of the inefficiency of that description of troops.

Journey into Wilderness

When will Congress awake to the worse than useless squandering of the public money in the employment of these useless and unwieldy hordes of unorganized militia! The country has suffered often enough by the inefficiency and undisciplined volunteers, to say nothing of the great and useless expense attending the support of them for only short periods. In action they have seldom done anything. In Col. Taylor's battle, it was reported on good authority, that the volunteers fled the field after the first fire; leaving their commander to perish alone, while the Regulars manfully stood the brunt of the fight, and beat the enemy though unsupported, and consequently suffering great loss. Some of the volunteers with whom I have come in contact in the field have also invariably refused to do any of the labour even, incident to a campaign; always exclaiming "they did not come to work, but to fight"; and when called upon to fight, declaring that their lives were too valuable to be exposed to the contingencies of a contest with savages. In the present instance their conduct from want of discipline met its reward. They suffered severely, from the confusion into which they were thrown; having five of their number killed, and twenty three wounded; many of whom died soon after. On all occasions, experience has shown, the regular troops to have been a far more economical force than the militia. And as it is well known from constant observation that regular troops always suffer less from the various hardships of a campaign; objections might be made to the employment of militia for the emergencies of military service, both on the score of economy and of humanity. There can be do doubt that our militia are brave individually, but the difficulty with them is the want of those habits of subordination, implicit obedience, and perfect method, which none but regular troops can acquire, and which are all important for efficiency in the duties and labours of the camp and field. It is by regular discipline only, and the circumspection and system, which results from it, that any safeguard against disease also can be expected among the soldiery. Witness the greater misery, and waste of life, among the volunteers who were sent to Florida, than among the regular troops; a very small part of those volunteers who never

The Journal

lived to return to their homes fell under the stroke of an enemy.

On emerging into the open pine woods on the south side of the hammock, we found ourselves in the midst of the enemy's camp; where many of them had left their packs and other chattels. In the vicinity we came across the remains of one of Lt. Powell's sailors, lying as he fell, with a bullet hole through his skull, which was divested of its scalp. This proved that we were on Powell's battle ground, and had been engaged with the Indians by whom he was defeated. Lts. Davidson and Anderson in their zeal to overtake the retreating enemy, advanced several miles beyond the hammock; and in consequence of their prolonged absence, we felt apprehensive for a time that they were among the slain.

We recrossed the *Locha-Hatchee* to the north side; and encamped upon the battle field. Many of the soldiery were employed in collecting the killed and wounded; and bringing them to the foot of a spreading oak, beneath whose widely-flung branches were strewn a score of dead and dying. There before us lay death in his most horrible forms; bodies pierced with ghastly wounds, and locks begrimed with gore. In one direction, leaning against a tree, there reclined a soldier of the Artillery; his face pale, and o'erspread with an expression of anguish; one hand pressed to his side, from which the blood slowly oozed. In another direction lay stretched upon the ground, with face turned upwards, and glazed eyes wide open, one whose marble cheek too plainly told that the rifle ball which had entered his temple had truly done its mission;—that he "slept a sleep that knows no waking." In one spot sat a party of wounded upon the ground, a surgeon binding up their bleeding wounds, with hasty but skilful hands; a little farther off, reclined one upon a cloak; his closed eyes, and calm smiling expression of features like that of a sleeping man, indicated an exemption from pain; true, his sufferings were over; he had gone to that place where physical pain is unknown.

That night as I sank tired and exhausted upon my saddle, which served for a pillow, my eyes were long kept from sleep, by reflecting upon the occurrences of the day.

After such events as the day brought forth, it was but natural

197

that distant friends, and their social hearth, should recur to our minds; that we should compare their life of quiet and repose, of domestic comfort and happiness, with the erratic one we had; one of constant privations and dangers; in which we had no right to feel the assurance of existence from one moment to another. Such thoughts were dissipated after a night of refreshing sleep; and the dawn found us as ready as ever for new trials and hardships.

The day after the battle we remained at our encampment, occupied in taking care of the wounded; preparing litters for their removal; and in the sad offices of interring the dead. Also in ranging the country round about with a portion of the Dragoons; and collecting the horses and cattle left by the enemy in the vicinity, of which we found a great many ponies, and over two hundred head of cattle. The day was also occupied in throwing a bridge over the *Locha-Hatchee,* and cutting a road through the hammock.[8] [Both of which were accomplished under the skill and supervision of Col. Gates.][9]

CHAPTER XXIX

*A*fter all, Florida is certainly the poorest country that ever two people quarrelled for. The climate in the first place is objectionable; for even in winter, while persons further north were freezing, we were melting with heat. In the next place, the larger portion of Florida is a poor, sandy country in the north; and in the southern portions nearly all wet prairies and swamp; healthy in winter but sickly in summer; and in the south even the Indians said they could not live a month without suffering, and in summer not at all. It is in fact a most hideous region to live in; a perfect paradise for Indians, alligators, serpents, frogs, and every other kind of loathsome reptile. The whole peninsula is alluvial, having been formed by successive encroachments on the Atlantic; and offers but feeble allurements to an agricultural population, the only land fit for cultivation being on the margin of the rivers, and inconsiderable as to extent, and barely sufficient to raise the ordinary subsistence for small families. The only resources are ranges for cattle, wrecking,[1] and the fisheries; the sea-beach is constantly enriched by the misfortunes of the enterprising;—which I in truth believe formed the strong attraction of the Indians to the country;—and the reservoirs of valuable fish are inexhaustible. Such can be the only allurements to emigrant adventurers. Then why not in the name of common sense let the Indians have kept it? We all know that there is a feeling implanted in the human breast which defies the hand of time to eradicate, the "amor patriae." The Hottentot will tell you that his country is the most desirable in the world; the Seminole said his country was "good"; and in that little word expressed more than could be said in the most elaborate speech.

Every day served but to convince us of their inflexible determination to fight or die in the land of their fathers. The latter they seemed as devoted to do as any martyr for his religion. And should we blame them? Their indomitable and long uncompromising spirit cannot but excite admiration in every breast. Unfortunately for us, the trade of war every day became more and more familiar to them, and they soon learnt that the white man was mortal as well as the red. They, throughout the whole war, conducted affairs with a bold and resolute hand. Every engagement proved their superiority in *bush-fighting;* and it is no disparagement to our troops to say, "the war was only a succession of disasters"; for Florida with its many advantages for Indian warfare, offered nothing but obstacles to the operations of our troops. True, the Indians yielded before our superior discipline; but not before they had left their bloody mark behind them. Florida has been the grave of many gallant soldiers, ornaments to their profession, and beyond price in social life. Alas! that a narrow policy should have converted that land for a time into a slaughter house! A heavy debt is due; oh! Florida, and the day of reckoning will some day come. When the pale face, and the red-man shall stand before their common God, to be judged each according to his deeds; the red-man will say,—"Wherefore hast thou done this? When thou wert a-hungered, did I not feed thee? And when thou wert a-thirst, did I not give thee to drink? When tossed on a boisterous sea you landed a weary few on my native shores, did I not clothe, and nurse thee in my wigwam? And what was my reward? Go! thou hast been unjust; the last red-man of my nation is now beyond the Rocky-mountains."

On the day after our battle, Capt. Fowler of the Dragoons, who had been despatched with his company to Fort Pierce when we left Camp Lloyd, joined us; bringing with him an Indian and two squaws, with one child and three ponies, whom he met in the woods, on their way, as they started to give themselves up. About 1 o'clock on the same day, the bridge over the *Locha-Hatchee* being completed, we struck our tents, and took up the line of march for Jupiter river, five miles further south. We encamped after dark on the north branch of Jupiter creek. On the afternoon of the 26th we changed our position to Jupiter Bay,

The Journal

near the spot where Lt. Powell disembarked at the time of his fight, three miles lower down the creek, and nearer to Jupiter Inlet. Here we expected to receive supplies by water from Ft. Pierce, and immediately commenced raising a stockade, intending to establish this place as a depot for supplies.

On the 27th, when out of forage, and but two days' rations remaining on hand, Major Kirby and Lt. Powell fortunately arrived in barges with the 1st Artillery; bringing supplies from Ft. Pierce, via the St. Lucie, where they had stopped according to prior orders, to establish a post, which however was soon after abandoned.

On the 28th the Stockade was completed, and designated as Fort Jupiter.[2] We were delayed here several days, before our preparations were completed for again taking the field. The principal cause of delay was the destitute condition of the troops; being without shoes, and almost without clothes, which were torn to pieces by scrambling through the saw-palmetto; and until a fresh supply could be received they were disabled from proceeding, from the nature of the country.

The Dragoons, however, were not kept idle; but were constantly employed in ranging the country round. A party which had been sent to look for Dr. Leitner's body, returned without success; finding not even a trace of him at the spot where he was seen to fall. They discovered the other dead bodies, and buried them; also the chest belonging to Midshipman McArthur, but rifled of everything except his papers. On the 29th Major Ashby with a hundred and fifty Dragoons were ordered out, with two days' rations, to scout in the neighbourhood, and endeavour to find traces of the enemy. They returned on the afternoon of the 30th, bringing thirty ponies,—some with their saddles on,—and twenty head of cattle, having trailed the Indians into an extensive prairie of saw-grass six feet high, towards the south-west. On the 1st Febry Hagan and Sanchez, two of our guides, returned from making a reconnaissance; and reported that the Indians had fled to an impregnable cypress swamp twenty eight miles south of us; where they lay concealed, resting after their flight; and probably

201

Journey into Wilderness

awaiting an opportunity to try their hand with us again. In the evening of the same day, an express arrived from Col. Taylor, who informed us that the Colonel with his division was twenty one miles north of us, at one of our old camps near the head of St. Lucie river, or *Alpatioka*. One hundred and twenty of the Dragoons and a company of Alabamians were immediately sent by Gen. Jesup to reinforce his command.

After dark on the evening of the 1st Febry we were startled by hearing the shrill scalp-whoop emanating from the quarter where the Delaware Indians had encamped. On enquiring the cause, we ascertained that it arose from a party of our Indian allies, just returned from a scout, in which one of their number had been exercising the polishing art upon the cranium of a luckless Seminole, whom he encountered. It was an act of individual daring, frequently the result of this desultory mode of warfare. While scouting, the party came across a fresh trail of several of the enemy, whom they pursued; and soon overtook one of them. The Seminole immediately hid himself in a cypress swamp. During the search which ensued, one of the Delawares, apart from the rest, approached a large cypress tree, under the root of which the Florida Indian was concealed, but who supposing himself discovered, suddenly jumped up, and so frightened the Delaware's horse that it threw him off. Quickly recovering his feet, he was in the act of raising his rifle, when the more eager Seminole levelled his, and shot his opponent through the left hand, the ball coming out at the wrist. The Delaware supporting his rifle on his left elbow, with his right hand shot the Florida savage through the heart, and uttering his war-whoop, sprang upon his prostrate foe, tore away his reeking scalp, ere life had departed, and rushing into camp, flew to the General's head-quarters, flourishing in triumph his bloody trophy, and uttering a succession of exciting yells. The event was celebrated at night with a scalp dance by our Indian allies.

On the 2d Febry I dined with Capt. Tompkins of the Dragoons *en famille;* he had also invited one of the Volunteer Captains to favour him with [the honor of][3] his company on the same occasion.

The Journal

At the appointed hour, lo and behold! there came marching to Tompkin's tent, a whole company of volunteers, by invitation as they said to dinner, their captain sending an apology that indisposition prevented his coming. A ludicrous mistake, certainly.

CHAPTER XXX

*O*n the 3d Febry I felt the symptoms of serious indisposition, but as we were expecting soon to take the field again, I said nothing about it, not wishing to be left behind.

On the 5th Febry, the shoes and every other necessary thing having arrived, we took up the line of march in pursuit of the enemy; proceeding south towards the cypress swamp where our scouts had reported them to be concealed, having discovered them by the numerous trails leading into it; and where it was expected they would certainly give us another fight, it being their last defensible position. We proceeded twelve miles through mud and water, and most gigantic saw-palmetto; and encamped, or rather bivouacked for the night. Riding on horseback under a scorching sun, by no means alleviated the burning fever which coursed through my blood, and with difficulty could I sit my horse.

On the 6th we resumed our march; and I determined to suffer in silence, as long as I could hold up my head. This, however, soon became an impossibility; and before the day's march was finished, I was reluctantly compelled to leave my horse, and take to an ambulance. There I lay, enduring the tortures of the damned, both bodily and mentally. On the eve of a battle, and put "hors du [de] combat"![1] This caused reflections more agonising than the racking head-ache which was crazing me.

When within a few miles of the cypress swamp, where the enemy lay concealed, we halted; and it being late in the day, encamped, that we may have a whole day for the anticipated battle.

On the morning of the 7th the column was put in motion at 8 o'clock, every one prepared for a bloody conflict. Before making the attack Gen. Jesup concluded to send a messenger to the enemy; offering peace, and inviting the chiefs to a conference.[2] For this purpose, *Sandy,* our Indian negro, was despatched. He proved a joyous messenger to the enemy; for very soon after, it was reported that several Indians were advancing from the cypress swamp with a white flag. Gen. Jesup met them, and heard their talk, which was delivered by a young chief, named, *Hallec-Hadjo.* He began by alluding to the wretched condition of his people, and stated how anxious they were for peace; but begged that they should not be sent out of the country. They were willing, he said, to do anything, rather than fight any more; they had lost all their cattle and ponies, and their wives and children were dying from the hardships of being chased about so much; that, being driven from land into the water, they must submit, and even emigrate if required; but earnestly prayed that we would let them remain in the country; they would thankfully receive the smallest piece of ground that might be given to them, no matter how bad, so that it was only in Florida, and big enough for them to spread their blankets upon. Gen. Jesup, requiring that *Tus-ke-gee,* their principal chief, should attend, was assured that on the following day he would make his appearance. After this, there was a grand shaking of hands, and the Indians retired.

We encamped on the spot; and next morning, *Tus-ke-gee* made his appearance, attended by a large suite. A repetition of yesterday's talk was made; and Gen. Jesup promised to send his recommendation to Washington, that they might be permitted to remain in the southern part of Florida. In the meantime, it was agreed, that while awaiting the President's decision, they should bring in their families, and encamp near us at Ft. Jupiter, within ten days.

These Indians we discovered were all Seminoles proper; and they offered to guide us to where the Micasukeys, with whom they were not on very friendly terms, were concealed in their fastnesses; if [they were] permitted themselves to remain in Florida. They said that the Micasukeys under *Apiaka,* alias Sam Jones, had retreated to islands in the *O-ke-cho-bee* lake; and could only be got at with boats, which would have to be transported across land.

These Micasukeys principally occupied Middle Florida before the treaty of Moultrie Creek; and were not only the first instigators of the war, but in conjunction with the negroes under Abram,[3] were mainly instrumental in keeping it up.[4] They were represented as the worst set of Indians in the U. States, being in fact criminals and fugitives from the Creek Nation, and distinct from the Seminole Indians, who were over awed and controlled by them, and who were in some measure forced into this war through fear of the Micasukies. Could terms have been made with the Seminoles, which I have no doubt they would have at any time been glad to enter into, it would have proved more effective in saving many valuable lives and much expenditure of the public treasury, by more speedily closing the war, than all the pitched battles which we were so eagerly endeavouring to bring about.

On the 10th we commenced our march back to Ft. Jupiter. Too sick to ride on horseback, I was obliged to be conveyed in an ambulance, which by constantly pitching and jolting over the saw-palmetto roots in a most awful manner, very nearly proved my last ride.

We reached Ft. Jupiter on the 11th Febry; and there I lay in the dirt on my back for fifteen days, with nothing but a thin and threadbare old tent, of the smallest dimensions to protect me from the maddening rays of the sun above; and one blanket beneath separating me from the bare ground, my saddle for a pillow to my aching head. On the day after our return Lt. Linnard[5] was despatched express to Washington by Gen. Jesup, bearer of the proposals for permitting the Indians to retain part of Florida.[6] We, of course, rested on our oars until his return.[7]

My sickness produced at the time feelings of perfect disgust for Florida, and the life we necessarily led there. Oh! that I could only have escaped from its detested soil, thought I! That I might once more live like a human being; that is, as human beings should live. For four continuous months had I been compelled to sleep, without a night's exception, with all my clothes on, even to boots and spurs. Indeed, the ceremony of disrobing was rendered quite superfluous, going to bed being nothing else but wrapping oneself up in a blanket, and tumbling upon the dewy ground; sometimes sheltered by a tent, but often, alas! too often!

206

pavillioned only by the starry vault of heaven. From long habit, however, it is astonishing how soundly one can sleep; and how pleasantly one can dream on this primitive couch; as much, and from attending circumstances such as fatigue even more so, than when reposing upon softer beds. The privations we were subjected to in the field of Florida were not altogether of a physical nature; for nearly two years had I been kept perfectly ignorant of all the acquisitions to the literary world. Not a book could be procured to read; for where transportation was scarce, no superfluous baggage was allowed; all mine had been left at St. Augustine. Oh! how I longed for even the sight of an old almanac to refresh my eyes with something in print. Tis true, the fluctuating contingencies of an Army life in the field brought me acquainted with many interesting excitements, and wild adventures; but what are they compared to the delights of civilized and social life? It is not astonishing that those persons who had once campaigned in Florida in the commencement of the war, should have shrunk from revisiting a country where they must have suffered such hardships.

In conformity with the agreement, the Indians very soon after our return to Ft. Jupiter, followed; and encamped within a mile of us. There were about four hundred of them and a great many negroes, awaiting the will of their great father, the President. They might have been constantly seen wandering about our camp like domesticated animals; the men begging of every one some tobacco; which being given, they smoked with a great deal of dignity; the squaws engaged in the less dignified employment of picking up the corn which our horses dropped from their mouths while eating; and which being sifted from the dirt, and pounded in mortars, was made into *sofka;*[8] a dish the Indians devour with great goût [gusto]. From their appearance, I should judge the burden of the war to have principally fallen upon the female portion of the natives; for while the men looked in good health, spirits, and conditions, the squaws with but few exceptions presented a most squalid appearance; being destitute of even the necessary clothing to cover their nakedness; many having nothing around them but the old corn bags we had thrown away, and which they had picked up in camp, and along our trail. A group of these swarthy worthies was constantly collected around my tent, being attracted there by my sympathy causing me to furnish them with food. They declared that if their great father said they must go, go they would but that they only petitioned to have a slip of the vast country that once owned them masters. They would be contented with the swamps, the hammocks, the barren spots, nay "the everglades," so that they might live and die in their native wilds. But, the decree had gone forth for their extermination. Alas! It is too surely being fulfilled.

CHAPTER XXXI

$\mathscr{O}$n the 24th Febry, having recovered sufficiently to walk about, I attended a grand pow-wow or *talk* that was held with *Tuskegee, Hallec-Hadjo,* and other chiefs, with most of their tribe, at Gen. Jesup's tent, in the Artillery camp, which was situated a mile from that of the Dragoons where I was. About 10 o'clock in the morning, the two principal chiefs *Tuskegee* and *Hallec-Hadjo*[1] entered the camp at the head of a procession of Indian warriors, dressed in all the paraphernalia of Indian finery. They were preceeded by two warriors dancing a peace dance, and cutting the most fantastic capers. This ceremony continued until they arrived at the General's head-quarters, frequently stopping on the way, and uttering a peculiar shrill whoop in concert, commenced by their chief and taken up in chorus by the rest. In front of the General's tent, which was the place of council, a ring was formed, and the dance concluded. The warriors then shook hands or rather elbows with the officers. This they did in a very peculiar manner, grasping you by the elbow, and making you take a corresponding hold; at the same time touching the head of each one they saluted with a white feather tied at the end of a stick; no doubt the emblem of infusing peace into their minds. All having taken seats, the calamut [calumet][2] was smoked; and the council was opened by an ancient squaw, the eldest in the tribe. She said, pointing to the warriors, "They were all her children; that she was tired of the war; that her warriors were slain; her villages burnt; her little ones perishing by the road side; that the great spirit frowned on his red children; that the star of her nation had set in blood. She desired that the hatchet should be buried forever, between her children, and her white brethren."

To this talk the General made a suitable reply; expatiating on the "maternal" affections of their great father at Washington, there being no great mother for his red children. The chiefs were then asked if they were willing, as they had promised, to abide the will of their great father *the President.* Whereupon *Hallec-Hadjo* replied, "that he did not understand the terms contemplated their leaving the country." At this reply Gen. Jesup was in a quandary. He appealed to *Tuskegee,* who replied, "that his understanding of the treaty was, that if their great father said they must leave the country, they *would go."*

The General then turned to *Hallec-Hadjo* and said he would give him two days to consider whether he would have peace or war; and appointed the 27th for holding another pow-wow; and for receiving his answer.

The council was then dissolved, by another shaking of elbows. Our Legislative bodies should certainly take lessons from the stern dignity of an Indian council.

This then was the state of things. About thirty or forty warriors had surrendered unconditionally, and were constantly in our camp. There were also many negroes; who by the bye, were the most diabolical looking wretches I ever saw; their style of dress contributing much to render them ferocious and oriental in aspect. They had none of the servility of our northern blacks, but were constantly offering their dirty paws with as much hauteur, and nonchalance, as if they were conferring a vast deal of honour, of which we should have been proud.

About a hundred and forty of this sable gentry, belonging to Indians who had already emigrated west, were sent off from our camp, on the 1st March under an escort, for Tampa-Bay, where they subsequently embarked to join their masters in their new homes west of the Mississippi. *Abram,* who was now constantly in our camp, said there would not be more than twenty or thirty negroes left in the nation after the departure of the above.

This *Abram* was a negro of some note in the Florida war. He was a perfect Talleyrand of the savage court; having been the prime minister and privy counsellor of *Micanopy* for a long period; and through his cunning, and the influence he exercised over his imbecile master, enjoyed entire sway in all the councils and actions of the Indians in Florida; and was supposed to have been very instrumental in getting up and continuing the war at first. He was sometimes honoured with the title of *"Prophet"* by the Indians, on account of his superior discernment.

An incident occurred while we were at Fort Jupiter which was highly creditable to the good feelings on the part of an Indian. When we left Ft. Jupiter to pursue the Indians south, on the 5th Febry, one of the soldiers was taken sick when about two miles on our march, and ordered back to the fort. When we returned, it was found that he had not made his appearance; nor was he heard off [of] until nineteen days after his disappearance; when an Indian brought him into camp, having found him asleep under a tree about twelve miles north. When the savage aroused him up, he was very much frightened; but soon became reassured by his friendly behaviour. Being very much exhausted by long fasting, and distressed of mind, his new friend kindly carried his musket, knapsack, and accoutrements for him while conducting him in safety to our camp.

It seems he lost the trail, after leaving the Army, and unable to find it again, had spent the whole nineteen days in wandering about the wilderness. At the time he was lost, he had but two days' rations in his haversack; and his distress of mind so affected his apetite, that when found, he had still remaining a biscuit and a half, and a small piece of meat. He had with him a pocket bible; on the blank leaves of which he had amused himself by noting down during his solitary peregrinations reflections upon his situation, after the manner of a diary; and expressed very much, as I heard an officer say, in the lugubrious style of Jeremiah's lamentations.

On the 2d March, Lt. Anderson with his company of pioneers, and Major Lauderdale[3] with two companies of Tennessee Volunteers, were sent out to explore the country, as far south as New River, about forty five or fifty miles distant; with orders to establish a post on its banks.

About the same time, in consequence of learning from Indians that had recently come in, that *Apiaka* with the Micasukeys were in the everglades near New River, Gen. Jesup ordered Lt. Col. Bankhead[4] to proceed with six companies of the 1st and 4th Artillery, by way of Ft. Pierce, to *Key Bis-cayne;*[5] and there to take barges and proceed up New River into the everglades; and endeavour to find and dislodge the Indians. Lt. Powell of the Navy was also directed to cooperate with Col. Bankhead in this undertaking.[6]

We frequently amused ourselves during this short armistice, by rowing to Jupiter Inlet, three miles off, and there strolling along the sea-beach, gathering the beautiful shells and other marine substances thrown up by the sea.

The beach about there we found lined with regular sand hills, not bare like those of the more northerly sea-coast, but covered with a peculiar kind of grass. On one of our visits, we found the Inlet completely closed up, by a dry sand bar formed across its mouth in one night. The day previous we had left it a broad, deep channel, capable of admitting the smaller vessels that sail the ocean. These sandy seals are said to be frequently formed upon all the Inlets of this coast; one day closing them up, the next day opening at some other spot; and "the whole Atlantic coast of Florida presents evidences of these struggles between the sands set in operation by the agitation of the ocean, and the currents of the rivers; the one striving to close, and the other to maintain an outlet for their waters."[7]

CHAPTER XXXII

$\mathcal{I}$ one day accompanied several of my brother officers on a visit to the Indian camp. The scene was exceedingly pictur-esque as we approached their rude lodges of bark and palmetto leaves, arranged among the trees in beautiful confusion.[1] We found the occupants variously occupied; here a squaw was pound-ing corn in a hollow log to make *sofka;* there a grave warrior was leaning on his elbow muttering guttural sounds to a companion, who lay extended on the ground muffled up in a deer skin; in all directions ugly little nudities, ycleped papooses, were rolling in the sand; appearing and disappearing in the most marvellous manner; tumbling over each other, and mimicking their progeni-tors; who now and then would suspend their conversation to utter a hasty *"Sta"* (be quiet); in one spot might have been seen several coy beauties squatted in a circle, and conversing in their musical language; probably on the deeds of their lovers; perchance dis-cussing a little scandal; prolonging their sentences with a mur-muring sound, which has a delightful effect. Farther on, an old and hideous hag was seated on a log, sawing her limbs to and fro, croaking forth some primitive war-song, and insensible to the blandishments of a great-grand-child, who was making vain efforts to get into her lap. How often had these very same Indians imbrued their hands, which they offered to us in token of friend-ship, in the blood of the white man; of weak woman and helpless infants! How many reeking scalps have dried in the fires of their wigwams.

In the course of our visit, we received an invitation to attend a dance, from the chief *Tuskegee;* who said, his warriors intended to give one that evening for our edification; and at the same time intimated that it would not be amiss should we bring a supply of that necessary stimulant, whiskey; assuring us that liquid libations were essential requisites in getting up to dancing pitch under their existing depression of spirits.

We accordingly in the evening armed ourselves with several bottles of the needful; and hearing the preparatory whoop from the Indian camp a mile off, which announced that the ball had opened, left ours about 9 o'clock at night.

We were immediately conducted to *Tuskegee* the chief, who, arrayed in the insignia of savage finery, received us with all the barbarian courtesy of the forests; and invited us to share with him the seats of distinction; which were skins spread upon the ground in his august vicinity. The scene presented to our eyes appeared that of some dark enchantment. Near the middle of their camp, and in the centre of a cleared circle, some fifteen feet in diameter, was blazing a large fire, whose flame threw its fitful gleam on the dark trees and glaring visages of the younger savages; who decked out in all their savage paraphernalia flitted to and fro before the blaze; their gaudy dress and animated figures, as they emerged from the shade of the trees, forming a lively contrast to the more sobre garb of the elderly ladies and gentlemen, who wrapped up in blankets on the ground in an assembled mass, looked fierce and grim in the flickering light of the fire. The moon also occasionally peeped from beneath a heavy cloud; and sent its beaming light through the straggling branches of the trees, which swayed gracefully in the light breeze, and gave a finishing touch to the scene.

On every side extending far into the gloom and shadow of the distance, might be seen a large fire before each lodge; in the glare of which, were visible the mothers and wives dressing their coarse food; and around which their more juvenile offspring were gambolling in unrestrained nudity.

We waited sometime in silence, expecting the dance to commence; but becoming impatient at the delay;—which feeling we no doubt exhibited in our countenances,—*Tuskegee* gave us to understand through the interpreter, that imbibing whiskey was an essential preliminary to the performance; and without which his warriors would not have *spirits* to dance. Upon the hint we acted;

214

and *Tuskegee's* eyes brightened as we pulled the bottles from our capacious pockets, and handed them over to him, as being the "chief cook and bottle washer." At first the wily old chief seemed reluctant to part with a drop; and exhibited strong indications of appropriating the whole to himself; his warriors, however, were not to be humbugged, and after receiving a drink all round, the dancing mania soon got into full operation among them. The young warriors at a signal of invitation, sprang from their seats on the ground; and forming a ring around the fire in the cleared space, commenced dancing; one, distinguished by his skill in the saltatory art leading the way. The dance commenced by all moving around the ring in single file, with a very slow pace; and such very grave countenances, that it had all the appearance of a religious ceremony; this was soon changed into a kind of ambling motion; the leader uttering all the time a monotonous whine somewhat resembling one of Weber's[2] waltzes; and which the others take up, or respond with a chorus of different words. Having completed the circumference of the fire once or twice; the motion becomes accelerated, and consists in stamping the ground with each foot alternately; the left hand, which is always the one nearest the fire, being held in a peculiar manner to the mouth; the leader all the time chanting with vociferous excitement, and in loud melodious strains, his "wild, woodland notes,"[3] consisting sometimes of the word *"U-han-a-way,"* or *"Dolly-heh,"* or *"Yo-halin-ah-way-ha,"* followed by a chorus of *"Yo-yo,"* in which all the dancers join; and which have some meaning, as the leader suits his actions to what he is saying; putting himself into strange and fantastic attitudes, which the other dancers imitate with religious correctness. Sometimes when the leader is a wag, he cuts a variety of the most extraordinary capers; distorting his countenance and exerting his ingenuity to display droll antics and grotesque gesticulations, that the attempts of the others to imitate may appear ridiculous, and excite laughter among the spectators; which they at times are unable to restrain, but indulge in very heartily. At intervals, the dancers utter a shrill yell with a peculiar intonation of voice, which is immediately taken up by the treble pipes of the papooses in a prolonged yell that dies far away in the echoing forest. As the excitement of the dance increases, the leader throws his limbs wildly about, leaping very high, and displaying all the agility he can; now he goes through the motions of taking a scalp; now creeping on his enemy, his body becomes distorted in the most ludicrous manner; the perspiration flows from him in torrents; and his movements become rapid beyond description; here a warrior bows his body to the centre of the ring, the others imitate him, then he faces about, cutting the most grotesque capers, which the others religiously imitate, with a solemnity that would do credit to a board of aldermen.

There is one warrior who seems to perform the duties of master of ceremonies; continually going around and shouting out words of encouragement for others to join the dance. The lookers on soon feeling the spirit move, utter a yell of excitement, and bound into the magic ring. Thus the dance goes joyously on, until the leader becoming fatigued, suddenly stops; utters a shrill whoop which his followers take up; and the dance ceases. They then leave the ring to give room for a fresh set, while they recuperate their exhausted energies by imbibing more whiskey.

The young squaws also, arrayed in their festive attire, and decorated with a profusion of gaudy trinkets, but with feet and legs unconscious of shoes or stockings, joined in the dance. There were many whose sparkling dark eyes and classic cast of features would have done no discredit to the belles of a more refined and fashionable coterie; and which fully counterbalanced the defect of their swarthy complexions.

The Indians are not entirely void of gallantry, or deference to the softer sex, for I noticed in the dance they always yielded to the ladies the place of honour; which is next to the leader, and preceeding the male dancers.

The demeanour of the fair sex in the dance was rather more staid and demure than that of the men; their movements being so gentle as to be scarcely perceptible, as with eyes bent upon the ground they glide after each other around the circle. Many of the women have a number of box-terrapin shells filled with small pebbles or the dried seed of the palmetto, which being tied together, and bound around the leg as high as the knee, make a great rattling when the feet are moved in the dance; harmonizing well with the various other noises, and forming a concert of sounds which the Indians seem to enjoy exceedingly.

There was one dance in which the men did not join, being performed by the women alone, who to the number of fifty or sixty, stood up at once to this singular and selfish performance. It was called by the Indians the *"Cat-fish dance,"* tho, wherein lay the resemblance I could not discover. The music was also different for this dance, the women alone singing, which they all do in a melancholy chant and without intermission during the continuance of the dance, their voices accompanyed by the rattling of the shells bound around their legs, and by that of a cocoa-nut shell filled with pebbles, which one of the oldest warriors present holds in his hand, he alone of the male sex chiming in with his voice. In this dance the women do not confine themselves to the circle around the fire but form on one side in a mass closely packed together not changing their position but merely beating the ground with their feet in singular harmony with their voices and the noise of the terrapin shells; their position and motion being that of a company of soldiers marking time in [a] solid square.[4]

Many of the officers, I among the rest, accepting the invitation of the master of ceremonies, took our places in the ring, and danced with the utmost gravity depicted on our faces; imitating the various grotesque evolutions of the arms and body; and chiming in with the chorus, our voices rendered awfully distinct by their rough tones, amid the softness of the Indians' musical notes; like a few thorns projecting from a bouquet of roses.

We retired about 1 o'clock to our camp, leaving the dancers going the merry round. This they kept up all night; and judging by the unearthly yells and demoniacal whooping and shrieking which continued to wring [ring] in our ears until daylight, the party must have been a very agreeable one.

From what one sees of these dances, they are as sensible as our own; and if we analyse the two, we will find it very difficult to determine which is preferable except our waltz, which I shall always admire.

*O*n the 20th March Lt. Linnard returned from Washington, whither he had been sent by Gen. Jesup with proposals for permitting the Indians under *Tuskegee* to remain in Florida. This proposition had been instantly rejected by the President, who sent back instructions that the Indians, unless they surrendered unconditionally, must be pursued and captured or destroyed.[1] Gen. Jesup knowing full well that should he leave it to the option of the Indians what to do, on hearing the result of this mission they would only break for the swamps again, and give us the trouble of hunting them down and perhaps of destroying many lives, very prudently determined to secure them first, and then communicate the answer from the President to their application.[2]

In pursuance of this plan, on the night of the 20th their camp was completely surrounded about midnight by our troops, both horse and foot, while the Indians were too much absorbed with the attendant delights of a grand frolic they were enjoying to notice what was going on in the distant darkness; and at daylight when their faculties had become completely obumbrated by the plentiful libations of whiskey which always characterize an Indian frolic, and the whole camp was buried in profound sleep, the order was given to close in upon them, and in this way we succeeded in capturing the entire band, without shedding a drop of blood, the Indians being unable to make the least resistance. There were about five hundred made prisoners and marched into the centre of our camp, *Tuskegee* and *Hallec Hadjo* included. Several endeavoured to escape the vigilance of our men by hiding under the hollow roots of trees in the swamp, and under a hollow cypress was found stowed away an entire family, who with difficulty could be distinguished from the mud in which they had promiscuously rolled themselves.[3]

The Journal

On the 22nd part of this band was sent off in boats to Fort Pierce, to be shipped thence via St. Augustine for emigration to the west. Great was the destruction among the numerous dogs left in our camp by the Indians who had been sent away, their dogs which they were not permitted to take with them outnumbering the Indians, as every man, woman, and child generally owned two or three apiece, and the most miserable curs in the world.

On the 29th the Indians who had been detained at our camp requested permission to amuse themselves by playing ball, which was allowed them. In consequence of there being so few men and the women very numerous [most of the male sex having been sent off], they decided to admit the latter to a participation of the game, which was not an unusual thing among them. The game in which the women join differs essentially from that of the men, the ball-play of the male Indians in all tribes requiring the most violent exertions, and frequently proving destructive of life to the players. The game as played on this occasion was very simple; a tall pole was erected in the center of a clear space, around which the players of both sexes were distributed, the two opposing sides consisting each of a separate sex. The individual who holds the ball throws it up perpendicularly into the air, and on its falling a general scramble ensues among all hands to secure it; the successful person then endeavours to hit the pole with it, which if he does it counts one towards the game, but if not, counts nothing. The women were always the winners at this game, but whether owing to their superior skill and agility, or the gallantry of the men in allowing them to be victorious, I could not positively decide, for these qualities on both sides were extensively exhibited.[4] In the evening of the same day they had a dance, which showed that their captivity did not produce a very depressing effect upon them.

While at Fort Jupiter we were visited by Mr. Colt,[5] the inventor of the repeating rifle, who came out to submit his invention to the examination of a Board of Officers appointed for that purpose, who reporting favorably, [the] Government directed that

219

fifty of his rifles should be immediately purchased and put into the hands of as many picked Dragoons, in place of the carbines they were armed with. The Indians exhibited considerable astonishment on witnessing the wonderful performances of this weapon, and came to the unanimous conclusion that it was *"great medicine,"* and the first day after witnessing the capabilities of this rifle they were very particular in avoiding any approach to that part of the camp where they knew it was.[6]

Col. Harney of the 2nd Dragoons being ordered to proceed south with a detachment of men, with the purpose of taking *Abiaka* [Sam Jones] by surprise, who we heard had retreated to the fastnesses of the everglades, he determined to take with him only the fifty Dragoons armed with Colt's rifles; I was ordered to accompany him; and on the 30th March we left our Camp at Jupiter, and took the direction for New River, whither some of the Artillery, and the Tennesseans under Major Lauderdale, had a short time previously gone, and established a fort which they called Fort Lauderdale,[7] after the brave volunteer officer of that name. The first night we bivouacked at an old deserted Indian encampment. The second night, we stopped near a marshy alligator pond, it being the only spot where water was to be procured, the whole surface of the country which a short time before had been entirely submerged, being now as remarkable for dryness, and even many of the streams about those parts had become dried up, which made it difficult for us to find suitable watering places. In the course of the day's march however we crossed several ugly cypress swamps with deep streams flowing through the centre, which proved disagreeable obstacles to our comfortable progress, having to wade through mud and water of all depths.

In the middle of our second night, while resting our wearied limbs upon the lap of mother earth, stretched luxuriously before a pine fire,—for although it was March and the country Florida yet the nights were sometimes cool,—I was suddenly startled from a sound sleep by some noise, and opening my eyes, the first objects presented to my vision were two fierce and savage-looking Indian warriors standing immediately over me. Not expecting to see

220

LAKE

OKEECHOBEE

PAY-HAI-O-KEE

OR

GRASS WATER

(THE EVERGLADES)

MAJOR LAUDERDALE'S ROUTE

TO ST. AUGUSTINE AND CHARLESTON

HILLSBORO INLET

Ft. Lauderdale

SAM JONES ISLANDS

MIAMI RIVER

Ft. Dallas

KEY BISCAYNE

Ft. Bankhead

Cape Florida Lighthouse

ROCK PINE LAND

ROCKY PINE-LAND

LONG KEY

BISCAYNE BAY

MANGROVE SWAMPS

FLORIDA KEYS

KEY LARGO

ATLANTIC

OCEAN

LOWER EAST COAST
OKEECHOBEE TO
KEY LARGO

REPRODUCED FROM THE
MACKAY & BLAKE MAP
1840

MOTTE'S ITINERARY ·····

such a sight at such a time, I was somewhat startled at first, but soon recovered my equanimity on finding they evinced no particular desire for polishing my cranium by the process of scalping. They proved to be messengers sent by Gen. Jesup, and had that instant overtaken us at our bivouac, and were only warming themselves at my fire.

On the third day's march we passed over the site of an Indian camp, which presented every appearance of having been very recently deserted; and on our arrival at Fort Lauderdale we found there forty five Indians that had been captured at this place only the day previous to that on which we passed it. We suffered very much during this march from the scarcity of water, every part of the ground being parched by the excessively hot sun. Our only mode of procuring it on many occasions was to dig holes in the ground, it being generally found at a depth of one or two feet from the surface; but of the colour and consistency of ink. We had to drink that or go without.

On the 2nd April at 11 o'clock A.M. we arrived at Fort Lauderdale. New River upon whose banks this fort was first located is called by the Indians *Coonte Hatchee,* the country around it being the great *coonte* region, where this root abounds; which being prepared by the Indian women for making their bread by a simple process of grating and washing, constitutes the arrow-root of many Apothecaries throughout the United States, and which I frequently used as such with the sick in Florida. This river arises five miles above or West of where our encampment was, in the *Pay-hai-o-kee* or *great grass water,* as the Indians call the everglades of Florida. On the southern bank of the river immediately opposite to our camp were the remains of an old palmetto house, the scene of quite a romantic but tragic affair; romantic as far as the heroine was concerned, but such romance as young ladies would always prefer reading about in novels, to acting *in propria persona.* At the commencement of hostilities, the Indians in this neighbourhood made an attack one night upon this house, all the occupants of which were butchered except a young girl of sixteen years of age, who eluding the savages by

The Journal

aid of darkness and great presence of mind, succeeded in making her way *en dishabillé* to Cape Florida [on Biscayne Bay]. Barefooted, and barely clad with only the lightest of all female garments, she traversed alone and under most agonizing circumstances many wide and deep lagoons, and almost impassable swamps and morasses, her delicate feet and limbs lacerated by the briers and brambles and bruised by the knotted roots and branches encountered in her hurried flight.

On the same side of the river with us, and within a mile of our station, we also saw the remnants of a house, which we learnt had been the once happy abode of a Mr. Cooly,[8] and his family, all of whom with one exception, had been massacred by the Indians in their own house and by the very individual Indians who had never known other than the kindest treatment at the hands of their victims, and always had received hospitality under that roof to which they applied the firebrand. Mr. Cooly was the only one who escaped, and by mere accident. Having resided among these Indians for many years, and having always treated them with the utmost kindness and liberality; and having moreover received from the Indians themselves, even after the outbreak of their people, repeated assurances of their friendship for him and his family, one of whom was even named after one of the Indians, he deemed himself safe, and not considering that treachery is an invariable characteristic of all Indians, he complied with their request of not moving away with his family, in consequence of the war. Dearly did he pay for this confidence; for feeling secure under these false manifestations of friendly disposition, he continued his usual tenor of living, and being on one occasion absent from home for a few days, on his return found it desolate, his whole family murdered, and his house reduced to ashes; all "at one fell swoop," wife, three children, and tutor, the latter named Flinton, basely massacred by the very Indians who had never received from them other treatment than such as should have ensured the warmest gratitude in return. This conduct is but too truly a prominent feature in all Indian character. The attack must have been made while the family was sitting in the

223

hall of their dwelling, the children occupied with their lessons; for when found they still held the books from which their lessons were usually learnt, tightly grasped in their stiffened fingers. After plundering the house of every thing valuable previous to setting it on fire, the Indians shot all the cattle about the place, and took away with them two negroes. The only indication of feeling on the part of the Indians was exhibited in their not scalping the wife and children; the tutor however was found divested of his.

Soon after our arrival at Fort Lauderdale, Col. Bankhead of the Artillery whom we found there, took his departure with the 4th Artillery in a Steamer, being ordered to the northern frontier of Florida. Major Lauderdale and his Tennessean Volunteers also left the day after our arrivel *for home* via *Fort Jupiter* and *Tampa Bay,* their term of service having expired.

CHAPTER XXXIV

*O*n the 15th April Col. Harney with his party of Dragoons accompanied by several companies of the 1st Artillery left Fort Lauderdale, and proceeded on his contemplated expedition south. We crossed New River at Fort Lauderdale, and pursuing a southerly course passed an old deserted Indian village at a distance of about five miles from the river. Very little, or rather nothing occurred that was interesting on this day's march; the country presenting nearly the same features already described as characterizing this part of Florida. We marched across a wet prairie or Savannah ten miles in length, and in the afternoon arrived at the northern bank of the Rio Ratones.[1] Some preparations being requisite previous to fording this stream, we encamped for the night, intending to be ready for crossing at an early hour on the following morning.

The Rio Ratones presented difficulties in crossing for which we were unprepared; so it was found necessary to send the wagons and horses back to Fort Lauderdale, while those men without horses wading through mud and slime up to their necks effected a landing on the southern bank. Being one of the mounted I was ordered back with the wagons and Dragoons with instructions to proceed by water to Key Bescayno and again join the rest of the command who would continue the march on foot.

We reached New River in the afternoon of the 16th April, and immediately swam our horses over, in the midst of alligators, to our late position at Fort Lauderdale.

In pursuance of instructions to embrace the first opportunity of joining Col. Harney at Fort Dallas[2] near the mouth of the Miami river, on the 19th April we embarked on board the Steamer Isis, and descending New River proceeded on our way to Key Bescayno, at which place some of our troops had been sent to

225

establish a depot, and which was but a few miles from Col. Harney's position on the main-land.

On reaching the mouth of New River, we did not find sufficient water on the bar to permit our crossing, so dropping anchor, we remained stationary all night, waiting for high tide next morning.

This river seems to have been very appropriately named, for there is sufficient evidence that what is now called New River, was at no very remote period a part of the ocean. The river is separated from the Atlantic by only a narrow neck of land, about ten miles long and fifty yards wide, its course being for that distance south and perfectly straight, parallel with the sea-beach. Its waters were actually alive with fish of every description, immense numbers of which were seen swimming about the Steamer. We were struck also with the beautiful colour of the bottom, which resembled a magnificent brussels carpet, the water towards the mouth of the river being so pellucid and clear that we could see the bottom at a depth of twenty feet. We saw sharks, which are very numerous about there, and other large fish, swimming at a depth of fifteen feet, their huge, unwieldy forms relieved against the clear sandy bottom looking like fleeting shadows, but so near and true that one would suppose he could grasp them with his hands. A vast number of shells of every description and of the most vivid hues were interspersed at the river bottom with all kinds and colours of pebbles, presenting at every movement the various arrangements of the kaleidoscope, which with every turn presents a new and if possible more beautiful combination. The river, the scenery, and in fact everything around appeared to wear a different aspect from the rest of the world which I had seen.

On the morning of the 20th April we crossed the bar, and proceeding out to sea turned the head of our Steamer towards Cape Florida, which we reached at 11 o'clock A.M. of the same day. We stopt a few moments at Key Bescayno where some of our troops were encamped around the ruins of the light-house, the wooden parts of which had been burnt by the Indians since the commencement of hostilities, and where occurred one of those

Light Tower at Key Biscayne   E. Glover
with Cocoa nut Tree   Feb 3 1849

Indian tragedies which but too frequently were enacted in unfortunate Florida during the Seminole war, but which in this instance resulted in the miraculous escape of the keeper of the light-house from flame and the deadly rifles of the savages.[3] The details of this affair may partake more of the nature of romance than of reality, but Indian massacres have generally appeared to those at a distance more like the workings of an excited imagination than the sad recital of real sufferings. The circumstances alluded to were as follows. On the 24th July 1836 John Thompson the keeper of this light-house, was attacked about 4 o'clock P.M. by about fifty or sixty Indians. He and a negro man, who were the only occupants of the Island at the time, receiving timely notice of the threatened attack, had retreated from their dwelling house close by into the light-house, and securing the door, deemed themselves safe from any efforts the Indians could make against the mossy brick walls and thick door of that building. The savages, however, succeeded in burning the door, when the fire communicating with the wooden spiral staircase within, threatened the most horrible death to the two besieged men, that of being roasted alive. They, however, retreated through the trap-door to the top of the light-house, which being arched over with brick offered some prospect of escape or temporary relief from immediate contact with the fire. Having carried with them a keg of gun-powder, it was thrown down into the flames, with the view of blowing up the staircase, lest the Indians should succeed in extinguishing the fire and thus secure them alive for the torture, to which immediate death would have been far preferable. The destruction of the stairs was effected, but the situation of the poor men was not much improved in comfort by the process, for the explosion failing to destroy their lives, and the flames bursting through the trap-door at [the] top almost in contact with their bodies, and the bricks upon which they were extended becoming heated by the intense fire beneath, their sufferings became excruciating. If at any time they exposed the smallest particle of their bodies over the edge of the roof it instantly became a target for fifty or sixty rifles in the hands of the yelling savages,

227

who surrounded the building, watching for such opportunities to destroy their victims. It was therefore impossible for them to diminish the space of contact with the hot bricks by standing up. The negro, however, less prudent than the white man, or not having the power of forbearance in so great a degree, was finally killed, having five rifle-balls shot through him; and Thompson, who had unawares exposed one of his feet over the edge of the roof, was instantly shot in it. After the death of the negro, he avoided in some measure the intense heat of the bricks by lying upon his dead body, and to this may possibly be ascribed his not having been roasted to death. The Indians unwilling to leave either of their victims alive finally attempted to reach them by tying sticks across the lightening rod, and by that means ascend to the top of the light-house which was ninety feet in height. They persevered in this attempt to a distance of forty feet, when becoming alarmed by part of the conductor giving way, they made no farther progress in that mode, and no doubt with heavy hearts left without bearing with them any trophy of their exploit in the shape of a scalp. They destroyed all the outhouses attached to the dwelling as well as the dwelling of the keeper, and carried off all the valuable contents. The next morning, a vessel that was accidentally passing, commanded by Lt. Leib of the Navy, approached near the spot, and the appearance of things on shore not being right or as usual, a boat was sent to reconnoitre and ascertain the state of affairs. On landing and approaching the light-house, those from the boat discovered the keeper on top of the light-house, still surviving but very much burnt, and totally incapacitated from helping himself. Every means were used to extricate Thompson from his perilous position; but those brought with them being inadequate, it was necessary to return to the vessel to procure what was requisite, and it was not until the succeeding day he was got down, by first shooting up twine attached to an iron ramrod, and eventually sending up men in a girt-line, which he had hauled up with a log-line, and made fast to the iron frame of the lantern at [the] top. The men who went up had to sling him, he was so much exhausted and lamed. The dead body of the negro had been thrown by him from the top previous to the arrival of the boat, and when burying it, he had been so much burnt, that in lifting the body into the grave, the skin wherever it was touched would slip from the flesh.

I have added a view of this light-house at Key Bescayno, drawn by Capt. Vinton as it appeared when I visited it, with the tents of our troops encamped there. Nothing remained of it but the brick walls and iron lantern, yet its appearance at a distance was not that of a burnt building, all that had been wood about it and destructible by fire never having been seen externally. The officers had built a tolerably comfortable house near the ruins, and from it there was a pleasant prospect of the sea. This Island is not of any very great extent, and consists of white sea sand, the only growth upon it being the mangrove trees, which we had to use even for fuel aboard the steamer, there being no other kind of tree, except a couple of cocoa-nut trees near the light-house, and which I suspect had been carried there from the main-land.

While at this place I was exceedingly annoyed by a species of fly, which possessing the size of horse flies, had the domestic habits and number of the common house fly, with the additional accomplishment of biting worse than mosquitoes.

We remained but a short time there, on this occasion; and proceeded at once towards the main-land, where Col. Harney had fixed his encampment, at the deserted settlement of a Mr. Lewis.[4]

The spot where I found Col. Harney encamped could with very little trouble be converted into a perfect Eden. The cocoa-nut, the banana, the orange, the lime, and tamarind flourished around us, the spontaneous growth of the soil. Swarms of deer abounded in the forests close by; and most delicious spring water flowed from the rock under the bluff of the shore. This was indeed the land of flowers, and no wonder that the Seminoles desired to remain in a country where food was as plentiful, and as easily procured as manna by the Israelites; for here no necessity existed for labour, and the sojourner reaped what he sowed not. The site of the encampment was not far from where Fort Dallas had been established, a few miles north of us, at the mouth of the Miami river.[5]

CHAPTER XXXV

*C*ol. Harney in pursuance of his intention to attempt a surprise upon *Abiaka,* in his southern retreat, had ordered a part of the detachment under his command to be in readiness for proceeding in small boats along the coast towards the southern extremity of Florida. Accordingly on the evening of the 21st April about 8 o'clock, the party selected for this secret expedition embarked in fifteen canoes, and immediately got under way, proceeding along the coast in the open sea; a rather hazardous position for such small and frail boats; but from the character of this part of Florida horses could not be used as means of transportation, and with difficulty could the men get along even without any extra rations. The party consisted of Col. Harney with his fifty picked Dragoons armed with Colt's rifles, and Lt. Anderson of the 3rd Artillery with part of his company armed with muskets. Lt. A. Rutledge of the 1st Artillery and myself comprised the Colonel's staff. We pursued our course all night, both to avoid being seen by the enemy, and in hopes of detecting their position by the light of their camp fires. At daylight the following morning we found ourselves about twenty miles south of Cape Florida, without having seen any signs of the foe during the night. With the view therefore of looking for them on foot, we approached the shore for the purpose of landing; but from the nature of this part of the Florida coast, we found it impracticable to effect our object, the coast presenting as far as the eye could see, a low, and at high water, an inundated shore, protected from the sea by a natural breakwater of tangled mangroves, their roots forming a perfect network higher than the knee, and thereby rendering these swamps, even where accessible, places of most laborious locomotion. The entire coast about there seemed to be formed of one mass of mangrove islands packed in upon each other, and separated from the water of the everglades by a lagoon, fresh or salt, by turns it was said, according as the waters of the glades or the tides of the ocean prevailed. We succeeded in finding a narrow strip of beach, it being low water, upon which we rested for awhile by stretching our cramped legs, while the men endeavoured to make some coffee, which was very much needed after the night's fatigue.[1] Near this spot we discovered a freshly impressed moccasin track, and in hopes of catching the individual who made it, we started off with the intention of following it up to its termination. We continued our pursuit for a distance of several miles through the mangrove swamp, constantly wading in water which was from knee deep to waist deep, and occasionally stumbling over the network of roots hid beneath its surface whenever we neglected to raise our feet to a sufficient elevation in stepping. Such a fatiguing mode of locomotion soon exhausted us, and finding it a difficult task to keep the tracks which were under water in sight, we returned to our boats. Again embarking we pushed off, and proceeding along the shore in search of a suitable landing place, after going three miles northwards discovered a part of the coast free from mangrove, and where the country back off the beach appeared open and having a growth of pine. We there landed and encamped, having drawn our boats upon the beach for better security against the force of the sea. We were fortunate in hitting upon this spot, for we there found a remarkable spring of fresh water, of the coolest and most delicious flavour I ever drank. This spring was remarkable from the circumstance of its being upon the beach considerably below high-water mark, and consequently covered by the salt-water twice every twenty-four hours.[2]

On the 24th April, we started on foot for the interior in search of *Abiaka,* with a part of our detachment, taking in our haversacks one day's rations, and leaving as a guard for the boats and camp the rest of our force, under charge of a sergeant. Our first six miles [of] progress was through a saw-grass prairie, when we struck a trail which led us to an Indian camp that had not been long deserted.[3] We were at first somewhat bothered by the

Journey into Wilderness

numerous trails leading from this place, and knew not which to take, until after a careful examination we selected the one which presented signs of being the most and the last trodden, when following it up, we pursued our way through a pine-barren, the ground being formed of coral-rocks jutting out in sharp points like oyster-beds, which caused us great suffering by cutting through our boots and lacerating our feet at every step, as much as if we were walking over a surface from which protruded a thick crop of sharply pointed knives. The whole of this part of Florida seemed to present this coral formation protruding through the surface of the earth, and which rendered it impracticable for horses, and almost impracticable for men unless well shod. We were puzzled in guessing how the moccasined Indians got over such a rough surface, until we subsequently ascertained that they protected their feet from the sharp rocks by making their moccasins of alligator hide when in this part of Florida. We suffered also very much for want of water, not a drop even of that which was stagnant to be met with in this parched up region. We consequently suffered more under the excessive heat of the sun's rays from this absence of everything like moisture. It was certainly the most dreary and pandemonium-like region I ever visited; nothing but barren wastes, where no grateful verdure quickened, and no generous plant took root,—where the only herbage to be found was stinted, and the shrubbery was bare, where the hot steaming atmosphere constantly quivered over the parched and cracked land,—without shade,—without water,—it was intolerable—excruciating. Oh! for the murmur of some brook,—and the chirp of some solitary bird to break the stillness and dreary aspect of the place! But there was neither brook, nor bird, nor any living thing except snakes to be met with. About 1 o'clock P.M. we emerged from this rocky pine-barren, and were doggedly following the Indian trail across a prairie when a distant but loud and repeated shout struck upon our ears;[4] it could be none but a hostile shout; and immediately after, while we were rounding a small projecting point of woods, there arose to our view from the edge of the prairie right before us, and a mile distant, the

232

smoke of an Indian camp. We could see that a terrible sensation pervaded the camp, and considerable excitement prevailed there, caused by our sudden and miraculous appearance in their vicinity, for the warriors appeared to be seizing their arms for defense while the women were bundling up their packs for flight. We lost no time in preparing for attack, and dividing our small party into three divisions, immediately charged forward at double quick, one consisting of the Artillery under Lt. Anderson extending to the left to intercept the Indians in flight, the second of part of the Dragoons to the right for the same purpose, while the third under Col. Harney accompanied by his staff advanced directly for the enemy. As we approached near, we found the Indian warriors with rifle in hand standing behind trees awaiting us, and on getting within the open pine-forest, we followed their example, and each of us taking to a tree immediately commenced our fire upon the enemy. The Indian warriors held their ground for some time, but finally began gradually to retreat from tree to tree; as they fell back, we advanced in the same cautious manner, only leaving the shelter of one tree to seek another nearer the enemy. In this way we followed them up some time, until finding that we were pressing them too hard, they at last broke cover and ran. We gave chase, and in the ardour of pursuit our men became scattered in all directions in small parties of two or three, and in the most extended order. At one moment Col. Harney was left with only Rutledge and myself, the Indians keeping up a brisk fire and yelling in every direction. One of the warriors, more courageous than the rest, stood out in open ground before us, and throwing up his arms yelled out his defiance, until the whistling of a ball from our Colonel's repeating rifle, warned him off in a most expeditious manner, for it told him that he was in dangerous proximity to a good marksman. By the rapid firing and loud yelling of the Indians heard in the direction in which Lt. Anderson with the few men of his company had gone, and by their delay in joining us, the Colonel was apprehensive they had encountered the enemy in greater force than themselves, and therefore ordered all hands to proceed to their assistance. On approaching the spot it was found that the Indians having retreated in greater force in the direction where Lt. Anderson was with his party of only ten men armed with muskets, had hemmed them in, and were keeping up a hot fire, and would no doubt have soon destroyed the whole of them had they not received timely assistance, for nearly all their ammunition was expended when rescued. This desultory fight lasted two hours and a half, from the moment we discovered the enemy, until we found ourselves in complete possession of their camp. We captured one prisoner only, owing to the difficulties of making rapid progress over the rocky ground with our lacerated feet; and not possessing the experience of the Indians in locomotion over such a surface, they beat us in running. We left another Indian on the ground, shot through the body.

The enemy being taken so much by surprise, had to decamp without carrying off their chattels, which we found in their camp strewed about everywhere, as they dropt them in their hurried flight. We found any quantity of cooking utensils, *coontee*-graters, bows and arrows; also large supplies of prepared *coontee* or arrow root, and some fresh venison, as well as skins of cattle, bear and deer, and of alligators; the latter for making moccasins in which they traverse those rocky parts of the country. Among other things we found a bag of gun-powder.

After the severe march of the morning, and the fatiguing exertions of the fight, we found ourselves too wearied to return to our boats without some previous repose; so after supping upon the enemy's *coontee* and venison, our own scanty rations having given out, we built large fires, and not having any blankets with us lay down upon the bare ground around them, their genial warmth very necessary during the excessively cold nights, which in temperature were diametrically the reverse of the days.

Upon questioning our prisoner, we ascertained that this was *Abiaka's* encampment; and that he himself had been present when we first appeared, but ran away from the prospect of being captured. We counted twenty-five fires in their camp; and allowing three warriors,—which is the usual proportion,—to each, the Indian force must have amounted to seventy-five warriors, exclusive of women and children. Our captive gave this as the number in camp at the time of our attack, consisting of Seminoles and Micasukies. Although when first captured, our prisoner was very much depressed at the loss of her liberty, she soon got over her distress, and talked and laughed as freely as with her own people. She stated herself to be a niece of my friend *Blue-Snake,* and from her having at least a pound of silver ornaments on her person, I should have judged that she belonged to the nobility. She told us that Abiaka had upwards of a hundred warriors, altogether, and that this was the same party that Col. Bankhead had attacked on Pine Island in the everglades a short time before our arrival at New River; and also informed us, that if he had continued the pursuit one day longer, he would have come upon the whole tribe, without the possibility of their escaping. We also learned from her, that *Alek-Hadjo,* the chief of the Indians whom we captured at Jupiter, and who afterwards had been sent out from Fort Jupiter with five other Indians, to persuade the rest of his people to come in, were met at the South Fork of the *Coontee-Hatchee* or *New River,* and the whole of them shot dead by a party of their own people, who accused them of being spies for the whites, and did not therefore deserve to live.[5] When asked if she knew where *Abiaka* would retreat to with the party we had just routed, she gave it as her opinion, that they would take refuge on some island in the *Oahatka,* or ocean; evidently meaning some of the numerous Southern Keys.

On the 25th April, the morning after the above skirmish, we returned to our boats. In consequence of several of our men being taken sick, and there being no means of carrying them over the sharp rocks, our progress was very slow and tedious. The night had been very cold, and the men not having their blankets with them, the contrast of temperature with the burning days, easily accounted for the sickness, which was much augmented in suffering by the absence of water. When within a mile of our boats, I found my strength fail me; and completely knocked up, I was compelled to knock under, not being able to budge one step further, my boots being cut into ribbons and my feet severely lacerated by the sharp rocks. I threw myself on the ground, feeling perfectly indifferent at the time as to what should become of me; but Lt. Arthur Rutledge who would not quit my side, persuaded me after resting awhile, to make some exertion, and with his friendly assistance I was enabled to regain our boats long after our party had reached them.

On the 26th April, we remained quiet, to recruit ourselves after the recent fatigue; and on the 27th, a part of us embarked in seven canoes to proceed south on an exploring expedition among the islands or Keys. The party consisted of Col. Harney, Lt. Rutledge, and myself, with the Colt's-rifle company, Lt. Anderson being left in command of the Artillery to guard the other boats and camp. We commenced our voyage early in the morning, and continued all day progressing in a southerly direction. About sun-set we attempted to land, but found it impracticable on account of the dense mangrove swamps. Night overtook us in the canoes, not being able to find a place to land; and long after dark while cruising about in search of a landing, we discovered a small rock near *Key Largo* sufficient to hold a part of our men.[6] Making fast our canoes to the rock, as many as could stretched themselves on its hard surface for repose; the rest spent the night in the boats.

On the morning of the 28th observing a small schooner at anchor a few miles off the Key, some of us were sent to board her to ascertain what she was doing there, but she proved to be only a wrecker, of whom so many infest this dangerous coast, seeking a hardy livelihood from the misfortunes of others. We also saw another schooner at anchor further out, engaged in the same business; and still further off, near the distant horizon, appeared a ship heading north in the gulf-stream. In returning to shore, or rather to the rock, the Colonel amused himself in harpooning the denizens of these waters, through whose clear depths they could be distinctly perceived, slowly moving about. Among others he succeeded in securing an immense *Sting-ray* and *Whip-ray,* the latter so called from the length and appearance of its tail. On regaining the rest of our fleet at the rock, the whole command was got under way, and we took up the *line of sail* for our encampment, without being able to see or hear anything of the enemy. Having fine fair-wind, we dispensed with our oars, and raising sail, made such rapid progress, that we reached camp a little after sunset of the same day.

On the morning of the 29th April, our whole detachment embarked in the canoes, and in consequence of our rations being expended, returned to *Camp Center* at Lewis' settlement near Key Bescayno, which we reached a little after sun-set of the same day.

CHAPTER XXXVI

*T*he very night of our return, an order was received from Head Quarters[1] directing the 1st Artillery to proceed without delay to the Cherokee Nation, via St. Augustine and Charleston, in consequence of that tribe of Indians refusing to emigrate to the west in accordance with their treaty, and indications of hostility being consequently manifested by them against the U. S. Government.[2] The same express brought orders for the 2nd Dragoons to march immediately across Florida to Tampa Bay.[3] Col. Harney feeling reluctant to give up the pursuit after *Abiaka,* when he had him almost in his power; and in consequence of information received from our Indian captive, had made preparations for another boat expedition among the Southern Keys, for the purpose of prosecuting his search after this wily chief. He therefore permitted only Lt. Anderson's company of 3rd Artillery to leave for Tampa Bay via New River; retaining the 1st Artillery and 2nd Dragoons for his contemplated expedition. As the Colonel intended to follow up the pursuit until he found the enemy, and give them a general engagement, it was necessary that our men should be first furnished with shoes, the recent tramp over the sharps rocks having left them barefoot. For this purpose he despatched orders to the depot at New River for a large supply of shoes; in the mean while directing us to furnish ourselves with ten days' rations, to be carried in our haversacks.

While waiting the arrival of the shoes, a party was sent out on the 3rd May to explore the country bordering upon the Miami river. Several villages were discovered, and destroyed. In one of them were found traces of the Indian diabolical custom of burning their captives. These were two stakes to which were still tied the wrist and armbones of some poor victim to their barbaric cruelty, who had suffered by fire.[4]

The Journal

In consequence of the non arrival of the shoes sent for, Col. Harney had to abandon his contemplated expedition; and on the 5th May we broke up our camp, and moved over to Fort Bankhead at Key Bescayno, preparatory to proceeding on our march to Tampa Bay and the Cherokee Nation. The 1st Artillery having no Surgeon with them but myself, I had every reason to expect that I should be ordered to accompany them to St. Augustine; for being one of the Medical Staff who had served longest in the field of Florida, I felt not the slightest doubt that I was among those destined for duty in the Cherokee country, and for two reasons was particularly desirous to leave Florida, via St. Augustine; one, because all my baggage had been left at St. Augustine on taking the field; the other, because I should then have a chance of visiting my native city, dear old Charleston; and though 'twould be but a flying visit, yet one hour in Charleston was worth a month spent elsewhere:—

> *"Home of our childhood! how affection clings*
> *And hovers round thee with her seraph wings!*
> *Sweeter the fragrance of thy summer breeze,*
> *Than all Arabia breathes along the seas!*
> *The stranger's gale wafts home the exile's sigh,*
> *For the heart's temple is its own blue sky!"*

While thus indulging in the sweet hope that I should at last escape from wading swamps, and hunting Seminoles;—that I should once more visit civilized scenes, and enjoy the delights of civilization and social life, and again mingle with my fellow man, not as an enemy, but a friend; that I should soon know the exquisite pleasure of again visiting childhood's scenes, after two years' absence, two years spent in scouting with Dragoons, or crawling through swamps and hammocks with Artillery and Infantry;—with an occasional divertisement of boating on lagoons etc. While indulging in these delightful anticipations, which caused the heart to dilate and pulse to beat high, I was unexpectedly told by the Colonel commanding that I must accompany the Dragoons to Tampa Bay;—that I was still destined yet awhile to hear naught but the loon's wild cry, and see naught but the alligator's splash in the dark lagoon; instead of directing my course to Charleston, "O'er the glad waters of the dark blue Sea." That I was still destined for awhile in Florida,

> *"To scorch beneath the vernal sun,*
> *Amid the hurried rout;*
> *To scare the vulture from his feast,*
> *Where the foremost steed gave out;*
> *To seek in vain for gushing spring,*
> *Upon a thirsty waste,*
> *To sink amid the mazy wood,*
> *With the homeward path effaced."*

Oh! the sudden revulsion of feeling, when this destiny was told me! Never had I felt before what it was to be indeed depressed in spirit. I could now fully realize the horrid situation of those affected with nostalgia, for I found myself suffering from its attack in its heaviest form. Ah! thought I, little do the pampered butterfly fops of a city know the real value of their situation, which to them is filled with *ennui;* for they cannot know how much a city life may be enjoyed unless they should be deprived of its advantages and enjoyments for a while.

I could find naught to cheer me, in the saddening view presented by my unlucky fate; even my usual source of consolation at last failed me; for heretofore when distressed, I have always derived comfort from the thought that "there is a day of sunny rest for every dark and troubled night"; but now, even this stream of consolation and comfort seemed to flow back in an alpine torrent upon my heart.

On the 6th May Lt. Aisquith embarked with his company of 1st Artillery in the schooner Lebanon, and at 7 o'clock A.M. got under way for St. Augustine. This sight did not tend much to raise my drooping spirits, for they would soon be in Charleston, and I not with them. At 12 o'clock the same day I embarked on board [the] Steamer Isis for New River, with Col. Harney and the 2nd Dragoons, on our way for Tampa Bay, and arrived at Fort

Lauderdale the same evening about dark, where we found part of the 1st Artillery preparing for their departure as soon as the Steamer Isis had landed us.

On the 7th May at an early hour in the morning, all who were destined for Tampa Bay were in the saddle, and ready to commence their long and dreary march across the Peninsula of Florida. When about to issue the order to proceed, Col. Harney turning to me, quietly directed that I should stay and accompany the 1st Artillery to St. Augustine.[5] The criminal under the gallows, who, when just about to be swung off, receives a reprieve, could not have experienced more enviable sensations than I did at that moment. How my heart throbbed, and pulse quickened, unable seriously to realize the glorious certainty of my soon seeing Charleston, to me the sunniest spot of earth, to which the magnetic needle of my affections ever pointed.

In the afternoon of the same day, I embarked in the Steamer Isis, with part of the 1st Artillery under Major Kirby; and Fort Lauderdale was abandoned to its primitive loneliness, until some stray Indian should choose to assume command of its vacant *Block-House.*

In descending the river we unfortunately got aground; and owing to the consequent delay, failed in reaching the bar before dark, and had to anchor for the night within the river mouth.

The next morning, May 8th, at half past seven o'clock, we crossed the bar and directed our course northwards. We were favored with fine weather during the day, and made considerable progress; but during the night the winds suddenly rose to a gale, and flung their wild and clamorous voices in fearful discord o'er the stormy sea, the roar of whose waves, careering wildly in their midnight gloom, kept up an accompaniment of dulcet harmony. Our little steamer, beneath the medium size, being built for harbour navigation, and never intended for buffeting the open sea,

> *"At every flap of wave*
> *Quiver'd to her keel."*

Thus passed the night of the 8th; and on the following morning, the sun rose beautifully, and gleamed brightly on the blue expanse of waters around us. Our brave little bark gallantly dashed aside the blue waves with her prow, flinging the glittering spray high in the air, and leaving a long white wake, whose snowy foam sparkled with a rainbow beauty. We found ourselves far out at sea, having been driven by the violence of the storm across the Gulf Stream, and far beyond sight of land, a glimpse of which we did not regain until 2 o'clock P.M. About midnight we reached St. Augustine bar, and came to anchor outside, it being necessary to have the aid of daylight in navigating the very dangerous intricacies of its channel. At an early hour the following morning we raised anchor, and steam, and by 7 o'clock A.M. made fast to the head of the only wharf, at St. Augustine.

After remaining three days at this ancient city, enjoying the hospitalities of its kind inhabitants, and indulging for the last time in the fascinating society of its beautiful ladies, which we had opportunities every night of doing while we remained, balls being given to us by various persons on "hospitable thoughts intent," on the 13th May before sunrise we took up the line of march for Picolata on the St. Johns, where a steamboat [the Camden] was waiting to transport us to Charleston, from whence we were to proceed by rail-road to Augusta, Ga., and thence march across the northern part of Georgia to the Cherokee Nation.

We reached Picolata about sun-set of the same day, and immediately embarked on the steamer "Camden," which got underway at once. We reached the mouth of St. Johns river that night, but the bar possessing the characteristic of all the Florida bars, that of very great shoalness, and it being low-water at the time, we anchored until 8 o'clock next morning, when we endeavoured to get to sea; and finally effected our object, after thumping upon the hard sandy bottom once or twice, without other detriment than disturbing the economy of our breakfast-table, we being at the time occupied with this pleasant and useful repast.[6]

We touched at St. Mary's, a small town in Georgia, and

242

continued on our way without any interruption until dark, when getting aground among the intricate channels of the marsh flats, it being the inland passage which we took after leaving St. Mary's, we were compelled to remain stationary until daylight, when flud [flood] tide again came to our relief.

We reached Savannah about 12 o'clock M. on the 15th May, and ascertaining that our boat would remain here three or four hours, many of us embraced the first opportunity of seeing this neatly laid-out little city, and also of enjoying a civilized meal in a civilized manner; so repairing to a hotel, we ordered dinner to be prepared as expeditiously as possible, while we strolled through some of the principal streets.

At 3 o'clock P.M. we were again under way, steaming towards Beaufort, S.C.; which place we reached after dark, and anchored in the stream opposite to the town; of which, however, we saw nothing but a few lights glimmering here and there from the windows of the houses, for by daylight next morning, we had weighed anchor, and resumed our progress towards Charleston.

Some little excitement occurred during the night, from one of our men having either rolled overboard from the hurricane deck where he was sleeping, or having jumped overboard with the view of swimming ashore for whiskey. In whatever way he got into the water, upon finding himself drifting out to sea with a strong ebb tide, he bellowed out lustily for help; which after some little delay,—every one being asleep but the sentinel,—was extended to him; and he was brought on deck more dead than alive, having swallowed more water than he had in his whole life before done voluntarily perhaps.

We were soon again in the open sea, where we continued our voyage

"With the blue above and the blue below,"

for we were blessed with charming weather and a clear sky.

Every thing conspired to render my return to the place of my nativity bright in its influence over my feelings; and with every mile of return struck off from the lengthened chain of absence, endured with dragging fetters, my spirits rose; and at [the] sight of Charleston Light house, I cried out in extacy,

"From the wide world of waters
In rapture I come
To the land of my fathers,
My dear native home!"

I have ever felt a strong and devoted attachment for Charleston,—for every thing and every body belonging to it; wherever I have been, and under whatever circumstances, my heart—not to be changed by place or time—has always turned to it with a wistful longing and anxiety. Twas not that my home was there; for home no longer existed for me; twas only to be found in the memory of past times and joyous youth, when hopes were bright, and the very air I breathed seemed impregnated with delight. There was now no hearth-stone in Charleston to which I might turn like others after the dangers and privations of the war, and say, this is my sacred asylum of home! No "heart still true in joy and woe" was there to pour forth its sympathy. That peculiar happiness was not for me, which those who lead a wandering life, or who quit their homes for a time, so frequently enjoy; that of returning to the home of past enjoyments, and again meeting those loved faces which render home so dear, and hearing the thousand tender inquiries which flow from the heart to the lips. Tis true, I left some friends in Charleston, who had twined themselves round my heart; to meet whom, after the wandering and cheerless life I had for the last two years been leading would be like entering upon the enjoyments of a new existence. Yet, there existed other reasons for the deep and abiding affection for Charleston, which neither time nor absence could shake from my heart. I loved it as the home and the burial-place of my ancestors,—as the spot of my birth,—the haunt of my boyhood, and scene of my earliest enjoyments;—enjoyments, which became embalmed and consecrated in the memory, by their striking contrast with the many harassing perplexities and anxieties which more or less characterize every man's progress in life, after passing his early years;—generally the happiest period of existence with most persons, because experience has not yet commenced the rigors of her discipline, nor has care yet found an abiding place in the heart.

Such were my reflections, as sitting upon the deck of our steamer, I caught the first glimpse of this dear and glorious old city looming in the distance, with its steeples and well known localities opening rapidly upon my vision. There stood Sullivan's Island stretching away to the right with its fort and neat cottage-like abodes greeting my eyes with the familiarity of old friends. Dear old sand-bank! although I had been long a wanderer from thy shores and myrtle groves, thou wert still as dear to my heart as ever! For,

> *"Still to thee, oh! still to thee,*
> *My spirit turned where'er I'd roam;*
> *Still in my midnight dreams I'd see*
> *Thy hills, thy groves, my Island home."*

and now I could add the rest of the couplet,

> *"Once more thy ocean waters sound*
> *Like sweetest music on mine ear;*
> *And old familiar scenes around*
> *Speak to my heart of hours most dear."*

About 2 o'clock P.M. we touched the wharf at Charleston, but nothing more; for our boat was immediately directed to Castle Pinckney, one of the forts in the harbour, where we were to be quartered until the arrangements had been completed for our transportation over the Hamburg rail-road. I obtained permission to return to the city; and lost no time in so doing.

Thus on the 16th May 1838 I once more found myself in the place of my nativity, of my friends, and of my affections, after an absence of two years spent in Camp and Field, exposed to all the vicissitudes, dangers, and privations of Indian warfare; a warfare, in which the assurance of existence was never felt from one moment to another.

Finis.

Editor's Notes

CHAPTER I

1. The depot was on Mary's Street, about five blocks from the city line. Citizens of Charleston opposed extension of the tracks within the city limits because flying sparks from the engine could easily ignite their frame buildings. Besides, the distance between depot and wharf created an opportunity for draymen to make a living. Samuel Melanchthon Derrick, *Centennial History of South Carolina Railroads* (Columbia, 1930), 117-118.

2. Hamburg, a small, bustling village, was located on the South Carolina side of the Savannah River, across from Augusta, Georgia. Old Railroad map, P. K. Yonge Library of Florida History, University of Florida.

3. The Creek Nation was a once powerful confederation of the Upper and Lower Creek tribes who belonged to the Muskhogean family of Indians. Hernando de Soto found this confederation of town-dwelling natives the largest and most feared in the southeast, and possessing a warlike heritage and advanced culture. The Upper Creek villages dotted the Tallapoosa and Coosa river areas in Alabama. Those of the Lower Creeks nestled on the banks and in the valleys of the Chattahoochee and Flint rivers in Georgia. At the height of power the confederation controlled a vast area in the southeast. By the 1830's, however, their territory had dwindled to a small section in eastern Alabama. John R. Swanton, *Early History of the Creek Indians and Their Neighbors*, Bureau of American Ethnology, Bulletin 73 (Washington, 1922), 215-216; Frederick Webb Hodge (ed.), *Handbook of American Indians North of Mexico*, Bureau of American Ethnology, Bulletin 30 (Washington, 1912), I, 362-363;

Richard Peters (ed.), "Treaties Between the United States and the Indian Tribes," *United States Statutes at Large* (Boston, 1846), VII, 366-367 (cited hereafter as *United States Statutes at Large*); and the various Creek land cessions outlined on the map (page 378) in Angie Debo, *The Road to Disappearance* (Norman, 1941).

4. The proud surgeon rode the unique coaches of the old South Carolina Railroad which, in 1833, was considered the longest in the world. The 135 miles of track connecting Charleston with Hamburg was covered in the amazing time of 13 hours. Today it is a part of the Southern Railway System. Robert Selph Henry, *Trains* (Indianapolis, 1934), 9.

5. Brigadier General John Roger Fenwick began his military career as a marine second lieutenant in 1799. Cited for gallantry on the Niagara Frontier during the war of 1812, Fenwick was made brigadier general in 1823. He was assigned to command the troops in the Creek Nation on May 13, 1836. *Army and Navy Chronicle*, May 19, 1836, 320; Francis B. Heitman, *Historical Register and Dictionary of the United States Army, from Its Organization, September 29, 1789, to March 2, 1903*, House Document 446, 57 Congress, 2 Session (Washington, 1903), I, 149 (cited hereafter as Heitman, *Historical Register*).

6. The Second Creek War, 1836. The main causes for this Indian uprising can be traced to the actions and attitudes of restless, land-hungry American frontiersmen and their notorious followers—land speculators. British pressure for Creek lands was applied in Colonial days. After American Independence land seizure continued with greater fury. During the War of 1812 a segment of Upper

247

Creeks, instigated by British agents and propaganda, initiated a short and bloody insurrection against the United States. Known as the First Creek War, this bloodletting episode was hastily and methodically crushed by the capable and inveterate Indian exterminator, General Andrew Jackson. By the terms of the Treaty of Fort Jackson, the Creeks ceded vast areas of land in Georgia and Alabama. Negotiating a treaty with the United States in 1833, the Creeks traded all claims to land east of the Mississippi River for lands in the west. This document, however, contained a clause stating emigration was not mandatory and could be accomplished only by consent of the individual. The majority of the Nation resolved not to emigrate. For those wishing to remain, provision was made for the distribution of individual reservations. Over 2,150,000 acres were parcelled into 6,696 reservations. One-half sections went to the heads of families; whole sections to ninety principal chiefs. By 1834 the task of relocating 21,672 Indians was finished. Ignorant of land or money values and unaware of responsibility implied in landownership, the Creeks were approached by a flock of unprincipled and infamous land speculators and subjected to what have been termed the greatest frauds ". . . ever perpetrated upon mankind." Stealing land became the order of the day. Speculators employed many forms of swindling to relieve the Creek of his property. Creeks who sold their land to the speculators soon found their money gone. Hungry and homeless, many of the radical "anti-removal" Creeks reverted to a life of vagrancy, robbery, and even murder in order to exist and gain revenge for their loss. By 1836 ill feeling between the white settlers and hostile Creeks of the confederation became critical. Threats of full-scale Indian war prompted the government to marshal over 10,000 armed troops near

the Creek territory for the purpose of rounding up all the Indians and forcefully removing them to lands west of the Mississippi. E. Merton Coulter, *Georgia, A Short History* (Chapel Hill, 1947), 26, 91-92, 99, 181-187, 225; Elbert Herring to Lewis Cass, Secretary of War, June 6, 1836, in *American State Papers, Military Affairs* (Washington, 1861), VI, 574-576; John O. Howard to Lewis Cass, May 9, 1836, *ibid.*, 577-578; George Dewey Harmon, *Sixty Years of Indian Affairs, Political, Economic, and Diplomatic, 1789-1850* (Chapel Hill, 1941), 224; Thomas H. Crawford and Alfred A. Balch (appointed to investigate the causes of the Creek Indian hostilities under a resolution passed by the House of Representatives on July 1, 1836), "Hostilities With the Creek Indians," Executive Document 154, 24 Congress, 2 Session (Washington, 1837), (cited hereafter as Executive Document 154); and Debo, *op. cit.*, 98-103.

7. Major Mann Page Lomax, Third Regiment, United States Artillery. *Army and Navy Chronicle*, June 2, 1836, 348.

8. Sparta straddled the Old Federal Road in Hancock County, Georgia.

9. Major General Winfield Scott (1786-1866) began his military career in 1808 as a captain in the First Heavy Artillery. His distinguished services in the battles of Chippewa and Lundy's Lane during the War of 1812 hastened Scott's promotions. By 1814 his broad shoulders sported brevet major general's insignia. In January, 1836, he fell heir to command of the troops operating against the Seminole Indians in Florida. Failing to meet High Command expectations for the quick defeat of a few impertinent and unruly Florida Indians, the apologetic Scott was "elevated" in May, 1836, to over-all command of military forces in the Creek Nation. Two months later he was recalled from this command for delaying the prosecution

Editor's Notes

of the Creek War, and arraigned before a Military Court of Inquiry. Exonerated of any default during the Seminole and Creek campaigns and praised for his ". . . energy, steadiness, and ability, . . ." he was appointed Commanding General of the United States Army in 1841. On March 27, 1847, Scott was promoted to lieutenant general for eminent services during the Mexican War and presented with a special Congressional Citation for distinguished services at Vera Cruz, San Juan de Ulloa, Cerro Gordo, and the capture of Mexico City. He retired from command of the United States Army in 1861. Heitman, *op. cit.*, I, 870; John T. Sprague, *The Origin, Progress, and Conclusion of the Florida War* (New York, 1848), 113-114 (cited hereafter as Sprague, *The Florida War);* Charles Winslow Elliott, *Winfield Scott, the Soldier and the Man* (New York, 1937), 291, 311-312, 319-320, 330-331; and "Proceedings of the Military Court of Inquiry in the Case of Major General Scott and Major General Gaines," Senate Document 224, 24 Congress, 2 Session (Washington, 1837), III, 730 (cited hereafter as Senate Document 224).

10. First Lieutenant Carlos Adolphus Waite served in the Quartermaster Corps during the Florida Indian War. Cited for gallantry in the Mexican campaigns of Contreras, Churubusco, and Molino del Rey he rose to the rank of brigadier general in the Union Army during the Civil War. Heitman, *op. cit.*, I, 993.

11. Hostile Creeks from Alabama made numerous forays into Georgia stealing cattle, horses, hogs, corn, and such other articles as they could carry away. These raiding parties destroyed bridges, attacked and burned isolated cabins of settlers, and even small villages. Fearful frontier inhabitants abandoned homes and crops and took refuge in nearby fortified stockades. The entire countryside in the vicinity

of the Chattahoochee was in a state of terror when the federal troops, Motte among them, began to pour into the Columbus area. William Schley to Thomas H. Crawford and Alfred A. Balch, October 7, 1836, in Executive Document 154, 5-6; William Mitchell to Major John Howard, May 7, 1836, in *American State Papers, Military Affairs,* VI, 576; and *Apalachicola Gazette,* May 21, 1836.

12. Motte's revised manuscript, 15 (cited hereafter as Revised MS).

13. Major Edmund Kirby, a veteran of the War of 1812, received special commendation for efficient service during the January, 1837, campaign in eastern Florida. During the Mexican War Kirby was cited for gallantry in the battles of Contreras, Churubusco, and Chapultepec. Sprague, *op. cit.*, 173; Heitman, *op. cit.*, I, 603.

14. These were the Georgia Volunteers, called up by Georgia's Governor William Schley on May 13. Between four and five thousand gathered in the Columbus area and were subsequently stationed at various points along the Chattahoochee River. Since arms and ammunition were slow in arriving, it was near the end of June before these "invincible patriots" were able to take an active part in the campaign which officially ended on July 5. William Schley to Thomas H. Crawford and Alfred A. Balch, October 7, 1836, in Executive Document 154, 5-6.

15. Four-fifths of the Creek Nation remained at peace during this uprising. Many friendly Creeks assisted the federal troops in rounding up their hostile brothers. Chief Opothleyoholo and 1,150 friendly warriors volunteered their services to General Jesup. Other chiefs who served under Jesup included Jim Boy, Tukabachee Hadjo, and Tukabachee Micco. A total of 1,806 Creeks assisted the 10,000 federal and volunteer troops in suppressing the hostilities. The hostile faction, loosely organized and with

249

divided leadership, were hard pressed to muster more than one hundred warriors at any one time despite their total numbers, estimated from five hundred to five thousand. Most of the hostiles came from the Uchee, Eufaula, Hitchiti, and Chehaw villages of the Lower Creeks. These villages, after relinquishing their lands in Georgia, had moved within the 1814 treaty boundaries in Alabama. The hostiles were splintered into three major parties. One was led by Eneah Mathla, venerated as the active leader of all opposition; another by Eneah Micco, recognized as the head chief of the Lower Creeks; and the third by an avid anti-removal chieftain named Jim Henry. All three groups were outlawed by the legal government of the Nation, which recognized Opothleyoholo as the head chief. Although the war parties roamed at great distances from their villages, they were to be found principally between the Hatchechubbee and Cowikee creeks in Russell and Barber counties, Alabama. John O. Howard to Lewis Cass, May 9, 1836, in *American State Papers, Military Affairs*, VI, 577-578; Executive Document 154, 52; "Report of Mr. Toombs," Senate Report 226, 33 Congress, 1 Session (Washington, 1854), II, parts 2, 5; Senate Document 224, 455; and Grant Foreman, *Indian Removal: The Emigration of the Five Civilized Tribes of Indians* (Norman, 1932), 148, 150 (cited hereafter as Foreman, *Indian Removal*).

16. An honorary or state militia rank. He is not listed in the official register of the United States Army officers.

17. Whiskey was the principal source of Creek misery. In "establishments" near the reservations white "shopkeepers" sold the Creeks abundant supplies of liquor. In return for credit they took liens on Creek property. Speedy foreclosures were common. When intoxicated the Indian frequently fought and occasionally killed. Creek men and women would lie promiscuously on the ground in drunken stupor all through the night. When their senses returned they found themselves heavily indebted or their land gone. They were not permitted to contradict accusations alleged against them. Executive Document 154, 16.

18. Captain John Munroe (Monroe), commander of Company G, Fourth Artillery, received a personal citation from General Jesup for outstanding service during the Seminole War in Florida. Heitman, *op. cit.*, I, 736; Sprague, *op. cit.*, 209.

19. The exact location of Woolfolk's plantation is unknown. It was probably near the present site of Fort Benning, Georgia.

20. Fort Mitchell was constructed in 1813 by General John Floyd on the west bank of the Chattahoochee River about ten miles south of Columbus. General Floyd, with 3,600 Georgia troops, used the fort as a base for operations against the Creeks in the First Creek War. During the second Creek uprising it was headquarters for the army in Georgia and Alabama. Coulter, *op. cit.*, 212.

21. First Lieutenant William Phillips Bainbridge of the Fourth Artillery served through the Florida War and was cited for gallantry in the Battle of Cerro Gordo during the Mexican War. Heitman, *op. cit.*, I, 182.

22. Revised MS, 18.

23. First Lieutenant Richard H. Peyton, a graduate of the United States Military Academy, was commanding officer of Fort Peyton—seven miles southwest of St. Augustine, Florida—at the time Osceola was taken prisoner near the fort.

24. Second Lieutenant Robert Harris Archer, Company I, Fourth Artillery. Heitman, *op. cit.*, I, 168.

25. Roanoke, Georgia, was situated on the east bank of the Chattahoochee, about thirty miles below Colum-

bus. Map in Theodore Irving, *The Conquest of Florida, by Hernando de Soto* (New York, 1851).

26. Revised MS, 20.

27. Major Benjamin Kendrick Pierce, First Artillery, was promoted to brevet lieutenant colonel on August 21, 1836, for distinguished service at Fort Drane, Florida. Sprague, *op. cit.*, 551.

28. Revised MS, 20.

29. Most of the hostile Creek chiefs realized that the war was a hopeless cause, and that full-scale conflict would mean extermination for the red man. Attempts to restrain the warriors, however, were unsuccessful. Seminole Indian victories in Florida set the pace for Creek acts of violence. The Creek warriors, possessing as they did an exaggerated idea of Seminole strength, dreamed of unlimited success in arms. They even entertained faint hopes that the Cherokees to the northeast would join in a concerted frontier struggle. Should they lose in Alabama and Georgia they planned to plunder the deserted white settlements, cause as much damage as possible, and, in the interval of panic and consternation, skulk or fight through to the Seminoles where a final stand could be maintained. T. H. Crawford to B. F. Butler, January 9, 1837, in Executive Document 154, 52; J. S. McIntosh to Robert Jones, May 9, 1836, in *American State Papers, Military Affairs*, VI, 579; and *id.* to *id.*, May 2, 1836, *ibid.*, 581.

30. Upon the outbreak of Creek hostilities Paddy Carr, son of an Irish father and a Creek Indian mother, offered his services to the United States Army. His role of warrior, guide, and interpreter made him popular among the troops. In the fall of 1836 he volunteered for service in Florida and was placed second in command of a band of Creek Volunteers who took part in the campaigns against the Seminole Indians. Frederick W. Hodge and David I. Bush-

nell, Jr. (eds.), Thomas L. McKenney and James Hall, *The Indian Tribes of North America* (Edinburgh, 1933-1934), II, 46-48 (cited hereafter as McKenney and Hall, *Indian Tribes of North America*).

31. The Indians considered white ". . . their fixt emblem of peace, friendship, happiness, prosperity, purity, holiness, etc." Samuel Cole Williams (ed.), *Adair's History of the American Indians* (Johnson City, Tennessee, 1930), 167.

32. Revised MS, 22.

33. Revised MS, 23.

CHAPTER II

1. Fort Henderson, Lee County, Alabama, was garrisoned by marines. Heitman, *Historical Register*, II, 507; Revised MS, 25.

2. Revised MS, 26.

3. Fort McCrary was eight miles north of Roanoke, Georgia.

4. The advance guard of an army on the march.

5. An account of the destruction of Roanoke is given in the *Apalachicola Gazette*, May 28, 1836.

"On Sunday morning last, at about daylight and after the sentinels who had been placed round the town had gone in, the citizens were aroused from their slumbers by the discharge of rifles and the yelling of savages. There were 70 or 80 persons in the town, including a small company of infantry under Capt. Horne, all of whom immediately gathered their arms, and rushed for the streets in the direction of the alarm. The Indians had placed a man or two, and at some places six or eight, at every door in the village, who of course made a simultaneous attack upon the citizens as they left their houses. Their fire was returned with as much spirit and effect as the circumstances would permit. By the time the number of the enemy being ascertained, (about 300), it was thought prudent to retreat, which they did in disorder;

they were pursued by the Indians some distance, who, failing to overtake them, returned to the town, plundered all the houses, and then applied the torch."

All but one house was destroyed. Casualties numbered seven whites and five blacks killed, one wounded, and fifteen persons missing. Three Indians were "supposed to have been killed"; the rest fled across the Chattahoochee to Alabama.

When news of the attack spread, a company of the armed men from Randolph County hurried to the aid of the village. Arriving on May 27, they found "the site . . . in possession of a company of Indians, headed by a white man." Three of the Indians and their white leader were killed—the rest escaped into the swamps.

6. Brigadier General John W. A. Sanford was appointed to command the Georgia Militia by Governor William Schley on May 27, 1836. Prior to the outbreak of hostilities Sanford was head of John W. A. Sanford and Company, composed of Alfred Iverson, John D. Howell, Benjamin Marshall, Luther Blake, Stephen Ingersoll, and Sanford. This company obtained, on September 17, 1835, a government contract for the removal of the Creek Indians to lands west of the Mississippi River. Unable to budge the Creeks from Alabama, Sanford resigned from the company on November 3, 1835. *American State Papers, Military Affairs,* VI, 756, 782.

7. Revised MS, 28.

8. The following was crossed out of the original manuscript: ". . . for Dr. Elwes was so beatified in the enjoyment of a leg of boiled fresh pork as to exceed the bounds of discretion, and was consequently attacked with the colic."

9. Dr. Mills was aboard the ill-fated steamboat *Dolphin* which blew up on December 17, 1836, off the bar of the St. Johns River, in Florida, killing fifteen and wounding nine. To make room for the women and children in the lifeboats, Dr. Mills clung precariously to a piece of timber for nine hours until rescued. *Niles Weekly Register,* December 31, 1836.

10. Revised MS, 30.

11. *Ibid.,* 30.

12. The "general"—a signal by the roll of the drums for striking tents, packing, and loading the wagons for marching.

13. This was probably a log raft. The army, however, maintained a small number of flatboats on the Chattahoochee for the purpose of ferrying troops.

14. The term "Indian negro" designates a Negro who lived with the Indians either as a slave or a free man.

15. Revised MS, 31.

16. Thomas Lawson was appointed Surgeon General on November 30, 1836. Previously Lawson served as a lieutenant colonel in the Louisiana Volunteers—part of the brigade brought from New Orleans to Fort Brooke, Florida, by Major General Gaines after hearing of Dade's Massacre. Heitman, *op. cit.,* I, 619; Sprague, *The Florida War,* 107.

17. General Scott's plan to bring a quick end to the Creek uprising was based upon defensive strategy, due, in the main, to a lack of arms and ammunition for his troops. He deployed the Georgia Volunteers along the east bank of the Chattahoochee from Columbus south to Irwinton to prevent any Creeks from escaping into Florida. Two steamboats patrolled the river to maintain open communications. The Alabama Volunteers were garrisoned at Tuskegee and Irwinton, thus closing a ring around the hostile country. The general offensive, when it unfolded, would see the Georgia forces cross the river, combine operations with the Alabama troops, marines, and regulars, and close in

on the hostile country in the fashion of a giant roundup.

Scott's delay foiled his grand plans. The Alabama troops, under General Jesup, hearing of constant Creek depredations, became impatient at Scott's procrastination. They took the initiative and made several sorties into hostile country. Disregarding Scott's order to "stop all offensive movements" until the general offensive would occur, Jesup seized the village of Eneah Mathla, capturing the aging chief and his deputy Eneah Micco. As a result the hostiles began surrendering in large numbers. On June 22, nearly one thousand surrendered, with smaller groups coming in each day. This offensive action by Jesup broke the power of the hostile faction and left only scattered resistance.

Scott finally began his offensive on June 25. The result was one Indian and one Indian Negro captured and a few worn-out Indian trails discovered. Three days later Scott was recalled to Washington and Jesup assumed supreme command of the troops in the Creek Nation. Scott to Jones, June 12, 1836, in Senate Document 224, 433; *id.* to *id.*, June 14, 1836, *ibid.*, 437; Scott to Jesup, June 16, 1836, *ibid.*, 441-442; Jesup to Lewis Cass, June 25, 1836, *ibid.*, 475-478; and Scott to Jones, July 2, 1836, *ibid.*, 481.

18. "The component parts of a ration are as follows: Three-fourths of a pound of pork or bacon, or one and one-quarter pound of fresh or salt beef; eighteen ounces of hard bread, or one and one-quarter pound of corn meal, to each man, per day; —and at the rate of four pounds of soap, one and one-half pounds of candles, two quarts of salt, four quarts of vinegar, eight quarts of peas or beans, four pounds of coffee, and eight pounds of sugar to each hundred men, per day. . . . The officers are . . . enabled to draw the full rations in preference to the privates, where the supplies are, for instance, limited. The private is entitled to one ration a day, in value about eighteen or twenty cents; the officers, according to their rank or grade, are entitled to two, three, four, to eight rations a day. In case the rations are not drawn, the soldier or officer has the privilege of drawing its value in money." Woodburne Potter, *The War in Florida: Being an Exposition of its Causes, and an Accurate History of the Campaigns of Generals Clinch, Gaines, and Scott* (Baltimore, 1836), 135 (cited hereafter as Potter, *The War in Florida*).

19. Motte undoubtedly was referring to the "Cowikee Lands," located along the Cowikee and Bear creeks and their tributaries in Russell and Barbour counties, Alabama. "These are gently undulating tracts . . . forming a kind of prairie. . . ." Saffold Berney, *Handbook of Alabama* (Birmingham, 1892), 439-440.

20. Revised MS, 32.

21. No organized Indian resistance existed in the Creek territory. Danger lay in small, roving bands of Indians who would attack if reasonably sure they held the advantage. Senate Report 226, II, parts 2, 3.

22. Revised MS, 32.

23. *Ibid.*, 32.

24. By 1836 twelve steamboats plied the Chattahoochee River. During the Creek War steamboating became stirring and exciting. The Indians attacked the "Hyperion" seven miles below Columbus, killing the pilot, mortally wounding a number of the crew, and causing the boat to run aground. Several attacks were made on other boats; and the Creeks carried audacity to an extreme in attacking the "Metamora" with 150 troops on board. John H. Goff states, "After this attack, five or six heavily armed steamers began to ply the river to intercept any Redskins attempting to cross to the Georgia side." "The Steamboat Period in Georgia," *The*

Journey into Wilderness

Georgia Historical Quarterly, XII (September, 1928), 247-248.

CHAPTER III

1. General Scott proclaimed the Creek War unofficially ended on July 5. Reporting the majority of the hostiles either captured or voluntarily surrendered, he estimated two hundred still at large in the swamps and a few on their way to Florida. Under these conditions it was deemed safe to discharge many of the troops. The total number prior to mustering out the volunteers was 10,158. This figure included some 1,103 regulars, 4,755 Georgians, and 4,300 Alabamans. Thomas J. Lee to Robert Jones, July 5, 1836, in Senate Document 224, 490; General Scott to General Wool, commander of the Alabama Volunteers, July 4, 1836, *ibid.,* 491-492.

2. Returning reports from those who had emigrated told of the "wretched existence" and denial of "the necessities promised them in this western country." Creeks feared the decimating fevers which wiped out over five hundred of their people in three years, and the chronic epidemics of influenza, cholera, and smallpox which ran rampant in that faraway and unknown land. Grant Foreman, *The Five Civilized Tribes* (Norman, 1934), 150.

3. "It is sweet and honorable to die for one's fatherland."

In fits of desperation many warriors went into the woods and hanged themselves with grapevines. Creek women displayed devout reverence for their homeland by burning piles of light wood over the graves of relatives and friends in honor of their memories. Others cut down fruit trees which shaded the graves of their children, declaring that the white man was unworthy to eat the fruit. Alfred A. Balch to Benjamin F. Butler, January 14, 1837, in Executive Document 154, 17.

4. Captured Creeks, rounded up by the troops, were herded into parties from one to three thousand, and hurried off to lands west of the Mississippi. The largest emigration took place in the winter of 1836 when Chief Opothleyoholo and more than eleven thousand of his people arrived at Fort Gibson in Arkansas. Grant Foreman (ed.), *A Traveler in Indian Territory; the Journal of Ethan Allen Hitchcock, Late Major-General in the United States Army* (Cedar Rapids, 1930), 119. For an excellent account of the removal of the Creek Indians, see Foreman, *Indian Removal.*

5. Eneah Mathla was a former chief of the Florida Seminoles. Terms were written into the Treaty of Moultrie Creek (United States-Seminole treaty) in 1823 allowing Eneah Mathla to remain on his ancestral land—a tract two miles square embracing the village of Tupholga on the waters of Rocky Comfort Creek in West Florida —while the rest of the Seminole Nation moved into a reservation farther down the peninsula. This favor was granted because the United States government and Florida territorial officials held the sage chieftain in high regard. Eneah Mathla's refusal to move with his people to East Florida, along with his subsequent opposition to the United States government's Indian policy, caused him to be deposed by his people. Embittered, he moved to the Creek Nation, where he was well received and became quite influential in their councils. In early 1836 he became the active head of the hostile war party, and was captured by a group of friendly Creek Indian scouts on June 15. Along with other captured warriors, the eighty-four-year-old Eneah Mathla, manacled and chained, was marched ninety miles from Fort Mitchell to Montgomery without uttering a complaining sound. At Montgomery the

Editor's Notes

prisoners were placed on a river boat and began the long journey to their new homes in the West. Charles H. Coe, *Red Patriots: The Story of the Seminoles* (Cincinnati, 1898), 24; Gad Humphries to William P. Duval, *American State Papers, Indian Affairs* (Washington, 1834), II, 616-617; McKenney and Hall, *The Indian Tribes of North America,* II, 264; *American State Papers, Military Affairs,* VII, 359; and Foreman, *Indian Removal,* 153.

6. Major General Thomas Sidney Jesup (1788-1860) was given command of the troops in Georgia and Alabama on May 19, 1836. Meanwhile, Scott, who was directing the campaign against the Indians in Florida, received orders to proceed to the Creek Nation as soon as he successfully checked Seminole hostilities. Scott prematurely left Florida, "where much certainly remained to be done," and met Jesup in Augusta, Georgia. Both general officers possessed orders to direct the Creek campaign. Jesup agreed to be second in command so that General Scott could recover "the military reputation lost in Florida." On June 9, Jesup took command of the troops in Alabama— the western half of the theater. This official collision between the two officers hindered harmonious cooperation. Jesup's strategy proposed seeking, finding, and destroying the enemy, while Scott posted guards along the Chattahoochee to prevent Creeks from escaping to Florida. This friction, along with the subsequent delay in terminating the Creek hostilities, led to the recall of General Scott by order of President Andrew Jackson. *American State Papers, Military Affairs,* VII, 356-360.

7. In early days interior Alabama was reached by means of a horse path, the right of way granted by the Creeks in 1805. Federal troops expanded this path into a road in 1811.

Called the "Three-Chopped Way," because surveyors cut three blazes on the trees marking the course, the road entered Alabama at Fort Mitchell and extended west to New Philadelphia (now Montgomery). From there it proceeded southwest. From Fort Mitchell eastward it snaked through Milledgeville, Augusta, Columbia, Raleigh, and Richmond, joining the Piedmont Road to Washington, D.C. At the time of the Second Creek War improper maintenance turned many sections of the road into gutted wagon trails which, at some places, were almost impassable. Albert Burton Moore, *History of Alabama* (University, Alabama, 1934), 67-69.

8. Lieutenant Colonel Alexander Brooks, Fourth Artillery, lost his life in the explosion of the steamboat *Dolphin* in St. Johns Bay, Florida, on December 17, 1836. *American State Papers, Military Affairs,* VI, 1019.

9. David Moniac, a half-breed Creek Indian, was graduated from the United States Military Academy in July, 1822. Five months after his graduation he resigned his regular commission and returned to his tribal home in Alabama. Upon the outbreak of Creek hostilities he volunteered for service and was commissioned a first lieutenant. In August, 1836, he was promoted to captain in the Creek Mounted Volunteer Regiment. While accompanying the Creek Volunteers to Florida, Captain Moniac was killed in the Battle of Wahoo Swamp on November 15, 1836. Heitman, *Historical Register,* I, 719.

10. Captain John F. Lane, promoted to colonel in September, 1836, was given command of 759 Creek Volunteers, among whom were Paddy Carr, Jim Boy, Captain Moniac, and other Indian notables. These volunteers played an important part in the campaigns against the Seminoles in Florida. Sprague, *The Florida War,* 162.

CHAPTER IV

1. There are a number of mineral springs in Meriwether County, Georgia, situated from thirty to forty miles northeast of Columbus. The most famous of this group is Warm Springs, vacation resort of the late President Franklin D. Roosevelt. The water is a constant ninety-two degrees and provides the "most delightful baths in all the Union." Others in the area include Chalybeate Springs, Cold Spring, and White Sulphur Springs. Motte undoubtedly was referring to Warm Springs, which at that time was well known for its beneficial health-giving qualities. Even the Indians regarded it as a health resort where, "according to tradition, warriors came to immerse their wounded bodies in the warm waters and soft mud. Believing that a beneficent Great Spirit stoked the fires under the earth to warm the waters, they respected the place as neutral ground where sick men could be free from attack by enemy tribes." *Georgia, Historical and Industrial* (Atlanta, 1901), 758-759; Federal Writers' Project, *Georgia: A Guide to Its Towns and Countryside* (Athens, 1940), 354.

2. Captain Harvey Brown commanded a company of the Fourth Artillery. An old Indian fighter, Captain Brown had been one of the witnesses to the signing of the Treaty of Moultrie Creek in 1823. In June, 1836, Brown was mustered as lieutenant colonel in the Creek Volunteer Regiment commanded by Colonel John F. Lane, and after the death of Colonel Lane took over command of the regiment. Sprague, *The Florida War*, 22, 162; *Niles Weekly Register*, November 26, 1836.

3. Big Warrior Stand refers to the area in which the Big Warrior, one of the principal chiefs of the Creek Confederation, made his home. The folding map in Saffold Berney's *Handbook of Alabama* locates Warrior Stand

southeast of the Tallapoosa River, south of Tuskegee, and west of the headwaters of the Hatchechubbee and Cowikee creeks.

4. Revised MS, 47.

5. Echo Hadjo, a friendly Creek sub-chieftain, was respected by friend and foe. Many hostile warriors surrendered to him rather than to army officials, hoping thereby to receive more favorable treatment. Exceptionally capable of handling warriors, Echo Hadjo was brought to Florida by Colonel Lane and used as a mediator to the Seminoles. Senate Document 224, 475.

6. "The ceremony of the black-drink is a military institution, blended with religious opinions. The black-drink is a strong decoction of the shrub well known in the Carolinas by the name of Cassina, or, the Uupon tea. The leaves are collected, parched in a pot until brown, boiled over a fire in the center of the square, dipped out and poured from one pan or cooler into another, and back again, until it ferments and produces a large quantity of white froth, from which, with the purifying qualities the Indians ascribe to it, they style it white drink; but the liquor of itself, which, if strong, is nearly as black as molasses, is by the white people universally called black-drink.

"It is a gentle diuretic, and, if taken in large quantities, sometimes affects the nerves. . . . Except rum, there is no liquor of which the Creek Indians are so excessively fond. In addition to their habitual fondness for it, they have a religious belief that it infallibly possesses the following qualities, viz.: That it purifies them from all sin, and leaves them in a state of perfect innocence; that it inspires them with an invincible prowess in war; and that it is the only solid cement of friendship, benevolence, and hospitality." John R. Swanton, *Religious Beliefs and Medicinal Practices of the Creek Indians*, Forty-second

Editor's Notes

Annual Report of the Bureau of American Ethnology, 1924-1925 (Washington, 1928), 538; see also James Adair, *History of the American Indians* (London, 1775), 46-48.

7. "After drinking copiously, the warrior, by hugging his arms across his stomach, and leaning forward, disgorges the liquor in a large stream from his mouth, to the distance of six or eight feet. Thus, immediately after drinking they begin spouting on all sides of the square and in every direction. . . . it is thought a handsome accomplishment in a young fellow to be able to spout well." Swanton, *op. cit.,* 539.

8. Revised MS, 49.

9. "After an Indian had chased a bear, deer, or other game animal for a long time until he had become tired and sweaty he would take a fish-tooth scratcher and scratch one thigh until the blood ran. This would prevent him from getting tired. Long ago the Indians scratched their bodies all over so that the loss of blood would lighten them and they would be able to run long distances without becoming weary." Swanton, *op. cit.,* 445-446.

10. Revised MS, 51.

11. *Ibid.,* 51.

12. *Ibid.,* 51.

13. *Ibid.,* 52.

14. *Ibid.,* 52.

15. *Ibid.,* 52.

16. *Ibid.,* 52.

17. *Ibid.,* 53.

18. *Ibid.,* 54. The language spoken by those Creeks and Seminoles who belonged to the Muskhogean linguistic family is similar. There were, however, elements in the Seminole tribe; for example, the Mikasukis, who belonged to the Hitchiti-speaking peoples. They spoke the Hitchiti language, which bore no resemblance to the Muskhogean Creek.

The original Seminoles were a Hitchiti-speaking people, and constituted a group of Oconee Indians who, led by their chieftain, Cowkeeper, moved into Florida around the year 1750. They migrated from their home along the Oconee River in central Georgia and settled near the Alachua savannah in north Florida. Here they occupied territory formerly inhabited by various pre-Seminole Indians, who, under Spanish control and domination for several centuries, had rapidly declined in numbers and strength. The small Oconee band was welcomed in Florida by the Spanish government, and became known as the Seminoles. The term *Seminole,* according to Benjamin Hawkins, who lived many years among the Creeks, was derived from the Creek "Isty-Semole," which meant "wild men," and was given to those groups of Indians who detached themselves from the Creek Confederacy "on account of their being hunters, and attending but little to agriculture." The nucleus of the Seminole Nation, therefore, was principally Hitchiti in character—non-Muskhogean.

Between 1750 and 1800 both Hitchiti- and Muskhogean-speaking tribes left the Creek Confederacy and joined the newly formed Seminole Nation, which slowly became a blend of Muskhogean and Hitchiti peoples. Out of the Hitchiti branch emerged the most important element among the Seminoles—the determined, resolute, and vindictive Mikasuki Indians.

After the First Creek War in 1814, large numbers of Muskhogean Creeks fled to Florida, thereby swelling the ranks of the Seminole Nation. Subsequent migrations of Muskhogean Creeks to Florida continued to increase the Seminole population. A census in 1823 revealed 4,883 Indians. This increase in population resulted in a predominance of the Muskhogean peoples, customs, and language. Leadership, however, remained with the matrilineal descendants of Cowkeeper, the original Seminole. John R. Swanton, *The Indians of the Southeastern United States,* Bureau of American

257

Journey into Wilderness

Ethnology Bulletin 137 (Washington, 1946), 150, 181-182; Swanton, *Early History of the Creek Indians and Their Neighbors,* 398-414, 440-448; Kenneth W. Porter, "The Founder of the 'Seminole Nation,' Secoffee or Cowkeeper," *The Florida Historical Quarterly,* XXVII (April, 1949), 362-384; and James F. Sunderman (ed.), "Life in Camp and Field: The Journal of an Army Surgeon, 1836-38," unpublished master's thesis, University of Florida (1949), xlviii-cxviii.

CHAPTER V

1. Four hundred marines, including the First and Second Battalions of United States Marines, served with the army in the Creek Nation. They were commanded by Colonel Archibald Henderson. Senate Document 224, 491; Edwin North McClellan, "History of the United States Marine Corps" (1932), II, Pt. 2, 29-30, unpublished manuscript in the P. K. Yonge Library of Florida History, University of Florida.

2. Captain John Harris commanded Company B, Second Battalion, United States Marines. In the campaigns against the Florida Indians, his company was mounted (the horse marines), and Captain Harris promoted to major for gallantry in the Battle of Hatchee-Lustee Creek near Lake Tohopekaliga on January 26, 1837. In March of 1837, Harris was appointed a courier for General Jesup and carried Jesup's message concerning the temporary cessation of hostilities to Washington. In 1839 Harris (then a lieutenant colonel) succeeded Brigadier General Archibald Henderson as Commandant of the Marine Corps. *Ibid.,* 39, 52, 61, 65; Clyde H. Metcalf, *A History of the United States Marine Corps* (New York, 1939), 189-190.

3. The Creek Nation agreed to furnish six hundred to one thousand warriors for service against the Seminoles. In return the United States

government promised to advance the Creek annuity of $31,900 to be applied to the payment of their debts. Creek warriors were paid and equipped like regular army soldiers and entitled to such plunder as they might take from the Seminoles. "The offer of 'plunder' was understood to authorize the Creek warriors to keep such slaves as they could capture in Florida,"—a tempting incentive to volunteer. Besides, while the regiment was engaged against the Seminoles, their families were promised protection by the United States government and remained in concentration camps in Alabama.

"Believing the Seminole war would be of short duration, 776 Creek warriors under their chief Jim Boy . . . enlisted for service in Florida with the assurance that they would be discharged on the first of February, 1837, so they could begin their journey to the west with their families in time to put in a crop in their new country that would sustain them the following year." But the Seminole War did not end in six months and the regiment was detained seven months beyond its enlistment period, causing considerable dissatisfaction in the ranks. In addition, many warriors fell sick in the Florida climate. To reconcile their ill feelings, General Jesup promised further government subsistence for a year after their arrival in the West and until they could harvest their first crop.

The services of the Creeks were invaluable. They were especially utilized as guides and scouts for an army which at times was completely baffled by the terrain over which it was operating. From the Seminole point of view, however, the Creek volunteers were vile traitors deserving only a traitor's death.

From time to time segments of the regiment were discharged, the last sailing from Tampa Bay on September 11, 1837. Foreman, *Indian Removal,*

258

160-161, 179-180, 348; Sprague, *The Florida War,* 162, 165, 169.

4. A "matross" was an artillery soldier who ranked inferior to the gunner. During the Revolutionary War the term was used to designate the American private soldier in the artillery service. Today it is synonymous with a "private" in the artillery. The term itself is a corruption of the French "matelot" soldier. James A. H. Murray and others (eds.), *A New English Dictionary on Historical Principles* (Oxford, 1888-1933), VI, 239; William A. Craigie and James R. Hulbert (eds.), *A Dictionary of American English on Historical Principles* (Chicago, 1940), III, 1496.

5. Colonel Lane's "road to Glory" ended shortly thereafter in a "melancholy death" at Fort Drane, Florida. He and his regiment of Creek Volunteers reached Fort Brooke, Tampa Bay, Florida, on October 5, 1836, and proceeded immediately into the interior. They examined the country in all directions, and had several spirited encounters with the enemy. Proceeding northward they joined Governor (Brigadier General) Richard K. Call and his Florida Militia at Fort Drane, where several days later Colonel Lane committed suicide. The following account of his death appeared in the *Florida Herald* (St. Augustine) on October 27, 1836:

"He [Colonel Lane] had been sick several days and complained of a great distress in his head. Just before the melancholy event took place, he complained of the heat of the weather. Captain Galt, in whose tent he was, proposed raising the tent and went out for that purpose . . . he heard a fall and then a groan within. On going in he saw Colonel Lane on his knees with the point of his sword thrust into his left eye, and the hilt resting on the ground, and which penetrated into the brain. It is supposed that he committed the fatal

act while in a fit of insanity produced by brain fever."

Colonel Lane was only twenty-six years of age. His military career had been brilliant, his promotions rapid, and the prospects for the future extremely bright. Jim Boy, one of the Creek chiefs of the regiment, addressed the assembled warriors at the funeral, saying "it was to be regretted that their white brother had left them so soon but there was no use lamenting his decease, for all here below, the white man as well as the red, had a certain race to be fulfilled, and these must be accomplished. Their white brother had fulfilled his, and now the Great Spirit had called him away from among them." J. W. Phelps to John Phelps, July 10, 1837, in "Letters of Lieutenant John W. Phelps," *The Florida Historical Quarterly,* VI (October, 1927), 71. (Cited hereafter as Phelps, "Letters.")

6. Revised MS, 59.
7. William Schley was governor of Georgia from 1835 to 1837.
8. Revised MS, 61.
9. *Ibid.,* 62.
10. "I found the water so beautiful, That I bathed in it."

CHAPTER VI

1. En route from Nashville, Tennessee, in January, 1818, to subdue the Seminoles in Florida, General Andrew Jackson passed through the Indian town of Cheraw (Chehaw), in Georgia. The warriors of the village under Howard, their aging chieftain, met Jackson and volunteered for service under him against the Seminoles. Jackson accepted their services and at the same time guaranteed the safety of the women, children, and old men left behind in the village. Shortly thereafter Captain Wright and 275 Georgia Militia, under an order from Governor William Rabum, advanced upon this village and massacred the

inhabitants. Their chief, the aged Howard, was shot down while carrying a white flag in his hand. Howard's little grandson shared the same fate. The militia left the entire village in desolate ruins. The news of this massacre by the Georgia Militia reached General Jackson after he had passed Fort Gadsden en route from St. Marks to Pensacola, Florida. In heated correspondence with Governor Rabum, Jackson demanded Captain Wright be arrested and court-martialed.

This massacre attributed to Jackson by his political enemies was used as propaganda during his presidential campaigns. John Henry Eaton, *The Life of Major General Andrew Jackson: Comprising a History of the War in the South; from the Commencement of the Creek Campaign to the Termination of Hostilities Before New Orleans* (Philadelphia, 1828), 299-300.

2. Pindartown, a small community on the east bank of the Flint River, north of Albany, Georgia, was built on the site of an old Indian village called "Thronateeska." It faded out of existence after 1836, when Albany received its first charter. Lucian Lamar Knight, *Georgia's Landmarks, Memorials, and Legends* (Atlanta, 1914), II, 1054.

3. "Hurrying Clouds! Sailors of the air!

Happy he who travels and sails with you!

Give my friendly regards to the land of my youth!"

4. Franklinville was founded in 1828, seven years after the first settlers moved into Lowndes County. It was located a few miles east of what is now Hahira, Georgia. *History of Lowndes County, Georgia, 1825-1941* (Valdosta, 1941), 5.

5. T. O. Townsend was one of the first settlers in Lowndes County. *Ibid.*, 6.

1. Places like Camp Townsend were temporary encampments and not official army posts.

2. Tattoo was a signal or call, sounded by the drum, trumpet, or bugle, shortly before taps, notifying the men to retire to their quarters for the night.

3. Revised MS, 74.

4. *Ibid.*, 75.

5. Captain Bernard Romans, early Florida traveler, mentions the groundnut which was "introduced by the Blacks [slaves] from Guinea." It became one of the favorite crops of the early settlers in the southeast, since it was easy to cultivate, yielded great quantities, and produced a type of oil which would keep for long periods of time without growing rancid. Bernard Romans, *A Concise Natural History of East and West-Florida* (New York, 1776), 131.

6. Henry Kirk White (1785-1806) was an English poet who drew praise from Lord Byron and was claimed by Robert Southey as a protégé. "He is known only today as the author of a few happy lyrics and several hymns." Stanley J. Kunitz and Howard Haycraft (eds.), *British Authors of the Nineteenth Century* (New York, 1936), 652-653.

7. Motte's expression "eat them out of doors" is an interesting variation of the popular phrase "eat them out of house and home."

8. A series of twenty periodical pamphlets published from January 24, 1807, to January 25, 1808, by Washington Irving, William Irving, and J. K. Paulding, under the title of *Salmagundi: Or, The Whim-Whams and Opinions of Launcelot Langstaff, Esq. and Others.* James D. Hart, *The Oxford Companion to American Literature* (New York, 1948), 664.

Editor's Notes

CHAPTER IX

1. Major Greenleaf Dearborn commanded this detachment of regular troops consisting of two companies and totaling two hundred men. *Niles Weekly Register,* October 15, 1836.

2. Samuel M. Clyatt was commissioned the first county surveyor of Lowndes County on May 29, 1826. He later served in the state senate (1841-1844). The Clyatt farm was probably a few miles east of the present town of Clyattville, Georgia. *History of Lowndes County, Georgia, 1825-1941,* 54, 64.

3. This refers to a figure quite similar to the quadrille—a dance which was popular in the nineteenth century. The phrase, in translation, signifies a movement of the legs to the right, then in the opposite direction, followed by a swing or twirl.

4. That is, exaggerated.

5. The arrival of Lieutenant Casey meant sufficient officers for a foursome in their game of whist. Various spellings of the word "dummy" were listed as correct in the nineteenth century: dumby, dummie, dumbie, dummee, and dumbee. Murray (ed.), *A New English Dictionary on Historical Principles,* III, 713.

The following was crossed out of the original manuscript—"Such an addition is particularly gratifying to myself, for the two old Majors [Staniford and Dearborn] were not exactly birds of a feather with myself; their only or principal pursuit being the replenishing [of] the body; particularly Major Dearborn; Ye Gods! what extraordinary powers of making victuals disappear that man possesses; his speed in swallowing is greater than that of any high-pressure steam-boat going down stream; and the quantity,—but that exceeds all description; nothing comes amiss to his maw [jaws], and he always takes his meals by himself from the same motive that actuated Sancho Panza to a like proceeding. He, however, has a large body to supply, and that may be some excuse for employing every hour of night and day in the gross pursuit of eating."

6. This evidently refers to being beaten up in some particular way.

7. Motte is referring to a tornado which leaves a narrow wake of destruction as compared to the wide swath left by a hurricane.

8. John Warner Barber (1789-1885) was an American writer, traveler, and engraver. Prior to 1836, his principal works, "remarkable for their odd bits of information and antiquarian flavor," were *Historical Scenes in the United States* (1827) and *New England Scenes* (1833). Stanley J. Kunitz and Howard Haycraft (eds.), *American Authors, 1600-1900: A Biographical Dictionary of American Literature* (New York, 1938), 53.

CHAPTER X

1. Squire E. Swilley was among the original settlers who moved into Lowndes County in 1821. Knight, *Georgia's Landmarks, Memorials, and Legends,* I, 754.

2. The following was crossed out of the original manuscript: "Home no longer exists for me; tis only to be found in the memory of past times and joyous youth, when hopes were bright, and the very air I breathed seemed impregnated with delight. There is no hearthstone to which I may turn, like others, when the dangers and privations of this war are over, and say, there is my sacred asylum of home! no 'heart still true in joy and woe' will pour forth its sympathy. That peculiar happiness is not for me, which those who lead a wandering life, or who quit their homes for a time, so frequently enjoy; —That of returning to the home of past enjoyments, and again meeting those loved faces which render home so dear, and hearing the thousand tender inquiries which flow from the heart to the lips. Tis true, neither

time nor absence can shake from my heart the memory of Charleston;—to me the dearest spot on Earth;—Yet I can only love it as the home and the burial-place of my ancestors; as the spot of my birth; the haunt of my boyhood, and scene of my early pleasures. There are indeed some friends there, who have twined themselves round my heart; to meet whom, after the wandering and cheerless life I now lead, will be like entering on the enjoyment of a new existence;— Yet I cannot anticipate the pleasurable *certainty* that my return to the place of my nativity would cause a single eye to brighten, a lip to smile, or a single countenance to emanate with friendly welcome."

3. Motte and the troops were scouting near the western edge of the Okefinokee Swamp. The Creeks and Seminoles were using this impenetrable morass as a refuge and hide-out, and its many trails, which only they knew, as a means of passing into Florida. The difficulty and near impossibility of conducting military operations into the swamp can be clearly ascertained from the following account:

"The Creeks had been harassing the settlers near the southern boundary-line of Georgia, and a detachment of troops, having too closely scrutinized their movements, saw the Indians melt away into the dim recesses of the Okefinokee. This swamp was of immense extent, more difficult to access than any previously mentioned, and had, up to this time, never been penetrated by a white man. In the month of August [1838] Captain [Benjamin Lloyd] Beall [of the Second United States Dragoons], with his company [I], determined to attempt an exploration of this terra incognita. Finding a fresh Indian trail, he soon discovered that it could not be followed mounted, as his horses mired the first step taken. Dismounting his men, he entered the swamp. The heat soon became so oppressive as almost to impede respira-

tion. It seemed like a spot where the breath of heaven was forbidden to enter, while the rays of the sun poured down, as through a convex glass, upon the aching heads of the party. After following the trail for about four miles, on a surface that continually trembled under foot and at last became entirely obliterated, the ground began to give way, the soldiers frequently sinking to the waist in black mud, the stench from which soon became so intolerable as to induce vomiting. Convinced himself, by sickness, of the impracticability of continuing the route, Captain Beall directed a counter-march, and once more gained the open, where the grateful shade of the pine breezes from the north were hardly sufficient to revive the failing energies of his half-poisoned command." Theo. F. Rodenbough, *From Everglade to Cañon with the Second Dragoons* (New York, 1875), 31-32 (cited hereafter as Rodenbough, *From Everglade to Cañon*).

4. Tustenuggee John was a minor chief. Tustenuggee, a corruption of the Creek word *Tastanagi,* which means warrior, was given to one who had distinguished himself in battle. The title generally carried with it a position of official capacity in the clan or town councils. Creek executive organizational flow and authority was relatively simple: after the head chiefs of the nation came the chiefs of the different towns, each town having a principal chief and a sub-chief. John R. Swanton, *Social Organization and Social Usages of the Indians of the Creek Confederacy,* Forty-second Annual Report of the Bureau of American Ethnology, 1924-1925 (Washington, 1928), 101, 316.

5. It was not uncommon for the Indians, when in flight, to lighten their load by destroying their children. *The Floridian* (Tallahassee), on August 13, 1836, printed several accounts of this practice. One account reads as follows:

Editor's Notes

". . . a party of Lowndes County, Georgia volunteers fell in with a party of Creeks near the Florida line, and killed ten warriors, and took eight women and children prisoners. The prisoners were taken to a house under guard. In the evening one of the squaws was observed to give her children drink from a coffee pot. Shortly after, she obtained leave of absence, and not returning, search was made for her, but she had made her escape. Her children were all found dead, from poison administered by their unnatural mother."

Another account, perhaps the one to which Motte referred, relates how "mud moss" was stuffed in the mouth and nostrils of the children.

Occasionally they would desert their offspring. Thus, during the Battle of Brushy Creek, July 10, 1836, in Berrien County, Georgia, when the Indians realized their defeat was imminent, ". . . one by one they began to slip from the scene, taking advantage of the thick swamp . . . in their flight many of the squaws threw away their children . . . these children being found dead and deserted." *History of Lowndes County, Georgia, 1825-1941*, 11-12.

CHAPTER XI

1. The following was crossed out of the original manuscript: " . . . and of a sister most dear,—my sister in whose smiles I lived, and whose happiness I made my study,—around whom the tendrils of my love were so closely twined, that on her welfare alone depended my happiness."

2. The following was crossed out of the original manuscript: "My brightest hopes at that time, however, beheld this 'el dorado' only through a lengthened vista."

3. Motte is referring to the Suwannee Springs, located about seven miles north of Live Oak, Florida. The

springs, situated in a hollow of the high bank of the Suwannee, are enclosed in a concrete-rock flood wall which is fifteen feet high. The average temperature of the spring water is 70° Fahrenheit. C. W. Lingham and others, in *Springs of Florida*, Florida Geological Survey Bulletin No. 31 (Tallahassee, 1947), 18, 158-160.

4. Revised MS, 109.

5. "To pass the time."

6. In 1837, according to John Lee Williams, the town of Micco was situated in the forks of the Alapaha River and was the county seat of Hamilton County. Today it no longer exists. *The Territory of Florida: Or, Sketches of the Topography, Civil and Natural History, of the Country, the Climate, and the Indian Tribes, from the First Discovery to the Present Time* (New York, 1837), 133 (cited hereafter as Williams, *The Territory of Florida*).

7. The old Indian town of Micco was situated across the Alapaha from the 1837 village. It has been located and identified by Dr. John M. Goggin, associate professor of sociology and anthropology, University of Florida.

8. The Alapaha River bed at this point goes dry only during extreme droughts, when all the water is carried through underground channels. C. Wythe Cooke and Stuart Mossom, *Geology of Florida*, Florida Geological Survey, Twentieth Annual Report, 1927-1928 (Tallahassee, 1929), 91.

9. After several months of scouting in the southern regions of Georgia, including sorties into northern Florida, Motte's detachment was transferred to the army in Florida, commanded by Brigadier General Thomas Sidney Jesup.

The Seminoles had been on the warpath over a year when Motte arrived in Florida. Jesup was the fifth commanding general in this short period of time to attempt a successful campaign. His predecessors in command had failed to bring hostilities to an expected quick termination. Their failure resulted from a number of varying conditions and circumstances not considered nor anticipated by the higher echelons of command and the American public in general. Not only had they to cope with a determined, sagacious, and intelligent foe, whose diplomatic stratagems and guerilla tactics outmaneuvered the armchair strategy of a peacetime army, but also with insurmountable problems of supply and transportation, inadequate intelligence and courier service, an apathetic Floridian citizenry, the morale and deployment of "short term" volunteer troops, climate, and disease, limited cooperation of higher and lower commands, and an inability to understand the Indian mind.

Hostilities in Florida began in late 1835, culminating many years of ill-feeling between the Seminole Indians and the ever-advancing American frontiersmen. Border warfare and frontier skirmishes over property, "runaway" slaves, "stolen" cattle, and constant encroachment dated back into the period of Spanish Florida. After the transfer of the peninsula to the United States, in 1821, these problems increased. The Treaty of Fort Moultrie (or Moultrie Creek) in 1823, was an attempt to solve the differences by giving the Seminole his own inviolate five-million-acre reservation in East Florida for a period of twenty years. Though workable, Fort Moultrie proved unsatisfactory owing to the attitudes and determinations of both the whites and Indians. The Indian Removal Act, passed by the United States Congress in the early days of the first Jackson administration, established the governmental policy towards all Indians residing east of the Mississippi River. It called for their removal to lands in the West. In accordance with this policy, the Seminoles, after constant pressure, signed the Treaty of Paynes Landing

in 1832, thereby nullifying Fort Moultrie and pledging removal if a delegation of their chiefs found the lands in the West satisfactory. Six Seminole chiefs journeyed to the West under government supervision. They inspected and approved the lands, and signed the Treaty of Fort Gibson pledging the Nation to emigrate. This action met with disapproval back in Florida and split the Seminole Nation into a "removal party" and an "anti-removal party"—the latter becoming known as the hostile or war party. The anti-removal faction vehemently maintained that the six chiefs were not empowered to speak for all the Seminoles. They accused the United States of bad faith and deceit in the execution of the Treaty of Paynes Landing, and maintained that the terms of Fort Moultrie guaranteed their residence in Florida for twenty years. Some even denied the existence of Paynes Landing.

General Wiley Thompson, government agent to the Indians, however, proceeded according to the terms of Paynes Landing and Fort Gibson, and set January 1, 1836, as the date for emigration. He deposed the anti-removal chieftains from their position of tribal authority and threatened force if his terms were not complied with by January 1. The anti-removal party immediately began preparations for war, collecting ammunition and supplies and recruiting warriors throughout the Nation.

On November 14, 1835, five "removal-party" chiefs, along with 450 of their people, fled to Fort Brooke, Florida, and sought the protection of the United States Army. About two weeks later, Charlie Emathla, a removal chief of considerable influence in the Nation, was murdered by Osceola and a group of hostile warriors. The purge continued. Fearing the refugees at Fort Brooke had divulged many of their war plans, the hostile chiefs forced all the remaining towns

Editor's Notes

in the Nation to join in a general war against the white man. Refusal meant death.

On November 30 General Thompson warned the inhabitants of Florida against possible Indian attacks. By the end of the first week in December, the entire countryside of east and central Florida was in a state of terror. The inhabitants fled to fortified stockades seeking protection and safety, for several skirmishes, involving either Florida Militia troops or private citizens, had taken place during the summer and fall of 1835. These typical frontier skirmishes indicated the determination and the potential destructivity possessed by the hostile Indians. On the afternoon of December 28, General Thompson and Lieutenant Constantine Smith were ambushed and murdered near Fort King by Osceola and his warriors. The murder of General Thompson was the first major blow struck by the Seminoles. The second occurred several hours later on the same day when Major Francis Dade and two companies of United States troops were ambushed along the Fort King road about five miles from the Wahoo Swamp. It was one of the worst disasters in the annals of American Indian warfare. Only three privates survived the horrible massacre. Before the first of January, the removal date set by Thompson, another significant battle was fought in the dense undergrowth and thick hammock-land along the Withlacoochee River.

The murder of Thompson, the massacre of Dade and his command, and the Battle of Withlacoochee left little doubt as to the hostile intentions of the Seminoles. The war had begun.

When Motte entered Florida, the countryside appeared a deserted land. The inhabitants were congregated in towns and stockades, living on government subsistence. No place was free from the fear of sudden attack.

Outside the fortifications, every thicket, swamp, or hammock concealed a possible unseen foe. For a more detailed account of the causes and early actions of the war see Sunderman (ed.), "Life in Camp and Field; The Journal of an Army Surgeon, 1836-38," xlviii-cxv.

CHAPTER XII

1. The Apalachicola River was the dividing line between East and West Florida during British control (1763-1783) and the second Spanish period of occupation. Andrew Jackson, appointed first United States Territorial Governor after transfer of the peninsula to the United States in 1821, used the Suwannee River as a dividing line creating two counties, Escambia to the west and St. Johns to the east. Politically, however, the territory remained as one unit. Kathryn Abbey Hanna, *Florida, Land of Change* (Chapel Hill, rev. ed., 1948), 75, 143, 146.

2. The mail road between Jacksonville and Tallahassee ran four miles south of Suwannee Springs. This road is shown on the original 1846 map of Florida by J. Goldsborough Bruff, located in the P. K. Yonge Library of Florida History, University of Florida (cited hereafter as the Bruff Map of Florida).

3. Sikes' rapid-fire technique was due to the assistance of his wife, who loaded one gun while he shot another. A contemporary account stated four Indians were killed and several wounded. *Niles Weekly Register,* February 25, 1837.

4. The statement that a white man led the band of Indians is questionable. It is not doubted that renegade whites carried on illicit trade in weapons, ammunition, and supplies with the Seminoles, but their actual leadership of Seminole bands is unsubstantiated. There were a number of half-breeds able to speak English remarkably well. Motte mentions sev-

eral: Paddy Carr, Lieutenant Moniac, and Jim Boy. These, however, were not hostile. It is possible that an English-speaking half-breed warrior could have appeared "white" to Sikes in a time of such great excitement.

5. The term "hammock" refers to a dense group of broad-leaf trees which, in comparison to the surrounding country or landscape, appears jungly. Generally hammocks cover small areas, and when found in treeless sections, flatwoods, or marshy regions they are silhouetted against the horizon-like islands of trees. Hammocks flourish both on high and low ground and along the borders of lakes, swamps, and streams. "The soil . . . is of the most luxuriant character, . . . with dense forests of pine, oak, mahogany, cedar, cypress, magnolia, lob-lolly, cabbage [cabbage-palm], palm, palmetto, and every variety of magnificent vegetation . . . presenting one of the most imposing sights in nature. . . . The edges and interior are covered with an immense variety of small bushes, shrubs, etc.; . . . the density of these hammocks in some places almost excludes every ray of light." John H. Davis, Jr., *The Natural Features of Southern Florida,* Florida Geological Survey Bulletin No. 25 (Tallahassee, 1943), 166; Potter, *The War in Florida,* 4.

6. Shortly after the commencement of Indian hostilities, James S. Bell, planter and former judge of the Hamilton County Court, was nominated colonel in the Thirteenth Regiment of Florida Militia by Governor John H. Eaton. The Thirteenth was composed of men of Hamilton and Madison counties. Bell's "place," as Motte calls it, was undoubtedly in the vicinity of the present town of Belleville, Hamilton County. *A Journal of the Proceedings of the [Florida] Legislative Council,* 12 Session, 1834, 177; 14 Session, 1836, 118 (cited hereafter as *Journals of the Legislative Council).*

7. Hickstown, built upon the site of the favorite camping place in the early 1800's of the Mikasuki chieftain, John Hicks (Tokse Emathla), was located about seven miles west of San Pedro, in Madison County. At the outbreak of the Seminole hostilities it was a city "in its infancy," with a population from two to three hundred. Today it no longer exists. Several efforts to locate the site have failed although some residents of that Madison County area are familiar with the name. It is shown on a map of Florida in M. M. Cohen, *Notices of Florida and the Campaigns* (Charleston, 1836); Federal Writers' Project, *Florida: A Guide to the Southernmost State* (New York, 1939), 437; and *Jacksonville Courier,* September 3, 1835.

8. Prior to the Seminole War, and like Hickstown, San Pedro was also a city "in its infancy." The site of one of the early Spanish missions in Florida, San Pedro was established as the county seat of Madison County on December 26, 1827. Its location, as shown on the Bruff Map of Florida, was about five miles southwest of the present city of Madison. Today it no longer exists. A. H. Phinney, "Florida's Spanish Missions," *The Florida Historical Quarterly,* IV (July, 1925), 19; *Jacksonville Courier,* September 3, 1835; and Williams, *The Territory of Florida,* 133.

9. Newnansville, a flourishing community in territorial days, was a short distance northeast of the present town of Alachua, Florida. One of the first towns in Alachua County, it was selected by the Territorial Legislative Council as a court-house site in 1825. F. W. Buchholz, *History of Alachua County, Florida* (St. Augustine, 1929), 147. The site of old Newnansville has been located and identified by Dr. John M. Goggin and a group of archeological students from the University of Florida.

10. Livingstons Ferry crossed the

Editor's Notes

Suwannee five miles south of the junction of the Upper Withlacoochee and the Suwannee River. See the Bruff Map of Florida.

11. Fort Alligator stood about two miles east of the present Lake City, Columbia County, Florida. H. J. Chaffer, "Military Posts of Florida Fortified Prior to 1860," with sources cited, MS in the P. K. Yonge Library of Florida History, University of Florida.

12. On March 5, 1837, the Seminole chieftains Holatoochee, Jumper (representing Micanopy), Cloud, and the interpreter Abraham, along with Jim Boy and John Opaunee, two friendly Creeks, met in council at Fort Dade on the Withlacoochee River with General Jesup. They expressed a desire to make peace. Jesup demanded cessation of hostilities and immediate emigration to lands west of the Mississippi. Jumper, objecting to an immediate emigration, maintained the earliest they could leave would be "in the fall." Since no agreement was reached, the council adjourned to enable the chiefs more time to decide on a date of departure. The following day, the parley resumed its deliberations with the additional Seminole chieftains Alligator, Coacoochee, and Peace Creek John present. Jesup remained adamant on his "immediate emigration" demands, and after fruitless argument the Seminole chiefs agreed to sign the "Treaty of Camp Dade." The stipulations of this treaty were: (1) the entire Nation would cease hostilities; (2) the entire Nation would emigrate; (3) the members of the Nation would be moved at government expense and be permitted to take their Negroes with them; (4) the government would buy their cattle and ponies before they left; (5) they would assemble by April 10 near Tampa Bay, where transports would be ready; (6) the chiefs, warriors, and families would receive government subsistence from the time they arrived at Tampa Bay until they settled in their new homes west of the Mississippi, and for twelve months thereafter; (7) Micanopy would remain near General Jesup as one of the hostages; and (8) all the advantages to the Indians, stipulated in the Treaty of Paynes Landing (1832), which were not enumerated in this treaty would be recognized by the United States government. *Niles Weekly Register,* March 25, 1837. Thus, according to treaty, hostilities ceased and the hopes for early negotiated peace with the Seminoles were realized.

13. According to the Treaty of Camp Dade, the Seminoles agreed to encamp near Tampa Bay, ready to emigrate, by April 10. By April 10, however, few had gathered at the designated spot—located ten miles from Fort Brooke. In defending their procrastination the Indians utilized every argument and excuse they could invent, and there was little Jesup could do to speed their movement towards Tampa Bay. Aware that the sovereignty of the tribe did not reside in the head chief, Micanopy, or any particular group of chieftains, Jesup hoped that all tribal factions would adhere to and honor the Treaty of Camp Dade. Believing that the use of strong measures to make the Indians comply would be interpreted by some chiefs and warriors as an abrogation or violation of the treaty, Jesup chose patience and perseverance lest the delicate diplomatic balance be upset and hostilities again be resumed. His policy seemed likely to succeed, for, by the middle of May, large numbers had gathered near Tampa Bay under the direction of Micanopy. Osceola sent word he would come. Alligator, Jumper, Coacoochee, and Cloud frequently visited the camp. Jesup, believing the war was over, discharged the volunteers and militia and sent the marines north. The citizens returned to their homes and

267

settlements from the stockades and blockhouses where they had been congregated for protection. Around midnight, however, on June 4, Osceola and Coacoochee, with about two hundred Mikasukis (a radical and resolute anti-removal faction of the Seminole Tribe), appeared at the camp, and before the break of day the entire body, numbering over seven hundred, had disappeared into the swamps. *Niles Weekly Register,* June 24, 1837; Sprague, *The Florida War,* 177-180.

Whether Micanopy and his followers were forced by the Mikasukis to break their treaty, or whether it was the culmination of a brilliant piece of Indian diplomatic strategy, it proved extremely embarrassing to General Jesup. He submitted his resignation but it was not accepted. His interpretation of the incident runs as follows:

"Our cunning enemy has again foiled us, and has shown himself as successful in the cabinet as in the field. During their protracted negotiations [three months], they were enabled to supply themselves with provisions, clothing, and ammunition; they brought in large droves of cattle, the captured property of our citizens, which they sold to the government, and received certificates therefor at a certain valuation: these were taken by traders as so much money, and they were enabled to purchase supplies. They obtained ammunition from the Creek volunteers, who received it from the ordnance officers, for the purpose of hunting."

Immediately after the escape of the Indians, Jesup ordered all post commanders to be on the alert, recommending they advise the inhabitants to abandon crops and retire to the forts. *Florida Herald,* June 9, 1837, as quoted in *The Floridian,* July 1, 1837.

CHAPTER XIII

1. General Jesup assumed command of the Army in Florida on December 8, 1836. He succeeded Brigadier General Richard Keith Call, who took over command in Florida after General Scott left for the Creek theater in the spring of 1836. It was hoped that Jesup, whose measures and strategy had effectively broken Creek resistance, would quickly terminate the Florida War.

From the beginning of his military career as a second lieutenant in 1808, Jesup displayed the qualities of a capable officer. During the War of 1812 he rose rapidly to the rank of colonel, receiving citations for distinguished service in the battles of Chippewa and Niagara (Lundy's Lane). In the latter engagement Jesup was seriously wounded. In 1814 President Madison sent Jesup to Connecticut to watch for any serious secession movement in the Hartford Convention. He received promotion to brigadier general in 1818 and to major general in 1828.

Jesup commanded the army in Florida for about a year and a half, being succeeded by Brigadier General Zachary Taylor in May of 1838. From Florida he was transferred to Washington where, until his death in 1860, he served as Quartermaster General of the Army. Heitman, *Historical Register,* I, 573; Allen Johnson and Dumas Malone (eds.), *Dictionary of American Biography* (New York, 1933), X, 62-63.

Although Jesup did not succeed in terminating the Seminole hostilities, it was under his direction that a majority of the principal hostile chiefs and large numbers of their people and slaves were captured. These prisoners were either on their way or awaiting removal to the West when the general turned over his command to Taylor. Hostilities continued after Jesup left but on a much reduced

Editor's Notes

scale and in a more sporadic, guerilla-like fashion.

2. Charles Ferry crossed the Suwannee River about ten miles south of Livingstons Ferry, and served the traffic on the Pensacola-St. Augustine Highway, known as the "Bellame Trail." Bruff Map of Florida.

3. Itchetucknee Springs, located five miles northeast of the present town of Hildreth, Columbia County, consisted of seven or more individual springs. The headspring to which Motte refers forms a somewhat circular pool about one hundred feet in diameter. This spring today can be seen in its natural, unspoiled beauty as Motte witnessed it in 1837. C. W. Lingham and others, in *Springs of Florida*, Florida Geological Survey Bulletin No. 31, 18, 62.

4. Six miles north of the present town of High Springs in O'Leno State Park, the Santa Fe River disappears into a sink hole and reappears three and one-half miles to the south. In Spanish days "El Camino Real" (The King's Highway), stretching from St. Augustine to Pensacola, passed near the present town of Alachua and crossed the river at this point. The Bellame Trail, the first American road in Florida, followed a course similar to the Spanish road and crossed the Santa Fe over this natural bridgeway. Federal Writers' Project, *Florida: A Guide to the Southernmost State*, 386-387; William E. Myer, *Indian Trails of the Southeast*, Forty-second Annual Report of the Bureau of American Ethnology (Washington, 1928), 828-829; Mark F. Boyd, "The First American Road in Florida," *The Florida Historical Quarterly*, XIV (January, 1936), map opposite page 139.

5. In 1837 Alachua County was famous for its production of corn, indigo, sugar cane, timber, and cattle. After the establishment of the Bellame Road (Bellame Trail), long-staple cotton culture attracted settlers from the states to the north, especially from the sea islands of Georgia and the Carolinas. Buchholz, *History of Alachua County, Florida*, 107; Williams, *The Territory of Florida*, 135.

6. William J. Mills of Duval County was a lieutenant colonel in the Fourth Regiment of Florida Militia. During the Battle of Withlacoochee on December 31, 1835, Lieutenant Colonel Mills was one of the small group of Florida Militia who saw action. This was the engagement in which Brigadier General Richard Keith Call and 460 Florida Volunteers sat as spectators on the north bank of the river watching a severe engagement taking place on the opposite shore between 250 Indians (under Osceola and Alligator) and 200 regular troops commanded by Brigadier General Duncan J. Clinch. Colonel John Warren and Lieutenant Colonel Mills, along with twenty-seven men from General Call's force, crossed the hazardous Withlacoochee "in spite of every obstacle" and assisted the regulars in their battle with the Indians. *Jacksonville Courier*, January 29, 1835; Sprague, *The Florida War*, 92.

7. Captain Daniel D. Tompkins was promoted to brevet major for his part in this engagement. This promotion, awarded belatedly in 1838, stemmed from a resolution passed by the Legislative Council of the territory petitioning President Martin Van Buren to reward the captain for his bravery at San Felasco Hammock. *Journals of the Legislative Council*, 16 Session, 1838, 100; Sprague, *op. cit.*, 552.

8. According to Williams' account of the battle which occurred on September 11, 1836, Colonel John Warren, commanding the Fourth Regiment of Florida Volunteers, led a combined force of one hundred mounted volunteers, twenty-five gentlemen citizens, and twenty-five United States regulars under Captain Tomp-

kins to San Felasco Hammock, four
miles from Newnansville. Here the
Indians were known to be entrenched.
In the fight which ensued, the Indians
charged with reckless daring four
times but were driven back each time.
Williams, *op. cit.*, 225.

9. Over two years before Motte
visited Newnansville, the *Jacksonville
Courier*, December 24, 1835, reported
"upwards of 200 people had assembled at Newnansville where the
Court House . . . is turned into a
fort, and the Jail into a block-house."

Beyond the towns and fortified
stockades, East Florida was a deserted
countryside. Most of the settlers and
their families had "abandoned their
homes and assembled at the different
places where the inhabitants . . .
erected, or are erecting forts for protection."

10. Revised MS, 128.

11. The "double trouble" was a
dancing step which consisted of "moving both feet without lifting them
from the floor, in such a manner as
to keep time to the music." It has
often been referred to as a Negro
dancing step. Craigie and Hulbert
(eds.), *A Dictionary of American
English on Historical Principles*, II,
802.

12. This phrase implies the heavens
resounded with cheering from the
crowd.

13. Joseph M. White, the congressional delegate from the territory, had
written three letters to the Secretary
of War protesting drafting men of
Middle Florida to suppress the Indian hostilities, and pointing out they
had enough to do protecting their own
frontiers. Receiving no answer, White
called on President Jackson to clarify
his request. "Let the damned cowards protect their country," roared
the President in a tirade of indignation, sarcastically boasting "that he
could take fifty women, and whip
every Indian that had crossed the
Suwannee, and that the people of

Florida had done less to put down the
war, or to defend themselves than any
other people in the United States.
He said if five Indians had approached into the white settlements
of Tennessee and Kentucky not one
would have ever got out alive. . . .
The men [of Florida] had better run
off or let the Indians shoot them,
that the women might get husbands
of courage, and breed up men who
would defend the country." *Florida
Herald*, March 29, 1837.

14. The resentment this incident
produced was reflected editorially in
the *Florida Herald*, March 29, 1837,
as follows:

"We belong to no political faction,
have few party predilections, and
neither fear the frowns or court the
smiles of Whig or Democrat; but we
belong to Florida. Our character and
interests are identified with hers; and
no man; or set of men, however high
in office, of any party, shall trample
with impunity upon her rights or
wantonly her honor, without receiving
merited censure."

15. Captain Gilleland was murdered by the Indians a short time
later (on June 4) near Itchetucknee
Springs while on his way from Suwannee to Newnansville. Williams,
op. cit., 272.

16. Captain Benjamin Lloyd Beall
was promoted to brevet major on
March 15, 1837, for "gallant and
successful services in the war against
the Florida Indians." Rodenbough,
From Everglade to Cañon, 449.

17. Major James A. Ashby, a veteran Florida campaigner, displayed
extraordinary bravery at Welika Pond
early in the war. This action took
place one mile from Micanopy on
July 19, 1836. Captain Ashby, with
52 men, was escorting a wagon train
of quartermaster stores from Fort
Drane, which was being abandoned.
A short distance from the fort they
were attacked by 250 Indians. Vastly
outnumbered, the troops held their

Editor's Notes

position until reinforcements arrived. Though badly wounded, Captain Ashby continued directing the fire and ordered a final charge which put the Indians to flight. *Ibid.,* 449; Williams, *op. cit.,* 247.

18. The following was crossed out of the original manuscript: "He [Major Ashby] must have made a profitable use of his time while there, for he not only got well, but also got engaged to a very handsome girl."

19. Suwannee Old Town was located on the west bank of the Suwannee River in the present Dixie County. It was an old Indian town, one of the largest in Florida. The Kolomi Indians were a large part of the town's inhabitants. They migrated from the vicinity of the present Stewart County, Alabama, in 1778. General Andrew Jackson approached the village in 1818 only to find the chief, "Billy Bowlegs," and his people scattered into the swamp. During the night of General Jackson's encampment there, Lieutenant Robert C. Ambrister, of the Royal Colonial Marines, blundered into an American picket and was taken prisoner. During the second Seminole War there were two military fortifications near the town, Fort McCrabb to the north, and Fort Fanning to the south. Federal Writers' Project, *op. cit.,* 417; Swanton, *The Indians of the Southeastern United States,* 146-147; Marquis James, *The Life of Andrew Jackson* (New York, 1940), 288, map opposite 285; and Bruff Map of Florida.

20. First Lieutenant Charles Spalding distinguished himself in a battle between 110 regulars and 300 Mikasuki Indians (commanded by Osceola) near Fort Drane on August 12, 1836. The battle lasted over an hour before the Indians retreated into ". . . recesses which could not be penetrated by our exhausted and inferior force." Rodenbough, *op. cit.,* 472; Sprague, *op. cit.,* 160.

21. First Lieutenant Seth B.

Thornton, a gallant and active officer in the Florida War, was severely wounded on the Rio Grande in the action which precipitated the Mexican War. Later he was killed by a cannon shot near San Antonio, Valley of Mexico. Rodenbough, *op. cit.,* 451.

22. First Lieutenant Nathaniel W. Hunter saw action at Lochahatchee on January 24, 1838, and in the Everglades on December 3-20, 1840. *Ibid.,* 452.

23. Assistant Surgeon G. R. Clarke participated in the Battle of Withlacoochee on December 29, 1836; during this action his horse was shot from under him. He resigned his commission on June 17, 1840. Sprague, *op. cit.,* 92; Heitman, *op. cit.,* I, 307.

CHAPTER XIV

1. Fort Mellon rested on the southwest bank of Lake Monroe. Originally called Camp Munroe (Monroe), the name was changed in honor of Captain Charles Mellon, killed when 300 to 400 Indian warriors led by Coacoochee, King Philip, and Louis Pacheco attacked the fort on February 8, 1837. "The United States forces, with the aid of a cannon on a boat near the fort routed the Indians at the expense of what would be considered a slight loss—fifteen wounded and one killed." The fort later grew into the town of Mellonville—the site of the present city of Sanford. *The Florida Historical Quarterly,* XV (April, 1937), 280-282. The location of the fort is shown on the 1840 Map of East Florida, by Captain John Mackay and Lieutenant J. E. Blake, published by order of the Senate of the United States for *Drake's Book of the Indians* (cited hereafter as Mackay and Blake, Map of East Florida).

2. Assistant Surgeon Charles Henry Laub received citation for bravery in the Fort Mellon engagement. Sprague, *The Florida War,* 169.

3. Fort Harlee, situated on the Santa Fe River about four miles north of the present town of Waldo, Alachua County, was established in March, 1837, and abandoned in November, 1838. William D. Hoyt, Jr., "A Soldier's View of the Seminole War, 1838-1839," *The Florida Historical Quarterly,* XXV (April, 1947), 357; Bruff Map of Florida.

4. Garey's Ferry, established as an army depot for the Florida campaign in early 1836, was located on the north side of Black Creek near the present town of Middleburg, Clay County, Florida. Between seven hundred and eight hundred civilians left their homes in the surrounding area and gathered there seeking safety and protection from the warring Indians. Housed in miserable shanties—four sticks supporting a roof with boards on the ground for a floor—these refugees existed in poverty and squalor. Sickness and disease ran rampant. A visitor to Garey's Ferry in 1836 wrote that in each of the three hundred huts he visited he found two or three people sick with some type of serious disease. In one shanty the mother and father were found dead and the five children, the oldest of which was thirteen, were deathly ill. Conditions such as these were typical of the fortified stockades and protected areas in the first few years of the war. Bruff Map of Florida; Sprague, *op. cit.,* 123; and *Niles Weekly Register,* September 3, 1836.

5. Fort Heilman stood across the river from Garey's Ferry at the fork of the north and south branches of Black Creek. Mackay and Blake, Map of East Florida.

6. The *Essayons,* a small river steamboat commanded by a Captain Peck, plied the treacherous inland rivers and creeks carrying supplies and personnel deep into the enemy's country. Captain Peck received commendation from the Army for his willingness to run his boat through

"unknown waters" of the Florida peninsula. Sprague, *op. cit.,* 169-170.

7. Picolata (not to be confused with the present town of Palatka) was located on the east bank of the St. Johns River due west of St. Augustine. Originally a strong fortress described by William Bartram as "very ancient," Picolata served to control the western approaches to the Spanish capital of St. Augustine. In his *Travels* in 1773, Bartram found "the fort dismantled and deserted. It is a square tower," he wrote, "thirty feet high, invested with a high wall, without bastions, about breast high, pierced with look holes and surrounded with a deep ditch. The upper story is open on each side, with battlements, supporting a cupola or roof; these battlements were formerly mounted with eight four pounders, two on each side. . . . The Works are constructed with hewn stone, cemented with lime."

The Old Spanish Road (St. Augustine to Pensacola) and later the "Bellame Trail" crossed the St. Johns at Picolata.

During the Seminole War Picolata was a supply depot for the troops in Florida, a base of operations against the Indians, and the location for one of the army general hospitals. Situated on the navigable St. Johns River, it was the terminus for many of the troops and supplies coming by boat from Charleston and other northern ports. Mackay and Blake, Map of East Florida; Mark Van Doren (ed.), *The Travels of William Bartram* (New York, 1940), 87; and Sprague, *op. cit.,* 116, 136, 139-140, 257.

8. Fort Volusia, located three miles south of Lake George on the east bank of the St. Johns River, was built on a large shell mound. Today State Highway #40 passes directly over the mound.

9. Dismissed on June 11, 1836, Major William Gates was reinstated

Editor's Notes

on January 7, 1838, and given a lieutenant colonel's rating in the Third Artillery. This commission was effective as of December 17, 1836. Gates rose to the rank of a brigadier general during the Civil War. Heitman, *Historical Register*, I, 449-450.

10. Lieutenant Colonel William Selby Harney, a veteran of Black Hawk's War, was promoted to brevet colonel in 1840 for gallant and meritorious conduct at Fort Mellon in February, 1837, and on the Caloosahatchie River in July, 1839. Described as a man of "fine physique and soldierly appearance, an experienced Indian fighter, and a good judge of men and horses," Colonel Harney played a colorful role in the fighting in the Everglades in 1840 and 1841. He was promoted to brevet brigadier general for bravery in the Battle of Cerro Gordo during the Mexican War. In 1855-1856 Harney commanded the Sioux Expedition and received permanent brigadier general rating in June, 1858. He retired from active service in 1863. Rodenbough, *From Everglade to Cañon*, 19-20, 436; Oliver Griswold, "William Selby Harney; Indian Fighter," *Tequesta* (Number 9, 1949), 73-80.

11. This is one of five pencil sketches to which Motte refers in his Journal. They were obtained from Captain John R. Vinton in 1845, along with a letter authorizing their use as illustrations in Motte's proposed volume on the Seminole Indian War. They were, therefore, a part of Motte's original manuscript, but in time became separated from the text. Four of the five drawings (Fort Mellon, the Indian mound at Fort Taylor, Osceola, and the Lighthouse at Key Biscayne) are reproduced in this volume through the courtesy of Dr. Mark F. Boyd, Tallahassee. The whereabouts of the fifth—the sketch of the old Barracks at St. Augustine—is unknown.

12 Captain John Rogers Vinton

led a small expedition into the Big Cypress in 1842. Cited for gallantry at Monterey, Mexico, during the Mexican War, he was killed on March 22, 1847, by the concussion from a shell at the siege of Vera Cruz, Mexico. Captain Vinton was noted for his unusually strong religious interest. Assistant Surgeon Forry, writing from Fort Taylor on March 4, 1838, to Lieutenant J. W. Phelps, says: ". . . here almost isolated from the world . . . we have become the most religious community imaginable . . . a Bible Class . . . meets every evening to hear the word of God expounded in familiar lessons, and on Sundays we have a regular dove-tailed sermon. The gentlemen who officiate on these pious and interesting occasions are the Rev. Brevet Major John L. Gardner and Captain J. R. Vinton. The congregation consists of the other officers, the soldiers, and two negro guides, *one of which never attends.* As Sampson guided us in pursuit of the Indians, the least we can do is to guide him to heaven. To carry out the parallel might prove an interesting subject, that is, to determine which is the better acquainted with the country to which he professes to pilot the other." Sprague, *op. cit.,* 380; Heitman, *op. cit.,* I, 988; and Assistant Surgeon Samuel Forry to Lieutenant J. W. Phelps, March 4, 1838, in "Letters of Samuel Forry, [Assistant] Surgeon U. S. Army, 1837-38," *The Florida Historical Quarterly,* VII (July, 1928), 97-98. Parts I and II of this series are published in Volume VI (January and April, 1928), (cited hereafter as Forry, "Letters").

13. Sprague estimated the attacking force at two hundred. *The Florida War,* 168.

14. King Philip (known to the Indians as Emathla) was the father of Coacoochee (Wildcat) and the principal chief of the Indians east of the St. Johns River. Philip was the

273

brother-in-law of Micanopy, the head chief of the Seminoles, and ranked high in the Seminole councils. A good-natured and sensible Indian, nearly sixty years old at the time, he opposed the execution of the treaty to move west, and was determined to die upon Florida soil. *Ibid.,* 98.

15. Coacoochee, or Wildcat (1808-1857), the twenty-eight-year-old son of King Philip, was one of the most dangerous chieftains in the field. Rather slim, and agile as a deer, he was attractive in appearance. "When hostilities commenced, he assembled his warriors, and in a fearless manner dictated the mode in which the war was to be conducted." Acting according to the dictates of his own conscience and judgment, he "ranged throughout the country . . . with a fleetness defying pursuit." Responsible for carrying on the war after the capture of Osceola, Coacoochee was the last important chief to surrender. *Ibid.,* 98; Kenneth W. Porter, "Seminole Flight from Fort Marion," *The Florida Historical Quarterly,* XXII (January, 1944), 132.

16. Motte took no part in this action and is only giving his account of it. By "our party" he refers to the garrison troops who fought the battle.

17. John T. McLaughlin, U. S. N., a passed-midshipman, had charge of supplies for the Camp Munroe detachment. He was one of a number of naval personnel serving with land forces during the Florida War. These navy men were assigned to the West Indian Squadron and detached for duty with the army. From 1838 to 1842 McLaughlin commanded the "mosquito fleet" (the Florida Squadron), operating along the coast and in the Everglades in conjunction with army operations. Sprague, *op. cit.,* 168; Dudley W. Knox, *A History of the United States Navy* (New York, 1936), 158; "Records Relating to the Service of the Navy and the Marine Corps on the Coast of Florida, 1835-

42," MS in National Archives, Washington (Microfilm in the P. K. Yonge Library of Florida History, University of Florida); and Alfred J. and Kathryn A. Hanna, *Florida's Golden Sands* (Indianapolis, 1950), 115-127.

18. Lieutenant William P. Piercy was a captain in the regiment of Creek Volunteers commanded by Col. John F. Lane. Sprague, *op. cit.,* 162.

19. The six officers: Captain William Gordon resigned his commission on September 27, 1837; Lieutenant James W. Hamilton died of an unknown disease at Fort Marion, St. Augustine, on November 26, 1837; Lieutenant John W. S. McNeil was killed in action at Mosquito Inlet on September 10, 1837; Lieutenant Charles E. Kingsbury died of fever at Fort Mellon on June 9, 1837; Lieutenant John Graham died at Tallahassee on September 16, 1841; and Lieutenant William B. Davidson died on an expedition into the Everglades under Colonel W. S. Harney in December, 1840. One out of six died as a result of enemy action. This ratio was typical of the entire Florida War. A sketch of the military records of the above-mentioned officers can be found in Rodenbough, *op. cit.,* 436-496.

20. After relating several incidents which occurred prior to his arrival at Fort Mellon, Motte returns to his own account at this point.

21. After the Indians' flight from Fort Brooke, which was a direct violation of the Fort Dade agreement, all expectations pointed toward a renewal of warfare. An officer, writing from Fort Brooke to his friend at Black Creek, expressed the consensus of opinion by stating "hostilities are again about to commence. . . ." But aside from several incidents—an attack on Fort Armstrong on the Manatee River and several murders near Fort King—nothing happened. "Our situation," wrote Lieutenant Phelps in September, 1837, "relatively to the

Indians, for the past summer . . . has been very singular. On the elopement of Miconope last June, it was expected that hostilities would be renewed, but nothing of the kind occurred, and both parties seemed to agree in an armistice. It was policy undoubtedly on both sides; our troops were sickly . . . and the enemy . . . evidently needed and desired time to recuperate."

The chiefs, as well as the warriors, frequently visited various forts and "appeared so friendly that hopes were entertained they would be ready to go in the fall." General Jesup, hoping to accomplish this end (emigration) through a policy of conciliation and leniency, refrained from measures of military force. But ". . . the rampant Micasookies began to act so impudently that the Gen. was induced to discover, if possible, their intentions. He found several chiefs to whom he talked very plainly, and concluded by telling them that he would extend their time for emigration to the first of October. He however gave Gen. Hernandez orders to scout."

By the first of October the Indians were not ready, nor the least inclined, to leave Florida; whereupon General Jesup, already having King Philip, Uchee Billy, Uchee Jack, and Coacoochee behind the bars of Fort Marion, seized Osceola under a flag of truce. *Florida Herald,* June 9, 1837; J. W. Phelps to Helen Phelps, September 19, 1837, in Phelps, "Letters," *The Florida Historical Quarterly,* VI, 80-81.

22. The supreme or highest good, from which others are derived.

23. This statement should be enlarged to include the white man, who, because of the scarcity of liquor during the first part of the Seminole War, paid exorbitant prices for it. An officer of the Georgia Volunteers wrote from Fort King in 1836 that whiskey sold for "$1. per gill . . . $20 per

gallon was offered . . . and would have been given readily. I think in one instance $100 was offered for one gallon. Money was of no use, grog usurped its place, and would buy anything in the eating line, even biscuits, which sold for three dollars apiece. I offered a U. S. soldier twenty-five cents for his cup of coffee and he would not take it, but would have given it up instantly for a drink of liquor." *Niles Weekly Register,* March 26, 1836.

Perhaps the Indians and the whites were of the same opinion as Bernard Romans, who, travelling in Florida in the 1770's, wrote, "Liquor is as necessary as victuals, I would therefore recommend the culture of vines, which will here succeed with certainty. . . ." Romans, *A Concise Natural History of East and West-Florida,* 131-132.

CHAPTER XV

1. Sickness and disease were by far the greatest enemy of the troops in Florida. Dropsy, typhus, inflammation of the bowels, consumption, chronic diarrhea, congestive fever, yellow fever, malaria, and "disease unknown" cut through the ranks with relentless fervor. "The prevailing disease was dysentery, caused by drinking turbid water from stagnant pools, and aggravated by the long continued and unvaried heat of the summer." Sprague, *The Florida War,* 257.

2. Brigadier General W. R. Armistead commanded a separate infantry brigade composed of regular troops, Florida Militia, and the regiment of Creek Volunteers. On May 1, 1840, he succeeded Brigadier General Zachary Taylor as commanding general of the army in Florida. Thirteen months later, in compliance with instructions from the War Department, he turned his command over to Colonel W. J. Worth. *Ibid.,* 243,

Journey into Wilderness

265; *Niles Weekly Register,* December 24, 1835.

3. Summer campaigning had been tried and failed. During this season "the troops sunk under the debility arising from exposure to noonday suns, constant rains, cool nights, turbid water, and the heavy marches through deep sand. Defeat, discouragement and disease had been the result. On the other hand, the summer was the Indian ally. It was to him what the depot and the magazine is to a civilized force." Sprague, *op. cit.,* 273.

4. The following was crossed out of the original manuscript:

"However strongly tempted by the allurements of a military life, or any other inducement of whatever magnitude, let me here warn you young physicians, who may feel desirous of entering our Army as surgeons. If you possess an impatient temper, or a character honorably proud and finely sensitive, as you value your peace of mind, do not think of taking such a step while the Medical Staff has for its chief the present incumbent, or more properly incumbrance. Should you yield to the temptation you will soon find yourself subjected to the liability of insult, and your self respect constantly assailed without being able to avail yourself of any power of self-protection except with the certainty of receiving greater insult and injury. This advice is based upon the long experience of not only myself but of many others who have been, or still are, under the authority and subjected to the vindictive prejudices of Surgeon General Thomas Lawson."

5. Major John Harlee served in the regular army from 1812 to 1815. During the Florida War he commanded a battalion of South Carolina Volunteers. Heitman, *Historical Register,* I, 501; Williams, *The Territory of Florida,* 269.

6. Woodburne Potter recalled that all forts in Florida were of similar construction. "The Pickets," he explained, "are made by splitting pine logs about eighteen feet in length into two parts, and driving them upright and firmly into the ground close together, with the flat side inwards; these are braced together by a strip of board nailed on the inside. The tops are sharpened, and holes are cut seven or eight feet from the ground for the fire arms. A range of benches extends around the work about three feet high, from which the fire is delivered." Potter, *The War in Florida,* 98.

7. In reminiscing of his whereabouts in past years, Motte recalled other Fourth-of-July events. These recollections, though crossed out of his original manuscript, are interesting for their glimpse into his pre-army life. In 1836 he was riding through a pine forest in Georgia. The same time a year previous found him enjoying the life of a citizen M.D. at the United States Arsenal near Augusta, Georgia. The Fourth of July, 1834, was spent on Sullivan's Island; that of 1833 in Charleston; and that of 1832 at Harvard University awaiting the commencement exercises at which time he received his A.B. degree. The year previous to graduation found him studying "within the walls of Cambridge College." After quite a lengthy summary he concludes, "But what use raking up past times, when the present requires my attention?"

8. "Dining Room."

9. Mr. William Levingston, august proprietor of the City Hotel, boasted his modern accommodations, which included private apartments, a bar well furnished with wines and liquors, plenty of servants, stables, carriages, and a "cistern containing 3,000 gallons of rain water for washing, etc." *Florida Herald,* February 6, 1836.

10. "Tabby is formed by mixing a quantity of lime with the fine coquina shell cast on shore by the tide. These materials are with fresh water mixed into a stiff mortar, and then spread

276

from four to six inches thick, either on the ground, or on a flooring of boards. It is then beat with a heavy stamper, similar to that used by pavers to smooth their work. When beat till no more water appears on the surface, it is left to dry. It is then in substance very similar to the coquina rock, except that the surface, by beating, becomes very smooth. Most of the old houses in St. Augustine are two stories high, the lower floor of which is of tabby; in some instances the upper floor and roof are of the same material." Williams, *op. cit.,* 118.

11. Joseph L. Smith, "a gigantic man both mentally and physically," served as Judge of the Superior Court of Eastern Florida from 1822 to 1832. He was the father of the famous Confederate General Edmund Kirby Smith. Judge Smith died in St. Augustine in 1841. Francis P. Fleming (ed.), Rowland H. Rerick, *Memoirs of Florida* (Atlanta, 1902), II, 64-65.

12. Robert Raymond Reid, appointed Judge of the Superior Court of the eastern district of Florida in 1832, succeeded Richard Keith Call as governor of the territory, serving one term—1839-1841. *Ibid.,* I, 200.

13. Brigadier General Joseph M. Hernandez, a Florida plantation owner, took an active part in operations against the Seminoles from the beginning of their hostilities. In 1835 he mustered a brigade of Florida Militia for the purpose of protecting the cities of St. Augustine and Jacksonville and the settlements south along the St. Johns River. On December 20, 1836, he was mustered into the service of the United States Army as a brigadier general and assigned command of the forces east of the St. Johns River under General Jesup. In this capacity and "in cooperation with General Jesup, who was operating west of the St. Johns River, he carried out a series of energetic measures on the eastern side along the Atlantic coast, a considerable distance south of St. Augus-

tine." Among the important chiefs Hernandez captured were King Philip, Uchee Billy, Uchee Jack, and Osceola. Sprague, *op. cit.,* 215-216.

14. On February 11, 1838, the auditor's office of the Treasury Department reported forty steamboats chartered since the commencement of hostilities in Florida. They "were generally employed in the transportation of troops, military stores, provisions, horses, mules, Indians, etc. . . ." In addition to the chartered vessels "many others were used and paid freight for purposes similar."

The rates paid for chartered vessels varied with circumstances. The "Forester" was chartered from December 31, 1836, to July 30, 1837, at $3,500 per month; the "Dolphin" in 1836 and the "McLean" in 1837 at $4,000 per month. The "Metamora" was paid $3,000 for one trip in December, 1836, from Fort Mitchell, Alabama, to the Withlacoochee River, Florida. The "Merchant," chartered on March 24, 1837, collected $10,000 for one trip from Fort Brooke to New Orleans, transporting Indians to their new homes west of the Mississippi. Many were chartered by the day at rates ranging from $60 to $450. Half a dozen were purchased by the government at $11,000 to $27,000 apiece. *American State Papers, Military Affairs,* VII, 994-996.

15. The feat of Captain Justin Dimick resulted in his promotion to major and drew much favorable comment from northern newspapers. *Niles Weekly Register,* September 10, 1836.

CHAPTER XVI

1. Major Benjamin D. Heriot served in the regular army from 1808 to 1815. Prior to the outbreak of the Seminole War he operated a large sugar plantation in the vicinity of New Smyrna. On December 26 or 27, 1835, a band of attacking Uchees and Indian Negroes under King Philip

burned all the buildings on his plantation with the exception of his corn shed, and carried away seventy-five of his Negro slaves. Heitman, *Historical Register,* I, 525; *Florida Herald,* January 13, 1836.

2. Koonti (coonti, coontie, coonte, kunti), or Indian bread flour, was usually made from the turnip-like roots of the plant *Zamia integrifolia* found in abundance in Florida. Preparation of the flour consisted of first mashing the roots, washing the pulp thoroughly, and straining it through a cloth deer hide suspended below. The starch residue in the water, after fermenting for several days, was then spread on palmetto leaves to dry. After drying, this yellowish-white flour was used for baking bread—relished by both white men and Indians. Clay MacCauley, *The Seminole Indians of Florida,* Fifth Annual Report of the Bureau of American Ethnology (Washington, 1887), 513-514. See also note 13 of this chapter.

3. Here Motte is referring to a boundary violation according to the Treaty of Moultrie Creek (Treaty of Fort Moultrie), signed on September 18, 1823. In this document the Seminoles forfeited claim to all land in Florida except a reservation of about five million acres in the peninsula of East Florida. The boundaries of this five-million-acre reservation were outlined as follows: on the north, a line from five miles north of Okahumkee to five miles west of Setarky's settlement on the Withlacoochee River; on the west, a line paralleling the Gulf of Mexico, fifteen miles inland; on the south, a line running east-west, five miles north of the Charlotte River; and on the east, a line which at no point was less than twenty miles from the Atlantic Ocean. Within these boundaries the United States pledged the territorial integrity of the Seminoles. Technically the Treaty of Paynes Landing, signed on May 9, 1832, nullified the Treaty of Moultrie

Creek, for in Paynes Landing the Seminoles traded claim to all land in Florida for real estate west of the Mississippi. A large segment of the Seminoles, however, did not recognize the Treaty of Paynes Landing. *United States Statutes at Large,* VII, 224-226, 368-370.

4. Revised MS, 162.

5. First Lieutenant John Graham was aide-de-camp to General Hernandez from September to November, 1837. A veteran soldier of the Florida campaign, Graham served garrison duty at Fort King in 1834-1835. Between 1835 and 1838 he saw action in the Battles of Withlacoochee, Fort Mellon, Mosquito Inlet, and Locha-Hatchee. Resigning his commission in 1838, Graham died at Tallahassee three years later at the age of twenty-seven. Rodenbough, *From Everglade to Cañon,* 450.

6. They were travelling along the King's Road constructed during the English occupation of Florida. Originally extending from the St. Marys River through St. Augustine to New Smyrna, the lower section had been abandoned in 1835. Motte's military expedition re-opened it all the way to New Smyrna. Williams, *The Territory of Florida,* 144.

7. Bulowville, the plantation of Mr. Charles W. Bulow, lay near the King's Road on Smith's Creek—a little stream running into the Halifax river head about eleven miles north of the present town of Ormond, Florida. It was the most extensive plantation in the Halifax country, comprising, before the Seminole War, over eight hundred cultivated acres. Purchased by Bulow in 1821 and extensively improved, the plantation employed hundreds of slaves in the cultivation of sugar cane, cotton, starch, and indigo. Upon the elder Bulow's death it was bequeathed to his son, John J., during whose occupancy the place was destroyed. At the beginning of the Seminole hostilities, Bulowville was

headquarters for the military forces south of St. Augustine. Bales of cotton formed breastworks around the quarters, and a fort was built in front of the dwelling house. General Hernandez ordered it abandoned on January 13, 1836, due to insufficient defending personnel. Soon after the troops withdrew the Indians moved in and in wild frenzy laid the place in ruins. John Pikula, "Historical Landmarks of My County," *The Florida Historical Quarterly*, XV (April, 1937), 255-257; Williams, *op. cit.*, 139; and T. E. Fitzgerald, *Volusia County, Past and Present* (Daytona Beach, Florida, 1937), 53.

8. Revised MS, 164.

9. The Tomoka River emptied into the Halifax about eight miles south of Bulow's Plantation. See the map of Florida in Williams, *op. cit.*

10. Dunlawton was another large sugar plantation. Situated on the Halifax River about twenty-five miles south of Bulow's, it was the scene of an early battle in the Seminole War. After sixteen large plantations in the Halifax River country were ransacked by the Indians within one month's time, Major Benjamin A. Putnam, a distinguished St. Augustine lawyer, marched two companies of Florida Militia to Dunlawton. On January 11, 1836, his outnumbered force was attacked by King Philip's warriors and forced to retreat northward, suffering two killed and fifteen wounded. Dunlawton was left to the mercy of Indian torches. Pleasant Daniel Gold, *History of Volusia County, Florida* (DeLand, 1927), 44; George R. Fairbanks, *History of Florida* (Philadelphia, 1871), 295; and Sprague, *The Florida War*, 216.

The low number of casualties in the Dunlawton engagement—typical of subsequent battles during the entire war—was explained by one of the participants who wrote in the *Florida Herald* on January 20, 1836: "Some of their [the Indians'] rifles

went off like pop guns with hardly strength enough to go through the men's clothes . . . a ball hit me in the breast and fell at my feet. . . ." The Indians were not the only inadequately armed fighters. When General Hernandez called up the Florida Militia in December of 1835 he faced the difficult problem of providing them weapons. The *Jacksonville Courier* on December 10, 1835, commented: "At such a time as this a great want of muskets is felt. Such as have rifles, have taken them. But a great part have been compelled to take their fowling pieces, or such guns as they could lay their hands upon."

11. It was under the command of King Philip that all the settlements along the east coast from St. Augustine south were attacked and destroyed. Williams, *op. cit.*, 275.

12. Revised MS, 166.

13. The white koonti was a product of the plant *Zamia integrifolia*, whereas the brick-red koonti came from the China-brier root referred to by some as the "ah-ha," or the wild potato. Its method of production was similar to that of the white koonti. According to the following observation both the white man and Indian considered koonti a tasty food: "A small quantity . . . mixed with warm water and sweetened with honey when cool becomes a beautiful delicious jelly, very nourishing and wholesome." The Indians also used it to make hot cakes or fritters by adding corn flour and frying it in fresh bear oil. Williams, *op. cit.*, 79; F. A. Ober, "Ten Days with the Seminoles," *Appleton's Journal*, XIV, July 31 and August 7, 1875, 142-144, 171-173.

14. Uchee Billy (or Billy Hicks, the son of old Hicks), chief of a band of Uchee warriors, resided in the Spring Garden area. "At the commencement of the war he went into the Creek Nation, and induced one hundred, or more, of his tribe to return with him to Florida, professing

to be friendly; but on his return he was induced to join [King] Philip." Billy and his band of Uchees, who "may have consisted of between 50 and 100 warriors . . . made Volusia and the vicinity the scene of their hostilities. . . ."

Uchee Billy was rumored to have been killed the year previous to his capture when, after a skirmish along the St. Johns River near Fort Volusia, a dead Indian was found and identified by the guide of the troops and "a gentleman who knew him" as the Uchee Chieftain. When found, however, the body had been stripped of all distinguishing marks, which left some doubt as to its identity. Uchee Billy died in the prison at Fort Marion, St. Augustine, on November 25, 1837. Williams, *op. cit.,* 274; W. W. Smith, *Sketch of the Seminole War, and Sketches During a Campaign, by a Lieutenant of the Left Wing* (Charleston, 1836), 244-247; and *The Floridian,* December 23, 1837.

15. Revised MS, 168.

16. *Ibid.,* 169.

17. This is another instance of the low number of casualties during a pitched fight with the Indians. Woodburne Potter claimed the inaccuracy and apparent harmlessness of Indian gunfire was due to careless loading of guns.

"Their first fire is generally dangerous, as the rifle is well loaded and the bullet patched. But when the Indian enters into battle, he fills his mouth with bullets, guesses at the quantity of powder, and the bullet is then dropped from the mouth into the barrel without a patch, and, hitting the butt a tap or two, he is ready to shoot again. These shots cannot, of course, be effective, and hence it is that many of our men who were wounded . . . received the shot from the rear, the bullet having passed by the object to which it was directed and gone to the other side of the camp, whilst others struck the trees

in the enclosure as high as twenty or thirty feet. This is in consequence of the large charge of powder, which makes the bullet fly wild. Too little powder drives the bullet with more precision, but not so far." Potter, *The War in Florida,* 152.

18. Lieutenant J. W. Phelps gives the account of Lieutenant McNeil's death in greater detail. "Euchee Billy, when surprised, donned his equipments like a hero, took fatal aim at Lieut. McNeil, and shot him thro' the body. McNeil saw him aiming at him, and he clapped his hand to his pistol; at that instant the ball came and carried away his little finger with it." J. W. Phelps to Helen Phelps, September 19, 1837, in Phelps, "Letters," *The Florida Historical Quarterly,* VI, 81.

19. Revised MS, 170.

20. General Hernandez, in a letter to General Jesup, recommended Motte for brevet promotion based on his participation in the capture of Uchee Billy and King Philip. Failure to get the promotion may help to explain some of the bitterness Motte entertained towards army life in general and his superior officer Surgeon General Lawson in particular. Hernandez to Jesup, September 16, 1837, in *American State Papers, Military Affairs,* VII, 850.

Chapter XVII

1. Lieutenant J. W. Phelps, writing from Fort Heilman to his sister, Miss Helen M. Phelps, in New York City, described this festive occasion: "So Gen. Hernandez returned to town with his prisoners. Handbills minutely detailing the affair were immediately posted up, balls and fetes were given, the Gen. got drunk, the captured property was disposed of at a high rate, the officers concerned were astonished at their own chivalry, and there was such rejoicing as was never surpassed." Phelps to Phelps,

Editor's Notes

September 19, 1837, in Phelps, "Letters," *The Florida Historical Quarterly*, VI, 82.

2. John Winfield Scott McNeil, a graduate of the Military Academy at West Point, received his second lieutenant's commission in the Second Dragoons in June, 1836. Heitman, *Historical Register*, I, 679.

CHAPTER XVIII

1. "Prog" is a slang term for food.

2. Before the hostilities began Messrs. Cruger and DePeyster were planters in the New Smyrna vicinity. In late December, 1835, their plantation fell victim to the torches of King Philip's warriors. Some of their Negro slaves volunteered to join the attackers; others—about sixty in all—were forcibly carried off. One very old Negro man, adamant in his refusal to leave, was shot and thrown into a burning building. *Florida Herald*, January 13, 1836.

3. "On the alert."

4. Blue Snake, a chief of the Tolofa tribe of Seminoles, came as an envoy to Philip from Coa-Hadjo, another influential chieftain. Blue Snake and Tomoka John became excellent guides for the troops. They were "always in advance examining trails, and at night proceeded several miles looking for the fires of the enemy." Jesup to Jones, September 27, 1837, in *American State Papers, Military Affairs*, VII, 848; Forry to Phelps, October 14, 1837, in Forry, "Letters," *The Florida Historical Quarterly*, VII, 92.

5. "Coa-cuchee has the countenance of a white man—a perfect Apollo in his figure—dresses very gaudily, and has more than the vanity of a woman." Forry to Phelps, October 19, 1837, *ibid.*, 89.

6. Coacoochee was permitted to visit his people. On October 17, he returned with the news that approximately one hundred Indians and as many Negroes were en route to St. Augustine. Sprague, *The Florida War*, 187.

CHAPTER XIX

1. Kenneth W. Porter, "Seminole Flight from Fort Marion," *The Florida Historical Quarterly*, XXII, 132.

2. Forry, "Letters," *The Florida Historical Quarterly*, VII, 93.

3. Osceola, son of a full-blooded Creek mother and a half-breed (Creek-Scotch) father, was born sometime between 1800 and 1806 near the Tallapoosa River in Alabama. During the first Creek War he was still a young lad but joined the "Redsticks" (hostile Creeks), and fought General Jackson and his Tennessee troops. After the war "he was one of the many unruly spirits who emigrated to Florida where the Redsticks became known as a party hostile to the United States. In 1817, when the repeated depredations of the Florida Indians resulted in the invasion of that country by General Jackson, he was in arms, and being driven across the Suwannee, retreated with a small party of his companions down into the peninsula and settled upon Peas' Creek." He remained there until several years before the opening of hostilities in 1835 when he moved ". . . to the Big Swamp in the neighbourhood of Fort King, and united himself with the Micocukees [Mikasukis]. . . ."

Although a minor figure at the beginning of the war, Osceola associated himself with the mass of warriors who made up the anti-removal party—a faction which possessed as much influence as the principal chief—and rose to a position of leadership and power. This rise to prominence was due to his natural ability as a leader, to his bold, desperate, and reckless spirit, and to the " . . . thousand fires of passion, animation, and energy, . . . " the indomitable firmness and withering scorn " . . . which his expressions and emotions could portray."

McKenney and Hall, *The Indian Tribes of North America,* II, 364-368.

4. Colonel John C. Cleland, Adjutant of the Second Brigade of Florida Militia, participated in the Battle of Dunlawton in January, 1836. Cohen, *Notices of Florida and the Campaigns,* 95.

5. With a detachment of troops General Hernandez met the advance guard of the Indians at Pellicier's Creek and ordered their camp moved to Fort Peyton. Sprague, *The Florida War,* 187.

6. Motte often comments on the beauty and sociability of the St. Augustine females. Lieutenant J. W. Phelps wrote a few observations on the same subject:

". . . there are a great many women here [St. Augustine], and marriage with its appliances is of frequent occurrence, and a topic of open, most free, and not unoften of delicate conversation. A young man who is apparently admitted into the first society, tells a woman of the same case with himself that such and such young women are beautiful, and confirms his assertion with an emphatic oath. He descants upon their ankles, eyes, lips, and so on, going how much farther into details I do not know. The young women themselves are pleased with this, and they manifest a readiness to throw themselves in the way of such men, which would tend, one might suppose, to immoral consequences; but, I believe, it does not, at least as far as appearances are concerned, and otherwise I have no Armsdens to show me the contrary, provided even it did exist." J. W. Phelps to Helen Phelps, November 12, 1838, Phelps, "Letters," *The Florida Historical Quarterly,* VI, 83.

7. Assistant Surgeon Samuel Forry, in describing the party, revealed an interesting and peculiar twist to the Florida hostilities—the presence of captive Indian dignitaries at local social functions. This stratagem was doubtless an attempt to woo the chieftains through the medium of firewater.

"Last night we had a grand party at Gen. Hernandez. Waltzes and Spanish dances were the order of the day. After midnight we had quite a splendid supper. About sixty ladies were in attendance, and some of them were passably handsome. I have never, however, participated in such amusements; but last night I most anxiously wished I could Waltz, for no other reason than merely to feel and be felt by the ladies. Coacuchee was the lion of the night, attracting the special attention of the ladies. His remarks were always to the point, prompted by the impulses of nature. A lady and gentleman being introduced to him he enquired if they were married. Being answered that the pair had lately been yoked, he added that she was very pretty, and that her husband no doubt enjoyed her very much, but that after bearing several children, she would be scarce worth having. . . . King Philip's brother got so drunk that it was necessary to carry him off. When he saw the display of liquors, he was really transported to the third elysium. He gulped down draught after draught . . . Coa-cuchee also drank immensely; but by being led between two men, he contrived to maintain the perpendicular. . . ." Forry to Phelps, October 19, 1837, Forry, "Letters," *The Florida Historical Quarterly,* VII, 88-89.

8. Micanopy, the nephew of King Payne, was the legitimate head chief of the Seminoles, having ascended to that position by hereditary right in 1814. In 1825, and at, the suggestion of Colonel Gad Humphries, government agent to the Indians, this position became elective. John Hicks (Tokse Emathla), head of the Mikasuki tribe and an extraordinarily talented red man, was duly elected. Although Hicks recognized the legitimacy of Micanopy he exercised pow-

Editor's Notes

erful control over the whole of the Seminoles. He foresaw the impossibility of the Indian remaining in Florida, and the impracticability of any attempts to stem the tide of white advance. In 1835, however, Hicks died, and Micanopy (who was always opposed to emigration, but inclined to peace as far as policy and personal safety was concerned) again became the head chief without the formality of an election. Micanopy was described by a contemporary writer as a man ". . . of low, stout, and gross stature, and what is called loggy in his movements—his face . . . bloated and carbuncled, eyes heavy and dull . . . and a mind like his person." About fifty years old at this time, the dark-skinned Micanopy was very fat, and so exceedingly lazy that many considered him unfit as a war leader. Contemporary sources claim he was forced by the younger and more radical warriors into hostilities. Williams, *The Territory of Florida,* 214; Sprague, *op. cit.,* 97; Cohen, *op. cit.,* 64, 238.

As titular head of the Seminoles, a role for which he was miscast, Micanopy was surrounded by a number of highly individualistic and anti-removal sub-chiefs, warriors, and advisors who were the "real powers" in the Indian councils. Chieftains like King Philip, Osceola, Alligator, Jumper, Holatoochee, Sam Jones, Abraham, John Cavalho, and Coacoochee were the "brains" of the Indian resistance and controlled powerful segments of warriors.

9. Holatoochee, thirty-five-year-old nephew of Micanopy and second chief of the Nation, carried his muscular five-feet-ten-inch frame with dignity and military bearing. Possessing a thoughtful and rather melancholic expression, his influence in Seminole councils was considerable. At the outbreak of hostilities he rejoined his band after a four-year banishment for adultery. During his exile he had re-

sided with Indians in the Everglades. His own residence was in the region of Charlotte Harbor. Sprague, *op. cit.,* 98; *Niles Weekly Register,* March 25, 1837; Porter, *op. cit.,* 129; and Forry, "Letters," *The Florida Historical Quarterly,* VI, 140.

10. Jumper, or Otee-Emathla, a bush-lawyer and capable advisor of Micanopy, was a Creek Indian and one of the leaders of the Fort Mims (Alabama) Massacre (First Creek War, 1813). After Jackson subdued the Creeks, Jumper escaped to Florida, married a sister of Micanopy, and made his home with the Seminoles. The forty-year-old warrior was a full six feet tall, with lean physique—an active, brave, cunning, intelligent, and deceitful Indian and extremely fond of talking. His peculiar musical voice aided him in becoming one of the most important men in councils and consultations. One writer described him as follows: "The crafty and designing Ote-mathla, is tall and well made, his face narrow but long, forehead contracted, eyes small but keen, nose prominent, countenance repulsive, and its expression indicative of sinister feelings." Sprague, *op. cit.,* 97; Williams, *op. cit.,* 214; Cohen, *op. cit.,* 239; and *Niles Weekly Register,* March 25, 1837.

11. Coa-Hadjo, or Mad Partridge, chief of the Seminoles east of Lake "Topkapolika" (Tohopekaliga), was one of the delegation sent west of the Mississippi River to examine the country in accordance with the terms of the Treaty of Paynes Landing. Originally he favored emigrating, but after the murder of Charlie Emathla (a chief who also favored emigration) Coa-Hadjo was informed by Sam Jones and other hostile warriors "that if even he should mention the word 'Arkansaw' they would cut his throat. . . ." Confronted with this threat Coa-Hadjo joined the hostile party. Williams, *op. cit.,* 275; Forry to Phelps, August 15, 1837, in Forry,

Journey into Wilderness

"Letters," *The Florida Historical Quarterly,* VI, 146.

12. The ball game occupied an important place in the social and ceremonial life of the Indians. Two perpendicular poles at each end of an open field served as goals. The distance between varied with local circumstances. The carrying of the ball or throwing of it between the poles constituted a goal. The common number of players on each side was nine to twelve, although at times as high as twenty-two and even fifty participated. The ballsticks were similar to our lacrosse sticks, each stick bent over at one end to form a loop with a cage constructed of deer- or raccoon-skin thongs on the end. Each hoop likewise was bent sideways so the ball could be held in the cage between the two. The ball itself, about the size of a man's fist, was made of deer hair, covered with deer hide, and sewed with deer sinews. The game was usually played between tribes or towns. It ". . . was exceedingly rough and deliberate efforts were made to put good players out. After each goal, the chief of the side which had made it, threw up the ball to put it into play again, the other chief facing him." An enormous amount of betting was done at ball games, while one of the high lights of the occasion was a huge dance the night before. Swanton, *The Indians of the Southeastern United States,* 674-679, 681-682.

13. John Cavalho [Cavallo], along with Coacoochee and Osceola, engineered the escape of the Indians from Fort Brooke, Tampa Bay, about four months prior to this. Cavalho "was of mixed Negro and Indian blood, with possibly a dash of Spanish, and although technically a 'slave' . . . he was a recognized Seminole sub-chief or chief; the brother-in-law of Holatoochee. . . ." After his capture he was sent to Indian Territory and became "spokesman of the Seminole

Tribe, but succeeded in returning to Florida in 1839 on the plea that he would be useful in inducing his relatives and friends there to go West. Under his nickname Gopher John . . . he became well-known as a guide and interpreter. In 1842 he was again shipped West, where he assumed leadership in the Negro element among the Seminoles. . . ." In 1849 he left, with Coacoochee, for Mexico. His subsequent career is described by Porter as follows:

"For about twenty years John Cavallo—known on the border either as Col. John Horse or *el Coronel* Juan Caballo—led his warriors against Apache and Comanche Indians and Texas filibusters, ranging from the banks of the Rio Grande in the north to the Laguna de Parrass in Southern Coahuila, receiving for their services a grant of land, in association with the Seminole Indians, at Nacimiento, in the Santa Rosa Mountains. In 1870 he led his band back to the United States and put them at the disposal of the army for scout service. . . . His death occurred, probably in 1882. . . ." Porter, *op. cit.,* 133, n. 7.

14. Osceola had encamped about a mile from Fort Peyton, and was standing beneath a white flag when General Hernandez approached for the proposed talk. Forry, "Letters," *The Florida Historical Quarterly,* VII, 90.

15. The following is a memorandum dated October 21, 1837, to General Hernandez from General Jesup concerning the specific questions to be addressed to Osceola:

"Ascertain the objects of the Indians in coming in at this time. Also their expectations. Are they prepared to deliver up the negroes taken from the citizens at once? Why have they not surrendered them already, as promised by Coa-Hadjo at Fort King? Have the chiefs of the nation held a council in relation to the subjects of the talk at Fort King? What chiefs attended that council, and what was their determination? Have the chiefs, Micanopy, Jumper, Cloud, and Alligator, sent a messenger, and if so, what is their message? Why have not those chiefs come in themselves?"

This "talk at Fort King" to which General Jesup referred was held on the nineteenth and twentieth of August between Jesup and several chiefs; the principal chief was Coa-Hadjo. At this parley the Indian leaders expressed their earnest desire for peace, but "declared the majority of the Indians to be averse to leaving the country." Coa-Hadjo promised Jesup that a conference of the tribal chiefs was scheduled to be held along the St. Johns River within several days and that this question would be discussed at that meeting. In addition he promised the general he would return to Fort King in twenty days and inform him whether the council had been held and what decisions had been made. Coa-Hadjo did not return, and later Jesup learned that very few chiefs had attended the council. This was another of the several broken promises which Jesup had experienced in dealing with the Seminole leaders. Sprague, *op. cit.*, 217, 185-186.

16. Forry, who witnessed the affair, commented, "The Indians bore it like philosophers." Forry to Phelps, October 21, 1837, in Forry "Letters," *The Florida Historical Quarterly*, VII, 90.

17. According to the *Florida Herald*, October 28, 1837, as quoted in *The Floridian*, November 18, 1837, the "other war-chiefs" were "Ya-a-hadjo, Powas-Hadjo; John Cavallo, No-co-co-sia-hola; Emathla Chamey, Co-hi-lo-clu-hadjo; (Doctor), and Hastano-micco." Forry adds to this list the chiefs "Micopotoka, John and Joe Hicks, . . . and old Tustenug." Forry to Phelps, October 21, 1837, in Forry, "Letters," *The Florida Historical Quarterly*, VII, 90.

18. Forry claims eighty-two prisoners, including half a dozen women

and children, were captured with Osceola. Sprague states, "There were seventy-one, the elite of the Mickasuky tribe, six women, and four Indian negroes." *Ibid.*, 91; Sprague, *op. cit.*, 218.

19. General Jesup's orders to Hernandez went as follows:

"Let the chiefs and warriors know that we have been deceived by them long enough, and that we do not intend to be deceived again. Order the whole party directly to town. You have force sufficient to compel obedience, and they must move instantly. . . . They can talk in town, and send any messengers out, if they please." Jesup to Hernandez, October 21, 1837, in Sprague, *op. cit.*, 218.

20. The Mikasuki Indians, a small but prominent Hitchiti-speaking tribe of Seminoles, were an offshoot of the "red" division of the Creeks. Benjamin Hawkins first mentions their presence in a list of Seminole towns made in 1799. The Mikasukis considered themselves legitimate owners of Florida, but being too weak to resist the invasion of later Creek bands from the north they amalgamated with them in efforts to resist the white man. Their first prominent appearance in Indian history came with the Seminole War of 1817 when they became ". . . conspicuous as a sort of political center for these Southern 'soreheads'. . . ." They were the most bitter opponents of white intrusion in Florida, the most resolute and vindictive, apparently disregarding all laws, opinions, and advice of the chiefs. They considered all others "as interlopers, and cherished the same vindictiveness towards their own color as they practiced towards the whites." Swanton, *The Indians of the Southeastern United States,* 150; Albert S. Gatschet, *A Migration Legend of the Creek Indians* (Philadelphia, 1884), I, 77; and Sprague, *op. cit.*, 19, 322-323, 428.

21. Sam Jones (Apeika, Apiaka,

Arpeik, Arpeika, Appiacca, Arpiucki) was chief of the Mikasuki tribe. An old man, near seventy years, he purported to be a prophet and medicine man. Violently opposed to emigration, his advice and opinions were highly regarded, due in great measure to the Indian regard for age. His territory was in the neighborhood of Lake Okeechobee. The active war-chiefs in the Big Cypress Swamps, along with their sub-chiefs and the warriors ". . . executed with fidelity the mandates . . . or wishes of Sam Jones." Declaring a policy of eternal hostility towards the whites, Sam planned many of the Indian attacks. In some he would fire the first gun to inspire his warriors with greater fanaticism and then retire. Sprague, *op. cit.,* 99, 252, 318-319.

22. Alligator, or Halpatter-Tustenuggee, was a "shrewd, crafty, politic, and intelligent chief of the Seminole Nation." About forty years of age, and a nephew of Micanopy, he possessed attractive manners and some ability to speak English. His knowledge of the country and the tactics of Indian warfare made him a topnotch war-chief as well as a dangerous enemy. Alligator commanded the Indians at Dade's Massacre, fought with Osceola in the Battle of Okeechobee in December of 1837. He surrendered in April, 1838, and emigrated to Arkansas. Along with five other chiefs, he returned to Florida in 1841 "in hopes of inducing relatives, still in the woods, to return with them." *Ibid.,* 97-98, 330; Porter, *op. cit.,* 129.

23. Cloud, or Yahalochee, was described as being "a fine looking fellow; soldierly in appearance; very robust, with a most benevolent countenance." He surrendered with Micanopy, Tuskegee, and Nocose-Yahola to General Jesup at Fort Mellon, December 3, 1837, after Jesup sent Coa-Hadjo and the Cherokee delegation to their villages assuring them

kind treatment. George Catlin, who painted portraits of the captive Indian chiefs, described Cloud as a "very good-natured, jolly man, growing fat in his imprisonment, where he gets enough to eat, and an occasional drink of whiskey from the officers with whom he is a great favorite." *Niles Weekly Register,* March 25, 1837; Jesup to Poinsett, December 6, 1837, in *American State Papers, Military Affairs,* VII, 890; and George Catlin, *Letters and Notes on the Manners, Customs and Condition of the North American Indians* (London, 1844), II, 220.

24. Chittee-Yoloho, a young sub-chief, had seen action in the Battles of Withlacoochee, Fort Mellon, and Wahoo Swamp. He was wounded in the hand at Fort Mellon. McKenney and Hall, *The Indian Tribes of North America,* II, 201-204.

25. Osceola's family surrendered to Jesup at Fort Mellon on November 30, 1837. Jesup to Poinsett, November 30, 1837, in *American State Papers, Military Affairs,* VII, 890.

26. An example of the public condemnation this act produced was expressed editorially in *Niles National Register,* November 4, 1837: "We disclaim all participation in the 'glory' of this achievement of American generalship, which, if practised towards a civilized foe, would be characterized as a violation of all that is noble and generous in war."

27. General Jesup may have been acting on his own initiative in taking Osceola prisoner under the flag of truce. Several weeks before the capture was made, however, Andrew Jackson, in a letter to the Secretary of War, Joel R. Poinsett, suggested the following advice and strategy: "Genl. Jessup, I hope, will profit by experience . . . and the moment he again gets powel [Powell, or Osceola] and the chiefs in his power, will hold them fast." Jackson to Poinsett, October 1, 1837, in John Spencer Bassett

Editor's Notes

(ed.), *Correspondence of Andrew Jackson* (Washington, 1931), V, 513.

28. The account of the capture of this group of Indians goes as follows: ". . . on the second day after the seizure of Powell, we captured 30 Indians, of whom 18 were male adults. They were met down the road by small parties of our people, who shook them by the hand very cordially—dealt out to them the contents of their haversacks, and invited them to the fort [Fort Peyton]. Arriving at the fort, unsuspicious of treachery, their rifles were seized, and they were marched off to St. Augustine." Forry to Phelps, October 31, 1837, in Forry, "Letters," *The Florida Historical Quarterly*, VII, 91.

29. Shortly after his capture, Osceola was taken to Fort Moultrie on Sullivans Island, Charleston, South Carolina. George Catlin, who painted Osceola's portrait five days before his untimely death and who was with him until the day before he died, stated that the fiery chieftain complained bitterly of the mode in which he was captured, ". . . grieving with a broken spirit, and ready to die, cursing the white man . . . to the end of his breath. . . ." His flesh and face rapidly declined after his imprisonment. Dr. Weedon, the physician at Fort Moultrie, gave Catlin an account of the great warrior's last moments.

"About half an hour before he died, he seemed to be sensible that he was dying; and although he could not speak, he signified by signs that he wished me to send for the chiefs and for the officers of the post, whom I called in. He made signs to his wives (of whom he had two, and also two fine little children by his side,) to go and bring his full dress, which he wore in time of war; which having been brought in, he rose up in his bed, which was on the floor, and put on his shirt, his leggings and moccasins —girded on his war belt—bullet-pouch and powder-horn, and laid his knife by the side of him on the floor. He then called for his red paint, and his looking-glass, which was held before him, when he deliberately painted one half of his face, his neck and his throat—his wrists—the backs of his hands, and the handle of his knife, red with vermilion; a custom practiced when the irrevocable oath of war and destruction is taken. His knife he then placed in its sheath, under his belt; and he carefully arranged his turban on his head, and his three ostrich plumes that he was in the habit of wearing in it. Being thus prepared in full dress, he laid down a few minutes to recover strength sufficient, when he rose up as before, and with most benignant and pleasing smiles, extended his hand to me and to all of the officers and chiefs that were around him; and shook hands with us all in dead silence; and also with his wives and his little children; he made a signal for them to lower him down upon his bed, which was done, and he then slowly drew from his war-belt, his scalping-knife, which he firmly grasped in his right hand, laying it across the other on his breast, and in a moment smiled away his last breath, without a struggle or a groan."

Dr. Weedon ascribed the cause of his death to a violent attack of quinsy, accompanied with intense pain and inflammation of the tonsils. Upon discovering the seriousness of Osceola's illness, Dr. Weedon attempted treatment. Blood was immediately drawn, after which an emetic and blister was prescribed. But at that moment an Indian, held in high esteem as a prophet and doctor, entered the room and prohibited further medical aid. Osceola died on January 31, 1838, and was buried near Fort Moultrie with full military honors.

"A few days after the burial, unknown persons opened the grave and decapitated the corpse, carrying off the head. Some time afterwards, according to the *New York Star* . . . the head was on exhibition at Stuyvesant Institute, New York City. It was believed . . . that this infamous act . . . was perpetrated with . . . the assistance of one of the physicians in the neighborhood." Catlin, *op. cit.,* II, 220-222; *Apalachicola Gazette,* February 26, 1838; and Coe, *Red Patriots, The Story of the Seminoles,* 112.

30. Spring Garden, a valuable plantation owned by a Colonel Rees of South Carolina, was situated on Spring Garden Creek, which emptied into the St. Johns River about twelve miles above Lake George—near the present De Leon Springs, Florida. In the latter part of December, 1835, it was totally destroyed by a group of Indians and Negroes led by King Philip. In addition to burning the buildings and destroying thirty-five hogsheads of sugar plus cane syrup to make seventy hogsheads, the raiding party stole the horses, mules, and 160 Negro slaves. The loss was estimated from $130,000 to $150,000. *Florida Herald,* January 13, 1836.

31. Assistant Surgeon Samuel Forry received his commission in the United States Army in August, 1836. He resigned in October, 1840, and died four years later. Heitman, *Historical Register,* I, 429. A number of his letters, written from various posts in Florida, have been published in *The Florida Historical Quarterly.* Several have been used as references in the footnotes of this Journal.

32. On January 1, 1838, the Indians, imprisoned at Fort Marion, embarked on the steamer "Poinsett" for Sullivans Island, Charleston, South Carolina. The main chiefs included Micanopy, Coa-Hadjo, Little Cloud, King Philip, Osceola, plus 116 warriors and 82 women. After languishing about two months in the prison at Charleston the entire party was placed on board the brig "Homer"

and on March 3, 1838, began the trip to their new home in the West. Upon reaching New Orleans they were transferred to a river steamboat and taken to Fort Gibson, Arkansas. On board the steamer the unreconciled old King Philip died. The whole party of migrating Indians, deeply moved at his loss, was allowed to attend the funeral. He was buried along the river about forty miles below Fort Gibson with all the honors due his rank and position, and one hundred guns were fired over his grave. *Florida Herald,* January 1, 1838, July 21, 1838; *Charleston Courier,* March 3, 1838.

CHAPTER XX

1. The people of Florida were anxiously anticipating this campaign and hoping it would be the last. "General Jesup is determined," commented the *Florida Herald,* "to end the war, if possible, and at all hazards, and if matured plans, fresh troops, ample supplies, energy and perseverance will accomplish so desired an end, it will be done. The eyes of all are now turned upon him with intense anxiety. His country holds him as one of her treasures, trembling for his success and fearing for his failure." The *Florida Herald,* October 28, 1837, as quoted in *The Floridian,* November 18, 1837.

2. His followers believed he "could make known the approach of troops, find game, and control the seasons, heal the sick, or inflict disease upon any one—even death." Sprague, *The Florida War,* 318.

3. General Jesup had this to say concerning military campaigning in Florida:

"If our operations have fallen short of public expectation, it should be remembered that we were attempting that which no other armies of our country had ever before been required to do. I, and my predecessors, in command, were not only required to fight, beat, and drive the enemy before us, but to go into an unexplored wilderness and catch them. Neither Wayne, Harrison, nor Jackson, was required to do this; and unless the objects to be accomplished be the same, there can be no just comparison as to the results." Jesup to Poinsett, July 6, 1838, *ibid.,* 197.

4. Among the critics of the Florida campaign was "Old Hickory" himself, the Creek and Seminole anathema of a decade before. Writing from his desk in Washington in August, 1836, Andrew Jackson reflected upon events south of the St. Marys: "The shameful proceedings in Florida, with the panic that pervaded everywhere which had tarnished the reputations of our army ought to have induced every military man to have exerted themselves to have regained the armies lost military character." Several months later, with the apparent increase of hostilities, he remarked: ". . . the whole Florida war from the first to the present time has been a succession of blunders and misfortunes . . . I have tried all the Generals and as General Jesup is now there and in command, he I hope will finish this unfortunate business." As for his own solution in obtaining a quick termination to what he called a "disgraceful war to the American Character," he offered a bit of sage advice: "The Commanding Genl. ought to find where their women are, and with his combined forces and forced marches reach and capture them—this done they [the warriors] will at once surrender."

Writing from The Hermitage in December, 1837, to J. R. Poinsett, Jackson remarked, "I am truly surprised at the force collected in Florida—[on November 30, 1837, there was a total of 455 officers and 8,411 men, including volunteers, militia, Indian allies, and regulars]—half that force was sufficient to put a speedy end to the war. Genl. Jesup wrote me that he was in great need of three or four

companies of good spies—if he had them he could put down the war in twenty-one days. He has them from Tennessee, and I trust he will realize his promise." Jackson to Francis P. Blair, August 12, 1836; Jackson to James Gadsden, November, 1836; Jackson to Poinsett, October 1, 1837; *id.* to *id.,* December 13, 1837, in Bassett (ed.), *Correspondence of Andrew Jackson,* V, 418, 434, 512, 521.

5. Brigadier General Abraham Eustis was transferred to Florida in January, 1836, from his peacetime command at Charleston, S. C. He was accompanied to Florida by regular troops from Charleston and Savannah, and South Carolina volunteers and militia. In March of 1836, General Eustis set up headquarters at Fort Volusia. His Carolinians, along with Major Kirby's battalion of First Regiment Artillery, composed what was termed the Left Wing of the army in Florida, which operated along the east coast; General Winfield Scott commanded the Right Wing. General Eustis's operations in the Everglades during the campaign of 1837-1838 were interrupted by his recall to the northern part of Florida, owing to renewed Indian depredations in that section. Sprague, *op. cit.,* 106, 195; Cohen, *Notices of Florida and the Campaigns,* 158.

6. Colonel Zachary Taylor (1784-1850) began his military career as a first lieutenant in 1808. Promoted to captain in 1810, Taylor proved a capable Indian fighter during the War of 1812 in the Old Northwest and Missouri Territory. In 1815 he received a promotion to major, but with the reduction of the army to peacetime standing reverted to his permanent rank of captain. Disgusted with this action Taylor resigned, but was reinstated as major in the spring of 1816, and two years later promoted to lieutenant colonel. In 1832 he became full colonel in the First Infantry. Between 1816 and 1837 Colonel Tay-

lor served frontier and garrison duty at various frontier outposts and participated in the Black Hawk War. He and his regiment were ordered to Florida in the summer of 1837 and arrived at Fort Brooke, Tampa, on November 8, 1837. His successful handling of the Battle of Okeechobee, December 25, 1837, earned him promotion to brigadier general. On May 15, 1838, he succeeded Jesup as commander of the Army in Florida, serving in this capacity until May 6, 1840, when, upon his request, he was relieved of his command and succeeded by Brigadier General W. R. Armistead. During the Mexican War Taylor rose to major general for distinguished services in the successive victories of Palo Alto and Resaca de la Palma, with special congressional citation and a gold medal, for his services on the Rio Grande front. After defeating Santa Anna at Buena Vista he again received a gold medal and congressional citation. He resigned his commission in January, 1849, after being elected President of the United States. His death occurred sixteen months after inauguration. Heitman, *Historical Register,* I, 949; Brainerd Dyer, *Zachary Taylor* (Baton Rouge, 1946), 13, 18, 23, 27, 35-37, 46, 68-97, 301; Sprague, *op. cit.,* 221, 247, 551.

7. Colonel P. F. Smith, adjutant general of the state of Louisiana, commanded a regiment of Louisiana Volunteers. His range of operations covered the country south of the Caloosahatchee River to Cape Sable. His operations in this area included one or two skirmishes in which several Indians were killed and 243 taken prisoner. Sprague, *op. cit.,* 107, 189.

8. The post at Mosquito lay on the west bank of the Halifax River, opposite Mosquito Inlet.

9. The campaign plans for the winter of 1837-1838 divided Florida into sections which were parcelled out to various commanders. Each was responsible for operations within his assigned area. Major area dispositions included: Colonel Smith—the area between the Caloosahatchee and Cape Sable; Colonel Taylor—the area east of the Fort King Road, Tampa Bay, and the Gulf of Mexico from the upper reaches of the Withlacoochee River to the Caloosahatchee River and east to the Kissimmee River and the eastern shore of Lake Okeechobee; Brigadier General Nelson (with a brigade of Georgia Volunteers)— the area west of the Fort King road, middle Florida, and along 150 miles of the gulf coast from Tampa Bay northward; Colonel Snodgrass (with a battalion of Alabama Volunteers) —the area between the St. Johns and Ocklawaha rivers, and the swamps and hammocks between Black Creek and the Ocklawaha; Lieutenant Colonel Coffee (with four companies of Alabama Volunteers)—the area around the Okeehumka Hammock, Lake Apopka, and Lake Tohopekaliga; and Major Lauderdale (with the Tennessee Volunteers)—the area between the Atlantic Ocean and the St. Johns River. Other sections of the state were assigned lesser commands. General Jesup hoped that through these combined operations the enemy could be flushed from their secluded retreats and either killed or captured, bringing the war to a speedy end. Jesup to Poinsett, July 6, 1838, Sprague, *op. cit.,* 189-191; original "Orderbook of General Thomas S. Jesup, 1838," MS in P. K. Yonge Library of Florida History, University of Florida, 54-57; see Mackay and Blake Map of East Florida.

CHAPTER XXI

1. New Smyrna, situated near the present city of New Smyrna Beach, faced the inlet on Mosquito Lagoon. The settlement was founded in August, 1768, by Dr. Andrew Turnbull, a Scottish physician and former resi-

dent of London, and named in honor of his wife, daughter of a Greek merchant of Smyrna. The more than fourteen hundred colonists who settled on the twenty-thousand-acre land grant consisted of Minorcans, Greeks, and Italians from the Peloponnesus and Leghorn. The majority were from the British island of Minorca. It was a huge undertaking for that time and one of the outstanding colonization efforts in Florida history. By 1781, however, the project had failed, and Turnbull moved to Charleston. His colonists either deserted or had been released from their indentures on testimonies of cruelties and brutalities inflicted by the overseers of the plantation. Charles Loch Mowat, *East Florida as a British Province, 1763-1784* (Los Angeles, 1943), 71-72; Carita Doggett Corse, *Dr. Andrew Turnbull and the New Smyrna Colony of Florida* (Jacksonville, 1919), 19, 46.

2. John Ross was the son of a Scottish father and a Cherokee Indian mother. His father's royalist affiliations during the Revolutionary War prompted him to settle among the Cherokees after the British surrender. Though John did not inherit the Cherokee chieftainship "by regular hereditary descent, yet very many circumstances pointed to him, from early boyhood, as the prospective ruler of the Cherokees; and he . . . governed them, in the most absolute manner, for upwards of a quarter of a century. . . ." He was a well educated half-breed, capable of writing and speaking English, and possessed "soft, easy, gentlemanly manners, rather retiring and reserved . . . seldom speaking unadvisedly." Wilson Lumpkin, *The Removal of the Cherokee Indians from Georgia* (New York, 1907), I, 186-187.

3. Such missions as the Cherokee delegation agreed to perform "were dangerous, for the Seminole chiefs and warriors had decreed the penalty of death for Indians consenting to emigrate and for white or Indian emissaries seeking to confer with them on the subject." Foreman, *Indian Removal*, 353, n. 3.

4. The Cherokee delegation met a group of the Seminole chiefs at Chickasaw Creek, about sixty miles inland from Fort Mellon. The Seminole leaders listened to the Cherokee message—an invitation to visit General Jesup's headquarters and negotiate for the early fulfillment of the Treaty of Paynes Landing. With sincerity and good feeling the assembled delegates smoked the peace pipe. Upon conclusion of this ceremony Micanopy, the Seminole chiefs, Cloud, Tuskegee, Nocose-Yahola, and eight other chiefs, along with fifteen to twenty warriors, agreed to accompany the Cherokees to Jesup's headquarters at Fort Mellon.

At Fort Mellon on December 3, there was a conference called in which Micanopy stated his desire for peace and his intentions to emigrate to the west. General Jesup, however, answered Micanopy's words by seizing the whole group of Seminole chiefs and warriors and imprisoning them in the fort at St. Augustine.

The members of the Cherokee delegation were mortified at Jesup's action. They considered it a base violation of one of the most elemental rules of war—a treachery in which they appeared to have had a part. After begging to clear themselves of any participation in the episode, they were allowed to send one of their delegates to the imprisoned Seminole chiefs to plead their innocence in the seizure. John Ross, head chief of the Cherokees, was especially humiliated and incensed. He promptly sent an indignant note to the Secretary of State, protesting the seizure and pleading for the release of the Seminoles captured in this alleged act of treachery. His protest was of no avail. The Seminoles were not released, and General Jesup brushed off the incident by announcing that all hope of peace through the Cherokee mediation had failed. *Ibid.,* 352-355; Taylor to Jones, January 4, 1838, in Sprague, *The Florida War,* 191, 203.

5. This artesian submarine spring is located about three miles east of Crescent Beach, Florida. The circular slick is seventy feet in diameter. Robert O. Vernon, *The Hydrology and Geology of Florida Springs,* Florida Geological Survey Bulletin No. 31 (Tallahassee, 1947), 10.

6. David R. Dunham, an influential planter, was appointed Judge of the Mosquito County Court in February, 1833. His plantation, located near the mouth of the Tomoka River, was destroyed by an Indian raid in December, 1835. Gold, *History of Volusia County, Florida,* 47.

7. The large Mackinaw boats, used extensively by early American frontier traders and explorers, were pointed at both ends and named after Mackinac (pronounced *Mackinaw*), Michigan, where they originated.

8. The following was crossed out of the original manuscript: "I have caught as many as ten, and very large ones, in about as many minutes with the hook."

9. The plantation of Major Henry Woodruff was located near Spring Garden. Woodruff was killed by the Indians in the early part of 1836, while horseback riding one morning with his servant. The latter, wounded in the thigh, escaped. *Jacksonville Courier,* January 7, 1836.

10. Lieutenant Colonel John M. Hanson served in the regular army as a second lieutenant from 1818 to 1821. On November 3, 1836, he was appointed a captain in the Florida Volunteers, and in October, 1837, promoted to lieutenant colonel. Heitman, *Historical Register,* I, 498.

CHAPTER XXII

1. John Bankhead Magruder, a first lieutenant in the First Artillery, received decoration for gallantry at Cerro Gordo and Chapultepec in the Mexican War. He served as a major general of the Confederate Army during the Civil War. Heitman, *Historical Register,* I, 684.

2. William Whann Mackall, a West Point graduate and second lieutenant in the First Artillery, was decorated for gallantry at Contreras and Churubusco during the Mexican War and served as a brigadier general in the Confederate Army during the Civil War. *Ibid.,* I, 670.

3. William Henry French, a second lieutenant in the First Artillery, and a classmate of Lieutenant Mackall at West Point, displayed outstanding bravery at Cerro Gordo, Contreras, and Churubusco in the Mexican War. He was promoted to brigadier general in the Union Army for gallantry at Chancellorsville, and to major general for meritorious service during the Civil War. *Ibid.,* I, 437.

4. The first week in February, 1835, found Florida suffering from abnormal cold and windy conditions. This cold wave "entered West Florida the morning of February 7, and by mid-night had advanced far down the peninsula. The next morning . . . the sun rose upon a freezing Florida, held in the grip of the most severe cold wave in its history." Temperatures in degrees Fahrenheit, at various places, ranged as follows: Pensacola, 8°; Tallahassee, 4°; Jacksonville, 8°; Picolata, 7°; St. Augustine, 10°; Fort King (Ocala), 11°; and Fort Brooke (Tampa), 20°. Salt water froze along the margin of Pensacola Bay, and ice formed many feet off shore on the St. Johns River. The great freeze killed every orange, lime, and lemon tree in Florida north of Tampa Bay, and resulted in the destruction of the citrus industry in northeast Florida. The financial loss

Editor's Notes

was tremendous. The white residents of Florida, completely ignorant of meteorological conditions, attributed the cold to an iceberg which presumably floated down from the northern seas and lodged off the coast. T. Frederick Davis, "Early Orange Culture in Florida and the Epochal Cold of 1835," *The Florida Historical Quarterly,* XV (April, 1937), 232-239.

5. Fort Taylor was located on the west side of Lake Winder (a small lake near the headwaters of the St. Johns River), north of Wolf Creek. The mound, situated about 200 yards south of the Fort Taylor site and 150 feet west of the lake shore, was examined by Assistant Surgeon Forry in 1838, and found to contain many "relics" near the surface. Subsequent explorations of the mound revealed various European artifacts also found near the surface. Since no European artifacts have been found at the base of the mound, indications are that "construction of the mound took place during prehistoric times and historic burials were added from the top."

The mound, as described by Rouse, who examined it in 1944, had a "classic conical shape, its sides rising steeply upwards at an angle of about 40° to a bluntly pointed top, where the house had previously been situated. It appeared to be circular in plan and perfectly symmetrical. . . . We estimated that the mound was 12 feet high and 30 feet in diameter." It was probably several feet higher when Vinton sketched it. Irving Rouse, *A Survey of Indian River Archeology, Florida,* Yale University Publications in Anthropology, Number 44 (New Haven, 1951), 137-140; Bruff Map of Florida.

6. George Cruikshank (1792-1878), famous English artist, caricaturist, and illustrator, was the first important professional illustrator in England. His skill as an etcher has been compared with that of Rembrandt. Some of his more famous works include the illustrations in Charles Dickens' *Sketches by Boz, Nicholas Nickleby, Martin Chuzzlewit, Oliver Twist,* and the *Memoirs of Joseph Grimaldi. Encyclopedia Britannica,* VI (Chicago, 1945), 768; Ruari McLean, *George Cruikshank, His Life and Work as a Book Illustrator* (New York, n.d.), 21-28, 38-39.

CHAPTER XXIII

1. The following was crossed out in the original manuscript: "His chief delight is to dissect his friends characters and affairs which he does with as much relish as an epicure would a well roasted goose or turkey, and God help the poor soul whose character is intrusted to his tender mercy. He stands six feet three and in form and features bears a striking resemblance to the 'La Mancha' hero, although differing essentially in his moral qualities, as he does not possess much of his chivalry, and has been often heard to assert that the poetry of his profession was gone, and that he had now arrived at the prose, an assertion which could never be gainsayed, as he always enforced it with a gloomy frown, which was perfectly convincing."

2. There are various accounts of how Coacoochee and his cohorts escaped. One claims the Indians walked through the gates of the fort by courtesy of bribed guards. Another describes how they accomplished the spectacular and almost unbelievable feat of crawling through a small aperture high in the prison wall, and descending a rope to the moat and to freedom. One thing is sure, Coacoochee's reappearance among the Seminoles stopped any possible hope of terminating the war at this time. Upon escaping from Fort Marion the wily young chieftain fled southward and contacted Sam Jones, who, with his people, was headed towards Fort Mellon to confer with General Jesup.

Coacoochee's vivid account of his imprisonment ". . . and the treatment received by him and the other Indians captured near Fort Peyton, at once aroused the suspicions and indignation of that wary and hostile old chief; who not only immediately relinquished all idea of surrendering or communicating any further with the commanding general, but succeeded in preventing all the Indians who were out, from coming in or listening to any proposal for peace." Sprague, *The Florida War*, 219-220.

For an interesting and critical analysis of the conflicting escape stories see Porter, "Seminole Flight from Fort Marion," *The Florida Historical Quarterly*, XXII, 113-133.

3. Coacoochee became one of the mainsprings of Indian resistance for the next four years. Shortly after his escape he reappeared as one of the Indian leaders in the Battle of Okeechobee, December 25, 1837. In 1838 he was operating in central and northern Florida and out of the Okefinokee Swamp. He gave himself up in March, 1841—the last important chief to surrender. His subsequent career, as sketched by Porter, was active and colorful:

"After his removal to Indian Territory, he was chief advisor to the head-chief Micanopy, but was disappointed in his ambition to succeed him after his death early in January, 1849, and late in the year removed to the Mexican border with a following of about a hundred Seminole Indians, accompanied by John Cavallo with as many more Negroes. Coacoochee had the ambitious idea of establishing a sort of Free State on the Mexican side of the Rio Grande, to be populated by Indians from Texas and Indian Territory, and by runaway slaves from the same region, but, except for some hundred each of Seminole Indians and Negroes, and a few Kickapoo, he was unable to win and retain many recruits. His military colony of Indians and Negroes did, however, serve the Mexican Government effectively against wild Indians and Texas filibusters until his death of smallpox at Alto, near Musquiz early in 1857." Appointed a colonel in the Mexican Army, Coacoochee was awarded a silver medal by the Mexican government in recognition of his services. *Ibid.*, 132-133, n. 4; Sprague, *op. cit.*, 325-326.

CHAPTER XXIV

1. During the Florida War it was not uncommon for one command to consist of soldiers, sailors, and marines. Sprague commented on this admixture in the following way:

"As illustrative of the peculiarity of the service to which these various corps were subjected, there was at one time to be seen in the Everglades, the dragoon in water from three to four feet deep, the sailor and marine wading in the mud in the midst of cypress stumps, and the soldiers, infantry and artillery, alternately on the land, in the water, and in boats. . . . Here was no distinction of corps, no jealousies, but a laudable rivalry in concerting means to punish a foe who had so effectually eluded all efforts. Comforts and conveniences were totally disregarded, even subsistence was reduced to the lowest extremity. Night after night officers and men were compelled to sleep in their canoes, others in damp bogs, and in the morning cook their breakfast over a fire built on a pile of sand in the prow of the boat, or kindled around a cypress stump. Intermixed as the various detachments were, subjected to privations, fatigue, and disappointment; subordination, cheerfulness, and resolution marked the conduct of all engaged in the expedition." *The Florida War*, 354.

2. Joseph E. Johnston, a West Point graduate, resigned his commission in the regular army on May 31, 1837. He was reappointed a first lieutenant

in the topographical engineers on July 7, 1838, and given an immediate promotion to brevet captain for gallantry on several occasions against the Florida Indians. Johnston rose to brigadier general in the United States Army, and in April, 1861, resigned this commission to receive an appointment as major general in the Confederate Army. Heitman, *Historical Register,* I, 578.

3. Samuel Weller, a popular Charles Dickens creation and center of comic interest in *The Pickwick Papers* (1836), was known for his shrewdness, and his humorous and realistic powers of comparison. Henrietta Gerwig (ed.), *Crowell's Handbook for Readers and Writers: A Dictionary of Famous Characters and Plots in Legend, Fiction, Drama, Opera, and Poetry* (New York, 1925), 708.

4. "What, Liset, is it you?"—implying a high degree of musical versatility.

5. Second Lieutenant William E. Aisquith led a checkered military career. He was graduated from West Point in 1827. Five years later he was dismissed from the service. In 1837 he received an appointment as second lieutenant in the First Artillery. Promoted to first lieutenant in 1838, he was again cashiered in 1845. Between 1845 and 1848 he served as first sergeant in the Maryland and D.C. Volunteers and also as a private, sergeant, and captain in the First Artillery. He was dropped from the army roll for the third time in 1848 and ended his military career as a sergeant in the marines, 1848-1853. Heitman, *op. cit.,* I, 154.

6. Sam Jones occupied the country around the mouth of the Kissimmee River and the eastern shore of Lake Okeechobee. Sprague, *op. cit.,* 270.

7. A "sense keeper" was an intimate and very able counsellor.

8. In his own account of the events leading up to the Battle of Okeecho-

bee, Colonel Taylor states that Jumper did surrender and was sent under escort to Tampa Bay. Alligator, however, had early expressed the opinion that he desired to surrender and was prevented from doing so by Sam Jones and the Mikasukis. Alligator was one of the chiefs in command of the Indians at the Battle of Okeechobee. Sprague, *op. cit.,* 204, 213.

9. The following was crossed out in the original manuscript: "Much to his own [Captain Porter's] satisfaction, having gained, as he says, sufficient laurels in the field."

One of the outstanding services of Captain Porter in the Florida War was his participation in the Battle of Wahoo Swamp, on November 21, 1836.

10. Mrs. Felicia Dorothea Hemans (1793-1835) was a popular English poet during the first part of the nineteenth century. Kunitz and Haycraft (eds.), *British Authors of the Nineteenth Century,* 290-291.

11. Mosquitoes were no small problem to both the Indian and white man in Florida. The Indians devised several means of protection. The most popular was the building of huge and smoky fires. During the war, however, "fires were dead give aways for enemy scouts, so they would annoint their bodies with rank fish oil, mixed with the juice or ashes of indigo. This perfume, and its effluvia, kept off from them every kind of insect." Williams (ed.), *Adair's History of the American Indians,* 489.

CHAPTER XXV

1. Lieutenant Colonel Benjamin Kendrick Pierce.

2. This ancient fortification was constructed by two Jesuit priests, José María Monaco and José Javier de Alaña during the first half of the eighteenth century. These two Jesuits "set out from Havana in response to a request for religious instruction

from the Tekesta Indians, some of whom had been making periodic voyages to Cuba. Arriving in south Florida, the priests found that the Tekesta had gone north to Santa Lucia to celebrate making peace with 'the chiefs of four or five villages . . . and some other tribes.' " Learning that a child would be sacrificed during the ceremony, the Jesuits immediately hastened to the scene and prevented the sacrifice.

The Indians received the material gifts which the friars gave them, but were not cordial to an invitation to become Christians. That step, they considered, meant submission to the king of Spain. Their refusal also was based on the fact that the Jesuits brought them no liquor.

The two Jesuit priests and their companions, however, were impressed with the countryside and decided to settle there. They constructed a small fort for protection against the local Indians and for defense against attacks by northern Indians. This fort ". . . consisted of an embankment, ditch, and stockade in the shape of an equilateral triangle 24 *varas* on a side; it had a bastion in each corner defended by a stone mortar (pedrero) and was so placed that 'it dominated both the river and the road from the Hill to the town.' The flag of Spain was raised over it on August 8, 1743."

The missionary labors of the Jesuits were cut short by an order from Havana to abandon the fort, and it was torn down so that it would be of no value to Indian or white man thereafter. Rouse, *A Survey of Indian River Archeology, Florida,* Yale University Publications in Anthropology, Number 44, 58, 59.

3. Colonel David Emmanuel Twiggs was a veteran of the War of 1812. Like many ranking officers campaigning in Florida he believed the war should be terminated and the Indians allowed to retain a part of the country. Continuation of hostilities, he ar-

gued, was useless. Little hope existed that the army could extract the Indians from the swamps. So long as they remained there the troops could do nothing but shadowbox. His opinions were highly respected and later adopted by Jesup, who offered the Seminoles a truce and forwarded Twiggs' recommendations to Washington, where they were quickly turned down. Colonel Twiggs rose to the rank of brevet major general during the Mexican War, was decorated at Monterey, and appointed military governor of Vera Cruz in 1848. During the Civil War he served as a major general in the Confederate Army. Heitman, *Historical Register,* I, 976; Sprague, *The Florida War,* 194; and Rodenbough, *From Everglade to Cañon,* 436.

4. Fort Lloyd (Fort Floyd, Camp Lloyd), was about thirty miles west of Fort Pierce and eight miles north of Lake Okeechobee. Lieutenant J. C. Ives, Map of the Peninsula of Florida South of Tampa Bay (compiled from the latest and most reliable sources by order of the Honorable Jefferson Davis, Secretary of War), Washington, April, 1856 (cited hereafter as Ives Military Map).

5. First Lieutenant Frederick Searle was promoted to captain in July, 1838, and to brevet major in November, 1838, for gallantry and good conduct during the Florida War. He served as a captain in the Creek Volunteers regiment under Colonel John F. Lane, and later in the Quartermaster Department under General Jesup. Heitman, *op. cit.,* I, 871; Sprague, *op. cit.,* 162, 552.

6. Colonel Zachary Taylor arrived at Fort Brooke, Tampa Bay, on November 8, 1837. Awaiting were orders from General Jesup placing him in command of the troops in the area south of the Withlacoochee River, north of Charlotte Harbor, and west of the Kissimmee River. Taylor immediately established an advance de-

Editor's Notes

pot for supplies (Fort Fraser) on Pease Creek, about halfway between Tampa Bay and Lake Kissimmee. On November 27, he departed from Fort Brooke with the First Infantry. Arriving at Fort Fraser the next day, he stopped only long enough to leave orders for Colonel Gentry and his Missouri Volunteers, Major McRae and the Florida Volunteers, Major Morgan and his Spies, and other commands to follow and meet him at Lake Kissimmee. Upon arriving at the river between Lake Kissimmee and Lake Tohopekaliga, Taylor built a fortification to protect his supplies, threw a bridge across the river, and named the place Fort Gardiner.

Leaving Fort Gardiner on December 19, he moved south along the west side of the Kissimmee River, establishing a depot (Fort Bassinger) about fifteen miles above Lake Okeechobee, at one of the few "eligible sites for Military posts on this river. . . ." The other "eligible sites" were Fort Kissimmee, fifty-two and one-half miles above Fort Bassinger, and Fort Gardiner.

Here at Bassinger, he learned from several captured Indians that a large body of Seminoles under Coacoochee, John Cavallo, and Alligator, and another large body of Mikasukis, under Sam Jones, were encamped east of the Kissimmee River and near Lake Okeechobee. A dense hammock and a cypress swamp separated the two Indian camps.

On the morning of December 25, Taylor dismounted his troops, drew up a line of battle and advanced upon the Seminole camp only to find the warriors had withdrawn in confusion, their fires still burning. Proceeding past the camp and through a cypress swamp, the water-logged troops came into a large prairie, where they captured a well-armed young Indian warrior tending two or three hundred head of grazing cattle. The captured warrior pointed to a dense hammock

less than a mile away and across an almost impassable saw-grass swamp, indicating the place where all the hostile Indians (the Seminoles had joined the Mikasukis) were awaiting the attack of the troops. "Letters and Reports of Colonel Zachary Taylor to Major General Thomas Sidney Jesup, 1837-1838," MS in the National Archives, Washington, D. C. (on microfilm in the P. K. Yonge Library of Florida History, University of Florida); "Report of Lieutenant Benson on the Exploration of Lake Okeechobee and the Kissimmee River, June 7, 1855," MS in the National Archives, Washington, D. C. (photostatic copy in the P. K. Yonge Library of Florida History, University of Florida); and Taylor to Jones, January 4, 1838, in *American State Papers, Military Affairs*, VII, 986-989.

7. The total number of troops under Colonel Taylor's command during this engagement, exclusive of officers, was 1,032. *Ibid.*, 986.

8. The action lasted from "half-past twelve until after 3 p. m., a part of the time very close and severe." *Ibid.*, 989.

9. Halpatter-Tustenuggee (Alligator) claimed 380 warriors participated in this battle. Coacoochee, Sam Jones, Otolke-Thloco (The Prophet), Halleck-Tustenuggee, and Alligator were some of the more important chiefs commanding the Indians. According to Coacoochee, the Indian losses stood at eleven Indians and one Negro killed, and nine wounded. Sprague, *op. cit.*, 213-214.

10. Lieutenant Colonel Alexander Ramsay Thompson, of the Sixth Infantry, began his military career during the War of 1812. Commanding a regiment in this engagement along Lake Okeechobee "he received two balls from the fire of the enemy early in the action, which wounded him severely, yet he appeared to disregard them, and continued to give his orders . . . [until]

a third ball . . . deprived him of his life. His last words were, 'keep steady men, charge the hammock—remember the regiment to which you belong.' " Heitman, *op. cit.,* I, 955; Taylor to Jones, January 4, 1838, in *American State Papers, Military Affairs,* VII, 989.

11. First Lieutenant John P. Center was graduated from West Point in 1833. Promoted to first lieutenant in September, 1837, he was appointed a regimental adjutant on November 1, 1837. During this battle he was killed by "a shot through the head from a tree." Heitman, *op. cit.,* I, 292; *Niles National Register,* February 3, 1838.

12. Captain Joseph Van Swearingen, a graduate of West Point in 1824, was promoted to first lieutenant in May, 1829, and to captain in July, 1837. While leading his company in the attack on the hammock, he was shot in the lower part of the neck. Retiring to the rear of his company, he "raised both his hands above his head, and fell flat on his face, gave one groan, and was no more." *Ibid.;* Heitman, *op. cit.,* I, 939.

13. First Lieutenant Francis J. Brooke, a West Point graduate of 1826, served as regimental adjutant of the Sixth Infantry from 1833 to 1836. Promoted to first lieutenant in May, 1835, he was killed immediately during this action by a shot through the heart. *Ibid.,* 248; *Niles National Register,* February 3, 1838.

14. Captain George Andrews was promoted to major for his distinguished service during this engagement. Sprague, *op. cit.,* 555.

15. Second Lieutenant William Henry Talbot Walker, a West Point graduate of 1837, was promoted to brevet first lieutenant for gallantry during this action. He was wounded by "three separate balls" and carried from the field. During the Mexican War he rose to the rank of lieutenant colonel. Walker served as a major

general in the Confederate Army during the Civil War, and was killed in action in July, 1864, near Atlanta, Georgia. Heitman, *op. cit.,* I, 997; Taylor to Jones, January 4, 1838, in *American State Papers, Military Affairs,* VII, 989.

16. Colonel Taylor reported his losses at 26 killed and 112 wounded. The Indians, he estimated, "probably suffered . . . equally with ourselves, they having left ten dead on the ground . . . doubtless carrying off many more, as is customary with them, when practicable." *Ibid.,* 988.

17. Colonel Richard Gentry, at the head of 180 Missouri Volunteers, along with 47 of Morgan's Spies, formed the first line of attack in the advance on the hammock. The second line was composed of the Fourth and Sixth Regular Infantries. The Indians, strongly entrenched within the hammock, opened with deadly fire upon the volunteers and spies, mortally wounding Colonel Gentry. Seeing their commander down, the volunteers broke ranks, fled to the rear, and could not be induced to return into action as a body. Colonel Gentry's son, a youth of eighteen or nineteen years and sergeant major of the regiment, was severely wounded at the same moment his father was killed. *Ibid.,* 986, 987, 989.

18. Colonel Taylor summed up the results of this campaign as follows:

"This column in six weeks penetrated 150 miles into the enemy's country, opened roads, and constructed bridges and causeways, when necessary, on the greater portion of the route, established two depots, and the necessary defences for the same, and finally overtook and beat the enemy in his strongest position. The results of which movement and battle have been the capture of thirty of the hostiles; and coming in and surrendering of more than 150 Indians and negroes, mostly the former, including the chiefs Ou-la-too-che, Tus-ta-nug-gee, and other principal men; the capturing and driving out of the country 600 head of cattle, upwards of 100 head of horses; besides obtaining a thorough knowledge of the country through which we operated, a greater portion of which was entirely unknown except to the enemy." *Ibid.*, 989.

19. The site of the Battle of Okeechobee, which assumed the largest proportions of any pitched battle during the Seminole War, was marked, in 1939, by the West Palm Beach and Fort Pierce chapters of the Florida Daughters of the American Revolution. "The marker is a six-foot stone monument located on the right-of-way of Conner's highway, four miles southeast of Okeechobee City and on the shore of Lake Okeechobee." *The Florida Historical Quarterly*, XVIII (January, 1940), 239-240.

Chapter XXVI

1. Lieutenant Powell's detachment consisted of fifty-five sailors and twenty-five army regulars. *Niles National Register*, February 10, 1838.

2. The number of Indians was estimated to be from forty-six to eighty. *Ibid.*

3. Along with the keg of powder was a box of cartridges and a considerable amount of rum and whiskey. *Ibid.*

4. Doctor Frederick Leitner was a young and talented German naturalist who emigrated to the United States and made Charleston, South Carolina, his home. Financed by several well-to-do friends in Charleston, Leitner, between 1832 and 1835, spent many months each year exploring the Territory of Florida, especially the southern portions of the peninsula, including the Florida Keys. His objective was to make a detailed study of the botany, natural history, and topography of that relatively unknown wilderness. Leitner became well known to many of the Seminoles, with whom he made

friends and to whom he extended medical aid. The outbreak of hostilities in 1835 did not impede his determination to continue his work, and he attached himself to the armed forces in order to further his scientific investigations. In November, 1836, he accompanied a small naval force which, starting at Key West, explored the south Florida coast from Cape Florida to Charlotte Harbor. On January 15, 1838, while acting as a surgeon for a similar naval expedition, he was captured by the Indians in the region of the St. Lucie River and subsequently put to death. Lieutenant Benjamin Alvord, U. S. A., *Address Before the Dialectic Society of the . . . Military Academy . . .* (delivered at West Point, December 29, 1838), (New York, 1839), 32, 58-59.

Chapter XXVII

1. The Second Dragoons, under the command of Colonel Twiggs, left St. Louis on September 5, 1837, and arrived at Jacksonville, Florida, on October 31. The following account was given in the *Jacksonville Courier*:

"The detachment left Jefferson Barracks, Missouri, September 5, and marched through Illinois to Shawneetown, crossing the Ohio; thence through a portion of Kentucky to Nashville, Tennessee; thence over the Cumberland Mountains, crossed the Tennessee River to the Lookout Mountain at Ross's Landing; thence through the Cherokee country to Milledgeville, Georgia; and thence to this place, *marching, from an actual calculation, twelve hundred miles in fifty-five days.*" *Jacksonville Courier*, as quoted in Rodenbough, *From Everglade to Cañon*, 28.

2. The Halpatioke Swamp, or Alligator Swamp, is located by Sprague on the west side of Lake Okeechobee. The Bruff Map of Florida represents it as including the entire area between Lake Okeechobee

and the Atlantic Ocean. Sprague, *The Florida War*, 435.

3. The force under General Eustis, with artillery and baggage wagons, left Fort Mellon on December 18, after "sending Major Lomax, of the artillery, with two companies of dragoons and a battalion of the Fourth Artillery, in advance to construct bridges and cut through the dense hummocks which obstruct the line of march." An anonymous officer of the expedition, describing the twenty-day march from Fort Mellon to Jupiter Inlet, asserted it was ". . . one of the most extraordinary marches ever made in this or any other country, considering the obstacles to be overcome. For nearly two hundred miles we passed through an unknown region, cutting roads through dense hummocks, passing innumerable cypress-swamps and pine-barrens, interspersed with a nearly impassable growth of saw-palmetto, and, for the last three days, wading nearly up to our waists in water. Our privations have not been less than our fatigue, the men being almost naked, and one third of them destitute of shoes."

Another officer of the Second Dragoons wrote: "Our march from Fort Mellon to the southern portion of Florida was marked by . . . a great destruction of the finest horses that I have ever seen. Our regiment suffered a great loss—one that I fear will not be made up in some time; nearly the whole is now mounted, but on indifferent horses." Rodenbough, *op. cit.*, 29, 30, 31.

4. About twenty miles southeast of Fort Lloyd, Colonel Taylor with his command struck south, proceeding along the eastern shore of Lake Okeechobee. The other troops under Generals Eustis and Jesup headed in the direction of Jupiter Inlet. Ives Military Map.

5. "The sight."

6. First Lieutenant Robert Anderson, a graduate of West Point in 1825, was promoted to brevet captain in April, 1838, for gallantry and "successful conduct" in the Florida War, and to major in September, 1847, for meritorious conduct in the Battle of Molino del Rey during the Mexican War. In February, 1865, Anderson was promoted to major general for his gallant defense of Fort Sumter in Charleston Harbor, South Carolina. This engagement, which took place in 1861, officially began the Civil War. Heitman, *Historical Register*, I, 164.

CHAPTER XXVIII

1. The region embodying Lake Okeechobee and the Everglades became the center of extensive military operations during the Seminole War. Although little was known of the area prior to the war, it was not entirely fabulous. The Calusa and Miami Indians were quite well acquainted with the country, as were a few white men who had been there. After the war, particularly after 1850, the reports of hunters, various expeditions, adventure seekers, and, subsequently, surveying parties increased the knowledge of the region. The name Macaco, to which Motte refers, is mentioned by Fontaneda in his *Memoirs*, as a region or a body of water lying somewhere north of Okeechobee, while the lake itself (Okeechobee) he calls the "Lake of Mayaimi." Fontaneda evidently named the lake after the Miami Indians who lived in that area. Williams, *The Territory of Florida*, 49; Romans, *A Concise Natural History of East and West-Florida*, 285; James Mooney, "Calusa," in Hodge (ed.), *Handbook of American Indians North of Mexico*, 195; George Henry Preble, "A Canoe Expedition into the Everglades in 1842," *Tequesta* (Number 5, 1945), 30-51; W. L. Perry, *Scenes of a Surveyors Life in South Florida* (Jacksonville, 1859); and David O. True (ed.), *Memoir of D⁰*

Editor's Notes

d'Escalente Fontaneda (Miami, 1944), 16, 56 n. 3.

2. Second Lieutenant John R. Parker, of the Second Dragoons, served only six months in the Florida War. Appointed in October, 1837, he resigned his commission in March, 1838. Heitman, *Historical Register*, I, 770.

3. In his official report to Brigadier General Robert Jones, General Jesup stated the Indians were lodged in "an almost impregnable position. . . ." Jesup to Jones, January 26, 1838, in Sprague, *The Florida War*, 198.

4. The Tennessee Volunteers formed the left flank, the Second Dragoons the right, with the artillery bringing up the center. Rodenbough, *From Everglade to Cañon*, 30.

5. The Congreve Rocket was invented by Sir William Congreve (1772-1828), a British artillerist and inventor. His rockets were first fired at Boulogne in 1806, "in salvos from boats of special construction and were very effective. . . ." Probably the forerunner of our modern incendiary bombs, these rockets were used by the British during their Peninsular Campaign in attempts to burn the enemy's stores and supplies. It is doubtful they were used for any purpose during the Florida War except for the terror, fright, and consternation which the "terrible whizzing" certainly produced among the musket-armed Indians. *Encyclopedia Britannica*, VI, 254; J. W. Fortescue, *A History of the British Army, 1809-1810* (London, 1912), VII, 548.

6. This was the Locha-Hatchee River, which emptied into Jupiter Inlet.

7. General Jesup, in his official report, did not mention the disobedient volunteers. Rather, he said, "some confusion occurred among the Tennessee Volunteers, in consequence of which they suffered severely; but order was readily restored."

This incident took place about a month after Andrew Jackson, in a letter to Secretary of War Joel R. Poinsett, prophesied a speedy and marked turn of events in the Florida War because of the arrival of his indomitable and beloved Tennesseans in Florida. "If permitted," he confidently wrote, "to act together, they will reach the hiding places of the Indians in a few days—they march to put down this war or die in the attempt. The five companies from the mountain region of Middle Tennessee, are all efficient, composed of many of my old spy companies in Creek and Seminole Campaigns. These are experienced and brave and will do their duty. [Major] Lauderdales Batalion can and will beat the whole combined Indian force in Florida . . . they are pledged to me to do their duty and sustain the character of Tennessee and put a speedy end to that panic war."

The failure of the volunteers to follow Jesup's leadership may be answered in part by Jackson's admonition the previous summer, when the subject of raising Tennessee Volunteers for duty in Florida was under discussion. Jackson emphasized at that time that volunteers would not serve under officers they did not know or could not look to for advice and care "when exposed to the dangers of a southern sun." Jesup to Jones, January 26, 1838, in Sprague, *op. cit.*, 198; Jackson to Poinsett, December 13, 1837, in Bassett (ed.), *Correspondence of Andrew Jackson*, V, 521-522; and *id.* to *id., August* 27, 1837, *ibid.*, V, 506-508.

8. The following was crossed out of the original manuscript: "We have evidently distressed the enemy so much, that it will no doubt have a beneficial effect in hastening their submission. By this time nearly all their cattle have been destroyed, and their ponies captured."

9. Revised MS, 258.

Journey into Wilderness

Chapter XXIX

1. "Wrecking" was a "unique and picturesque" industry in Florida. Those engaged in this profitable occupation of salvaging shipwrecks lived aboard their vessels, waiting for misfortune to strike Gulf Stream merchantmen. The south Florida coast was a favorite haunt for wreckers. "Navigation of the Bahama banks and Florida Straits was very hazardous and the annual loss from shipwrecks ran into hundreds of thousands of dollars. It was said that in 1825 alone, 64 vessels were lost off the Florida coast and the loss was placed at nearly $1,200,000." In March, 1825, Congress decreed that all salvage from a shipwreck on the Florida coast should be brought to a port of entry within the United States. From December, 1824, to December, 1825, $293,353 worth of salvaged goods was sold in Key West. The government collected a cool $100,000 in duties. It is quite possible that the first lighthouse at Key West was not built until 1838 for quite definite reasons. Alice Whitman, "Transportation in Territorial Florida," *The Florida Historical Quarterly*, XVII (July, 1938), 36-37; Dorothy Dodd, "Railroad Projects in Territorial Florida," unpublished master's thesis, Tallahassee, May, 1929, quoted in Whitman, *op. cit.*, 36, n. 23.

2. Fort Jupiter, on the south bank of Jupiter River about three miles from the mouth of Jupiter Inlet, stood on the point formed by the junction of Jupiter River and Jones Creek. J. C. Ives, *Memoir to Accompany a Military Map of the Peninsula of Florida, South of Tampa Bay* (New York, 1856), 10.

3. Revised MS, 266.

Chapter XXX

1. "Out of the battle!"

2. General Jesup decided to offer the Indians a truce after the urgent pleadings of General Eustis and Colonel Twiggs convinced him that "most, if not all the officers of the Army" believed the Indians could never be defeated in the swamps. An officer of the Second Dragoons expressed the sentiment prevalent among the officers and men at this time: ". . . they [the Indians] can remain here until they deem it proper to surrender. To say that we can 'perish them out' is nonsense, as the whole country is filled with fine beef, the woods abound with deer and turkeys, and the streams and ponds have an abundance of fish. The enemy can elude us, at any moment when we are in pursuit, in the dense hammocks which afford a safe shelter to them. In many hammocks no troops can operate; but the enemy have small, beaten trails, with which they are familiar, and pass out of our reach." Sprague, *The Florida War*, 193; Rodenbough, *From Everglade to Cañon*, 31.

3. Abram, or Abraham, a runaway Negro slave from Pensacola, was the property of Micanopy, who subsequently released him from bondage. Prior to hostilities he was the principal interpreter at conferences between the Seminoles and the whites. Universally recognized as an able adviser to Micanopy, Abram exercised as much influence in the Seminole councils as did the principal chiefs of the nation. A modest, ambitious, avaricious, and very intelligent Negro, he enjoyed virtual dictatorial control over the Seminole Negroes who, although technically slaves to the Indians, "maintained a sort of ascendency over their masters through superior intelligence and a little education, made effective for the most part in . . . intercourse with the whites."

It has been claimed that Abram, while acting as interpreter at the Paynes Landing deliberations in 1832, purposefully mistranslated a proposed treaty article which he knew the chiefs would never accept. He did this to collect two hundred dollars offered him by Colonel Gadsden if the treaty was ratified by the Seminoles. Two hundred dollars was "a very large sum in the eyes of a runaway slave in a country where very little money was ever seen." The article in question concerned the delegation which would journey west of the Mississippi River to survey lands the government offered the Seminoles. As it reads today, the article clearly states the point in dispute; it provides that the six-member delegation would speak for the nation. Should they accept the government lands in the west, the entire nation would emigrate. Abram, knowing how unacceptable this would be to the chiefs, translated the article so that the Seminole signatories of the treaty believed the ultimate decision to emigrate rested with them, regardless of the report from the western deputation. This bribery, though denied by Colonel Gadsden, is indicative of the craftiness and wiles of such Indian Negroes as Abram. Williams, *The Territory of Florida*, 272-273; W. A. Croffut (ed.), *Fifty Years in Camp and Field, Diary of Major General Ethan Allen Hitchcock, U. S. A.* (New York, 1909), 78-82; and Gadsden to D. W. Whitehurst, July 3, 1839, in T. F. Davis, "The Seminole Council, October 23-25, 1834," *The Florida Historical Quarterly*, VII (April, 1929), 350-356.

4. The role of the Indian Negroes during the Seminole War is not to be underestimated. The Negroes living among the Seminoles either were legally purchased by their Indian masters or were runaways from their white masters. Among the Indians their status was changed from slave to dependent, and, in many cases, like that of Abraham, the Negro rose to advisory capacity in the tribe. In addition to the Indian Negroes there existed two other classes of Negroes in Florida—free Negroes and those who were slaves to the whites. These latter two classes, in many instances, served

as espionage agents and suppliers of ammunition, food, and equipment to the hostile.

The free, easy, and independent life of the Indian Negroes aroused discontent among slaves on the sugar plantations and in the towns, and posed a constant threat to the slave owners. As a result, Florida slave owners advocated complete elimination of all Indians and their Negroes from the peninsula.

By 1837, the Seminoles became hard pressed for food. Forced to move from place to place, unable to plant or harvest a crop, and hunted like wild animals, many Indian Negroes were happy to be taken prisoner by the troops. Motte mentions several instances when Negroes were overjoyed by capture. Others, however, and perhaps the more important Negro element, resisted emigration and openly refused to surrender with their masters. Their attitude was logical, for if they surrendered, "many of them would have been reclaimed by the Creeks, to whom some belonged. Others would have been taken possession of by the whites, who for years had been urging their claims through the government and its agents. In Arkansas, hard labor was necessary for means of support, while Florida assured them of every means to indulge in idleness, and enjoy an independence corresponding with their masters'." Thus, the Negro was active in preparing for hostilities, and "in the prosecution blood-thirsty and cruel. . . . The Negroes from the commencement of the Florida War, have, for their numbers, been the most formidable foe, more bloodthirsty, active and revengeful, than the Indians. . . . to surrender would be servitude to the whites; but to retain an open warfare secured them plunder, liberty, and importance."

General Jesup issued the following significant statement shortly after he was appointed commander of the armed forces in Florida: "This, you may be assured, is a negro, not an Indian war, and if it be not speedily put down, the south will feel the effects of it on their slave population before the end of the next season." Kenneth W. Porter, "Florida Slaves and Free Negroes in the Seminole War, 1835-1842," *The Journal of Negro History,* XXVIII (October, 1943), 390-421; Sprague, *op. cit.,* 81, 100, 309; and *American State Papers, Military Affairs,* VII, 820-821.

5. Captain Thomas Beasley Linnard, a graduate of the Military Academy in 1830, was promoted to first lieutenant in December, 1835, and to brevet captain in September, 1836, for "gallant conduct, activity, and enterprise in the war against the Florida Indians." At the time of his mission to Washington, he was serving as an aide-de-camp to General Jesup. Heitman, *Historical Register,* I, 634; Sprague, *op. cit.,* 173.

6. In the proposals carried by Captain Linnard to Washington, General Jesup emphasizes that although he is in favor of emigration he does not believe it should be enforced until "the white population are in contact with or intermingled among them [the Indians]. . . ." He justifies his opinion in the following manner: ". . . we have committed the error of attempting to remove them when their lands were not required for agricultural purposes; when they were not in the way of the white inhabitants; and when the greater portion of their country was an unexplored wilderness, of the interior of which we were as ignorant as of the interior of China . . . the prospect of terminating the war, in any reasonable time, is any thing but flattering. My decided opinion is, that unless immediate emigration be abandoned, the war will continue for years to come, and at constantly accumulating expense. Is it not then well worth the serious consideration of an enlightened govern-ment, whether, even if the wilderness we are traversing could be inhabited by the white man, (which is not the fact) the object we are contending for would be worth the cost? . . . I do not consider the country south of the Chickasa-Hatchee worth the medicines we shall expend in driving the Indians from it.

"If I were permitted—and it is with great diffidence that I venture to make the suggestion—I would allow them to remain, and would assign them the country west of the Kissim-mee, Okee-Chobee, and Panai-Okee, and east of Pease Creek, south, to the extreme of Florida. That would satisfy them; and they might hold it on the express condition that they should forfeit their right to it, if they should either commit depredations upon the white inhabitants, or pass the boundaries assigned to them without the written permission of the Military commander or agent." Jesup to Poinsett, February 11, 1838, in Sprague, *op. cit.,* 200-201.

7. General Jesup's proposals brought a blast from the Florida newspapers. Claiming to speak for all Floridians, the *Florida Herald* stated on February 15, 1838: "We do not like the proposition about remaining in a small portion of the territory. The breach is too wide between the Indians and the Floridian, ever to be healed. The people of Florida will not submit to it, and it has cost too much blood and treasure for government to give up the war in this style. The people of Florida are willing to emigrate and leave the Seminoles in full possession, provided [the] Government will pay them for their property and their losses they have incurred."

Agitating for complete removal of the Seminoles, the Floridians would consider no alternative. The chances of a compromise (such as Jesup proposed) succeeding were almost nil, at least while the Democratic administration remained in Washington.

Statehood for Florida was approaching and there was undoubtedly no inclination in Democratic circles to disturb the political plum ripening in the Florida sunshine.

8. *Sofki,* or *sofkey,* was "a thin, sour corn gruel prepared by the Creek and other Indians formerly of the Gulf region, from corn, water, and lye." The preparation of this gruel has been described as follows: ". . . two quarts of the meal [coarse corn meal] are put into a gallon pot of hot water, which is placed over a fire and allowed to boil. A perforated vessel is filled with clean wood ashes, on which water is poured to form a lye. The lye as it percolates through the ashes drops into the meal and water and turns the mixture yellow. Water is kept on the *sofki* for hours at a time, and, finally, after the mixture has become very thick, it is removed and allowed to cool." Hodge (ed.), *Handbook of American Indians North of Mexico,* part 2, 613.

CHAPTER **XXXI**

1. Tuskegee and Hallek-Hadjo were Mikasuki chiefs. The former was a lieutenant of Sam Jones and chief of the Mikasuki Indians along the lower southeast coast of Florida. Hallek-Hadjo was a young chieftain in Tuskegee's tribe. Sprague, *The Florida War,* 191, 192; Marjory Stoneman Douglas, *The Everglades: River of Grass* (New York, 1947), 215.

2. The calumet was the peace-pipe. Technically it "was not properly the pipe but a highly ornamented and symbolic stem. The stem used in a peace-making ceremony remained with the chief who had received the embassy while the pipe bowl was taken out and carried back by the visitors. This bowl was usually . . . made of red stone from the north. . . ." The Florida Indians, however, used an "earthen cup" in place of the stone bowl. Swanton, *The Indians of the Southeastern United States,* 546-547.

3. Major William Lauderdale, commander of the Tennessee Volunteers, served under General Jackson in the Creek War of 1813-1814. In 1837 he raised five companies of volunteers (totaling 500 men) from the mountain regions of Tennessee and marched them to Florida, reporting to General Jesup on November 26, 1837. Jackson to Poinsett, October 1, 1837, and *id.* to *id.,* December 13, 1837, in Bassett (ed.), *Correspondence of Andrew Jackson,* V, 513 n. 2, 521-522.

4. Lieutenant Colonel James Bankhead began his military service as a captain in the Fifth Infantry in June, 1808. Promoted to major in 1813 and to lieutenant colonel in 1832, he was transferred to the Fourth Artillery in July of 1838. During the Florida War Bankhead was cited for meritorious conduct and promoted to colonel. In the Mexican War he was promoted to brigadier general for gallantry at Vera Cruz. Heitman, *Historical Register,* I, 189; Sprague, *op. cit.,* 551.

5. Key Biscayne was the large island southeast across Biscayne Bay from the mouth of the Miami River.

6. The following is an account of the expedition:

"On arriving at New River, Lieutenant Colonel Bankhead, by means of messengers furnished by Toskeegee, communicated with the Indians. They promised to meet him, but failed to do so, and he prepared to attack them. He was joined by Lieutenant Powell, of the Navy, and Major Lauderdale, with their commands; and having captured, by a detachment under Lieutenant Anderson, Pahose-Mico, a sub-chief of Toskeegee, with his band of forty-seven persons, he proceeded into the Everglades in pursuit of Appiacca [Sam Jones]. The nature of the country was such, that the soldiers could not even carry their cartridge-boxes. They were compelled to deposit them, with their muskets, in light boats, which they pushed before them through the mud for many miles to an island where they found the Indians. Lieutenant Colonel Bankhead attempted to communicate with them, but they fired upon his flag. He attacked and dispersed them; but the troops were unable to find or follow them." Sprague, *op. cit.*, 195-196; Ives Military Map locates Sam Jones' Seven Islands about twelve miles southwest of Fort Lauderdale. Colonel Bankhead's attack undoubtedly was made on Pine Island—one of the larger of the group. Its location is southwest of Davie, Florida.

7. An interesting account of a similar action is given by Ives:

"The alternate opening and closing of this inlet is somewhat remarkable. Between the years 1840 and 1844, it was closed. At the latter period, Capt. Davis, the mail carrier from Fort Capron to Cape Florida, endeavored, with a party of four men, to excavate a channel. After digging for several hours, they succeeded by nightfall in starting outward a stream of water four inches in depth. Upon this they desisted from labor and went to their camp, which was some fifty feet from the ditch. The river inside was unusually high, from a freshet in the everglades, and a strong north wind was blowing. At night, the sleeping party was awakened by a flood of water, and had to abandon their camp equipage and run for their lives, barely escaping being carried out to sea. The next day there was a channel nearly a quarter of a mile wide, and the rush of water could be traced far out upon the ocean." Ives, *Memoir to Accompany a Military Map of the Peninsula of Florida, South of Tampa Bay,* 11.

CHAPTER XXXII

1. Seminole dwellings varied in style and type. In the southern portions of the peninsula, houses were relatively simple and sufficient merely to afford

protection from the elements. In the northern area they were more elaborate. William Bartram described the homes of the town of Cuscowilla, the capital of the early Seminoles in north Florida. They were "constructed of a kind of frame. In the first place, strong corner pillars are fixed in the ground, with others somewhat less, ranging on a line between; these are strengthened by crosspieces of timber, and the whole with the roof is covered close with the bark of the Cypress tree. The dwelling stands near the middle of a square yard, encompassed by a low bank, formed with the earth taken out of the yard, which is always carefully swept. Their towns are clean, the inhabitants being particular in laying their filth at a proper distance from their dwellings, which undoubtedly contributes to the healthiness of their habitations." The houses measured about thirty feet long, twelve feet wide, and twelve feet high. The door stood midway on one side or in the front. Each house was divided into two apartments, "one of which is the cook room and common hall, and the other the lodging room."

In 1880, Clay MacCauley found a Seminole house in southern Florida which he described as follows:

"This house is approximately 16 by 9 feet in ground measurement, made almost, if not wholly, of materials taken from the palmetto tree. It is actually but a platform elevated about three feet from the ground and covered with a palmetto thatched roof, the roof being not more than 12 feet above the ground at the ridge pole, or 7 at the eaves. Eight upright palmetto logs, unsplit and undressed, support the roof. Many rafters sustain the palmetto thatching. The platform is composed of split palmetto logs lying transversely, flat sides up, upon beams which extend the length of the building and are lashed to the uprights by palmetto ropes, thongs, or trader's ropes. This platform . . .

serves to furnish the family with a dry sitting or lying down place when, as often happens, the whole region is under water. The thatching of the roof is quite a work of art . . . the mass of leaves of which the roof is composed is held in place and made firm by heavy logs, which bound together in pairs, are laid upon it astride the ridge. This covering . . . is watertight and durable and will resist even a violent wind. Only hurricanes can tear it off. . . . A shelter from the hot sun and the frequent rains and a dry floor above the damp or water covered ground are sufficient for the Florida Indian's needs." Van Doren (ed.), *The Travels of William Bartram,* 168-169; MacCauley, *The Seminole Indians of Florida,* Fifth Annual Report of the Bureau of American Ethnology, 500-501.

2. Baron Karl Maria (Friedrich Ernst) von Weber (1786-1826) was a German composer, conductor, and piano virtuoso. *Encyclopedia Americana* (New York, 1948), XXIX, 144-145.

3. Concerning Indian singing, Robert Beverley wrote in 1705: "Their [Indian] singing is not the most charming that I have ever heard, it consists much in exalting the voice, and is full of slow melancholy accents. However, I must allow even this Musick to contain some wild Notes that are agreeable." Robert Beverley, *The history and present state of Virginia, in four parts . . . By a native and inhabitant of the place* (London, 1705), as quoted in Swanton, *The Indians of the Southeastern United States,* 747.

4. Motte's description of the catfish dance is an addition to the folklore of the Southeastern Indians. Swanton, in *Religious Beliefs and Medicinal Practices of the Creek Indians,* Forty-second Annual Report of the Bureau of American Ethnology (1922), states: "Regarding the catfish [dance] . . . I have no information other than that [it] . . . existed."

He does not mention the dance in a more recent publication, *The Indians of the Southeastern United States* (1946).

CHAPTER XXXIII

1. The reply to General Jesup's proposals came in the form of a letter from the Secretary of War, J. R. Poinsett, dated March 1, 1838, saying:

"In the present stage of our relations with the Indians residing within the states and territories east of the Mississippi, including the Seminoles, it is useless to refer to the principles and motives which induced the government to determine their removal to the west. The acts of the executive and the laws of congress evince a determination to carry out the measure, and it is to be regarded as the settled policy of the country. Whether the government ought not to have waited until the Seminoles were pressed upon by the white population, and their lands became necessary to the agricultural wants of the community, it is not a question for the executive now to consider. The treaty [Paynes Landing] has been ratified, and is the law of the land. . . . I cannot, therefore, authorize any arrangement with the Seminoles, by which they will be permitted to remain, or assign them any portion of the Territory of Florida as their future residence."

The communication authorized General Jesup, if he considered it advisable, to make temporary peace with the Indians to last through the summer months. This would protect the settlements during the season in which troops found it almost impossible to operate. The letter further urged that Jesup take some definite action to "put it out of the power of these Indians to do any further mischief. They ought to be captured, or destroyed." Poinsett to Jesup, March

307

Journey into Wilderness

1, 1838, in Sprague, *The Florida War,* 201-202.

Poinsett's answer, rejecting General Jesup's proposals, immediately met with the full approval of the citizens of Florida. "The President has promptly and nobly discharged his duty to the country. General Jesup's aide has returned from Washington bearing the President's answer to the Commanding General's Moral Treason against the inhabitants of Florida. . . . Any other policy must have depopulated Florida. It is but justice to concede the *patriotism* and *firmness* of the President in our Indian relations. His *perseverance* 'in the footsteps of his predecessor,' in this particular, entitles him to the commendation and gratitude of every resident and friend of suffering Florida." *Florida Herald,* March 22, 1838.

2. Captain Linnard returned to Fort Jupiter from Washington on March 17, 1838. On March 19 General Jesup called a council of the chiefs to inform them of the decision. Tuskegee sent word that he did not wish to come. Not one of the chiefs attended, so General Jesup ordered Colonel Twiggs to seize the entire party. This was done on March 21, and the "two succeeding days." Jesup to Poinsett, July 6, 1838, in *Niles National Register,* September 8, 1838.

3. Passac Micco (Pahose Micco), a sub-chief of Tuskegee, escaped with fourteen of his band. A short time later he and his followers (the band had increased to forty-seven persons) were captured by a detachment under Lieutenant Robert Anderson. *Ibid.*

4. There were many varieties of the Indian ball game. The "single post" game "was always between men and women though sometimes the women's side was reinforced by two good male players. The men used the regular ball sticks, the women their hands. Part way up the pole was a mark and whichever side made a hit upon the pole above this mark scored one point. On top there was a wooden image, or in modern times, a cow skull or a horse skull, and if a player hit this his or her side scored an extra number of points, usually five." Swanton, *The Indians of the Southeastern United States,* 681-682.

5. Samuel Colt (1814-1862) was an American inventor who netted one of the outstanding fortunes of his time. Among his inventions were the electrically discharged submarine mine and the submarine telegraphy, which utilized the first cable ever laid under water. On February 25, 1836, he patented a single-barreled repeating rifle with a multi-chambered rotating breech, which was locked and unlocked by cocking. The first military use of this rifle occurred in the Seminole War in 1838. It was also used by the Texas Rangers in the war between Texas and Mexico. *Encyclopedia Britannica,* VI, 74-75.

6. The Board of Officers appointed to test the rifle included Colonel Twiggs, Lieutenant Colonel Gates, Major Lomax, Captains Washington, Fulton, and Beall, and Lieutenant Tompkins. Their orders read as follows:

"Among other points the Board will examine particularly the structure of the arm, and whether its cylinder, in revolving, is invariably adjusted with perfect accuracy to the barrel by the process of cocking; and whether it is not liable to be frequently out of firing order by the loss of screws, sedges, and other essential parts of its works. The process of loading will be examined to ascertain whether the mode of the invention insures invariably the proper charge. The arm will be fired at various distances from fifty to three hundred yards, to ascertain the accuracy as well as the force of its fire." Special order 71, March 3, 1838, in "Orderbook of General Thomas S. Jesup, 1838," MS in P. K. Yonge Library of Florida History, University of Florida, 12.

7. Fort Lauderdale was on the right bank of the west branch of New River, about a mile from its mouth. Today the site is within the present city of Fort Lauderdale. Ives Military Map.

8. The attack on the Cooly plantation by a party of thirty Indians took place on January 6, 1836. It was a part of the grand strategy by which the Indians expected to drive the whites into the ocean. In December, 1835, and January, 1836, nearly all the plantations from Cape Florida to St. Augustine were destroyed. Cohen, *Notices of Florida and the Campaigns,* 79-81.

CHAPTER XXXIV

1. The Rio Ratones, or Boca Ratones, empties into the north end of Biscayne Bay. The trail which led from Fort Lauderdale to Fort Dallas paralleled the coast inland from two to five miles, passing to the west of a large saw-grass marsh. It crossed three streams—the Boca Ratones, Arch Creek, and Little River. The distance from Fort Lauderdale to Fort Dallas was about twenty-five miles. Ives, *Memoir to Accompany a Military Map of the Peninsula of Florida, South of Tampa Bay,* 19.

2. Fort Dallas, named after Commodore Alexander Dallas, commander of the Caribbean Fleet, was built on the north bank of the Miami River at its mouth. *Ibid.,* 20; Tracy Hollingsworth, *History of Dade County, Florida* (Miami, 1936), 24. It is commemorated today by Fort Dallas Park in downtown Miami.

3. The Cape Florida lighthouse, perched on the southern tip of Key Biscayne at the north side of the entrance to Biscayne Bay, was repaired after the Indian attack. The structure can be seen today standing in its original location.

4. In 1796 Charles IV of Spain granted a 640-acre tract of land, between Fort Lauderdale and the Miami River, to an Englishman named Frankie Lewis. A similar grant, south of the Miami River, was made in 1805 to Tolly Lewis. At the outbreak of the Seminole War, R. R. Fitzpatrick of Key West, to whom the holdings had been transferred and who was using the plantations for the production of cotton, moved his slaves and equipment to Key West. The United States government took over the plantation buildings for military purposes. Hollingsworth, *op. cit.,* 23-24.

5. They undoubtedly were encamped at the spring known as the "Devils Punch Bowl," located a few hundred yards south of the present Rickenbacker Causeway—the southernmost of the causeways in Miami, Florida. The spring flowed from a round hole in the rocks at the base of the cliffs bordering the south end of Brickell Hammock. This site is situated between the present Southwest Twenty-fifth Road and the north end of the Deering Estate.

CHAPTER XXXV

1. The troops landed at a small beach about two miles north of Black Point. See Soil Conservation Service Map 35, Everglades Drainage District, Washington, 1946.

2. Many springs in this section of Florida, including various bayside springs, have been dried up by lowered water tables. An example of this is Mangrove Springs at Coconut Grove which "supplied water for the United States Fleet at Havana in 1898 . . . flowing at 100 gallons per minute." Today it no longer exists. C. W. Lingham, and others, *Springs of Florida,* Florida Geological Survey Bulletin, No. 31, 65.

Indications are that Motte and the troops went ashore in the present Cutler Hammock, a large part of which is encompassed in the Deering Estate, directly east of Perrine, Florida. This is the only spot on the coastline of lower Biscayne Bay where pine land approaches the water's edge. Before the water table in the Everglades was lowered, there were many springs in this vicinity. The location is found on Soil Conservation Service Map 35, Everglades Drainage District.

3. The troops, after leaving their bayshore camp, ascended the transverse glade which today crosses Federal Highway Number One immediately south of Howard and one mile north of Rockdale. These transverse glades were strips of low-lying soil stretching like fingers through the rocky pine land from the coastal area into the Everglades. The Indians used them in dry weather as foot trails, and when they were inundated, in wet weather, as canoe trails. Today the transverse glades are productive tomato-growing areas. See Soil Conservation Service Map 35, Everglades Drainage District.

4. After proceeding over six miles, the troops left the transverse glade and struck out across the rocky pine land to the edge of the Everglades. The rim of the Everglades was the favorite camping spot of the south Florida Indians. The location referred to here was a few miles southwest of the present Dade County Hospital. See Soil Conservation Service Map 35, Everglades Drainage District.

5. The assassination was carried out by the order of Sam Jones. Many of the Seminoles, horrified by this murderous act, begged the troops to remain, offering their assistance in finding Sam Jones and his Mikasukis. *Savannah Republican* as quoted in the *Apalachicola Gazette,* May 17, 1838.

6. Key Largo is the largest of the Florida Keys lying directly off the southern coast of Florida. In the days of Spanish galleons and privateering, according to tradition, the rock was used by pirates as an anchorage for their ships. An iron pin driven into the rock served to hold fast their anchor ropes.

CHAPTER XXXVI

1. General Order No. 7, dated April 10, 1838, Adjutant General's Office, Washington, began by stating: "Major General Jesup having reported that the operations in Florida will have terminated by the 1st of May, and that a portion of the troops will be disposable, the following arrangements will be carried into effect as soon thereafter as practicable." The First and Sixth Regiments of Infantry, six companies of the Second Infantry, and four companies of Second Dragoons were ordered to remain in Florida as the regular force along with as many volunteers as the commanding general deemed necessary. In addition, three companies of the Sixth Infantry, stationed in Louisiana, were ordered to proceed to Florida. The First Regiment of Artillery, the Fourth Regiment of Infantry, six companies of the Second Dragoons, and a detachment of marines were ordered to proceed to the Cherokee country and report to Major General Winfield Scott, the commander of the troops in that area, with headquarters at Athens, Tennessee.

Upon executing this order General Jesup was instructed to turn the command in Florida over to Brigadier General Zachary Taylor, to report to Washington and take over the duty of Quartermaster General. *Niles National Register,* April 14, 1838.

2. The Cherokee Indians were a "powerful detached tribe of the Iroquoian family, formerly holding the whole mountain region of the South Alleghenies, in southwest Virginia, west North Carolina and South Carolina, north Georgia, east Tennessee, and northeast Alabama, and claiming even to the Ohio River." During the American Revolution they sided with the British, continuing the struggle until 1794. After 1800, missionaries and educators began working among them. In 1820 the Cherokee Nation

Editor's Notes

adopted a government modelled after that of the United States. Meanwhile many of the more conservative Cherokees, "wearied by the encroachments of the whites," emigrated and settled in the wilderness west of the Mississippi. Discovery of gold near Dahlonega, Georgia, increased the pressure to remove those who still lived east of the Mississippi. After local authorities resorted to violence in order to remove them, the federal government intervened. On December 29, 1835, the "Treaty of New Echota," providing for the removal, was signed by "an insignificant fraction of the tribe." The United States government, however, held the entire nation to the strict observance of the treaty. Refusing to emigrate, the bulk of the tribe, under its chief John Ross and other principal leaders, was moved by force in the winter of 1838-1839. The unwilling Cherokees were driven from their home by military force, making the long journey to the west on foot. During this operation the Nation, which numbered 16,542 souls, suffered considerable hardship, losing nearly one-fourth of their population. Hodge (ed.), *Handbook of American Indians North of Mexico*, Pt. I, 246-247; Swanton, *The Indians of the Southeastern United States*, 112-113. For an excellent account of the removal of the Cherokees, see Foreman, *Indian Removal*.

3. While the majority of the troops had been operating in the southern part of the peninsula during the winter campaign of 1837-1838, many of the Mikasuki and Tallahassee Indians had retired to the dense swamps and hammocks near the mouth of the Withlacoochee River. The order for the Second Dragoons to proceed to Tampa Bay was a part of the maneuvering of troops to the Florida west coast for a campaign into the Withlacoochee country. This enterprise was abandoned, however, upon the recall of General Jesup to Washington.

Sprague, *The Florida War*, 196.

4. By the nineteenth century, torturing of prisoners by fire was a rare occurrence, although in early times it was a custom practiced by the Indians throughout the eastern and southeastern United States. An excellent discussion of this and similar types of barbarity is given by Nathaniel Knowles in "The Torture of Captives by the Indians of Eastern North America," *Proceedings of the American Philosophical Society*, LXXXII (March, 1940), 151-225.

Several incidents of the type of torture mentioned by Motte occurred in both the First and Second Seminole Wars. See James Parton, *Life of Andrew Jackson* (New York, 1861), II, 406, 458; and Sprague, *op. cit.*, 316.

Torturing prisoners was a customary procedure among the Creek Indians. Swanton, in *Social Organization and Social Usages of the Indians of the Creek Confederacy*, Forty-second Annual Report of the Bureau of American Ethnology, 417-418, quotes Bernard Romans on the subject of Creek cruelties: "As hospitable as this nation is to friends, as irreconcilably inhuman are they to their enemies; there is hardly an instance of one miserable prisoner's ever having escaped their barbarity, the torments they put the wretched victims to, are too horrid to relate, and the account thereof can only serve to make human nature shudder." Swanton also gives a vivid description of one of these ceremonies. Since large numbers of Creeks had become well assimilated into the Seminole Tribe, it is probable that Motte's account of this practice among the Seminole Indians is true.

5. General Order No. 7 called for two surgeons and as many assistant surgeons as the service would require to remain in Florida. The ones selected to stay were to be chosen from those who had the shortest period of

311

service in the territory. All other medical officers were ordered to the Cherokee country. *Niles National Register,* April 14, 1838.

6. After Motte left Florida the hostilities continued intermittently and in a guerilla-like fashion for four more years. In its entirety the war lasted seven years at a staggering expense both in lives and money. On the military side several thousand soldiers died, the majority from fevers and countless diseases—the most deadly enemy an army of that time could face. During the first five years, 1835-1840, $19,480,000 was expended for militia and volunteers, and damage claims of the citizens of the territory. This did not include expenditures for the regular army and its equipment. Estimates of the total cost range from forty to eighty million dollars. In 1836 over four thousand troops were stationed in Florida. A year later the number was practically doubled. Although the military strength was reduced in subsequent years, in 1841 the government still maintained an army of nearly four thousand soldiers in the peninsula. In contrast, the Seminoles, at the peak of their strength in 1836, were estimated to number 1,660 warriors capable of bearing arms and 250 hostile Negro allies. As the war proceeded their numbers steadily decreased. It was this contrast that caused fiery, old Andrew Jackson caustically to term the war in Florida as "disgraceful . . . to the American character. . . ."

In 1842 Colonel W. J. Worth, commander of the troops in Florida, proclaimed hostilities at an end. Although most of the Indians were removed by force, groups of them still remained in the southern sections of the peninsula. On November 17, 1843, Colonel Worth reported a Florida Indian population of 95 warriors and 205 women and children. A more accurate account in 1845 listed 120 warriors (70 Seminoles proper, 30 Mikasuki, 12 Creek, 4 Uchee, and 4 Choctaw), 100 women, and 140 children—a total of 360 Indians of both sexes. Their chief was Billy Bowlegs, the thirty-six-year-old nephew of Micanopy, and a descendant of old Bowlegs, King Payne, and Cowkeeper. Sub-chiefs under Bowlegs included the ninety-two-year-old Sam Jones (who once vowed his determination to die on Florida soil), and Assinwar, a sixty-year-old veteran warrior. The majority of the Seminoles bowed to the wishes of the white man. Their destiny, in the lands west of the Mississippi, is recorded in the sad chapters of Indian removal. Sprague, *op. cit.,* 97, 101-107, 200; Jackson to Poinsett, December 13, 1837, in Bassett (ed.), *Correspondence of Andrew Jackson,* V, 522; Worth to the Secretary of War, November 17, 1843, in Sprague, *op. cit.,* 507; and John T. Sprague, Captain in charge of Indian Affairs, to the editor of the *St. Augustine Herald,* September 16, 1845, in *ibid.,* 508-512.

Bibliography

MANUSCRIPTS

CHAFFER, H. J., "Military Posts of Florida Fortified Prior to 1860," with sources cited; typed MS in the P. K. Yonge Library of Florida History, University of Florida.

DODD, DOROTHY, "Railroad Projects in Territorial Florida"; unpublished master's thesis, Tallahassee, 1929.

DOVELL, JUNIUS E., "A History of the Everglades of Florida"; unpublished doctoral dissertation, University of North Carolina, 1947.

"Letters and Reports of Colonel Zachary Taylor to Major General Thomas Sidney Jesup, 1837-1838"; MS in the Library of Congress, Washington, D. C. Microfilm copy in the P. K. Yonge Library of Florida History, University of Florida.

McCLELLAN, EDWIN NORTH, "History of the United States Marine Corps," 1932; mimeographed copy in the P. K. Yonge Library of Florida History, University of Florida.

"Records Relating to the Service of the Navy and the Marine Corps on the Coast of Florida, 1835-42"; typed MS in the National Archives, Washington, D. C. Microfilm copy in the P. K. Yonge Library of Florida History, University of Florida.

"Report of Lieutenant Benson on the Exploration of Lake Okeechobee and the Kissimmee River, June 7, 1855"; MS in the National Archives, Washington, D. C. Photostatic copy in the P. K. Yonge Library of Florida History, University of Florida.

"Orderbook of General Thomas S. Jesup, 1838," an original military orderbook; MS in the P. K. Yonge Library of Florida History, University of Florida.

OFFICIAL RECORDS AND DOCUMENTS

American State Papers, 38 vols., *Foreign Relations,* vol. IV (1815-1822); *Indian Affairs,* vols. I, II (1789-1827); *Military Affairs,* vols. VI, VII (1836-1838), Washington, Gales and Seaton, 1832-1861.

Everglades of Florida: Acts, Reports, and Other Papers, State and National, Relating to the Everglades of the State of Florida and Their Reclamation, 62 Congress, 1 Session, Senate Document No. 89, Washington, Government Printing Office, 1911.

Expenditure in 1841—Florida Indians, etc, House of Representatives, 27 Congress, 2 Session, Document 247, Washington, D.C., Gales and Seaton, 1842.

Florida (Territorial) Legislative Council Journals, 12 Session, 1834; 14 Session, 1836; 16 Session, 1838; original and microfilm copies in the P. K. Yonge Library of Florida History, University of Florida.

HEITMAN, FRANCIS B.; *Historical Register and Dictionary of the United States Army, from Its Organization, September 29, 1789, to March 2, 1903,* 2 vols., House of Representatives, 57 Congress, 2 Session, Document No. 446, Washington, Government Printing Office, 1903.

Journey into Wilderness

Hostilities With the Creek Indians, the report of the Honorable Thomas H. Crawford and Alfred Balch, Esquire, who were appointed commissioners to investigate the causes of the late hostilities of the Creek Indians, House of Representatives, 24 Congress, 2 Session, Executive Document 154, vol. 4, Washington, Blair and Rives, 1836-1837.

Indian Hostilities in Florida, Message from the President of the United States, upon the Subject of a System of Defence for the Territory of Florida, etc., House of Representatives, 27 Congress, 2 Session, Document No. 223, Washington, Blair and Rives, 1842.

Letter From the Secretary of War Transmitting Documents in Relation to Hostilities of Creek Indians, June 6, 1836, House of Representatives, 24 Congress, 1 Session, Document No. 276, Washington, Blair and Rives, 1836.

Proceedings of the Military Court of Inquiry in the Case of Major General Scott and Major General Gaines, 24 Congress, 2 Session, Senate Document 224, vol. 3, Washington, Gales and Seaton, 1837.

PETERS, RICHARD (ED.): "Treaties Between the United States and the Indian Tribes," *United States Statutes at Large,* vol. 7, Boston, Charles C. Little and James Brown, 1846.

Remarks of Mr. Biddle, on the Seminole War, Delivered in the House of Representatives, January 24, 1838, and June 5, 1838, Washington, Niles National Register, 1838.

Report from the Secretary of War Transmitting Copies of Correspondence Relative to the Campaign in Florida, January 23, 1837, 24 Congress, 2 Session, Senate Document 100, Washington, Gales and Seaton, 1837.

Report of Mr. Toombs to Accompany Bill S. 43, 33 Congress, 1 Session, Senate Report 226, vol. 2, Washington, Beverley Tucker, 1854.

Seminole Hostilities. Message from the President of the United States Transmitting a Supplemental Report Respecting the Causes of the Seminole Hostilities, and the Measures Taken to Suppress Them, House of Representatives, 24 Congress, 1 Session, Document No. 271, Washington, Blair and Rives, 1836.

Seminole War—Slaves Captured. Message from the President of the United States, Transmitting the Information Called for by a Resolution of the House of Representatives of August 9, 1841, in Relation to the Origin of the Seminole War, of Slaves Captured, etc., January 29, 1842, House of Representatives, 27 Congress, 2 Session, Executive Document 55, Washington, Blair and Rives, 1842.

Speech of W. O. Butler, of Kentucky, in Committee of the Whole, in Reply to Mr. Biddle and Mr. Hunt, upon the Appropriation for Suppressing Hostilities in Florida, Delivered in the House of Representatives, June 11, 1840, Washington, Blair and Rives, 1840.

ARTICLES IN PERIODICALS

BOYD, MARK F.: "The First American Road in Florida," *The Florida Historical Quarterly,* XIV (January, 1936).

...............: "Events at Prospect Bluff on the Apalachicola River, 1808-1818," *The Florida Historical Quarterly,* XVI (October, 1937).

CARTER, CLARENCE E.: "Observations of Superintendent John Stuart and Governor James Grant of East Florida on the Proposed Plan of 1764 for the Future Management of Indian Affairs," *The American Historical Review,* XX (July, 1915).

DAVIS, T. FREDERICK: "Early Orange Culture in Florida and the Epochal

314

Bibliography

Cold of 1835," *The Florida Historical Quarterly,* XV (April, 1937).

................: Milly Francis and Duncan McKrimmon, an Authentic Florida Pocahontas," *The Florida Historical Quarterly,* XXI (January, 1943).

................: "MacGregor's Invasion of Florida," *The Florida Historical Quarterly,* VII (July, 1928).

................: "The Seminole Council, October 23-25, 1834," *The Florida Historical Quarterly,* VII (April, 1929).

The Florida Historical Quarterly, XV (April, 1937); XVIII (January, 1940).

FORRY, SAMUEL: "Letters of Samuel Forry, Surgeon U. S. Army, 1837-1838," *The Florida Historical Quarterly,* VI (January, 1928; April, 1928); VII (July, 1928).

GOFF, JOHN H.: "The Steamboat Period in Georgia," *The Georgia Historical Quarterly,* XII (September, 1928).

GRISWOLD, OLIVER: "William Selby Harney; Indian Fighter," *Tequesta* (Number 9, 1949).

HOYT, WILLIAM D., JR.: "A Soldier's View of the Seminole War, 1838-1839," *The Florida Historical Quarterly,* XXV (April, 1947).

KNOWLES, NATHANIEL: "The Torture of Captives by the Indians of Eastern North America," *Proceedings of the American Philosophical Society,* LXXXII (March, 1940).

OBER, F. A.: "Ten Days with the Seminoles," *Appleton's Journal,* XIV (July, August, 1875).

"Obituary of J. Rhett Motte," *The Christian Register* (July, 1869).

PHELPS, JOHN W.: "Letters of Lieutenant John W. Phelps, U.S.A., 1837-1838," *The Florida Historical Quarterly,* VI (October, 1927).

PHINNEY, A. H.: "Florida's Spanish Missions," *The Florida Historical Quarterly,* IV (July, 1925).

................: "The Second Spanish-American War," *The Florida Historical Quarterly,* V (October, 1926).

PIKULA, JOHN: "Historical Landmarks of My County," *The Florida Historical Quarterly,* XV (April, 1937).

PORTER, KENNETH W.: "The Founder of the 'Seminole Nation,' Secoffee or Cowkeeper," *The Florida Historical Quarterly,* XXVII (April, 1949).

................: "Seminole Flight from Fort Marion," *The Florida Historical Quarterly,* XXII (January, 1944).

................: "The Negro Abraham," *The Florida Historical Quarterly,* XXV (July, 1946).

................: "Florida Slaves and Free Negroes in the Seminole War, 1835-1842," *The Journal of Negro History,* XXVIII (October, 1943).

PREBLE, GEORGE HENRY: "A Canoe Expedition into the Everglades in 1842," *Tequesta* (Number 5, 1945).

ROWLES, W. P.: "Incidents and Observations in Florida in 1836," *The Southron,* Gallatin, Tennessee (1841); photostatic copy in the P. K. Yonge Library of Florida History, University of Florida.

South Carolina Historical and Genealogical Magazine, IV (1903).

WHITMAN, ALICE: "Transportation in Territorial Florida," *The Florida Historical Quarterly,* XVII (July, 1938).

NEWSPAPERS

Apalachicola Gazette, May, 1836; February-May, 1838.

Army and Navy Chronicle, B. Homans (ed.), January-June, 1836.

Journey into Wilderness

Charleston Courier, March, 1838.
Florida Herald (St. Augustine), July, 1835; January-October, 1836; March-October, 1837; January-July, 1838.
Jacksonville Courier, January-December, 1835; January, 1836.
Niles Weekly Register (Name changed to *Niles National Register,* September 2, 1837), March-December, 1836; February-November, 1837; February-September, 1838.
New York Observer, January, 1838.
The Floridian (Tallahassee), August, 1836; July-December, 1837.

BOOKS

ADAIR, JAMES: *The History of the American Indians,* London, Edward and Charles Dilly, 1775.

ALDEN, JOHN RICHARD: *John Stuart and the Southern Colonial Frontier, A Study of Indian Relations, War, Trade, and Land Problems in the Southern Wilderness, 1754-1775,* Ann Arbor, The University of Michigan Press, 1944.

ALVORD, BENJAMIN, LIEUTENANT, U.S.A.: *Address Before the Dialectic Society of the Corps of Cadets, in Commemoration of the Gallant Conduct of the Nine Graduates of the Military Academy, and other Officers of the United States' Army, Who Fell in the Battles which Took Place in Florida, on the 28th of December, 1835, and the 25th December, 1837; the Former called Dade's Battle, the Latter, the Battle of Okee-cho-bee,* delivered at West Point, New York, on the 29th of December, 1838, New York, Wiley and Putnam, 1839.

BASSETT, JOHN SPENCER (ED.): *Correspondence of Andrew Jackson,* 7 vols., Washington, Carnegie Institution of Washington, 1926-35.

BERNEY, SAFFOLD: *Hand-Book of Alabama,* 2nd ed. rev., Birmingham, Roberts and Son, 1892.

BREVARD, CAROLINE MAYS: *A History of Florida from the Treaty of 1763 to Our Own Times,* James Alexander Robertson (ed), 2 vols., DeLand, Florida State Historical Society, 1924.

BREWER, W.: *Alabama: Her History, Resources, War Record, and Public Men. From 1540 to 1872,* Montgomery, Barrett & Brown, 1872.

BROWN, JOHN P.: *Old Frontiers; the Story of the Cherokee Indians from Earliest Times to the Date of Their Removal to the West, 1838,* Kingsport, Tennessee, Southern Publishers, 1938.

BUCHHOLZ, F. W.: *History of Alachua County, Florida,* St. Augustine, The Record Company, 1929.

CATLIN, GEORGE: *Letters and Notes on the Manners, Customs and Condition of the North American Indians,* 2 vols., London, David Bogue, 1844.

CAUGHEY, JOHN WALTON: *McGillivray of the Creeks,* Norman, University of Oklahoma Press, 1938.

CLAIBORNE, J. F. H.: *Life and Times of Gen. Sam. Dale, the Mississippi Partisan,* New York, Harper and Brothers, 1860.

COE, CHARLES H.: *Red Patriots: The Story of the Seminoles,* Cincinnati, The Editor Publishing Company, 1898.

COHEN, M. M.: *Notices of Florida and the Campaigns,* Charleston, Burges and Honour, 1836.

COLE, ARTHUR H. (ED.): *Charleston Goes to Harvard, Diary of a Harvard Student of 1831,* Cambridge, Harvard University Press, 1940.

316

Bibliography

COOKE, C. WYTHE: *Geology of the Coastal Plain of Georgia,* United States Geological Survey Bulletin 941, Washington, Government Printing Office, 1943.

COOKE, C. WYTHE, AND MOSSOM, STUART: *Geology of Florida,* Florida Geological Survey, Twentieth Annual Report, 1927-1928, Tallahassee, Florida Geological Survey, 1929.

CORSE, CARITA DOGGETT: *Dr. Andrew Turnbull and the New Smyrna Colony of Florida,* Jacksonville, The Drew Press, 1919.

COTTERILL, R. S.: *The Old South: The Geographic, Economic, Social, Political and Cultural Expansion, Institutions, and Nationalism of the Ante-Bellum South,* Glendale, Cal., Arthur H. Clarke Company, 1936.

COULTER, E. MERTON: *Georgia, A Short History,* rev. ed., Chapel Hill, University of North Carolina Press, 1947.

CRAIGIE, WILLIAM A., AND HULBERT, JAMES R. (EDS.): *A Dictionary of American English on Historical Principles,* 4 vols., Chicago, University of Chicago Press, 1940.

CROFFUT, W. A. (ED.): *Fifty Years in Camp and Field, Diary of Major-General Ethan Allen Hitchcock, U. S. A.,* New York, G. P. Putnam's Sons, 1909.

CURLEY, MICHAEL J.: *Church and State in the Spanish Floridas (1783-1822),* Washington, Catholic University of American Press, 1940.

DAVIS, JOHN H., JR.: *The Natural Features of Southern Florida,* Florida Geological Survey Bulletin Number 25, Tallahassee, Florida Geological Survey, 1943.

DEBO, ANGIE: *The Road to Disappearance,* Norman, University of Oklahoma Press, 1941.

DERRICK, SAMUEL MELANCHTHON: *Centennial History of South Carolina Railroads,* Columbia, The State Company, 1930.

DOUGLAS, MARJORY STONEMAN: *The Everglades: River of Grass,* New York, Rinehart and Company, 1947.

DYER, BRAINERD: *Zachary Taylor,* Baton Rouge, Louisiana State University Press, 1946.

EATON, JOHN HENRY: *The Life of Major General Andrew Jackson: Comprising a History of the War in the South; from the Commencement of the Creek Campaign to the Termination of Hostilities Before New Orleans,* Philadelphia, McCarty and Davis, 1828.

ELLIOTT, CHARLES WINSLOW: *Winfield Scott, the Soldier and the Man,* New York, The Macmillan Company, 1937.

ENCYCLOPEDIA AMERICANA, 30 vols., New York, Americana Corporation, 1948.

ENCYCLOPEDIA BRITANNICA, 24 vols., Chicago, Encyclopedia Britannica Incorporated, 1945.

FAIRBANKS, GEORGE R.: *History of Florida from Its Discovery by Ponce de Leon, in 1512, to the Close of the Florida War in 1842.* Philadelphia, J. B. Lippincott and Company, 1871.

Federal Writers' Project of the Work Projects Administration: *Florida: A Guide to the Southernmost State,* New York, Oxford University Press, 1939.

...............: *Georgia: A Guide to Its Towns and Countryside,* Athens, University of Georgia Press, 1940.

FITZGERALD, T. E.: *Volusia County, Past and Present,* Daytona Beach, The Observer Press, 1937.

FOREMAN, GRANT: *The Five Civilized Tribes,* Norman, University of Oklahoma Press, 1934.

317

FOREMAN, GRANT: *Indian Removal: The Emigration of the Five Civilized Tribes of Indians,* Norman, University of Oklahoma Press, 1932.

..............: *The Last Trek of the Indians,* Chicago, University of Chicago Press, 1946.

FOREMAN, GRANT (ED.): *A Traveler in Indian Territory: The Journal of Ethan Allen Hitchcock, Late Major-General in the United States Army,* Cedar Rapids, The Torch Press, 1930.

FORTESCUE, J. W.: *A History of the British Army, 1809-1810,* 13 vols., London, Macmillan and Company, Limited, 1899-1930.

GATSCHET, ALBERT S.: *A Migration Legend of the Creek Indians,* 2 vols.— Vol. I: Philadelphia, D. G. Brinton, 1884; Vol. II: St. Louis, privately printed, 1888.

..............: "Towns and Villages of the Creek Confederacy in the XVIII and XIX Centuries," *Report of the Alabama History Commission to the Governor of Alabama, December 1, 1900,* Thomas M. Owen (ed.), Montgomery, Brown Printing Company, 1901.

Georgia, Historical and Industrial, Atlanta, Department of Agriculture, 1901.

GERWIG, HENRIETTA (ED.): *Crowell's Handbook for Readers and Writers: A Dictionary of Famous Characters and Plots in Legend, Fiction, Drama, Opera, and Poetry,* New York, Thomas Y. Crowell Company, 1925.

GIDDINGS, JOSHUA R.: *The Exiles of Florida: Or, the Crimes Committed by our Government Against the Maroons, Who Fled from South Carolina and Other Slave States, Seeking Protection Under Spanish Laws,* Columbus, Follett, Foster and Company, 1858.

GOLD, PLEASANT DANIEL: *History of Volusia County, Florida,* DeLand, The E. O. Painter Printing Company, 1927.

HALBERT, H. S., AND BALL, T. H.: *The Creek War of 1813 and 1814,* Montgomery, White, Woodruff, & Fowler, 1895.

HAMILTON, PETER J.: *Colonial Mobile,* New York, Houghton, Mifflin and Company, 1898.

HANNA, ALFRED J., AND KATHRYN A.: *Lake Okeechobee, Wellspring of the Everglades,* Indianapolis, Bobbs-Merrill, 1948.

..............: *Florida's Golden Sands,* Indianapolis, Bobbs-Merrill, 1950.

HANNA, KATHRYN ABBEY: *Florida, Land of Change,* Chapel Hill, University of North Carolina Press, rev. ed., 1948.

HARMON, GEORGE DEWEY: *Sixty Years of Indian Affairs, Political, Economic, and Diplomatic,* 1789-1850, Chapel Hill, University of North Carolina Press, 1941.

HART, JAMES D.: *The Oxford Companion to American Literature,* New York, Oxford University Press, 1948.

Letters of Benjamin Hawkins, 1796-1806, collections of the Georgia Historical Society, vol. 9, Savannah, The Georgia Historical Society, 1916.

HEILPRIN, ANGELO: *Explorations on the West Coast of Florida and in the Okeechobee Wilderness,* Philadelphia, Wagner Free Institute of Science, 1887.

HENRY, ROBERT SELPH: *Trains,* Indianapolis, Bobbs Merrill, 1934.

HODGE, FREDERICK WEBB (ED.): *Handbook of American Indians North of Mexico,* Bureau of American Ethnology, Bulletin 30, 2 parts, Washington, Government Printing Office, 1912.

HODGSON, W. R., AND HAWKINS, COLONEL BENJAMIN: *Creek Indian History as Comprised in 'Creek Confederacy' and 'The Creek Country,'* a reprint of volume three, part one, of the Georgia Historical Society Publications, Americus, Americus Book Company, 1938.

Bibliography

HOLLINGSWORTH, TRACY: *History of Dade County, Florida*, Miami, Miami Post, 1936.

IRVING, THEODORE: *The Conquest of Florida, by Hernando de Soto*, New York, George P. Putnam, 1851.

IVES, J. C.: *Memoir to Accompany a Military Map of the Peninsula of Florida, South of Tampa Bay*, New York, M. B. Wynkoop, 1856.

JAMES, MARQUIS: *The Life of Andrew Jackson*, 2 parts, New York, Garden City Publishing Company, 1940.

JOHNSON, ALLEN, AND MALONE, DUMAS (EDS.): *Dictionary of American Biography*, 21 vols., New York, Charles Scribner's Sons, 1928-1944.

KNIGHT, LUCIAN LAMAR: *Georgia's Landmarks, Memorials, and Legends*, 2 vols., Atlanta, The Byrd Printing Company, 1913-1914.

KNOX, DUDLEY W.: *A History of the United States Navy*, New York, G. P. Putnam's Sons, 1936.

KUNITZ, STANLEY, J., AND HAYCRAFT, HOWARD (EDS.): *American Authors 1600-1900: A Biographical Dictionary of American Literature*, New York, H. W. Wilson Company, 1938.

...............: *British Authors of the Nineteenth Century*, New York, H. W. Wilson Company, 1936.

LANNING, JOHN TATE: *The Spanish Missions of Georgia*, Chapel Hill, University of North Carolina Press, 1935.

LINGHAM, C. W., AND OTHERS: *Springs of Florida*, Florida Geological Survey Bulletin Number 31, Tallahassee, The Florida Geological Survey, 1947.

History of Lowndes County, Georgia, 1825-1941, Valdosta, The General James Jackson Chapter of the Daughters of the American Revolution, 1941.

LUMPKIN, WILSON: *The Removal of the Cherokee Indians from Georgia*, 2 vols., New York, Dodd, Mead and Company, 1907.

MacCAULEY, CLAY: *The Seminole Indians of Florida*, Fifth Annual Report of the Bureau of American Ethnology, Washington, Government Printing Office, 1887.

McKENNEY, THOMAS L., AND HALL, JAMES: *The Indian Tribes of North America*, Hodge, Frederick W., and Bushnell, David I., Jr. (eds.), new ed., 2 vols., Edinburgh, John Grant, 1933-1934.

McLEAN, RUARI: *George Cruikshank, His Life and Work as a Book Illustrator*, New York, Pellegrini and Cudahy, n. d.

METCALF, CLYDE H.: *A History of the United States Marine Corps*, New York, G. P. Putnam's Sons, 1939.

MILLING, CHAPMAN J.: *Red Carolinians*, Chapel Hill, University of North Carolina Press, 1940.

MOORE, ALBERT BURTON: *History of Alabama*, University, Alabama, University Supply Store, 1934.

MOWAT, CHARLES LOCH: *East Florida as a British Province, 1763-1784*, Los Angeles, University of California Press, 1943.

MURRAY, JAMES A. H., AND OTHERS (EDS.): *A New English Dictionary on Historical Principles*, 10 vols., Oxford, The Clarendon Press, 1888-1933.

MYER, WILLIAM E.: *Indian Trails of the Southeast*, Forty-second Annual Report of the Bureau of American Ethnology, Washington, Government Printing Office, 1928.

PARTON, JAMES: *Life of Andrew Jackson*, 3 vols., New York, Mason Brothers, 1861.

PATRICK, REMBERT W.: *Florida Under Five Flags*, Gainesville, University of Florida Press, 1945.

Journey into Wilderness

PERRY, W. L.: *Scenes of a Surveyors Life in South Florida,* Jacksonville, 1859.

PICKETT, ALBERT JAMES: *History of Alabama and Incidentally of Georgia and Mississippi, from the Earliest Period,* Sheffield, Alabama, Robert C. Randolph, 1896.

POTTER, WOODBURNE: *The War in Florida: Being an Exposition of its Causes, and an Accurate History of the Campaigns of Generals Clinch, Gaines, and Scott,* Baltimore, Lewis and Coleman, 1836.

RERICK, ROWLAND H.: *Memoirs of Florida,* Fleming, Francis P. (ed.), 2 vols., Atlanta, The Southern Historical Association, 1902.

RODENBOUGH, THEO. F.: *From Everglade to Cañon with the Second Dragoons,* New York, D. Van Nostrand, 1875.

ROMANS, BERNARD: *A Concise Natural History of East and West-Florida,* New York, R. Aitken, 1776.

ROUSE, IRVING: *A Survey of Indian River Archeology, Florida,* Yale University Publications in Anthropology, Number 44, New Haven, Yale University Press, 1951.

SHAW, HELEN LOUISE: *British Administration of the Southern Indians, 1756-1783,* Lancaster, Pa., The Lancaster Press, 1931.

SIEBERT, WILBUR HENRY (ED.): *Loyalists in East Florida; 1774 to 1785,* 2 vols., DeLand, Florida State Historical Society, 1929.

SMITH, W. W.: *Sketch of the Seminole War, and Sketches During a Campaign, by a Lieutenant of the Left Wing,* Charleston, Dan J. Dowling, 1836.

SPRAGUE, JOHN T.: *The Origin, Progress, and Conclusion of the Florida War,* New York, D. Appleton and Company, 1848.

SWANTON, JOHN R.: *Early History of the Creek Indians and Their Neighbors,* Bureau of American Ethnology Bulletin 73, Washington, Government Printing Office, 1922.

...............: *The Indians of the Southeastern United States,* Bureau of American Ethnology Bulletin 137, Washington, Government Printing Office, 1946.

...............: *Religious Beliefs and Medicinal Practices of the Creek Indians, and Social Organization and Social Usages of the Indians of the Creek Confederacy* in Forty-second Annual Report of the Bureau of American Ethnology, 1924-1925, Washington, Government Printing Office, 1928.

TRUE, DAVID O. (ED.): *Memoir of D⁰ d'Escalente Fontaneda,* translated from the Spanish with notes by Buckingham Smith, Miami, University of Miami, 1944.

VAN DOREN, MARK (ED.): *The Travels of William Bartram,* New York, Barnes and Noble, 1940.

VERNON, ROBERT O.: *The Hydrology and Geology of Florida Springs,* Florida Geological Survey Bulletin Number 31, Tallahassee, Florida Geological Survey, 1947.

WHITE, GEORGE: *Historical Collections of Georgia,* New York, Pudney and Russell, 1854.

WILLIAMS, JOHN LEE: *The Territory of Florida: Or, Sketches of the Topography, Civil and Natural History, of the Country, the Climate, and the Indian Tribes, from the First Discovery to the Present Time,* New York, A. T. Goodrich, 1837.

WILLIAMS, SAMUEL COLE (ED.): *Adair's History of the American Indians,* Johnson City, Tennessee, The Watauga Press, 1930.

WILLIAMS, W.: *Appleton's New and Complete United States Guide Book for Travelers,* New York, D. Appleton and Company, 1854.

WRIGHT, ALBERT HAZEN: *Our Georgia-Florida Frontier: The Okefinokee Swamp, Its History and Cartography,* Ithaca, A. H. Wright, 1945.

Index

Index

323

Index

Twiggs, D. E., Col., 178, 299, 302, 308

Uchee Billy, 125, 129, 140, 275, 277, 280; capture of, 120-123
Uchee Indians, 120, 121, 277, 279, 312
Uchee Jack, 123, 275, 277

Van Swearingen, J., Capt., 180
Vinton, J. R., Capt., 100, 102, 111, 141, 229, 273
Volunteer troops, behavior of, 195-196, 301
Volunteers, Alabama, 21, 23, 38, 178, 188, 202, 252, 254, 290; Florida, 89, 117, 154, 269, 292, 297; Georgia, 249, 252, 254, 263, 275, 290; Louisi-ana, 252, 290; Missouri, 181, 297, 298; South Carolina, 107, 276, 289; Tennessee, 25, 154, 170, 178, 188, 195, 211, 220, 224, 290, 301, 305; Washington City, 168, 178

Waite, C. A., Lt., 2
Walker, W. H. T., Lt., 181
Warner's ferry, 83, 87
Warren, J., Col., 269
Watson, Col., 25
White, J. M., 270
Whitehurst, D. W., Lt., 117, 119
Woodruff, H., Major, 153
Woolfolk's plantation, 4
Worrell, E., Surg., 106
Worth, W. J., Col., 275, 312
Wrecking, 199

Journey into Wilderness

A map showing the travels of Jacob Rhett Motte
during the Creek and Seminole Wars of 1836-1838